Legal Issues of Faith-based and Other Nonpublic Schools

7th Edition of the Former Title

Legal Problems of Religious and Private Schools

by Ralph D. Mawdsley

Charles J. Russo and Steve Permuth, Editors

EDUCATION LAW ASSOCIATION

No. 98 in the K-12 Series

© 2018 by the Education Law Association
Cleveland, Ohio 44115-2214
Phone: 216-523-7377 / Fax: 216-687-5284
www.educationlaw.org

**Legal Issues of Faith-based and Other
Nonpublic Schools**
No. 98 in the ELA K-12 Series

Education Law Association Publications

Founded in 1954, the Education Law Association is a nonprofit, nonadvocacy member association that seeks to improve education by promoting interest in and understanding of the legal framework of education and the rights of students, parents, school boards, and school employees.

Both authors and editors who collaborate on ELA publications include many of the best-known experts in their fields: deans, professors of education or law, school administrators, and attorneys specializing in education law.

Whether you're doing research as an educational administrator, attorney, or student—or you are a professor selecting high-quality and affordable textbooks—help yourself succeed by choosing education law publications from ELA's bookstore on our website, www.educationlaw.org.

Editors

Charles J. Russo, M. Div., J.D., Ed. D., is the Joseph Panzer Chair in Education in the School of Education and Health Sciences, Director of its Ph.D. Program, and Research Professor of Law in the School of Law at the University of Dayton. The 1998-99 President of the Education Law Association and 2002 recipient of its McGhehey Award for outstanding service to education law, he has authored or coauthored more than 300 articles in peer-reviewed journals; authored, coauthored, edited, or coedited 66 books; and has been published in more than 1,100 publications. Dr. Russo also speaks extensively on issues in education law in the United States and has presented in thirty other nations. He has served as editor of ELA's annual *Yearbook of Education Law* for nearly 25 years and is one of the association's most prolific authors.

Steve Permuth, Ed.D., Professor of Education at the University of South Florida, worked with Ralph Mawdsley on the original *Legal Problems of Religious and Private Schools* and recently served as chief editor of *Religion and Law in the Public Schools*, published by the Education Law Association (ELA). With a background of teaching and administration in seven states, he has authored or coauthored eleven books, has published articles on many topics, and regularly presents at conferences. In addition to serving on the ELA Board of Directors, Dr. Permuth remains active with the National Association of Secondary School Principals, several journals, and is on the publication review board of ELA and other organizations. He particularly enjoys working with students on writing and presentation projects to help them become actively involved with ELA.

Authors

Bryan H. Beauman, J.D.: Attorney, Sturgill, Turner, Barker & Moloney, PLLC, Lexington, KY

Lynn M. Daggett, J.D., Ph.D.: Smithmoore P. Myers Chair and Professor of Law, Gonzaga University School of Law, Spokane, WA

Barbara M. De Luca, Ph.D.: Associate Professor, School of Education and Health Sciences, University of Dayton, Dayton, OH

Steven A. Hinshaw, Ph.D.: Adjunct Professor, University of Dayton, Dayton, OH

James L. Mawdsley, J.D.: Adjunct Professor, Cleveland State University, Cleveland, OH and Instructor, Stark State College, North Canton, OH

Ralph D. Mawdsley, J.D., Ph.D.: Chair/Professor (Retired), Cleveland State University, Cleveland, OH

R. Stewart Mayers, Ed.D.: Professor/Chair, Department of Educational Instruction and Leadership, Director of Teacher Education, Southeastern Oklahoma State University, Durant, OK

Steve Permuth, Ed.D.: Professor of Education, University of South Florida, Tampa, FL

Cristiana Ritchie-Carter, Ph.D.: Associate Director, Center for Catholic School Leadership, Graduate School of Education, Fordham University, New York, NY

Charles J. Russo, M. Div., J.D., Ed. D., Joseph Panzer Chair in Education and Director of Ph.D. Program, School of Education and Health Sciences; Research Professor of Law, School of Law, University of Dayton, Dayton, OH

Sr. Mary Angela Shaughnessy, SCN, J.D., Ph.D.: Attorney and Senior Distinguished Fellow of Catholic Education, Loyola Marymount University, Los Angeles, CA

Jennifer A. Sughrue, Ph.D.: Professor, Educational Leadership, Florida Gulf Coast University, Ft. Myers, FL

William E. Thro, J.D.: General Counsel, University of Kentucky, Lexington, KY

Dedication

On a more personal note, we both would like to recognize that the character and quality of this text reflect on the professional dedication and scholarly excellence demonstrated by our dear friend, Ralph Mawdsley, throughout a life dedicated to teaching, scholarship, and service.

Without Ralph's leadership, this text likely would not have been written. We would thus like to share a few things about Ralph.

Ralph D. Mawdsley, who holds a J.D. from the University of Illinois and a Ph.D. from the University of Minnesota, retired as a professor of law and education at Cleveland State University, where he held that University's Roslyn C. Wolf Chair in Urban Educational Leadership. He also was the recipient of two Fulbright Awards, one for the University of Pretoria, South Africa, and a second to Brisbane University, Australia. In 2010, he received an honorary doctorate by the University of Pretoria and, in 2014, was named a Professor Extraordinary by the Law Faculty of the University of the Free State, Africa. Ralph taught courses in the area of school law, sports law, and special education law, and has published over 600 articles, books, and book chapters. He was awarded Cleveland State University's highest awards for teaching, the Distinguished Teaching Award and the Dr. Jennie S. Hwang Award for Faculty Excellence.

In 2001, Ralph served with distinction as the President of ELA and, in 2004, was awarded the ELA's Marion McGhehey Award for Outstanding Service in the Field of Education Law. Ralph has been a regular speaker at education law conferences in the United States, South Africa, Australia, and various venues in Europe, and is a member of publication boards for a number of the leading educational law journals throughout the world. He recently retired from Cleveland State University, but will continue an active role supporting ELA and school law in general through publishing in areas of interest, including religion.

With the support of his wife, Alice, and his sons, James and Jonathan, we hope and expect that Ralph will continue to contribute to scholarship and leadership for many years to come.

Charles J. Russo and Steve Permuth

Table of Contents

Introduction
Steve Permuth and Charles J. Russo

Pages 1–4

Chapter 1 – History of Faith-based and Nonpublic Schools in America
Jennifer A. Sughrue

Introduction / 5
Private versus Public Education / 6
      Private Educational Establishment Types / 7
      Multiple Models for Multiple Purposes / 10
Homeschools / 13
Academies / 17
Charter Schools / 21
Church Schools / 24
Conclusion / 26
Discussion Questions / 27
Key Words / 27

Chapter 2 – Institution, Student, and Faculty Relationships
Ralph D. Mawdsley and James L. Mawdsley

Introduction / 30
Defining the Contract / 32
Constitutional Constraints / 38
      Concept of Fairness / 39
      State Action / 40
      Contractual Due Process / 48
Student/Employee Conduct and Violations of Contract / 50
      Prohibited Conduct / 50
      Compliance with Procedures / 51
      Adherence to Contract Terms / 54
Fundamental Fairness / 61
Recommendations / 65
Conclusion / 66
Discussion Questions / 66
Key Words / 67

Chapter 3 – Governing Board Responsibilities and Liability

Cristiana Ritchie-Carter

Introduction / 69
Board Structures / 70
Board Responsibilities / 73
       Defining and Maintaining the Missions of Religious Schools / 75
       Fiduciary Relationship / 80
       Standard of Care / 81
Liability / 83
       Use of Public Funds / 86
       Conflict of Interest / 87
       Vicarious Liability / 88
       Indemnification / 88
       Liability Insurance / 90
Conclusion / 90
Discussion Questions / 91
Key Words / 91

Chapter 4 – State Aid to Faith-based Schools

Charles J. Russo

Introduction / 93
State Aid to Faith-Based Schools / 96
       Setting the Stage / 96
       Types of State Aid / 97
              Overview / 97
              Transportation / 97
              Textbooks / 98
              Secular Services and Salary Supplements / 99
              Tuition Reimbursement to Parents / 100
              Reimbursements to Faith-Based Schools for Testing / 100
              Income Tax Benefits / 101
              Instructional Materials / 102
              Support Services / 103
              Vouchers / 104
              Facially Neutral State Aid Programs / 106
Conclusion / 106
Discussion Questions / 107
Conclusion / 107

Chapter 5 – Tort Liability

Charles J. Russo and Sr. Mary Angela Shaughnessy

Introduction / 110

Tort Theories / 110
Strict Liability / 110
Intentional Torts / 111
      Assault and Battery / 111
      Sexual Abuse / 112
      Corporal Punishment / 113
      Hazing and Bullying / 115
      Defamation / 116
      False Imprisonment / 118
      Intentional Infliction of Emotional Distress / 119
      Invasion of Privacy / 119
Negligence / 120
      Elements of Negligence / 121
          Duty / 121
          Supervision / 124
          Breach / 126
          Injury / 128
          Causation / 129
          Defenses / 130
              Consent/ Assumption of Risk / 130
              Contributory/ Comparative Negligence / 132
              Charitable Immunity / 133
Special Topics / 135
      Insurance Coverage / 135
      Exculpatory Clauses / 137
      Negligent Hiring, Supervision, and Retention / 142
      Self-Defense and Restraint / 145
      Field Trips / 147
      Medical Needs / 150
      Child Abuse Reporting / 154
Conclusion / 157
Discussion Questions / 157
Key Words / 158
Appendices A, B, C, D / 158–161

Chapter 6 – School Safety

R. Stewart Mayers

Introduction / 164
State and Local Safety Codes / 165
      Religious Land Use and Institutionalized Persons Act / 167
      Zoning Codes / 167
Higher Education Crime Reporting / 168
Crisis Management Plans / 171
Persistently Dangerous Schools / 173

School Safety and the Every Student Succeeds Act / 174
Student Searches / 175
    Generally / 175
    Defining Contraband / 176
    T.L.O. Reasonableness Standard / 176
    Contractual Language Authorizing Searches / 177
    Suspicionless Searches / 178
    Zero Tolerance Policies / 178
    Source of Information / 179
    Scope of Search / 180
        Intrusiveness / 180
        Age and Sex / 181
        Nature of Infraction / 182
    Special Types of Searches / 183
        Field Trips/Activities Outside of Schools / 183
        Car/Vehicle Searches / 186
        Metal Detectors / 187
        Sniff Dogs / 188
        Strip Searches / 189
        Breath Analysis / 191
        Cell Phone Searches / 191
        Cyber Speech / 192
Recommendations for Practice / 193
Drug Testing / 194
    Drug Testing Policies / 195
Employee Searches and Drug Testing / 198
    Employee Searches / 198
    Electronic Surveillance / 199
    Suspicionless Searches / 200
    Searches of Employee Computers / 200
    Guidelines for Employee Searches / 200
    Employee Drug Testing / 201
Conclusion / 202
Discussion Questions / 203
Key Words / 204

Chapter 7 – School Finance

Barbara M. De Luca and Steven A. Hinshaw

Introduction / 206
Constitutional and Legal Historical Background / 207
    Federal Funding / 207
    State Funding / 207
Revenues / 208
    Sources of Private Money / 208

Tuition / 208
Donations, Stewardship, Philanthropy / 210
Public Money / 211
Federal Level / 211
State Level / 213
Other Revenue Sources / 214
Budgets / 215
Budget Objectives / 215
Budget Allocations / 215
Budget Approaches / 216
Line Item Budgeting / 216
Incremental Budgeting / 216
Performance-Based Budgeting / 217
Planning, Programming, and Budgeting Systems / 217
Management by Objectives / 218
Zero-based Budgeting / 218
Cutback (Decremental) Budgeting / 219
Weighted Student Funding as a Budgeting Approach / 219
Budget Roles and Responsibilities / 220
Capital Budgeting / 221
Conclusion / 221
Discussion Questions / 222
Key Words / 222

Chapter 8 – Special Education and Students in Nonpublic Schools

Lynn M. Daggett

Introduction / 224
Overview of the Individuals with Disabilities Education Act and Students in Public Schools / 224
Individuals with Disabilities Education Act Eligibility Requirements / 225
The IDEA Eligibility Process / 226
Alternative Eligibility under Section 504 of the Rehabilitation Act / 227
Individualized Education Programs / 228
Free Appropriate Public Education / 229
Special Education Instruction / 231
Related Services / 232
Least Restrictive Environment / 233
Procedural Safeguards / 235
Parental Participation on Special Education Teams / 235
Notice and Consent; Independent Educational Evaluations / 236
Access to Special Education Records / 236
Disciplining Special Education Students / 237
Special Education Disputes / 238

The IDEA and Students in Private Schools / 240
    Child Find / 240
    Special Education and Students in Private Schools Generally / 241
    Children Placed in Private Schools by Public Agencies / 241
    Children Placed in Private Schools by Their Parents in FAPE Disputes with Public School Boards / 243
    Children Placed in Private Schools Due to Parental Preferences / 245
    Who Are the "Students in Private Schools" in This Category? / 245
        Proportionate Allocations of Federal IDEA Funds / 246
        Consultation Processes / 248
    Services Plan Requirement / 249
    Location of Services / 249
    Complaints by Parents Whose Children Attend Private Schools / 250
    By-Pass for Children in Private Schools / 251
    State Laws May Provide Additional Rights / 251
    Private School Obligations under Section 504 / 252
Policy Issues / 257
Conclusion / 259
Discussion Questions / 260
Key Words / 260

Chapter 9 – Governmental Regulations of Nonpublic Schools

Bryan H. Beauman

Introduction / 264
Basis for State Regulation and Restrictions on Governmental Authority / 264
    Free Exercise Expanded: *Wisconsin v. Yoder* / 265
    Free Exercise Limited: *Employment Division Department of Human Resources of Oregon v. Smith* / 266
    Free Exercise Targeted: *Church of the Lukumi Babalu Aye v. City of Hialeah* / 268
    Free Exercise Excluded: *Trinity Lutheran Church of Columbia v. Comer* / 270
    Protected Liberty Interests / 271
    Expanding Public School Requirements / 272
Government Regulation of Admission and Hiring in Nonpublic Schools / 274
    The Church Autonomy Doctrine / 275
    Religiosity to Qualify for the Ministerial Exemption / 276
    Hosanna-Tabor Evangelical Lutheran Church and *School v. Equal Employment Opportunities Commission* Affirms the Constitutional Rule / 277
    Qualifying for the Ministerial Exemption / 279
Participation by Nonpublic School Students in Public School Courses and Activities / 282

Nonpublic Schools Participating in State Activities / 282
Public School Opportunities for Students in Private Schools / 285
Governmental Regulation of Home Instruction / 287
Home Instruction Generally / 287
Opportunities in Public Schools for Students who are
Homeschooled / 289
Legislative and Organizational Involvement Public School
Activities / 290
Conclusion / 291
Discussion Questions / 291
Key Words / 292

Chapter 10 – Federal Antidiscrimination Legislation
William E. Thro

Introduction / 293
Title VII / 296
Overview / 296
The Ministerial Exception May Exempt Some Employees from
Title VII / 296
Faith-Based Schools May Require Employees to Adhere to the
Faith / 296
Faith-Based Schools May Have to Accommodate Employees'
Religious Beliefs / 297
Liability Theories for Title VII / 297
Intentional Discrimination / 297
Disparate Impact / 299
Harassment / 299
Americans with Disabilities Act / 300
Employment / 300
Reasonable Accommodation / 301
Drug Use / 301
Exemption for Selected Religious Tasks / 302
Participation in Educational Programs and Activities / 302
Age Discrimination in Employment Act / 303
The Equal Pay Act / 303
The Family Medical Leave Act / 304
Special Rules for Classroom Teachers / 305
Retaliation Claims / 306
Conclusion / 306
Discussion Questions / 307
Key Words / 307

Chapter 11 – Special Topics

Charles J. Russo

Introduction / 309
Copyright / 309
 Copyright Protection / 309
 Fair Use / 311
 Works for Hire / 313
 Educational-Use Exemption / 314
 Multiple Photocopying / 315
 Civil Penalties / 316
 Digital Millennium Copyright Act of 1998 / 316
 The Technology, Education, and Copyright Harmonization Act / 317
Immigration and Reform Control Act / 318
Family Educational Rights and Privacy Act / 319
Conclusion / 325
Discussion Questions / 325
Key Words / 325
Appendices A, B, C, D / 326–333

Case Index

Pages 335–352

Introduction to *Legal Issues of Religious and Other Nonpublic Schools*

Steve Permuth and Charles J. Russo

Private or nonpublic schools, primarily faith-based in nature, furnished the earliest formal education to children and young adults in the United States and remain a choice for quality education today. As with their public school counterparts, the amount of litigation involving nonpublic educational institutions from pre-K to graduate school continues to increase. Troublesome issues that have become commonplace in public schools, such as safety/security and bullying, have become equally challenging in nonpublic schools. Further, in efforts to keep students safe, parents and reformers call for better supervision of student and staff conduct, including background checks for employees. In addition, educational leaders in faith-based schools are likely to have special concerns about balancing religious beliefs with local, state, and federal laws.

The issues facing faith-based, private, or other nonpublic schools are not new, but are changing. This is also true of the Education Law Association's response to those issues. One constant for the Association, however, remains to provide school leaders and attorneys with up-to-date, practical research and information to help them develop proactive, preventive measures to keep their schools out of court.

The first edition of *Legal Problems of Religious and Private Schools* was published in 1983 under the auspices of the National Organization on Legal Problems of Education (NOLPE), founded in 1954. NOLPE changed its name to the Education Law Association (ELA) in 1996. In the first edition, Ralph D. Mawdsley (Editor) and Steve Permuth (Coauthor) developed a text based on key issues that generated substantial litigation in nonpublic schools, whether faith-based or secular. The chapters in the initial edition were Tort Liability, Student and Faculty Discipline, Governing Board Liability, Governmental Regulation of Nonpublic Schools, Federal Anti-Discrimination Legislation, and Copyright Law.

Subsequent versions of the text revisited and updated these topics through the sixth edition in 2012, with Ralph Mawdsley as the sole author. This edition, which continues to be among the most successful of all ELA publications, added chapters on school safety, special education, and contract law.

Following his retirement in 2016, Ralph Mawdsley relinquished authorship of the forthcoming seventh edition of the book, but remained as coauthor of a chapter. Charles J. Russo, the Joseph Panzer Chair in Education and Research Professor of Law at the University of Dayton, was asked to be Lead Editor, with Steve Permuth, Professor of Education at the University of South Florida, as Editor. Both also serve as chapter authors and coauthors throughout the text.

This 2018 edition offers important changes. First, in order to more accurately reflect the current status of nonpublic schools in the United States, its title was revised from *Legal Problems of Religious and Private Schools* to *Legal Issues of Faith-based and Other Nonpublic Schools*.

Second, authorship was extended to a group of skilled authors and scholars in the field, providing broader perspectives on wide-ranging subjects, now including such topics as the history of private schools in the United States, the Supreme Court and state aid to faith-based schools, and school finance. Tasked with the responsibility of updating the sixth edition's chapters or write new ones were Bryan Beauman, Lynn Daggett, Barbara De Luca, Steven Hinshaw, James Mawdsley, Ralph Mawdsley, Stewart Mayers, Steve Permuth, Cristiana Ritchie-Carter, Charles Russo, Sister Mary Angela Shaughnessy, Jennifer Sughrue, and William Thro.

Third, this edition incorporates key cases affecting nonpublic schools that have been litigated since the publication of the sixth edition. Three Supreme Court cases stand out with the potential to have major impacts on nonpublic schools, particularly those that are religiously affiliated. The first two cases, *Obergefell v. Hodges* (2015) and *Masterpiece Cakeshop v. Colorado Civil Rights Commission* (2018), involved disputes over sexuality and same-sex marriages. The third case, *Trinity Lutheran Church of Columbia v. Comer* (2017), concerned aid to faith-based schools.

In *Obergefell,* a non-education case, the Supreme Court held that under Fourteenth Amendment's Due Process and Equal Protection Clauses, state officials must grant marriage licenses to two people of the same sex, while also recognizing marriages between two people of the same sex when their marriages were lawfully licensed and performed out of state. In so ruling, the Court essentially made same-sex marriages legal throughout the United States.

In *Masterpiece Cakeshop,* the Supreme Court found that because Colorado's Civil Rights Commission failed to comply with the Free Exercise Clause's requirement of religious neutrality when resolving a dispute wherein it fined a baker who refused to bake a cake for a gay marriage, they violated his rights. As such, the Court entered a judgment in favor of the baker. However, the Justices sidestepped the constitutional issue of whether the baker's refusal to bake a cake for a same-sex marriage—just as he was unwilling to do so for other customers with whose viewpoints he disagreed (such as for Halloween)—is a form of protected speech or a manifestation of unlawful discrimination. In so doing, the Justices left the door open to future litigation. The way in which the Court ultimately resolves this thorny question is sure to have significant implications for faith-based institutions at all levels, as well as a wide array of small, and perhaps not so small, private businesses, a topic well beyond the scope of this book.

To date there has been little litigation over whether couples in same-sex marriages can enroll their children in faith-based schools. Yet, conflicts may well arise, because the teachings of the churches with which many faith-based schools are associated do not recognize same-sex marriages. In other words, litigation may result when educational officials do not allow same-sex couples to enroll their children in their faith-based schools because the parents are not abiding by the lifestyle and sexuality teachings of the religious bodies sponsoring the schools.

Since *Masterpiece Cakeshop* stopped short of answering definitively whether the baker—and by extension, schools—had a protected right not to sell to or work with those whose lifestyle choices and views he disagreed, including his refusal to offer his services for those commemorating Halloween, this issue may be far from settled. In fact, tensions are likely to continue over the rights of individuals to live openly as they wish and the rights of believers, along with their schools and/or churches, to the free exercise of their faiths, allowing them to practice their sincerely held religious beliefs.

Trinity Lutheran Church of Columbia v. Comer addressed a decidedly different issue from the first two cases. Here, the Supreme Court reasoned that the Establishment Clause does not allow states to single out faith-based institutions and/or believers, denying them generally available benefits simply because they are religious. On its face, *Trinity Lutheran* appears to open the door to allowing states to provide greater aid to students and their faith-based schools. Still, it remains to be seen how lower courts apply *Trinity Lutheran* and whether the case will be the game-changer some suggest.

As developments continue regularly in so many areas of education law, these are issues that bear close watching in coming years and are likely to be revisited in the next edition of this book.

Another important factor governing the writing and publishing of the seventh edition has been the impact on education stemming from the 2016 election of President Donald Trump. The change in administrations is significant because both the President and his Secretary of Education, Betsy DeVos, have spoken out on behalf of vouchers, charter schools, privatization, and school choice generally.

Judicial "originalism" appears to be growing in the U.S. federal court system as well, potentially spawning changes in areas impacting education. These judicial developments include the appointment of Associate Justice Neal Gorsuch to the United States Supreme Court, replacing Justice Antonin Scalia, as well as the naming of new members of federal appellate and trial courts with textualist credentials viewed as complementary to those of Justice Gorsuch and other members of the bench, such as Justices Alito, Roberts, and Thomas. One can only speculate as to the effects of future transitions on judicial outcomes.

In light of the changes that have transpired in education law over the past six years alone, it is worth keeping in mind the observation of the ancient Greek philosopher Heraclitis, who wrote that "one cannot step into the same river twice." In other words, Heraclitis suggested that while a river's location can remain unchanged, the constant flow of water means it is always a new body of water. Similarly, in light of the constant changes in education law impacting faith-based and other nonpublic schools, as well as the broader field, the next edition of this text certainly will address new issues that have yet to be recognized.

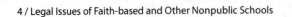

1

History of Faith-based and Nonpublic Schools in America

Jennifer A. Sughrue

Contents

Introduction / 5
Private versus Public Education / 6
      Private Educational Establishment Types / 7
      Multiple Models for Multiple Purposes / 10
Homeschools / 13
Academies / 17
Charter Schools / 21
Church Schools / 24
Conclusion / 26
Discussion Questions / 27
Key Words / 27

Introduction

Private schooling long preceded public education in the United States. Homeschooling, sometimes referred to as domestic education, was the foremost form of private schooling in the early colonial period and continues in earnest today.[1] During the colonial period, parents generally provided education in rural areas and in townships, while wealthier households relied on private tutors or older siblings to educate their children until they were old enough to be sent to Europe or to attend an academy to complete their formal education.[2] As colonial leaders grew concerned about parents failing to teach their children, particularly in the New England colonies, education became a community-

---

[1] *See, e.g.,* Milton Gaither, HOMESCHOOL: AN AMERICAN HISTORY (2008); Jennifer A. Sughrue, *Homeschooling: Parent Rights and Public Good* in the SAGE GUIDE TO EDUCATIONAL LEADERSHIP AND MANAGEMENT, 359-372 (Fenwick English, ed. 2015); Carl F. Kaestle, PILLARS OF THE REPUBLIC: COMMON SCHOOLS AND AMERICAN SOCIETY, 1780-1860 (1983); Nancy Beadie and Kim Tolley (eds.), CHARTERED SCHOOLS: TWO HUNDRED YEARS OF INDEPENDENT ACADEMIES IN THE UNITED STATES, 1725-1925 (2002).

[2] Kaestle, *Id. See also* Sarah L. Hyde, SCHOOLING IN THE ANTEBELLUM SOUTH: THE RISE OF THE PUBLIC AND PRIVATE EDUCATION IN LOUISIANA, MISSISSIPPI, AND ALABAMA (2016); Lawrence Cremin, AMERICAN EDUCATION: THE NATIONAL EXPERIENCE, 1783-1876 (1980); Lawrence A. Cremin, AMERICAN EDUCATION: THE COLONIAL EXPERIENCE, 1607-1789 (1970).

based function, initially funded by parents of school-aged children, but later by local revenues in large townships at the direction of colonial governments.

Of course, the nature and availability of education varied across the thirteen colonies, so care must be taken not to suggest that the purposes and types of American private education were uniform across regions. Likewise, as education assumed a more prominent position in American politics and society from the birth of the nation to contemporary America, no singular portrait of American private and public education is representative across all states and across national educational history.

The purpose of this chapter is to describe broadly the evolution and function of private education prior to and through the formation of the United States and up to the first two decades of the twenty-first century. This chapter first offers a brief explanation of modern distinctions between private and public education, before examining why those differences are not useful when describing educational organizations in early American history and are becoming less useful in the current educational environment in which school choice is touted. This chapter next briefly identifies and describes the various types of private institutions and schooling that contributed to the availability of education, from colonial examples to more contemporary models. Finally, the chapter provides more detail on the educational role of these institutional types, particularly in relationship to the social, political, and economic contexts in which they functioned.

Private versus Public Education

Typically, contemporary private and public schools can be distinguished by their sources of funding and governance structures. Broadly speaking, private schools are funded by tuition, endowments, charitable contributions, and other sources of nonpublic monies. Financial support for public schools comes primarily from state and local funding, as well as relatively modest amounts of federal money in the form of categorical grants. Public school systems are established and regulated by their state legislatures under the authority of their constitutions, with oversight provided by their state departments of education and local education agencies. Private schools are usually operated under the supervision of corporate sponsors or boards of trustees comprised of parents and perhaps representatives from businesses that provide major financial or operational support.

Historically, the distinctions between private and public institutions were not so clearly defined. It was not uncommon for private educational endeavors (that is, schools serving particular populations of students) to receive some public funding along with tuition and donations, or for "public" schools (those freely open to most school-aged students) to be funded and governed entirely by private or charitable organizations.[3]

There appears to have been no need to make clear demarcations between public and private because public education as it is structured today, a system of K-12 education both funded and regulated by state governments, had not yet been conceived; most viewed private schools as a partner in educating youth. The mingled nature of what was private and what was public served the educational needs of the day and were reflective of the communities in which they functioned. Education, particularly toward the end of the colonial period, "was a peculiar blend of public and private, classical and vocational, religious and secular."[4]

Private Educational Establishments Types

Dame schools, academies, homeschools, field schools, and seminaries are among the common terms used to describe private education options in the literature of American educational history. Identifying and describing these and other private educational types assists in understanding their functions and places in the history of American private education.

Venture schools

Historically, venture schools were unincorporated commercial enterprises supported entirely by tuition that competed with other private educational institutions for students.[5] The literature has described venture schools as "entrepreneurial in nature, characterized by market supply and demand."[6] Venture schools were the invention of entrepreneurial teachers who competed for working class and middle class students by being responsive to the particular educational demands of the families they served.

In her study of early private education, Tolley analyzed documents and advertisements related to eighty-one venture schools from 1808-1842.[7] What Tolley uncovered was that venture school instructors were individual men and women who sought students through marketing by offering instruction ranging from one or two subjects, such as dancing, languages, and/or mathematics, to diverse curricula going beyond the basics of literacy and numeracy.

Venture schools were prominent features of private education throughout the colonies and in states during the early national period. In large cities such as Boston and New York, venture schools were a primary source of formal

---

[3] *Supra,* note 2. *See also* Robert N. *Gross,* PUBLIC VS. PRIVATE: THE EARLY HISTORY OF SCHOOL CHOICE IN AMERICA (2018); Robert Middlekauff, *Before the Public School: Education in Colonial America,* 62 CURRENT HISTORY 279 (1972).

[4] Middlekauff, *supra* note 3, 307.

[5] Gross, *supra* note 3. *See also* Kim Tolley, *Mapping the Landscape of Higher Schooling,* in CHARTERED SCHOOLS: TWO HUNDRED YEARS OF INDEPENDENT ACADEMIES IN THE UNITED STATES, 1725-1925 (Nancy Beadie and Kim Tolley, eds. 2002).

[6] Tolley, *supra* note 5, at 20.

[7] *Id.*

education through the eighteenth century.[8] Venture schools expanded rapidly in the eighteenth century in response to a growing mercantile industry, offering specialized study directed at business or other subjects that suited the needs of their students in that context. Some of these schools focused on the education of males, while others catered to females.

Some successful venture schools later incorporated and became academies. Most came and went, depending on the fortunes of individual teachers and how many students they were able to attract. Eventually, families turned to town schools, parochial schools, or academies, leaving venture schools that did not convert to academies to disappear from the education marketplace.

Dame schools

Dame schools were considered a form of venture schools.[9] Typically, they were in the homes of female teachers, most often widows or single women who needed to sustain themselves economically.[10] Located in both rural and urban settings, dame schools usually offered basic literacy and mathematics education, perhaps along with a domestic skill such as sewing. Because the students the dame schools served were generally poor females, there were instances, primarily in the mid-Atlantic and northern town and cites, that the schools offered daughters of freedmen instruction in basic reading and writing.[11]

Dame schools were one of the few options available to women to teach during the colonial period and into the late 1700s, a situation that began to change in the early national period when "the ideology of the Republican mother" took hold.[12] The underlying principle of this ideology was that mothers needed to be educated so they could teach their children to be good citizens.

The next ideology to emerge in the early 1800s was what Jensen labeled as "the ideology of the teaching daughters."[13] According to this perspective, women should be educated and employed as teachers because they needed to be able to earn a living in a "profession offering influence, respectability and independence."[14] The private schools, dame schools, and later primary schools and boarding schools dedicated to the education of girls and young women offered the earliest employment opportunities for female teachers.

Academies

Academies, some of which were named institutes or seminaries, were institutions that provided "higher schooling."[15] Academies were legally

---

[8] Gross, *supra* note 3.

[9] Tolley, *supra* note 5.

[10] Gaither, *supra* note 1; Kaestle, *supra* note 1.

[11] *Id.*

[12] Joan M. Jensen, *Not Only Ours but Others: The Quaker Teaching Daughters of the Mid-Atlantic, 1790-1850*. 24 HIST. OF EDUC. Q. 3 (1984).

[13] *Id.*

[14] *Id.* at 3. (Catharine Beecher, cited by Jensen).

[15] Tolly, *supra* note 5, at 19. Tolley defined higher schooling as "any advanced variety of formal education beyond the common school level apart for that offered in colleges and universities."

incorporated and did not depend solely on tuition for funding their operations. Academies were established by diverse organizations such as religious entities, fraternal and educational societies, as well as by local communities and private individuals.[16]

Church schools

Sponsored by religious groups such as missionary societies, the Catholic and Anglican churches, the Quakers, and Protestant philanthropic societies, church schools took many forms: parsons' schools, charity schools, parochial schools, and Sunday schools.[17] These church schools provided instruction in basic subjects such as reading, writing, and mathematics, along with religious instruction.

Town schools

Town schools appeared in northern and southern localities during the late 1600s and early 1700s.[18] Perhaps the earliest forms of town schools were the products of the Massachusetts Bay Colony's "Old Deluder Satan Law," which required the establishment of a school in townships of fifty to 100 households so that all children would learn to read and write by studying the Bible. Teachers were paid by the parents of the children attending the town schools, or entire communities. Larger communities were required to set up grammar schools. Later versions of town schools usually were governed by elected officials and funded, at least in part, by local or state grants.

Charter schools

Charter schools are public schools subject to some government regulations that receive public funding, but are independently managed by nonprofit and for-profit companies, universities, or school councils comprised of parents and teachers; a few are associated with religious entities.[19] These schools operate under performance contracts, referred to as charters, which are agreed to by the school organizers and the state or local education agency in whose jurisdiction they intend to operate. The first public charter schools were established by law in Minnesota in 1991; they opened for business, according to their advocates, as attempts to improve public education through competition for students and to inspire entrepreneurial innovation in the delivery of instruction.

---

[16] Tolly, *supra* note 5.

[17] Kaestle, *supra* note 1; Cremin, *supra* note 1, Tolley, *supra* note 5.

[18] Kaestle, *supra* note 1; Cremin, *supra* note 1; Tolley, *supra* note 5. *See also* R. Freeman Butts & Lawrence A. Cremin, A History of Education in American Culture (1953).

[19] *See, e.g.*, National Charter School Resource Center, *What is a Charter School?* (n.d.); Janet R. Decker and Kari A. Carr, *Church-State Entanglement at Religiously Affiliated Charter Schools*, 2015 B.Y.U. Educ. & L.J. 77 (2015).

Homeschools

Homeschooling is the first form of private education.[20] Today, parents may educate their children at home if they adhere to state regulations that govern homeschooling.[21] However, homeschooling has evolved from solely an independent family endeavor to an array of options; these include highly organized homeschooling associations, as well as cyberschools facilitating the education of children in their homes or in groups outside of their homes.[22]

This handful of private school types represents those most frequently described in the literature on private schooling. While there are myriad private schools in today's education marketplace, they can be categorized as one or more of these types. An in-depth discussion of homeschools, academies, church schools, and charter schools follows.

Multiple Models for Multiple Purposes

Historically, the needs of the family and community dictated the forms and nature of education available to educate children and later, adults, along with groups that had been previously been denied access to education (particularly to higher schooling) such as women, Native Americans, the working poor, indentured servants, and slaves. Education was valued, but the reasons and purposes varied over time. In the New England colonies, education was about scriptural literacy and maintaining the values of the immigrant community, such as the Pilgrims, who sought religious freedom but attempted to deny that same freedom to others.[23]

Following the Revolutionary War, the Founders pressed education as the primary force through which to join diverse populations of people in a common endeavor, a representative democracy, which would unite them as a nascent republic. The Common School Movement in the nineteenth century spurred the development of an educated labor force with the introduction of compulsory education laws. This movement promoted the ideal of free universal public education through a system of schools with local oversight and state funding.

Leaping forward to the twentieth century, education was viewed, rightly or wrongly, as a mechanism for social and economic mobility and, conversely, for segregation and disenfranchisement. For the past twenty-five years, school reformers—who have influenced both public and private education—have advocated for school choice, claiming it affords parents greater authority in overseeing the education of their children, creates a variety of educational environments designed to meet the needs of diverse students, and prepares all school-aged children for the technological innovations impacting the workplace, the economy, and society generally.

---

[20] Gaither, *supra* note 1.

[21] Sughrue, *supra* note 1.

[22] *Id.*

[23] Deborah Jones Merritt and Daniel C. Merritt, *The Future of Religious Pluralism: Justice O'Conner and the Establishment Clause*, 39 ARIZ. ST. L.J. 895 (Fall 2007).

Perhaps the two most important influences over the purposes and expected outcomes of education, whether delivered by private or public providers, are the social and political contexts of time and place. Education is not provided in a vacuum. Rather, education is a reflection of social, political, and economic forces, along with community values.

> [The] interrelatedness of human experience forces upon one the view that education is not some discrete activity carried on outside the community of ideas and values of an age. Education is never an autonomous process divorced from the society it serves. It always operates within a given social framework and it finds its central purpose, its guiding principles, its ultimate goals in the particular social order within which it develops and functions.[24]

How education is provided is also a reflection of these same forces and values. Private schools, as much as their public counterparts, are social agencies. Purveyors of private education must be responsive to the families and communities they serve if they are to survive the competition for students and resources.

In recent decades, the number of private educational institutions and the percentages of students enrolled in them have fluctuated. During the school year 1980-81, there were 20,764 private schools, a number that swelled to 35,895 in 2001-02.[25] In 2015-16, the total number of private schools stood at 34,576.[26]

Between 1995 and 2015, student enrollment in private schools varied between a high of 11.7% (1995) and a low of 9.7% (2011).[27]

> In fall 2015, some 5.8 million students (10.2% of all elementary and secondary students) were enrolled in private elementary and secondary schools; 36% of private school students were enrolled in Catholic schools, 39% were enrolled in other religiously affiliated schools, and 24% were enrolled in nonsectarian schools.[28]

Fall 2015 demographic data indicate that White students comprise the largest percent of enrollment in private schools, with 65% of all students attending Catholic schools, 73% of those enrolled in other religiously affiliated schools, and 65% of students enrolled in nonsectarian schools.[29] Latinos are the second-largest demographic in Catholic schools (16%), while Black stu-

---

[24] Norton Edwards, *Social Forces in American Education*, 1 HISTORY OF EDUC. J. 70, 70 (Winter 1949).

[25] National Center for Education Statistics (NCES), FAST FACTS: EDUCATIONAL INSTITUTIONS (2016), available at https://nces.ed.gov/fastfacts/display.asp?id=84

[26] NCES, PRIVATE SCHOOL UNIVERSE SURVEY (2017), available at https://nces.ed.gov/surveys/pss/tables /TABLE14fl.asp

[27] NCES, DIGEST OF EDUCATION STATISTICS (2016), available at https://nces.ed.gov/programs/digest/d16/tables/dt16_205.10.asp ?current=yes. These data do not include children who are homeschooled.

[28] NCES, THE CONDITION OF EDUCATION: PRIVATE SCHOOL ENROLLMENT (2018), available at https://nces.ed.gov/programs/coe /indicator_cgc.asp

[29] *Id*. at Figure 5.

dents make up the second-largest demographic in other religiously affiliated schools (11%). Asian students make up a small percentage of the population in nonpublic schools, with 5% in Catholic schools and 5% in other sectarian schools. At 9%, Asians are the second-largest demographic enrolled in nonsectarian schools.

These data may suggest that only a fraction of the total number of school-aged students are enrolled in private schools and that their number and variety are small. Yet, private schools continue to occupy a place in American education. Even the Supreme Court recognized as much.

In its landmark judgment in *Pierce v. Society of Sisters,*[30] the Supreme Court observed that requiring school-aged children to attend only public schools, absent extenuating circumstances, was "arbitrary, unreasonable, and unlawful interference with [their] patrons and the consequent destruction of [the Appellees'] business and property."[31] The Court further pointed out that parents had a liberty right under the Fourteenth Amendment to choose a private institution at which to educate their children.

> The fundamental theory of liberty upon which all governments in this Union repose excludes any general power of the state to standardize its children by forcing them to accept instruction from public teachers only. The child is not the mere creature of the state; those who nurture him and direct his destiny have the right, coupled with the high duty, to recognize and prepare him for additional obligations.[32]

Myriad reasons guarantee the survival of private education. The most notable of these reasons are parental interests in overseeing the education of their children, providing them instruction in religion as well as in academic subjects, sending them to smaller and perhaps safer schools, taking advantage of school choice options that blend attributes of public and private schools, and seeking specialized curricula for their children.

Following are descriptions of how private schools were, and are, reflections of social and political contexts. These contexts do not adhere strictly to timelines. Forms of private schooling did not start and stop at fixed times in history; rather they flowed through American educational history, sometimes as ripples, sometimes as waves.

---

[30] 268 U.S. 510 (1925). As the result of a voter initiative, the Oregon Compulsory Education Act required, with a handful of exceptions, all children between the ages of 8 and 16 to attend their neighborhood public schools. Prior to going into effect, two private schools, the Society of Sisters and the Hill Military Academy, successfully sued for an injunction that the Supreme Court held. Among other allegations, the plaintiffs charged that the law interfered with the rights of parents to oversee the upbringing of their children, which included "choos[ing] schools where their children will receive appropriate mental and religious training." *Id.* at 532.

[31] *Id.* at 536.

[32] *Id.* at 535.

Homeschools

As noted, homeschooling was the primary educational mechanism in the early colonial period and remains an important feature in private education today.[33] For instance, it is well known that the Pilgrims came to the New World for the purpose of having the freedom to exercise their religious beliefs. What is often absent in the teaching of early American history is that a motivating factor for the Pilgrims was to have the freedom to educate their children in their values and religious doctrine without government or established church interference.[34]

Educating children in the home allowed Pilgrim parents to teach scriptural literacy, values, manners, and vocational skills. Educating children in the home is what some social historians refer to as the establishment of the family state; that is, the family was the foundation for the "holy commonwealth" and the education of the children was fundamental to that endeavor.[35]

> The prosperity and well-being of Comonweles doth much depend upon the well government and ordering of particular Families, which in an ordinary way cannot be expected when the rules of God are neglected in laying the foundations of a family state.[36]

The success of the colony thus depended on the success of the family, and vice versa. Concerned that the rural isolation and hardships faced by families were distracting parents from their responsibility to educate their children, colonial governments, as reflected in Massachusetts and Connecticut, passed laws obligating parents to meet their ordained responsibilities to educate their children. Petty officers and "tithingmen" were appointed to monitor the education of children in the home and were expected to report unruly children and

---

[33] Sughrue, *supra* note 1.

[34] Gaither, *supra,* note 1. Gaither illustrates this premise by tracing the first Protestant separatists who left Scrooby, England, and traveled to Amsterdam so they could practice their religion freely and educate their children according to their separatist beliefs. Their dreams to build a religious community did not materialize. After more than a decade of hard labor and few converts, these separatists would become what we now refer to as the Pilgrims who set sail for the New World. "Generations of Americans have learned in elementary school of the Mayflower, Squanto, Thanksgiving, and the other tropes that make up the romance of the Plymouth Colony, but it has not often been noted that one of the driving motivations behind the endeavor was the education of children" (p. 9).

[35] *Id. See also* John Demos, A LITTLE COMMONWEALTH: FAMILY LIFE IN PLYMOUTH COLONY (2nd ed.) (2000); Arthur W. Calhoun, SOCIAL HISTORY OF THE AMERICAN FAMILY: FROM COLONIAL TIMES TO THE PRESENT, VOL. 1 (1945).

[36] Demos, *supra* note 35, at 144.

adults to the authorities.[37] Families seemingly accepted this colonial oversight and intrusion into the home without complaint.[38]

Rurality and lack of public resources also required families in mid-Atlantic and southern colonies to rely on homeschooling; geographical isolation and low population density did not accommodate central schooling structures. Wealthy landowners often hired tutors for their children or set up field schools on their plantations to educate their children and those of the tradesmen, workers, freedmen, and sometimes slaves who lived there.[39] Older female siblings frequently functioned as teachers once their own education was nearly complete. After primary schooling, male adolescents were typically sent to academies or to Europe to further their studies. Farming families of more modest means often organized field schools and shared the cost of hiring teachers.

As the movement toward independence from England advanced and as colonies became larger and more complex economically and politically, other models of private education, as well as the emergence of public schoolhouses, competed for space. However, homeschooling neither disappeared nor was viewed antagonistically by community leaders. Education was education, regardless of the means. Homeschooling continued to offer families the option of educating their children according to their religious and cultural values.

The Revolutionary War, the Common School Movement, and the Civil War had profound impact on expanding the role of government in providing primary education and, in turn, diminishing the role of private schooling, particularly homeschooling. The Founders believed that the diffusion of knowledge was a bastion against tyranny, the preserver of freedom, and essential to the success of a representative democracy. While there was some disagreement initially, the Founders agreed that education should be under the purview of each state. State governments were thus charged with meeting the needs of their citizens, while creating national social and political cohesion by promulgating common values such as liberty, equality, and the common good.

In the 1830s, the Common School Movement took hold, leading to compulsory education laws beginning in the 1850s; Massachusetts was the first to adopt such a statute in 1852. These laws required all children to attend school to receive basic education, although no effort was made to mandate attendance only at public schools. The same laws are credited with helping the

---

[37] Gaither, *supra* note 1.

[38] Mary Beth Norton, FOUNDING MOTHERS AND FATHERS: GENDERED POWER AND THE FORMING OF AMERICAN SOCIETY (1997). Norton explains this passive acceptance of intrusion into the home as acquiescence to paternal authority, a theory posited by Sir Robert Filmer. Gaither further explained that "the family and the state were analogous institutions, both created by God and ground in the natural law of patriarchal authority. . . . [Both] family and state were created by God to serve the same purpose—the peaceful government of society according to Divine law" (p. 14).

[39] Middlekauff, *supra* note 3. The Nat Turner rebellion was a turning point in the education of Blacks in the lower mid-Atlantic and southern colonies, after which educating Blacks was outlawed.

enforcement of child labor laws by obligating young children to go to school, thereby getting them out of the factories, off the farms, and into classrooms.

The Common School Movement did not find a warm reception in the South, though. Because there was a growing political and social divide between Northern and Southern states, ideas birthed in New England were viewed suspiciously in the South. Further, the remoteness of plantations and the dispersed populations in Southern states made a system of free common schools unworkable. Homeschooling and field schools were primary forms of education. According to James DeBow, publisher of a popular Southern magazine, the *DeBow Review*, "in consequence of the population being scattered in the Southern states, the number of children educated at home by private tutors . . . is immensely greater in proportion to the whole, than in other parts of the Union."[40]

Following the Civil War, free education was viewed as a way to enable emancipated Blacks to find a "proper appreciation and employment of their liberty,"[41] as well as a means to help to avoid future rebellions. Ignorance was the enemy of freedom and democracy. Missionaries, many of them women, traveled to the South to teach freed Blacks, but were not well received. Likewise, there was opposition to taxation for public schools, regardless of whether the students were White or Black. Nonetheless, over time free schools were established for Blacks and Whites—but, as history taught, they were separate and not equal.

All of these events conspired to diminish the role of homeschooling in favor of public and private schools. Economic depressions, additional military struggles, as well as political fears of economic and religious polarization at the turn of the century further contributed to the demise of homeschooling as a prominent form of educating children.[42] With men at war and women working, children went to public schools. When World War I ended, economic depression hit; as parents struggled to scrape by, children continued to go to public schools. Public high schools drew children out of the home because parents believed their young would be better prepared for employment with high school diplomas. Homeschooling retreated as a common option, replaced by public and, to a lesser degree, parochial schools. Homeschooling lay relatively dormant for decades, except for a "fringe" element.

A resurgence in homeschooling occurred in the 1970s, thereby marking its "modern era."[43] The new popularity of homeschooling was the result of multiple factors: a renewed religious fundamentalism whose adherents rejected

---

[40] James D. B. DeBow, *The Progress of Education in the United States and Europe*, DeBow's Review (Jan. 1855), as cited in Mark Groen, *These Public Schoolhouses-The Citadels of our Liberties*, 32 Am. Educ. Hist. J. 153, 153 (2005).

[41] Harper's Weekly, *The Freedmen's Schools*. (3 October 1869), as cited in Groen, *supra* note 40, at 154.

[42] Groen, *supra* note 40; Sughrue, *supra* note 1. *See also* Joseph Murphy, Homeschooling in America: Capturing and Assessing the Movement (2012).

[43] Eric J. Isenberg, *What Have We Learned about Homeschooling?* 83 Peabody J. of Educ. 387 (2007).

the perceived replacement of God with secular humanism in public schools; the activism of progressive parents who believed their children deserved an education that fostered autonomy and self-directed learning; civil rights activists who viewed public schools as a source of perpetuated inequities; and others who simply did not trust government agencies, including public schools.[44]

Data from recent surveys of parents who homeschool their children evinced their desires to provide moral and religious instruction.[45] Other reasons included parents' perceptions of poor learning environments at schools, including safety and discipline issues; their objections to some of the curricular content, or their concerns that curricula lacked rigor; and their desire to provide nontraditional approaches to educating their children.

The percentage of students who are homeschooled, while small, has grown steadily. Current data indicate that from 1999 to 2012, the percentage of homeschooled students doubled, from 1.7% to 3.4%.[46] Data collected in 2016 point to a slight leveling off in the percent of students who are homeschooled, at 3.3%.[47]

Homeschooling advocates developed a cadre of powerful supporters. The Home School Legal Defense Association (HSLDA) and the National Home Education Institute (NHERI) work continuously to lobby for and defend the rights of parent to homeschool their children.[48]

The NSLDA, in particular, has been instrumental in lobbying state legislatures for laws relaxing governmental restrictions on and oversight of homeschooling. The NSLDA has staff members who readily come to the legal defense of parents or groups when they come up against local school authorities who hold them accountable to state regulations, or who limit the access of their children to advanced courses and athletics in the public schools, a topic discussed in Chapter 9.

At the same time, the NHERI generates research supporting the value of homeschooling. However, NHERI is not transparent about its research methods, data analysis, and/or sample populations. As such, it is difficult to confirm or challenge NHERI's findings.[49]

Homeschooling has taken on new forms, too, as it is no longer limited to hardcopy textbooks or even to the home. To this end, homeschooling associations are marketing curricular and instructional materials, as well as training and support, to parents. These groups provide online instruction, if preferred. Groups of homeschooling families have organized to provide academic, social, and extracurricular experiences.

---

[44] *Id. See also* Sughrue, *supra* note 1; Murphy, *supra* note 42.

[45] NCES, PARENT AND FAMILY INVOLVEMENT IN EDUCATION: RESULTS FROM THE NATIONAL HOUSEHOLD EDUCATION SURVEYS PROGRAM OF 2016 (2017). *See* Table 8, available at https://nces.ed.gov/pubsearch/pubsinfo.asp?pubid=2017102

[46] *Id.*

[47] *Id.* The NCES reported that the 2016 percentage was not statistically different from the 2012 data.

[48] Sughrue, *supra* note 1.

[49] *Id.*

Once state legislatures created opportunities for funding, local school boards encouraged homeschooling parents to enroll their children in public charter schools and virtual schools so they can access higher level and Advanced Placement coursework, as well as extracurricular activities and clubs. In this way, students who are homeschooled are assured certified teachers and curricula to prepare them for postsecondary opportunities.

Contemporary homeschooling is a reflection of changing attitudes about school choice and of the emerging hybrid of private and public educational offerings. Parents still can direct the education of their children and yet enjoy the flexibility of a combination of direct and online teaching. While homeschooling still has its detractors,[50] it is once again well-established in the mainstream of educational options.

Academies

Academies are mainstays in private schooling, having expanded the educational landscape for about three centuries. Educational historians place the height of the academy movement from the last decade of the 1700s up to the Civil War.[51]

Historically, academies served diverse populations, from rural families to wealthy urban and plantation families, while being located in all regions of the new republic.[52] The academies provided the bridge between grammar schools and colleges by offering higher schooling. Some academies functioned as college preparatory schools for boys, while others catered to females and offered instruction in French, embroidery, and dancing.[53] Academies in the North tended to be coeducational and offered a "liberal" education that included instruction in geography, mathematics, oratory, history, composition, and elocution.

While a few academies existed in the early colonial period, they grew in popularity after the Revolutionary War; political and educational leaders took greater interest in formal education when state and local governments were unable or unwilling to establish and maintain public schools.[54] In fact, Southern states tended to incorporate existing academies and seminaries, maintaining the burden of educating children in the private sector. Incorporation meant some financial support from the state and exemption from taxation, guaranteeing stability and educational continuity.

In seeking charters for incorporation, promoters claimed their academies would "be of great Utility to the Publick and especially to the rising

---

[50] *Id.* Among concerns express by opponents of homeschooling is child welfare. Unsupervised homeschooling means situations in which children who are denied an education or who are abused may go on undetected for years.

[51] Tolley, *supra* note 5. *See also* J. M. Opal, *Exciting Emulation: Academies and the Transformation of the Rural North, 1780s-1820s*, 91 J. Amer. Hist. 445 (2004).

[52] Beadie and Tolley, *supra* note 1.

[53] Opal, *supra* note 51.

[54] Beadie and Tolley, *supra* note 1; Opal, *supra* note 51; Hyde, *supra* note 2.

Generation."[55] Inasmuch as academies were really private enterprises, trustees often contrived an academy's value to the community by building impressive, commodious structures in the middle of the town or village, or atop a hill in clear view of the public. Academies were stocked with impressive teaching aids like globes, maps, and telescopes.[56]

The academies' promise of social and economic mobility generated detractors concerned about the disruption to established social and economic hierarchies, as well as to family stability.

> [M]any took issue with the central postulate of [academies] that, instead of following their parents' calling, children should seek distinction among their peers and within an expanded public. The entire spirit of the schools ran counter to forms of established and still-vital family cohesion and mutuality.[57]

In other words, academies encouraged youth to be ambitious and self-serving, attributes that did not sit well in families valuing modesty while focusing on family needs. Yet, the emergence of the industrial era and capitalism fostered this form of individualism, which helped drive the demand for academies.

As with other private school models, such as church schools and home-schooling, enrollment in academies has waxed and waned over time, a function of politics and economics. As public schools became well established, middle- and lower-income families chose to send their children to free public schools.

Conversely, both the number of private academies and their enrollment surged in the South in the 1960s when it was evident states had no choice but to integrate the public schools.[58] Segregation academies, which restricted matriculation to White students, were a mechanism for resistance to desegregation. In the wake of the Massive Resistance Movement championed by Senator Harry F. Byrd, Sr., some states repealed compulsory attendance laws, shut down integrated schools, created freedom-of-choice plans, and provided grants to White families to send their children to private nonsectarian schools, which were really segregation academies. After these efforts were challenged and found unconstitutional,[59] White families paid the tuition to maintain their children's enrollment in segregated private schools rather than send them to integrated schools.

The enactment of the Civil Rights Act of 1964 further spawned a growth in segregated academies.[60] Champagne shared a report compiled by plaintiffs' lawyers in preparation for challenging Mississippi's statutory program

---

[55] Opal, at 449. The trustees of Haverhill Academy in New Hampshire made this statement before the General Court as they argued for a state charter in 1793.

[56] *Id.*

[57] *Id.* at 448.

[58] Anthony M. Champagne, *The Segregation Academy and the Law*, 42 J. NEGRO EDUC. 58 (1973, Winter).

[59] *See* Harrison v. Day, 106 S.E.2d 636 (1959); Griffin v. County Sch. Bd. of Prince Edward Cnty., 377 U.S. 218; 84 S. Ct. 1226 (1964).

[60] Champagne, *supra* note 57.

that allowed the state to purchase and loan textbooks to public and private schools, including segregation academies.[61] The report included data about the growth of segregation academies in Mississippi from school years 1963-1964 to 1969-1970.[62] In 1963, there were sixteen such academies. By 1969, there were 124 academies, almost eight times the number that existed in 1963. Student enrollment grew from 2290 in 1963 to 30,939 in 1969, more than a fourteen-fold increase.

In light of losing state funding, many thought segregation academies would die out. However, they underestimated the amount of "guts and anger"[63] that resided within the members of the White community who refused to send their children to integrated schools. The Internal Revenue Service (IRS) was contributing to their survival as well, by "consciously, deliberately, and against continual objection" approving tax-exempt status to these academies under the charitable sections of the IRS code. Enjoying tax-exempt status made contributions to the academies attractive to supporters.[64] Under the code in 1970,

> Contributions made to a school classified as tax exempt entitle the donor to take a deduction from his taxable income. A donor who provides a building or land for a school site, if the basis of his property is below market value, may deduct the current market value without realizing capital gain. A wealthy donor who has used up his $60,000 lifetime tax exemption can avoid the payment of a gift tax (if the gift exceeds $3000), and take a charitable deduction instead. He, like the donor of low basis property, escapes one federal tax and reduces another.[65]

Leadership in segregated academies often relied on donations, particularly for capital expenditures, but when they lost state tuition grants, soliciting donations became a priority and they needed tax-exempt status to make it palatable to potential donors. As a 1969 letter from the Directors of Central Holmes Academy explained,

> Unless we receive substantial contributions to our Scholarship Fund there will be many, many students, whose minds and bodies

---

[61] *Id. See also* Norwood v. Harrison, 413 U.S. 455 (1973). Overturning an earlier order, the Supreme Court ruled that "the constitutional infirmity of the Mississippi textbook program is that it significantly aids the organization and continuation of a separate system of private schools. A State's constitutional obligation requires it to steer clear, not only of operating the old dual system of racially segregated schools, but also of giving significant aid to institutions that practice racial or other invidious discrimination." The Court ordered state officials to audit the private schools receiving textbooks to determine which were not discriminating against Black children. Children at those schools would continue to be eligible to receive textbooks.

[62] Champagne, *supra* note 57, at 59. These numbers represent private, non-Catholic schools.

[63] Reginald Stuart, *Segregated Academies Look to Congress for Tax Relief*, N.Y. TIMES (1982 February 2), available at https://www.nytimes.com/1982/02/02/us/segregated-academies-look-to-congress-for-tax-relief.html

[64] James M. Spratt, Jr., *Federal Tax Exemption for Private Segregated Schools: The Crumbling Foundation*, 12 WM & MARY L. REV. 1 (Fall 1970).

[65] *Id.* at 3.

are just as pure as those of any of their classmates and playmates . . ., who for financial reasons alone, will be forced into one of the intolerable and repugnant 'other schools', . . . or into dropping out of school entirely.[66]

The IRS halted this practice after the federal trial court in the District of Columbia enjoined it from awarding further exemptions to private schools engaged in racial discrimination.[67] Acknowledging efforts to establish and maintain a unitary school system, the court ruled that

The due process clause of the Fifth Amendment does not permit the Federal Government to act in aid of private racial discrimination in a way which would be prohibited to the States by the Fourteenth Amendment. . . .[Likewise,] the Federal Government is not constitutionally free to frustrate the only constitutionally permissible state policy . . . by providing government support for endeavors to continue under private auspices the kind of racially segregated dual school system that the state formerly supported.[68]

Some segregated academies still exist, most often buried in the Deep South in small towns and rural areas.

On the one hand, growth in the number of academies stagnated in the face of judicial decrees that pinched off their access to direct and indirect funding. On the other hand, some scholars argue that the purpose of segregation academies is being satisfied by public charter schools, magnet schools, open enrollment policies, and voucher programs, all of which provide families who have the knowledge and means to find private and public school niches that allow them to continue to segregate themselves under the cover of school choice.[69]

School choice has had the effect of smudging the lines between private and public schooling by creating a competitive marketplace in which private educational corporations and parochial schools can receive public dollars, if indirectly, by attracting students to their schools and by submitting to some modicum of government oversight. Among the most prominent options to emerge under school choice are charter schools. What follows is a brief history of the development of public charter schools, their place in the new educational marketplace, and how they have helped return a segment of public schooling to something less than public.

---

[66] Green v. Kennedy, 309 F. Supp. 1127, 1135 (1970).

[67] Id.

[68] Id. at 1137.

[69] See, e.g., Amy J. Borman, Understanding legal Issues in Private Education: Leading Lawyers on Managing Issues Affecting Students and Teachers, 2014 WL 4785758 (Oct. 2014); Louise Seamster and Kaey Henricks, A Second Redemption? Racism, Backlash Politics, and Public Education, 39 HUMANITY & SOC'Y 363 (2015).

Charter Schools

While they are public schools, charter schools represent a return to a public and private educational compact, a partnership that bears some resemblance to educational endeavors in the early national period and through the Civil War. The difference between now and then is that private schools were filling a space in educational delivery, with the assistance of some public financing, that was unavailable otherwise. Today, public schools are the major component of the American educational fabric that has become frayed after decades of underfunding and political backlash. School choice advocates have contributed to the struggles of public education by successfully introducing educational options that siphon students and money away from traditional schools and into those managed by private corporations and other non-public entities. Charter schools are the premiere example of this movement.

Under state laws, charter schools are privately managed public schools independent of most forms of governmental regulation. Charter schools gain autonomy and less regulation in exchange for meeting stipulated performance criteria. Nonprofit organizations, teachers, parents, and private corporations, including for-profit companies, are among those eligible to apply for charters. Per-pupil funding follows students to their charter schools, meaning that for-profit businesses and, in some instances, sectarian institutions are collecting taxpayer dollars, whether directly or indirectly.

The idea of "education by charter" was first proposed in 1974 by Ray Budd, a former school administrator who became a professor of educational administration in Massachusetts.[70] Budd proposed reforming the internal structure of school boards, in effect flattening them, so groups of educators could petition school committees, the name given boards in Massachusetts, for charters to form new schools. Citing Dewey, Budd claimed that if teachers were full participants in the structure and delivery of education, they would become fully invested in the success of their students and public education would be a more democratic institution.

Budd's ideas about education by charter did not garner support until *A Nation at Risk* was published in 1983, at which time Al Shanker took notice.[71] Shanker embraced Budd's idea of small schools and empowering teachers. However, being pragmatic, Shanker did not advocate the radical restructuring of school systems Budd proposed. Rather, Shanker was influenced by his visit to a teacher-led middle and high school in Cologne, Germany, in which a diverse population of students comprised of immigrant and native Germans were taught by small teams of teachers. These teams had considerable latitude on what subjects would be taught, when they would be taught, and by whom, as long as

---

[70] Ray Budd, EDUCATION BY CHARTER: RESTRUCTURING SCHOOL DISTRICTS (1988). Budd first floated the idea of charter schools in 1974, but the idea received no attention at the time. Fifteen years later, following *Nation at Risk*, he wrote his book.

[71] Richard D. Kahlenberg and Halley Potter, *A Smarter Charter*, 23 POVERTY & RACE 5 (2014). Al Shanker was president of the American Federation of Teachers from 1974-1997.

they met common sets of standards.[72] The innovative approach resulted in an unexpectedly high percentage of students pursuing post-secondary education.

In 1988, the Citizens League of Minnesota published a report, *Chartered Schools = Choices for Educators + Quality for All Students*.[73] The League advocated for an innovative approach for improving racial integration and quality of education in their public schools.

> Minneapolis and St. Paul have learned that school desegregation based solely on numbers and transportation produces neither sufficient integration nor assured access to quality education. We need a new approach to multicultural education that values quality as much as it does quotas, and that moves us closer to real integration as a community.[74]

To this end, the League urged the state legislature to embrace a "Minnesota difference" by enacting a charter school law to encourage cooperatively managed schools that would be autonomous and would inspire educational innovation by educators who understood how to address the needs of their student populations; all they needed was flexibility and support to do so. In 1992, the Minnesota's legislature passed the first law in the nation authorizing public charter schools. In 2017, Kentucky became the forty-fourth jurisdiction to enact charter school legislation.[75]

Nationally, while the numbers are small relative to traditional public schools, enrollment in charter schools has increased dramatically since their inception. The National Center for Education Statistics reported that in fall 2000, less than 1 million students enrolled (0.4 million), representing one percent of public school students in nearly 3400 charter schools.[76] By fall 2015, this number increased to 2.8 million, or 6% of public school students, in over 6700 charter schools.

After the District of Columbia, which has 43% of students enrolled in charter schools, Arizona follows with 16%. Nearly 30% of Arizona's public schools are charters.[77] In terms of whom the charter schools are serving, in the fall of 2000, 43% of charter school students were White, with 33% Black and

---

[72] *Id.*

[73] Available at https://citizensleague.org/wp-content/uploads/2017/07/PolicyReportEducation Nov-1988.pdf

[74] *Id.* at i.

[75] 2017 KY. REV. STAT. ANN. § 160.1592. The first charter schools are supposed to open in 2018, but there appears to be some doubt whether funding will be available. All links to charter school documents such as student applications, charter school applications, and charter school conversions and petitions, on the Kentucky Department of Education webpage were dead, available at https://education.ky.gov/CommOfEd/chartsch/Pages/default.aspx

[76] NCES, THE CONDITION OF EDUCATION: PUBLIC CHARTER SCHOOL ENROLLMENT (2018), available at https://nces.ed.gov/programs/coe /indicator_cgb.asp

[77] NCES, DIGEST OF EDUCATION STATISTICS, Table 216.90: Public elementary and secondary charter schools and enrollment, by state: Selected years, 1999-2000 through 2014-15 (2016), available at https://nces.ed.gov/programs/digest/d16 /tables/dt16_216.90.asp

19% Latino.[78] In the fall of 2015, Latino enrollment took the lead, with 32%. Whites represented 33% and Blacks, 27%. Charter schools tend to be racially distinct. Suburban charters typically have White schools, while urban charters are populated by racial minorities.

Findings from a study conducted in Michigan indicated that charter schools have negatively affected private school enrollment, albeit at a modest rate.[79] This should be no surprise insofar as charter schools have given parents, who otherwise had their children in private schools, options to meet the needs and interests of their young in tuition-free schools. The scope of curricular options and guiding philosophies in charter schools offer parents choices they might not have available in private schools. Still, whether charter schools deliver in terms of educational quality and equality of opportunities are issues subject to vigorous debate in the literature.

A concern for those who pay close attention to charter school funding and management is the involvement of for-profit education management organizations (EMOs).[80] Many states restrict charters to nonprofit organizations, but this does not constrain them from contracting with for-profit companies to manage their schools. Auditors have discovered that many charter schools depend on EMOs to run the business end of the schools. In so doing, charter school boards sign what are called "sweeps" contracts, termed as such "because nearly all of the school's public dollars—anywhere from 95 to 100%—is 'swept' into a charter-management company."[81]

The most disturbing aspect of these arrangements is that the boards often neither know how the money is spent nor question the numbers presented to them in the EMO budgets. Equally concerning is that this is happening in the absence of rigorous research on the merits of charter schools and whether these EMOs are giving taxpayers a return on their investment.

These revelations have not shaken state legislators into action, and the public does not seem to be sufficiently aware of the problem to pressure their state representatives. Skeptics assert that charter schools and other school choice options are a form of "opportunity hoarding that has its eyes locked

---

[78] NCES, *supra* note 76.

[79] Rajashri Chakrabarti andd Joydeep Roy, *Do Charter Schools Crowd Out Private School Enrollment? Evidence from Michigan*, 91 J. URBAN ECON. 88 (2016).

[80] *See, e.g.*, Natalie Lacireno-Paquet, *Charter School Enrollments in Context: An Exploration of Organization and Policy Influences*, 81 PEABODY J. OF EDUC. 79 (2006); General Accounting Office, *Public Schools: Insufficient Research to Determine Effectiveness of Selected Private Education Companies* (2002), Marian Wang, *When Charter Schools Are Nonprofit in Name Only*, Propublica (2014, December 9), available at https://www.propublica.org/article/when-charter-schools-are-nonprofit-in-name-only; Allison Graves, *Are All Florida Charter Schools Not-for-Profit?* Politifact in partnership with Tampa Bay Times (2017, April 27), available at http://www.politifact.com/ florida/statements/2017 /apr/27/bob-cortes/are-all-florida-charter-schools-not-profit/; Marian Wang, *Charter School Power Broker Turns Public Education into Private Profits*, Propublica (2014, October 15), available at https://www.propublica.org/ article/charter-school-power-broker-turns-public-education-into-private-profits

[81] *Id.* Wang, available at https://www.propublica.org/article/charter-school-power-broker-turns-public-education-into-private-profits

onto dollar sign,"[82] and that "these interests converge with entrepreneurs and profiteers who see education as a source of profit."[83] Adjustments to how charter schools are run and who may collect taxpayer funds depends on a reframing of the debate on public dollars being spent for the public good, and whether private-public partnerships are generating the promised outcomes or simply exacerbating the problems they were supposed to resolve.

Church Schools

Sectarian schooling and schools that have populated the educational landscape longer than public schools have been viewed by many politicians, and even the judiciary, as playing an important role in secular education. In *Board of Education of Central School District No. 1 v. Allen,* [84] affirming the constitutionality of a statute from New York requiring local school boards to loan textbooks in secular subjects to children in grades seven to twelve in nonpublic schools, the Supreme Court defended state action that indirectly aided private schools, including sectarian institutions. The Justices observed that such legislative measures were "recognition that private education has played and is playing a significant and valuable role in raising national levels of knowledge, competence, and experience."[85] The court added that the continued reliance on private school systems, including parochial systems, by states

> Strongly suggests that a wide segment of informed opinion, legislative and otherwise, has found that those schools do an acceptable job of providing secular education to their students. This judgment is further evidence that parochial schools are performing, in addition to their sectarian function, the task of secular education.[86]

The evolution of sectarian schooling is manifest in the early colonial period and into the national period. As amply described previously, religious instruction was paramount in the New England colonies, particularly in homes. Later, when the first town schools were founded, Puritan religious tenets were in evidence.[87] Education was a means of inculcating "biblical truths" and of "instilling obedience and proper behavior in children."[88]

---

[82] *Supra,* note 68, Seamster and Henricks, 366.

[83] *Id.*

[84] 392 U.S. 236 (1968), in which the Supreme Court ruled that indirect aid, such as loaning textbooks to children who attend parochial schools, served a public purpose.

[85] *Id.* at 247.

[86] *Id.* at 248.

[87] Jennifer A. Sughrue, *The Legal and Historical Links Between Public Schools and the Establishment Clause Through the Twentieth Century,* in Religion and the Law in Public Schools: History, Philosophy, Trends, 1-63 (Steve Permuth, ed. in chief, 2017)

[88] *Id.*

As public schools took hold in urban centers, particular in New York, Pennsylvania, Michigan, and Ohio, religious tensions arose.[89] Initially, "free schools" were established "for the education of poor children who do not belong to, or are not provided for by, any religious society."[90] However, they soon evolved into schools that would inculcate immigrant children into the established religious and cultural mores of the community.

> While early pauper and charity schools founded by philanthropic free school societies were not technically public schools, these schools and their missions enjoyed civic and political support. Prominent civic and political leaders, virtually all of whom were Protestant, believed these schools should be used to acculturate new non-English speaking, non-Protestant immigrant children to the Nativist Protestant cultures that prevailed in urban centers.[91]

The Catholic Church, in response, began establishing schools. This effort was in response to the anti-Papist sentiments permeating the curricula and textbooks of the day.[92] Bishop John Hughes, an Irish-born prelate, was a fiery advocate of establishing an equivalent Catholic free school system to educate Catholic children in New York. Hughes lobbied the state legislature to provide the Catholic Church its fair share of public funds with which to run its schools. Over time, religious tensions spilled over, resulting in riots, after which state legislatures took control of public education and denied funding to both Protestant and Catholic organizations. Catholic schools have been a mainstay ever since that time.

The number of faith-based schools dwindled in the early decades of the twentieth century. However, in the late 1970s and early 1980s, religious conservatism, primarily Christian fundamentalism, emerged.[93] The Moral Majority, the Religious Roundtable, and The Coalition took issue with the progressive, and Godless, nature of public education; this reignited interest in private religious schools and homeschooling.

> The Christian Right membership believed that public schools were a bulwark that denied students the true source of moral training, God's word, as revealed in the Bible. In their view, God is the final moral arbiter of right and wrong. In addition, they believed government authorities compounded the problem by being dismissive of parental and religious authority over issues such as sex

---

[89] *Kastler, supra* note 1. *See also* Steven K. Green, THE BIBLE, THE SCHOOL AND THE CONSTITUTION: THE CLASH THAT SHAPED MODERN CHURCH-STATE DOCTRINE (2012); David Tyack and Larry Cuban, TINKERING TOWARD UTOPIA: A CENTURY OF PUBLIC SCHOOL REFORM (1995); R. Freeman Butts, THE AMERICAN TRADITION IN RELIGION AND EDUCATION (1950); Diane Ravitch, THE GREAT SCHOOL WARS: A HISTORY OF THE NEW YORK PUBLIC SCHOOLS (2000).

[90] Sughrue, *supra* note 87.

[91] *Id.*

[92] *Id.*; Kaestle, *supra* note 1; Cremin, *supra* note 2; Ravitch, *supra* note 89.

[93] Sughrue, *supra* note 87

education, health education, gender roles, the origin of man, and values education.[94]

A recent trend in private schooling indicates that the number and enrollment in Conservative Christian schools has declined slightly. In 2011-2012, 14.8% of private schools were described as Conservative Christian, educating 14% of all private school students.[95] Catholic schools represented 22.3% of private schools and 42.9% of private school students. In 2014-2015, the numbers shifted away from both. The percent of Conservative Christian schools fell to 12%, with 13.5% of the students, while the percent of Catholic schools increased to 20.3%, while only capturing 38.8% of the students.[96] The percent of "other religious" schools increased slightly in 2014-2015.

Over the past forty years, church schools have enjoyed more state fiscal and legislative support. Tax deductions, tuition tax credits, vouchers, provision of textbooks, transportation, and instructional materials, reimbursements for testing and reporting requirements, and even school charters have aided church schools in maintaining their presence. As discussed in Chapter 4, decades of Supreme Court rulings have established that indirect aid to sectarian schools does not offend the First Amendment, opening the way for closer church-state partnership. What lies in store for this relationship is unclear. Surely, politics and religion will play a role.

Conclusion

Private schools will always be an option for families who want to provide a different kind of teaching and learning environment for their children, and who can afford the tuition. The political tension between families and lawmakers who believe parents should be able to choose the kind of school they want their children to attend, with some level of government financial support, and those who believe taxpayer dollars should be invested only in public goods, such as public schools, has sparked contentious political disputes over vouchers and school choice. These contemporary issues define the relationship between private and public education today.

Researchers from all fields with interests in public and private education, law, sociology, public policy, political science, and economics, must continue to investigate current trends in educational policy and practice and their impact on the lives of children, as well as their families and on society in general. Perhaps empirical data can inform policy makers and other decision makers if all use our human and fiscal resources to, as the Founders urged, educating for the common good, against tyranny and for freedom, or if we have unwittingly closed our eyes to their vision.

---

[94] Id.

[95] NCES, CHARACTERISTICS OF PRIVATE SCHOOLS IN THE UNITED STATES: RESULTS FROM THE 201L-2012 PRIVATE SCHOOL UNIVERSE SURVEY (2013).

[96] NCES, CHARACTERISTICS OF PRIVATE SCHOOLS IN THE UNITED STATES: RESULTS FROM THE 2014-2015 PRIVATE SCHOOL UNIVERSE SURVEY (2016).

Discussion Questions

1. What was the role of private education in the early history of American education, and how has that role changed over time?

2. How has the distinction between what is public and what is private schooling changed over time?

3. What are your views on the purposes of education, and in what ways private schools can fulfill those purposes, if any?

4. What are your thoughts on the public-private partnerships that are a part of the education landscape today?

5. What are your thoughts about the premise of a competitive educational marketplace, one in which there is a place for private schools?

6. How does taxpayer money play into today's educational marketplace?

7. How do you see schooling evolving in the future and the role of private schooling in that future?

Key Words

Academies
Charter schools
Church schools
Common school movement
Dame schools
Education management organizations
History of American education
Homeschools
Private schools
Town schools
Venture schools

2

Institution, Student, and Faculty Relationships

Ralph D. Mawdsley and James L. Mawdsley

Contents

Introduction / 30
Defining the Contract / 32
Constitutional Constraints / 38
      Concept of Fairness / 39
      State Action / 40
      Contractual Due Process / 48
Student/Employee Conduct and Violations of Contract / 50
      Prohibited Conduct / 50
      Compliance with Procedures / 51
      Adherence to Contract Terms / 54
Fundamental Fairness / 61
Recommendations / 65
Conclusion / 66
Discussion Questions / 66
Key Words / 67

Introduction

Most courts define the relationship between public and nonpublic[1] educational institutions, their faculties, and students under contractual, rather than constitutional, principles.[2] Moreover, while some courts have discussed these relationships in terms of the law of association, most simply treat them as matters of contract.[3]

Insofar as faith-based schools are not public actors, the constitutional principles often cited in contract disputes involving public educational institutions are inapplicable.[4] Courts expect fair treatment of students and employees in contractual relationships in nonpublic schools. Even so, the definition of fairness is less rigorous than the constitutional standards imposed on public institutions. Still, like their public counterparts, nonpublic educational institutions are subject to a wide variety of state and federal statutes that set requirements for, or limitations on, the contractual authority of nonpublic schools. For example, officials of nonpublic schools making gender-based employment decisions are subject to state and federal antidiscrimination statutes.[5] Chapter 10, Federal Antidiscrimination Legislation, discusses these statutes in detail.

When employees and students in public institutions experience adverse contractual actions, their relationship with these schools entitles them to due process rights under the Property and Liberty clauses of the Fourteenth Amendment. However, these rights and remedies are unavailable to the students and employees of nonpublic schools. Whatever contractual rights employees and students enjoy in nonpublic schools are limited to the language of their contracts, which may include applications, promotional literature, and stu-

---

[1] This chapter uses the terms nonpublic and faith-based interchangeably unless the context suggests otherwise.

[2] *See* Sharick v. Southeastern Univ. of the Health Sci., 780 So. 2d 136 [152 EDUC. L. REP. 448] (Fla. Dist. Ct. App. 2000).

[3] The law of association is based on the theory that membership in organizations should carry measures of "protection of the members' valuable personal relationship to the associations and the status conferred by those relationships. The loss of status resulting from the destruction of one's relationship to a professional organization at times may be more harmful than a loss of property or contractual rights." Napolitano v. Trs. of Princeton Univ., 453 A.2d 263, 271 [8 EDUC. L. REP. 74] (N.J. Super. Ct. App. Div. 1982) (upholding the delay in awarding a diploma to a student convicted of plagiarizing on an assignment during her senior year). While this concept differs from contract, its application to institutions of higher learning has generally been another way to assure that institutional official deals fairly with students and faculty. *See* Clayton v. Trs. of Princeton Univ., 608 F. Supp. 413 [25 EDUC. L. REP. 234] (D.N.J. 1985) (applying the law of association in agreeing that a student who was suspended for one year for cheating received fundamental fairness). *But see* Higgins v. Am. Soc'y of Clinical Pathologists, 238 A.2d 665 (N.J. 1968), *aff'd per curiam after remand*, 251 A.2d 760 (N.J. 1969) (rejecting the expulsion of a medical technologist as a member of a certification body as an unjustifiable penalty).

[4] For a discussion of contractual differences between nonpublic and public institutions of higher education, see Ralph D. Mawdsley, *Comparison of Employment Issues in Public and Private Higher Education Institutions* [65 EDUC. L. REP. 669] (1991).

[5] *See* Gallo v. Salesian Soc'y, 676 N.E.2d 580 [109 EDUC. L. REP. 1286] (N.J. Super. Ct. 1996) (allowing a lay teacher to sue a religious school for age and sex discrimination under the state statute prohibiting such behavior).

dent or employee handbooks. This chapter discusses the contractual rights of employees and students together, as the same principles apply in both instances.

In an age where online course offerings have become a vital part of the programs of many educational institutions, nonpublic and public, questions of jurisdiction have emerged. In such a case, the Third Circuit, in a non-precedential order, affirmed that a university in Alabama lacked sufficient contacts with students in Delaware to afford the judiciary in the latter state jurisdiction over a student's breach of contract and discrimination claims.[6] The upshot of the rejection of the jurisdictional claim meant that the aggrieved student would have had to file suit in Alabama if he wished to pursue a claim.

A similar dispute arose in Texas, where a federal trial court determined that it lacked jurisdiction over a dispute between two educational institutions. An online college employed 129 adjunct instructors in Texas, providing educational services to 12,281 residents of the state. Acknowledging that the college had no offices, bank accounts, or physical property in the state, the court treated the fact that it operated an interactive website used by state residents as insufficient to establish in-state jurisdiction.[7] One might argue that being able to solicit students to enroll in electronic courses, and then fight to restrict jurisdiction for them if disputes arise after they enroll, certainly puts education at cross-purposes.

In Illinois, while the case involved a faculty member rather than a student, an appellate court ruled in favor of a private, out-of-state university when a physician filed a defamation action against it and an unpaid faculty member, alleging they made false and defamatory statements about his qualifications after he received a prestigious award from a disease treatment foundation.[8] The court found that the university's lack of contacts with the state meant that it was not subject to general jurisdiction, adding that it had no campuses or offices located in-state, and only one of its approximately 6,000 employees had a primary work address in the state.

The cases in this chapter examine the rights students and employees vis-à-vis nonpublic educational institutions based on their relationships with their students.

In a case from Missouri, for instance, the Eighth Circuit affirmed injunctive and declaratory relief in favor of a church against a chief juvenile officer who removed 115 boarding students from its school based on inaccurate and stale information.[9] In an overwhelming victory for the church in Missouri against the officer's overreaching exercise of authority, the court rejected his claim for prosecutorial immunity while recognizing a host of constitutional claims for the church. The court found that school officials had associational standing to assert the Fourth Amendment rights of their students; the seizures

---

[6] Kloth v. Southern Christian Univ., 320 F. App'x 113 [245 Educ. L. Rep. 673] (3d Cir. 2008).

[7] Am. Univ. Sys. v. Am. Univ., 858 F. Supp. 2d 705 (N.D. Tex. 2012). For a similar outcome in an unreported case, see Hershman v. Muhlenberg Coll., 2013 WL 5929849 (D. Conn. 2013) (rejecting a claim of jurisdiction where a student sued his alma mater while living in a different state from which it was located).

[8] Wesly v. Nat'l Hemophilia Found., 77 N.E.3d 746 [345 Educ. L. Rep. 384] (Ill. App. Ct. 2017).

[9] Heartland Acad. Cmty. Church v. Waddle, 427 F.3d 525 [202 Educ. L. Rep. 629] (8th Cir. 2005).

were not reasonable under the Fourth Amendment; the officer violated both the school's right to family integrity and to procedural due process by removing the boarding students; the officer violated the school's First Amendment associational rights; and the injunction did not implicate a violation of the Establishment Clause.

Defining the Contract

The threshold challenge in litigation over contracts between nonpublic educational institutions and their students or employees is selecting which of the many documents have become part of the disputed agreements. Among the documents most nonpublic educational institutions rely on are application forms, brochures, handbooks, and board policies defining and describing relationships between and among the parties.

As demonstrated by a case from the Supreme Court of Arkansas, religious schools have unique opportunities to incorporate their beliefs into their contracts. The court thus overturned that part of an earlier order awarding $190,000 to the parents of a child its officials disenrolled. The court pointed out that the school contract which all parents signed each year contained a "Matthew 18 Principle [requiring the] … reconciling [of] differences by first conferring with the most immediate staff member related to the incident in question, and then only pursuing the proper, progressive chain of authority when matters are not acceptably resolved."[10]

When school officials received evidence that the parents were not following the Matthew 18 Principles, they disenrolled their son. Treating this "unaffiliated parochial school [as being] similar to a congregational or self-governing church,"[11] the panel observed that the trial court lacked jurisdiction because "any analyses of whether the school breached or interfered with its agreement with the [parents] would require us to determine whether the[y] did, or did not, comply with Matthew 18."[12]

---

[10] Calvary Christian Sch. v. Huffstuttler, 238 S.W.3d 58, 66-67 [227 Educ. L. Rep. 378] (Ark. 2006).

[11] *Id.* at 66, n. 6.

[12] *Id.* at 67.

Generally, student and employee handbooks form part of their contracts with educational institutions unless explicitly excluded.[13] Institutional boards and/or school officials can often change handbooks unilaterally from one year to the next, and occasionally during academic years, without going through the contract process with employees or students of offer, acceptance, consideration, and mutuality of benefit.

Having enforceable agreements without the formalities of contractual processes may be problematic from the perspective of contract law.[14] Yet, courts ordinarily accept the language in institutional documents as parts of contracts without inquiring into the processes leading to their formulations. In essence, this means that students and employees in nonpublic educational institutions must abide by the terms of the documents comprising their contracts, even to the point where breach actions can be forestalled if handbooks require exhaustion of administrative remedies.[15]

Contract challenges in nonpublic educational institutions involve a two-step analysis: first, defining the nature of the contract provision; second, identifying appropriate remedies if breaches occur. Because not all language in handbooks creates contractual rights, the Sixth Circuit affirmed that a provision in the Statement of Philosophy section of the Student and Parent Handbook of an Ohio Catholic school about "respecting pupils' differing abilities and styles of learning" did not form an enforceable promise to support a breach of contract claim parents filed on behalf of their son, who had an individualized education program and had not done well in the school.[16]

On the other hand, the federal trial court in the District of Columbia rejected the motion for summary judgment entered on behalf of a Catholic

---

[13] *Compare, e.g.*, Moffice v. Oglethorpe Univ., 367 S.E.2d 112 [46 Educ. L. Rep. 837] (Ga. Ct. App. 1988) (where the faculty handbook was incorporated by reference into the plaintiff's employment contract) *with* Hartz v. Administrators of Tulane Educ. Fund, 275 F. App'x 281 [234 Educ. L. Rep. 281] (5th Cir. 2008) (relying on state law in refusing to treat the medical school's faculty handbook as part of an employment contract). *See also* Wall v. Tulane Univ., 499 So. 2d 375 [36 Educ. L. Rep. 1041] (La. Ct. App. 1986) (rejecting the charge that a university's change in tuition benefit was not a violation of the plaintiff's employment contract where such benefits were identified in a staff handbook that was not part of the contract); Shannon v. Bepko, 684 F. Supp. 1465 [47 Educ. L. Rep. 150] (S.D. Ind. 1988) (remarking that a handbook did not apply to hourly employees); Love v. Duke Univ., 776 F. Supp. 1070 [71 Educ. L. Rep. 124] (M.D.N.C. 1991), *aff'd without opinion*, 959 F.2d 231 (4th Cir. 1992) (refusing to treat a university's academic bulletin about program completion requirements for graduate students as part of the student-university contract); Faur v. Jewish Theological Seminary of Am., 536 N.Y.S.2d 516 [51 Educ. L. Rep. 586] (N.Y. App. Div. 1989) (declaring that insofar as student admission policies were not part of the faculty contract, the seminary could alter its admission policy and admit women).

[14] *See* Dunfey v. Roger Williams Univ., 824 F. Supp. 18 [84 Educ. L. Rep. 219] (D. Mass. 1993) (indicating that a personnel manual that the administration could alter or revoke at any time did not create contractual rights under commonwealth law).

[15] *See* Dahlman v. Oakland Univ., 432 N.W.2d 304 [50 Educ. L. Rep. 895] (Mich. Ct. App. 1988). *See also* Dayton Christian Schs. v. Ohio Civil Rights Comm'n, 766 F.2d 932 [26 Educ. L. Rep. 108] (6th Cir. 1985) (upholding the nonrenewal of a teacher's contract and enjoining the commission's investigation of gender discrimination where she sought advice from an attorney without following the chain-of-command disagreement resolution in Matt. 18:15-17 and delineated in the teachers' manual).

[16] Ullmo v. Gilmour Acad., 273 F.3d 671 [159 Educ. L. Rep. 521] (6th Cir. 2001).

university when it was sued by a faculty member.[17] The court allowed the plaintiff's breach of contract claim because university officials failed to follow their published procedure for addressing a plagiarism charge against him, that was eventually treated as unfounded, while in the midst of his successful tenure review.

Breach of contract actions generally do not lie when school officials followed the procedures in their handbooks.[18] Even so, institutional practices are susceptible to breach of contract challenges if officials seek to enforce changes against students and/or parents who entered into contractual relationships under prior policies.[19] Educational institutions may also be subject to damages for negligent misrepresentation or fraud if officials make unfulfilled promises about program content.[20]

Contracts can involve external documents, understandings of the parties, or custom and usage. The most challenging cases involve interpretations of faculty tenure. In such a case, an appellate court in New York reversed the dismissal of a tenured teacher in a religious school.[21] The court held that the actions of school officials in dismissing the teacher for financial reasons and not for cause were arbitrary and capricious.

In the first of two cases from Illinois, an appellate court asserted that a faculty member was entitled to tenure when, among other letters, the Dean of the School of Medicine sent him pre-employment letters stating that he would approve the plaintiff for early tenure, but failed to do so. The court accepted the faculty member's claim that the letters were part of the contract, expressly

---

[17] Tacka v. Georgetown Univ., 193 F. Supp. 2d 43 [163 EDUC. L. REP. 740] (D.D.C. 2001).

[18] *See e.g.*, Sullivan v. Boston Architectural Ctr., 786 N.E.2d 419 [174 EDUC. L. REP. 1083] (Mass. Ct. App. 2003) (affirming the rejection of a student's claim that he had a right of appeal of his academic record that was different from the process identified in his handbook). *But see* McConnell v. Le Moyne Coll., 808 N.Y.S.2d 860 [206 EDUC. L. REP. 696] (N.Y. 2006) (affirming that once a student was matriculated, he was entitled to the due process procedures identified in the college's rule book before he could be dismissed); Morehouse Coll. v. McGaha, 627 S.E.2d 39 [207 EDUC. L. REP. 429] (Ga. Ct. App. 2005) (recognizing that a student had a breach of contract action where college officials had not followed the handbook during his expulsion procedures).

[19] *See* Bender v. Alderson Broaddus Coll., 575 S.E.2d 112 [173 EDUC. L. REP. 202] (W. Va. 2002) (affirming that college officials did not abuse their discretion by changing their grading policy during a student's final year) *with* Reynolds v. Sterling Coll., 750 A.2d 1020 [144 EDUC. L. REP. 314] (Vt. 2000) (treating the registration contract between the parties as affording a student and his mother rights to a tuition refund identified in the college catalog once they started paying tuition).

[20] *See* Troknya v. Cleveland Chiropractic Clinic, 280 F.3d 1200 [161 EDUC. L. REP. 782] (8th Cir. 2002) (upholding an award for actual damages in the amount of $1.00, but denying punitive damages of $15,000 per claimant, because they failed to demonstrate that institutional officials had the necessary knowledge of wrongdoing under state law to support such awards). *But see* Verni v. Cleveland Chiropractic Coll., 212 S.W.3d 150 [216 EDUC. L. REP. 150] (Mo. 2007) (rejecting the fraudulent misrepresentation claim of a student who was dismissed because he had not relied on representations in the student handbook).

[21] Bane v. Hebrew Acad. of Five Towns and Rockaway, 846 N.Y.S.2d 380 [226 EDUC. L. REP. 979] (N.Y. App. Div. 2007).

rejecting the institution's defense that the letters were only "expressions of good will and [were] not an enforceable promise creating a contractual obligation."[22]

A second appellate court in Illinois denied the claim of two faculty members who alleged that because university officials wrongfully ended their employment before they completed tenure review, they were entitled to have the process completed.[23] At the same time, the court rejected an earlier order that the plaintiffs would have been granted tenure because the publication of qualifications and procedures for it in university bylaws and the faculty handbook did not amount to contractual assurances that tenure would be granted to those who met the stated standards.

If handbooks are clear about the process for such an important academic function as tenure, though, assurances of its being granted outside of established processes are not enforceable under breach of contract or promissory estoppel claims.[24] The admission of oral statements or past practices to construe contractual language is generally governed by the interpretation of the normal parol-evidence rule as to whether it can be used to clarify ambiguities or rewrite contracts.[25]

Custom and usage, which refer to existing or past practices as a means of defining contract terms, can encounter problems in their application. As such, custom and usage do not translate at-will contracts into term contracts where state law clearly interprets contracts of indefinite duration as employment at will.[26] Still, custom and usage may be helpful in interpreting whether language about the length of contracts is sufficient to create term contracts.[27]

Handbook provisions may permit educational institutions to take specified actions with regard to employees and students or their parents. One of the most controversial contract enforcement issues concerns liquidated damages provisions specifying, for example, the amounts teachers who breach their

---

[22] Lewis v. Loyola Univ. of Chicago, 500 N.E.2d 47, 50 [35 Educ. L. Rep. 1199] (Ill. App. Ct. 1986).

[23] Hentosh v. Herman M. Finch Univ. of Health Sci., 734 N.E.2d 125 [148 Educ. L. Rep. 429] (Ill. App. Ct. 2000).

[24] See Kakaes v. George Washington Univ., 790 A.2d 581 [162 Educ. L. Rep. 388] (D.C. Cir. 2002) (affirming that language in the university's employment contract did not entitle the plaintiff to specific performance granting him tenure even if the contract had been construed as granting tenure as the remedy for breach).

[25] For a statement of the parol-evidence rule, see U.C.C. § 2-202 (defining the rule in terms of business dealings). See also Whitney v. Bd. of Educ. of Grand Cnty, 292 F.3d 1280 [166 Educ. L. Rep. 420] (10th Cir. 2002) (barring the use of parol evidence as adding a term to a teacher's contract that termination be preceded by a three-step remediation process). But see Tuomala v. Regent Univ., 477 S.E.2d 501 [113 Educ. L. Rep. 1337] (Va. 1996) (treating parol evidence as admissible as to the statements of board members where ambiguity existed about whether the law school contract conferred tenure on faculty members).

[26] See Roberts v. Wake Forest Univ., 286 S.E.2d 120 [2 Educ. L. Rep. 296] (N.C. Ct. App. 1982) (rejecting the claims of a golf coach who was dismissed after sixteen months that the contracts of golf coaches were long term based on custom and practice in the field, where state law defined all contracts of indefinite length as being at-will).

[27] See Rooney v. Tyson, 674 N.Y.S.2d 616, 617 (N.Y. 1998) (writing that under state law, language that boxing trainer Kevin Rooney would be Mike Tyson's trainer "for as long as [Tyson] fought professionally" was sufficient to create a term contract).

employment contracts must pay,[28] or parents who withdraw their children from schools after specified dates owe in back tuition,[29] as long as the amounts are fair measures when the parties entered the agreements.

Liquidated damages provisions do have an appeal by serving to provide measures of employee and student stability during school years.[30] Even so, such provisions may not readily be enforceable in all states. If educational officials wish to rely on liquidated damages provisions, they would be wise first to investigate whether their state courts enforce such terms. The two most frequent interpretations are that liquidated damages are unenforceable if their purpose is to punish employees or parents,[31] or if officials have not attempted to mitigate damages before seeking to enforce such clauses.[32]

What makes liquidated damages attractive to educational officials is that they not only have sums of money to attract replacement students or employees, but also retain flexibility in attracting replacements. In such a case from Tennessee, the Sixth Circuit upheld a liquidated damages provision in a football coach's contract that required him to pay more than $93,000 for each of three years remaining on his contract when he left to coach at another university.[33]

Similarly, an appellate court in Ohio affirmed a grant of summary judgment in its breach of contracts claim, including a liquidated damages clause, against a former basketball coach.[34] The coach, who quit before the expiration of his contract in order to accept a position at another college, had to pay his salary for each year remaining under the contract. Both courts upheld the liquidated damages clauses because the damage to the institutions over the loss of the coaches was not easily measurable.

Turning to cases from K-12 education, an appellate court in Nebraska affirmed that officials in a Catholic school did not breach a teacher's contract by enforcing its liquidated damages provision.[35] School officials deducted

---

[28] Parizek v. Roncalli Catholic High Sch. of Omaha, 655 N.W.2d 404 [172 EDUC. L. REP. 968] (Neb. Ct. App. 2002)

[29] *See* Sisters of the Holy Child Jesus at Old Westbury v. Corwin, 29 N.Y.S.3d 736 [329 EDUC. L. REP. 1036] (N.Y. App. Div. 2016) (upholding the liquidated damages clause in a registration contract obligating parents to pay tuition and fees for the full year after they withdrew their daughter from the school as not an impermissible penalty). For other cases affirming liquidated damages clauses for tuition, see, e.g., Western Reserve Acad. v. Franklin, 999 N.E.2d 1198 [300 EDUC. L. REP. 404] (Ohio Ct. App. 2013); Turner v. Atlanta Girls' Sch., 653 S.E.2d 380 [227 EDUC. L. REP. 357] (Ga. Ct. App. 2007); Barrie Sch. v. Patch, 933 A.2d 382 [225 EDUC. L. REP. 973] (Md. 2007).

[30] For a discussion of this issue, see Ralph D. Mawdsley, *Liquidated Damages Clauses in Educational Contracts*, 186 EDUC. L. REP. 587 (2004).

[31] *See* 24 RICHARD A. LORD, WILLISTON ON CONTRACTS § 65:1, at 216–23 (4th ed. 2002).

[32] *See, e.g.,* Barrie Sch. v. Patch, 933 A.2d 382 [225 EDUC. L. REP. 973] (Md. 2007) (refusing to treat mitigation as required before enforcing a liquidated damages clause).

[33] Vanderbilt Univ. v. DiNardo, 174 F.3d 751 [134 EDUC. L. REP. 766] (6th Cir. 1999).

[34] Kent State Univ. v. Ford, 26 N.E.3d 868 (Ohio Ct. App. 2015).

[35] Parizek v. Roncalli Catholic High Sch. of Omaha, 655 N.W.2d 404 [172 EDUC. L. REP. 968] (Neb. Ct. App. 2002) (also involving a breach of contract charge against the teacher for an unspecified violation of the doctrine of the Catholic Church that was precluded from the court's jurisdiction because the Establishment Clause prohibited it from addressing the merits of the claim).

$1,000 from the teacher's last paycheck after officials denied his request to be released from the subsequent year's contract.

On the other hand, an appellate court in Florida refused to permit officials in a private school to sue a teacher for liquidated damages equal to two months of pay.[36] Just prior to the beginning of the academic year, the teacher asked officials to vacate her contract so she could accept a job in a public school. The public superintendent required such consent from the private school before he would issue the teacher a contract such that absent it, she did not receive the job. Officials in the private school treated the teacher's request as a breach of contract, hired a replacement, and sued her to collect the liquidated damages. Rejecting the private school's liquidated damages claim, the court noted that its charges were mutually exclusive; officials could not hire a replacement, thus making it impossible for the teacher to fulfill her contract and sue for liquidated damages, alleging that she breached her contract.

The court in Florida chose not to address whether the teacher's having sought to vacate her contract prior to the beginning of the school year could have been treated as a breach without liquidated damages in the equation. In other words, a question arose over whether private school officials could have treated the teacher's request as a breach and then hired a replacement. Presumably, nothing would have prevented officials from treating such requests as breaches, but contracts would have to be unequivocally clear in making this part of their terms.

In a case from higher education, litigation arose when a former faculty member who received a two-year sabbatical leave of absence failed to return to campus on time, even though officials refused to extend his sabbatical. The Eighth Circuit affirmed that insofar as the plaintiff had not invoked the faculty handbook's dismissal provisions, college officials could treat his failure to return at the end of two years as a resignation, thereby not having to address his procedural rights associated with his dismissal.[37]

As reflected in the following four cases, disputes involving liquidated damages in K-12 schools can also involve parents and students. After a mother withdrew her children from a nonpublic school because she was dissatisfied with their educational progress, she unsuccessfully filed suit. An appellate court in Georgia affirmed the dismissal of the mother's breach of contract claim for tuition because school officials fulfilled their obligations under the contract by providing teachers and facilities to the children.[38]

A second appellate court in Georgia reached a like outcome in affirming a liquidated damages award of $12,539 plus interest in favor of a school when parents refused to send their daughter to classes after signing an enrollment contract. The court agreed that the liquidated damages provision was enforceable under state law where "(1) the injury caused by the breach is difficult or impossible to estimate accurately, (2) the parties intended to provide for dam-

---

[36] Weisfeld v. Peterseil Sch. Corp., 623 So. 2d 515 [85 EDUC. L. REP. 954] (Fla. Dist. Ct. App. 1993).

[37] Altimore v. Mount Mercy Coll., 420 F.3d 763 [201 EDUC. L. REP. 87] (8th Cir. 2005).

[38] Fuller v. Lakeview Acad., 583 S.E.2d 282 [179 EDUC. L. REP. 492] (Ga. Ct. App. 2003).

ages rather than a penalty, and (3) the stipulated sum is a reasonable estimate of the probable loss."[39]

Maryland's highest court upheld a liquidated damages provision obligating parents who removed their children from a private school without permission to pay the balance of the tuition owed for the year, plus 12% interest and attorney fees. The court treated the liquidated damages provision as "a reasonable forecast of just compensation for potential harm caused by a breach of the Agreement."[40]

Most recently, an appellate court in New York upheld the liquidated damages clause in a registration contract obligating parents to pay tuition and fees for the full year after they withdrew their daughter from a faith-based school as a permissible penalty.[41] Consequently, the parents were responsible for $14,800.68 in tuition and fees for one academic year.

Courts have upheld institutional actions in light of published statements in their materials. The first two of three key higher education issues, both of which were litigated in New York, were withholding a diploma and transcript at graduation where a student had outstanding financial obligations,[42] and refusing to forward a degree-holder's transcript to graduate schools he applied to because he had an outstanding balance for tuition owed.[43]

The third case affirmed the refusal of officials to grant a diploma to a student in Maryland who, between the completion of his courses and the date of graduation, murdered a peer, because the handbook expressly prohibited the types of violations he committed. The court added that individuals had to have had any and all charges of misconduct removed from their records before they could be awarded diplomas.[44] In a case involving a private K-12 school, the highest court in the District of Columbia affirmed that officials could exclude a student because his father had not paid his tuition, and that their doing so did not result in intentional infliction of emotional distress against the child.[45]

Constitutional Constraints

As discussed in this section, nonpublic schools generally are exempt from the substantive and procedural constitutional constraints imposed on public educational institutions. However, the absence of such rights has not prevented students and employees from alleging constitutional violations, nor has it stopped courts from discussing the treatment of students or employees using broad concepts of constitutional fairness.

---

[39] Turner v. Atlanta Girls' Sch., 653 S.E.2d 380, 382 [226 EDUC. L. REP. 357] (Ga. Ct. App. 2007)..

[40] Barrie Sch. v. Patch, 933 A.2d 382, 391 [225 EDUC. L. REP. 973] (Md. 2007).

[41] Sisters of the Holy Child Jesus at Old Westbury v. Corwin, 29 N.Y.S.3d 736 [329 EDUC. L. REP. 1036] (N.Y. App. Div. 2016).

[42] Martin v. Pratt Inst., 717 N.Y.S.2d 356 [149 EDUC. L. REP. 872] (N.Y. App. Div. 2000).

[43] Sheridan v. Trs. of Columbia Univ., 745 N.Y.S.2d 18 [167 EDUC. L. REP. 326] (N.Y. App. Div. 2002).

[44] Harwood v. Johns Hopkins Univ., 747 A.2d 205 [142 EDUC. L. REP. 980] (Md. Ct. App. 2000).

[45] Sibley v. St. Albans, 134 A.3d 789 [330 EDUC. L. REP. 193] (D.C. 2016).

Concept of Fairness

The Due Process Clause of the Fourteenth Amendment[46] protects the substantive and procedural rights of employees and students against actions of officials in public educational institutions. Substantive rights, such as free speech, protect students and employees from institutional rules that are unfair on their faces or are interpreted unfairly.[47] Procedural rights, such as the right to hearings, ensure that students and employees receive fair treatment by educational officials.[48]

Balancing the rights of individual employees and students with the need of public school officials to exercise and maintain control over education has not always been easy. During the 1980s, in four prominent cases—*New Jersey v. T.L.O.*,[49] *Bethel School District v. Fraser*,[50] *Hazelwood School District v. Kuhlmeier*,[51] and *Morse v. Frederick*[52]—the Supreme Court tipped the balance

---

[46] The Fourteenth Amendment, through which the substantive and procedural rights in the Bill of Rights are made applicable to the states, provides in part: "No State shall make or enforce any law which shall abridge the privileges or immunities of citizens of the United States; nor shall any State deprive any person of life, liberty, or property without due process of law; nor deny any person within its jurisdiction the equal protection of the laws."

[47] The seminal substantive due process case is Tinker v. Des Moines Independent School District, 393 U.S. 503, 506 (1969), where the Supreme Court, ruling in favor of students who wore black armbands to school, held that "students, and teachers, [do not] shed their constitutional rights to freedom of speech or expression at the schoolhouse gate." As to employees, the Court has treated their speech as protected only if it is on matters of "public concern" (Pickering v. Board of Educ. of Twp. High Sch. Dist. 205, 391 U.S. 563 (1968)). The First Amendment does not protect public employees if their employers would have taken adverse employment actions against them absent the protected speech (Connick v. Myers, 461 U.S. 138 (1983); Mt. Healthy City Bd. of Educ. v. Doyle, 429 U.S. 274 (1977)), or they speak out pursuant to their official duties, because they are not doing so as private citizens (Garcetti v. Ceballos, 547 U.S. 410 (2006)).

[48] The seminal procedural due process case for students is Goss v. Lopez, 419 U.S. 565 (1975), wherein the Supreme Court found that the nature of the hearings students receive depends on whether their removals from school would be more or less than ten days. In Honig v. Doe, 484 U.S. 305 [43 EDUC. L. REP. 857] (1988), the Court applied *Goss* to removal of students with disabilities from school. The leading case protecting the procedural due process rights of public employees facing dismissal is Cleveland Board of Education v. Loudermill, 470 U.S. 532 [23 EDUC. L. REP. 473] (1985), *on remand*, 763 F.2d 202 [25 EDUC. L. REP. 158] (6th Cir. 1985), *on remand*, 651 F. Supp. 92 [37 EDUC. L. REP. 502] (N.D. Ohio 1986), *aff'd*, 844 F.2d 304 [46 EDUC. L. REP. 523] (6th Cir. 1988), *cert. denied*, 488 U.S. 941 (1988), *cert. denied*, 488 U.S. 946 [50 EDUC. L. REP. 15] (1988).

[49] 469 U.S. 325 [21 EDUC. L. REP. 1122] (1985) (allowing school officials to search students based on reasonable suspicion rather than the Fourth Amendment's probable cause standard). The Court subsequently applied the *T.L.O.* standard to search of an employee's office in O'Connor v. Ortega, 480 U.S. 709 (1987).

[50] 478 U.S. 675 [32 EDUC. L. REP. 1243] (1986) (upholding the disciplining of a student for vulgar and lewd speech that would undermine the school's basic educational mission).

[51] 484 U.S. 260, 273 [43 EDUC. L. REP. 515] (1987) (upholding the removal of two pages of a school newspaper prepared as part of a journalism course on the basis that since the school curriculum was involved, educators had the power to act "so long as their actions are reasonably related to legitimate pedagogical concerns.").

[52] 551 U.S. 393 [220 EDUC. L. REP. 50] (2007) (upholding a student's suspension for displaying the sign reading "Bong Hits 4 Jesus" at a school-related parade because the principal interpreted it as being in violation of school policy prohibiting student drug use).

in support of school board control over education. As often seems to occur with Supreme Court cases, there subsequently seems to be little or no diminution in the number of federal and state cases involving constitutional claims by students and employees.

Fourteenth Amendment substantive and procedural rights applicable to students and employees in public educational institutions are inapplicable to those in nonpublic schools.[53] This does not mean, though, that courts are unwilling to distill a concept of fairness from the constitutional standards in examining the treatment of students and employees in nonpublic institutions.[54] On occasion, courts, in confusing and troubling judgments, have discussed constitutional due process standards in great detail when assessing whether officials in private institutions of higher education provided appropriate process to students or employees.[55] In nonpublic schools, generally, the concept of fairness means that their contracts with students and/or employees must clearly identify the appropriate, or inappropriate, standards or conduct, as well as the penalties for misconduct. Invariably, contracts can represent a variety of documents, including applications, promotional materials, and handbooks that may be incomplete, inconsistent, or inaccurate; to the extent that contracts contain conflicting or ambiguous language, students and/or employees are likely to contest adverse treatment on the basis of unfairness.

Officials in nonpublic educational institutions should be committed to writing clear expectations for conduct, along with setting forth the process they intend to use in evaluating whether individuals violated these standards. Accomplishing this goal requires educational officials to review contractual documents regularly with their attorneys. Fairness, then, is as much about what is done as it is about what is written in institutional documents.

State Action

Students and employees in nonpublic educational institutions lack constitutional rights similar to those of their counterparts in public schools. This difference arises because in nonpublic schools—absent express state statutory

---

[53] *See, e.g.,* Centre Coll. v. Trzop, 127 S.W.3d 562 [185 Educ. L. Rep. 1074] (Ky. 2004) (reiterating that private colleges are not held to the same standard of due process as public institutions).

[54] *See* Harvey v. Palmer Coll. of Chiropractic, 363 N.W.2d 443, 444 [23 Educ. L. Rep. 667] (Iowa Ct. App. 1984) ("requirements imposed by the common law on private universities parallel those imposed by the Due Process Clause on public universities."); Flint v. St. Augustine High Sch., 323 So. 2d 229, 235 (La. Ct. App. 1976) (decreeing that in expelling two students, "if there is color of due process, that is enough.").

[55] *See* Franklin v. Leland Stanford, Jr. Univ., 218 Cal.Rptr. 228 [27 Educ. L. Rep. 525] (Cal. Ct. App. 1985) (upholding dismissal of a tenured faculty member as a result of 1971 speeches encouraging physical damage to the university's computation center and which prolonged student disruption after applying Pickering v. Bd. of Educ., 391 U.S. 563 (1968) (free-speech balancing test) and Mt. Healthy City Bd. of Educ. v. Doyle, 429 U.S. 274 (1977) (mixed-motive test)); Napolitano v. Princeton Univ., 453 A.2d 263 [8 Educ. L. Rep. 74] (N.J. Super. Ct. App. Div. 1982) (in upholding a delay in awarding a degree for plagiarism, while acknowledging the inapplicability of constitutional due process to a private university, nonetheless discussed it at length, rejecting the student's claim that the university was subject to a higher standard under the state constitution).

language to the contrary,[56] or specific situations such as where there was collusion between institutional officials and local police to conceal evidence of a sexual assault after which the victim committed suicide[57]—lack sufficient connections to the government. The Fourteenth Amendment, according to which persons cannot be deprived of life, liberty, or property without due process of law, applies only to actions by states.

Unless private educational institutions are imbued with the authority of state governments, they cannot be rendered liable for alleged violation of constitutional rights conferred on citizens.[58] This lack of accountability means that students and employees in nonpublic institutions cannot seek damages for alleged constitutional violations under Section 1983 of the Civil Rights Act of 1871.[59] Section 1983 has become a favorite remedial vehicle by public school claimants alleging that state actors violated their federal constitutional or statutory rights.

---

[56] *See* Riester v. Riverside Cmty. Sch., 257 F. Supp. 2d 968, 972 [177 Educ. L. Rep. 187] (S.D. Ohio 2002) (treating the private parties operating a community school as state actors where a statute mandated that "[a] community school created under this chapter is a public school."). *But see* Caviness v. Horizon Cmty. Learning Ctr., 590 F.3d 806 [252 Educ. L. Rep. 53] (9th Cir. 2010) (affirming that even though Arizona statutes describe charter schools as public, officials in one were not engaged in state action disciplining a teacher because education is not a public function and the state did not regulate the personnel functions of charter schools).

[57] McGrath v. Dominican Coll. of Blauvelt, 672 F. Supp. 2d 477 [253 Educ. L. Rep. 635] (S.D.N.Y. 2009). *See also* Victory Outreach Ctr. v. Melso, 371 F. Supp. 2d 642 [199 Educ. L. Rep. 139], *aff'd*, 281 F. App'x 136 (3d Cir. 2008) (while conceding that a conspiracy between security guards at a private college and city policy can constitute state action, the court upheld the dismissal of the student's alleged free speech violation after he was arrested for preaching on a crowded street corner).

[58] *See* Jackson v. Strayer Coll., 941 F. Supp. 192 [113 Educ. L. Rep. 1191] (D.D.C. 1996), *aff'd*, 1997 WL 411656 (D.C. Cir. 1997) (affirming that absent state action, the federal courts lacked jurisdiction to stop a private college from prohibiting students from forming a student government).

[59] 42 U.S.C. § 1983 provides in relevant part that: "Every person who, under the color of any statute, ordinance, regulation, custom or usage, of any State ... subjects, or causes to be subjected, any citizen of the United States or other person within the jurisdiction thereof to the deprivation of any rights, privileges, or immunities secured by the Constitution or laws, shall be liable to the party injured ...."

Both the Fourteenth Amendment and Section 1983 are premised on the existence of state action.[60] Over the years, claimants from nonpublic schools have advanced four theories in arguing that private activity has sufficient involvement with government so as to create constitutional liability:[61] the state entanglement theory;[62] the state or public function theory;[63] the symbiotic

---

[60] Findings of state action requires plaintiffs to meet at least one of the tests in Blum v. Yaretsky, 457 U.S. 991 (1982) (Blum): (1) the extent to which the private entity is subject to state or federal regulations; (2) sufficiency of close nexus between the state and private entity so that action of the latter is treated as action of the former; (3) the presence of such coercive power or significant encouragement of the state that private decisions are essentially those of the state (rejecting the claim that Medicaid recipients were able to establish "state action" in a nursing home's actions in discharging or transferring Medicaid patients to lower levels of care). For a case agreeing that state action was present when officials at a private school satisfied one or more of the *Blum* tests, see Milonas v. Williams, 691 F.2d 931, 940 [7 Educ. L. Rep. 247] (10th Cir. 1982), *cert. denied*, 460 U.S. 1069 (1983) (affirming that former students in a private school for behavioral-problem youths had a Section 1983 claim alleging constitutional violations where the state "had insinuated itself with Provo Canyon School [so] as to be considered a joint participant in the offending actions."). *But see* Logiodice v. Trs. of Me. Cent. Inst., 296 F.3d 22 [167 Educ. L. Rep. 85] (1st Cir. 2002), *cert. denied*, 537 U.S. 1107 (2003) (affirming that where a local board lacking a high school placed students in a private school within its boundaries pursuant to a contract between the parties, officials in the private school were not state actors subject to the Fourteenth Amendment's due process requirements). For an article including a discussion of the *Blum* tests, see Ralph D. Mawdsley, *State Action and Private Educational Institutions*, 117 Educ. L. Rep. 411 (1997).

[61] *See* Brentwood Acad. v. Tenn. Sch. Athletic Ass'n, 531 U.S. 288, 295-96 [151 Educ. L. Rep. 18] (2001) (treating a state athletic association as a public actor in a suit filed by a private school that was disciplined allegedly for violating its recruiting rules; on remand, the association was found to have violated the free speech rights of the school, but on appeal to the Supreme Court for a second time, it reversed in favor of the private school). *See also* NCAA v. Tarkanian, 488 U.S. 179 [50 Educ. L. Rep. 17] (1988) (refusing to treat the NCAA as a state actor in a suit by a former coach who alleged that it violated his constitutional rights). For a discussion of the three theories in the context of a private school student's constitutional claim, see Huff v. Notre Dame High Sch., 456 F. Supp. 1145 (D. Conn. 1978).

[62] *See, e.g.,* Howard v. Pine Forge Acad., 678 F. Supp. 1120 [45 Educ. L. Rep. 115] (E.D. Pa. 1987) (refusing to treat compliance with state requirements, applicable to all public and private schools, as state action). *See also* Vincent v. W. Technical Corp., 828 F.2d 563 (9th Cir. 1987) (refusing to treat the receipt of funds from the federal government to perform contract work according to federal standards as state action where the regulations had no bearing on its personnel policies).

[63] *See, e.g.,* Logiodice v. Trs. of Me. Cent. Inst., 296 F.3d 22 [167 Educ. L. Rep. 85] (1st Cir. 2002), *cert. denied*, 537 U.S. 1107 (2003) (affirming that states have no federal constitutional obligation to provide education in light of Pierce v. Soc'y of Sisters, 268 U.S. 510 (1925) (holding that a state cannot prohibit nonpublic schools from operating); Gorman v. St. Raphael's Acad., 853 A.2d 28 [189 Educ. L. Rep. 784] (R.I. 2004) (upholding a challenge a Catholic school's hair length rule, rejecting the intimation that it performed a public function for state action purposes such that it infringed on the student's constitutional rights). *See also* NCAA v. Tarkanian, 488 U.S. 179 [50 Educ. L. Rep. 17] (1988) (refusing to treat the NCAA's regulatory role as a public function where the number of private colleges and universities in it was sufficient to balance the public members); Transport Careers v. Nat'l Home Study Council, 646 F. Supp. 1474 (N.D. Ind. 1987) (refusing to treat accreditation duties as not traditionally a public function). *But see* Missert v. Trs. of Boston Univ., 73 F. Supp. 2d 68, 72 [140 Educ. L. Rep. 554] (D. Mass. 1999) (suggesting in dicta that "an IRB's decision may well constitute state action under th[e] traditional government function.").

relationship theory; [64] and entwinement.[65] Using one or more of these theories, litigants have unsuccessfully alleged factual connections to support claims of state actions: the receipt of federal or state financial assistance;[66] accredita-

---

[64] *See, e.g.,* Williams v. Discovery Day Sch., 924 F. Supp. 41 [109 EDUC. L. REP. 748] (E.D. Pa. 1996) (refusing to treat a private day school that used space in a federal office building as a state actor when officials did not allow a father to see his son's records); Stone v. Dartmouth Coll., 682 F. Supp. 106 [46 EDUC. L. REP. 194] (D.N.H. 1988) (declining to treat the disciplinary actions of college officials against students by tearing down structures they built to protest investment in South Africa as a substitution for criminal prosecution so as to constitute a symbiotic relationship between the college and the state). *But see* Craft v. Vanderbilt Univ., 18 F. Supp. 2d 786 [130 EDUC. L. REP. 171] (M.D. Tenn. 1998) (decreeing that genuine issues of material fact existed as to whether a symbiotic relationship existed between the state and a private university concerning medical research conducted under state auspices, the results of which were concealed from participants).

[65] The Supreme Court acknowledged the entwinement argument in Brentwood Acad. v. Tenn. Sch. Athletic Ass'n, 531 U.S. 288 [151 EDUC. L. REP. 18] (2001) (treating the behavior of officials of a state athletic association as state action because although it was nominally private, it was so intertwined with public school boards that, due to their overwhelming numbers when compared with private schools, they represented the largest voting bloc interpreting and enforcing organizational rules).

[66] Rendell-Baker v. Kohn, 457 U.S. 830 [4 EDUC. L. REP. 999] (1982) (refusing to treat a private school's dismissal of employees as state action even though over 90% of its funding came from the state where state officials did not influence the decision); Martin v. Univ. of New Haven, 359 F. Supp. 2d 185 [196 EDUC. L. REP. 529] (D. Conn. 2005) (declining to treat the receipt of federal funds as the basis of a section 1983 claim where federal law did not compel the alleged adverse treatment of the plaintiff); Smith v. Duquesne Univ., 612 F. Supp. 72 [26 EDUC. L. REP. 604] (W.D. Pa. 1985), *aff'd*, 787 F.2d 583 [31 EDUC. L. REP. 422] (3d Cir. 1986) (rejecting an expelled graduate student's procedural constitutional claims for lack of state action where the state financial aid to the private university was only a miniscule part of its budget); Murphy v. Villanova Univ., 547 F. Supp. 512 [6 EDUC. L. REP. 715] (E.D. Pa. 1982), *aff'd*, 707 F.2d 1402 (3d Cir. 1983) (denying the claim of a former student that officials at his private university engaged in state action in violation of his civil rights when they transferred him from a work study program to the regular payroll after funds for the former were used up); Williams v. Howard Univ., 528 F.2d 658 (D.C. Cir. 1976) (refusing to treat the federal government's contribution of funds to a medical school as state action for the purposes of a student's due process claim for readmission); Spark v. Catholic Univ. of Am., 510 F.2d 1277 (D.C. Cir. 1975) (rejecting the request to treat financial aid to the university in the form of grants, student aid, payment for government contracts as not sufficient for state action involving a law professor's free speech claim, even though the federal aid amounted to 25% of the university's budget); Wahba v. New York Univ., 492 F.2d 96 (2d Cir. 1974) (refusing to treat a research program funded by the federal government as sufficient for state action where a research associate professor was dismissed without a hearing); Grafton v. Brooklyn Law Sch., 478 F.2d 1137 (2d Cir. 1973) (affirming that a student who was expelled for academic deficiencies failed to prove that officials engaged in state action to support his constitutional claim based on the location of the school on a site acquired in a public sale where the bidding was limited to nonpublic corporations for educational use).

tion or state licensure;[67] receiving state charters;[68] certification of teachers;[69] tax exemption;[70] filing of state forms;[71] performing the public function of

---

[67] Huff v. Notre Dame High Sch., 456 F. Supp. 1145 (D. Conn. 1978) (refusing to treat state accreditation as state action where the private school functioned on its own and was not drawn into a symbiotic relationship with other public schools or the state); Geraci v. St. Xavier High Sch., 13 Ohio Op.3d 146 [1978 WL 195016] (Ohio Ct. App. 1978) (rejecting the claim that the school's state approval was a form of state action); Bright v. Isenbarger, 445 F.2d 412 (7th Cir. 1971) (affirming that a private school's having received a first-class commission from the state board of education was not state action where the commission had nothing to do with the disciplinary rules the students who were expelled challenged).

[68] Fischer v. Driscoll, 546 F. Supp. 861 [6 EDUC. L. REP. 545] (E.D. Pa. 1982) (rejecting the claims of a student who was denied permission to complete specified classes that a private university's having received a charter from the commonwealth constituted state action); Blackburn v. Fisk Univ., 443 F.2d 121 (6th Cir. 1971) (affirming the denial of claims filed by a student who was suspended that the actions of officials constituted state action because officials of the private university neither derived revenues from the state nor did public officials control the its disciplinary policies).

[69] See Geraci, 13 Ohio Op.3d at 146, 1978 WL 195016 at *2 (Ohio Ct. App. 1978) (refusing to treat state certification of teachers as state action); Bright v. Isenbarger, 445 F.2d at 414 (affirming that curricular and training requirements were not sufficient state involvement to constitute state action).

[70] Browns v. Mitchell, 409 F.2d 593 (10th Cir. 1969) (affirming that a private institution's ability to benefit from a special tax exemption not enjoyed by other corporations did not qualify as state action, thereby allowing students who were suspended for disciplinary reasons to file suit alleging that officials acted under "color of state law") Williams v. Howard Univ., 528 F.2d at 660 (affirming that a federal tax exemption is not state action); Huff, 456 F. Supp. at 1148 (refusing to treat a tax exemption as state action where it did not result in state supervisory control); Wisch v. Sanford Sch., 420 F. Supp. 1310, 1314 (D. Del. 1976) ("mere exemption from taxation ... cannot be a basis for finding state action.")

[71] Albert v. Carovano, 851 F.2d 561 [48 EDUC. L. REP. 35] (2d Cir. 1988) (deciding that the actions of officials at a private college in disciplining students did not constitute "state action" within meaning of a civil rights statute even though state law required institutions to adopt disciplinary rules and file them with state because public authorities never sought to compel institutions to enforce their rules nor even inquired about enforcement).

education;[72] establishing policies required by the government;[73] meeting state minimum education standards;[74] and complying with state regulations.[75]

Courts have been resolute in refusing to find state action under the factors just identified and have been creative with terminology in maintaining their positions. Such a case arose when officials at a private university revoked the degree of a medical resident who failed his licensing examination. The Third Circuit affirmed the denial of the plaintiff's claim, reasoning that contacts between public officials and their counterparts at the university were "state-aided" rather than "state-related," and Pennsylvania's Department of Education neither coerced nor significantly encouraged the university regarding the revocation of the degree.[76]

The leading Supreme Court case on state action in private education is *Rendell-Baker v. Kohn* (*Rendell-Baker*).[77] In *Rendell-Baker*, teachers in Mas-

---

[72] Hu v. Am. Bar Ass'n, 568 F. Supp. 2d 959 [236 Educ. L. Rep. 826] (N.D. Ill. 2008), *aff'd* 334 F. App'x 17 (7th Cir.2009) (affirming that a private university was not a state actor for purposes of Section 1983 in an action by a former law student alleging that the state delegated an exclusive public function to it or its law school because education was not the exclusive province of the state); *Logiodice*, 296 F.3d at 26-27 (affirming that education was not a state function because in order to be so it must exclusively be reserved to the state); Martin v. Univ. of New Haven, 359 F. Supp. 2d 185 [195 Educ. L. Rep. 529] (D. Conn. 2005) (rejecting the claim that higher education was an exclusive governmental function); Berrios v. Inter-Am. Univ., 535 F.2d 1330 (1st Cir. 1976) (rejected the state-action claim a suspended student filed based on a provision in the Constitution of Puerto Rico respecting the rights of all persons to an education).

[73] Logan v. Bennington Coll., 72 F.3d 1017 [106 Educ. L. Rep. 51] (2d Cir. 1995) (agreeing that officials at a private college did not engage in state action because the Vermont Human Rights Commission was part of the impetus for adoption of its sexual harassment policy under which a faculty member was dismissed); Missert v. Trs. of Boston Coll., 73 F. Supp. 2d 68 [140 Educ. L. Rep. 554] (D. Mass. 1999), *aff'd without opinion*, 248 F.3d 1127 (1st Cir. 2000) (rejecting the claims of a student dismissed from a dentistry program that officials at his private college engaged in state action where the involvement of its institutional review board, which the federal government mandated to oversee research on human subjects, did not render his being excluded as state action).

[74] Nobles v. Ala. Christian Acad., 917 F. Supp. 786 [107 Educ. L. Rep. 851] (D. Ala. 1996) (rejecting claims that officials in a nonpublic school failed to provide a student with an adequate education because even if the state constitution mandated a minimum standard of education, this amounted to no more than a state regulation that was insufficient to constitute state action).

[75] I.H. by and through Hunter v. Oakland School for Arts, 234 F.Supp.3d 987345 Educ. L. Rep. 176 (N.D. Cal. 2017), Caviness v. Horizon Cmty. Learning Ctr., 590 F.3d 806 [252 Educ. L. Rep. 53] (9th Cir. 2010) (rejecting claims that charter schools were public schools for the purposes of alleging that their officials engaged in state actions); Tavolini v. Mt. Sinai Med. Ctr., 984 F. Supp. 196 [123 Educ. L. Rep. 195] (S.D.N.Y. 1997), *aff'd*, 198 F.3d 235 [140 Educ. L. Rep. 857] (2d Cir. 1999) (affirming that an affiliation agreement between a private medical school and a city university over space, personnel, and facilities was insufficient as a basis to raise a claim that officials engaged in state action when they allegedly breached a faculty member's contract); Moghimzadeh v. College of St. Rose, 653 N.Y.S.2d 198 [115 Educ. L. Rep. 1012] (N.Y. App. Div. 1997) (affirming the rejection of the claim of a former faculty member at a private college that the general public oversight of all colleges and universities in the state was insufficient for state action); Gardiner v. Mercyhurst Coll., 942 F. Supp. 1055 [114 Educ. L. Rep. 162] (W.D. Pa. 1996) (rejecting the claim that a private college's establishment of a police training program pursuant to a commonwealth statute was state action).

[76] Imperiale v. Hahneman Univ., 776 F. Supp. 189 [71 Educ. L. Rep. 83] (E.D. Pa. 1991), *aff'd*, 966 F.2d 125 [75 Educ. L. Rep. 1024] (3d Cir. 1992).

[77] 457 U.S. 830 [4 Educ. L. Rep. 999] (1982).

sachusetts unsuccessfully alleged that officials discharged them from a private school for maladjusted high school students for exercising their constitutional rights to free speech.

In *Rendell-Baker*, the Supreme Court affirmed the dismissal of the teachers' claims for lack of state action. The Court reached this outcome even though the school received virtually all of its referrals from public school boards; at least 90% of its operating budget came from commonwealth and federal funds; and its policies had to comply with regulations common to all public schools, such as record keeping, teacher-student ratios, maintenance of job descriptions, and written personnel standards and procedures. Because the dismissals were "not compelled or even influenced by any state regulation,"[78] the Court agreed that the behavior of the school's administration could not be treated as state action.

Following *Rendell-Baker*, lower federal courts have consistently refused to permit plaintiffs to pursue claims under Section 1983 for alleged constitutional violations. Twenty years after *Rendell-Baker*, the First Circuit illustrated that state action remains an elusive concept in nonpublic education. A public school board representing multiple communities in Maine which lacked high schools entered into a renewable, ten-year contract with a private school to educate all of its students in the ninth through twelfth grades for specified tuition payments. When the ten-day suspension of one of the public school students for threatening behavior was extended to seventeen days as he awaited a psychological evaluation, his parents sued, alleging that his exclusion in excess of ten days without a hearing violated both his rights to due process and state law.

Even though the private school "serve[d] as the school of last resort for students in the [public] district," the First Circuit refused to invoke the public function aspect of state action where "even publicly funded education of last resort was not provided exclusively by government in Maine." [79] The court affirmed that no evidence supported the entwinement theory of state action in light of the private school's contract provision that "the Trustees shall have the sole right to promulgate, administer, and enforce all rules and regulations pertaining to student behavior, discipline, and use of the buildings and grounds."[80]

The First Circuit recognized the student's dilemma, but ruled that creating new exceptions to state action is the responsibility of the Supreme Court. Although the First Circuit observed that the private school's affording due process rights might have been included in the contract, it nonetheless noted that even if its officials did not follow the contract, the responsibility under Maine's constitution ultimately fell on a public school board to provide education for the student.

Earlier, the Second Circuit reached a like result in a case involving a private college.[81] Students who were suspended pursuant to college rules after occupying its administration building alleged that officials infringed on

---

[78] *Id*. at 841. For a discussion of various issues, including contractual disputes in light of this case, see Ralph D. Mawdsley, *Emerging Legal Issues in Nonpublic Education*, 83 EDUC. L. REP. 1 (1985).

[79] Logiodice v. Trustees of Me. Cent. Inst., 296 F.3d 22, 27 [167 EDUC. L. REP. 85] (1st Cir. 2002).

[80] *Id*. at 28.

[81] Albert v. Carovano, 851 F.2d 561 [48 EDUC. L. REP. 35] (2d Cir. 1988).

their constitutional right to free speech. The students further claimed that the actions of college officials were state action because public officials required all colleges and universities in New York to submit rules adopted by their institutional governing boards pertaining to the maintenance of public order and providing for ejection, suspension, expulsion, or other appropriate actions for infractions. Rejecting the claim, the court agreed that this requirement failed to provide a sufficient nexus for state action to support a Section 1983 claim because the state's role was "merely to keep on file rules submitted by colleges and universities [but] [t]he state never sought to compel schools to enforce these rules and has never even inquired about enforcement."[82]

Rendell-Baker has made difficult the finding of state action by students or employees pursuing Section 1983 claims for violations of their constitutional or federal statutory rights. A federal trial court in Minnesota made a cogent observation in a case over whether officials at a private college violated a student's rights when she was suspended. According to the court, state action is not be bestowed on private colleges simply because they are "in the business of providing education" or because they receive government assistance "available to other educational institutions."[83]

As reflected in a case from Pennsylvania, the Third Circuit Court categorically rejected the public function argument advanced by a student who alleged that officials committed constitutional torts under Section 1983. The court reached this outcome even under a set of facts where the only schools in the commonwealth providing education to juvenile sex offenders were private schools.[84]

In like manner, a federal trial court in Pennsylvania pointed out that a student had not shown that officials at a private university acted under color of state law when they placed him in an independent study program due to his criticism of it and his instructor. In an online discussion board for a class, in response to an assignment asking students to report their post-graduation plans, he posted that he would "run…without ever looking back" and would "get out of City U ASAP."[85] The court granted the university's motion to dismiss on the ground it was not a state actor, pointing out that its officials had not exercised powers that were traditionally state prerogatives, had not acted in concert with public officials, and they were not in a position of interdependence with the state.

Finally, a federal trial court in New York granted a private school's motion to dismiss claims filed by a member of its non-teaching staff that officials fired for assaulting a student because the school was not a state actor.[86] The staff member claimed that officials at the school, which catered to students with

---

[82] *Id.* at 568. The court did suggest in dicta that officials' inconsistent enforcement of the rules as to African Americans and Latinos might have served as the basis for a claim under Section 1981 of the Civil Rights Act of 1964. *Id.* at 574.

[83] Ben-Yonatan v. Concordia Coll. Corp., 863 F. Supp. 983, 987 [94 Educ. L. Rep. 1321] (D. Minn. 1994).

[84] Robert S. v. Stetson Sch., 256 F.3d 159 [155 Educ. L. Rep. 129] (3d Cir. 2001).

[85] Becker v. City Univ. of Seattle, 723 F. Supp. 2d 807, 809 [261 Educ. L. Rep. 928] (E.D. Pa. 2010).

[86] Dawkins v. Biondi Educ. Ctr., 164 F. Supp. 3d 518 [334 Educ. L. Rep. 216] (S.D.N.Y. 2016).

special needs, were state actors for the purposes of a Section 1983 and Title VI claim because the state heavily regulated it, and the state also paid tuition for most of the children. Applying the Compulsion Test, the Joint Action Test, and the Public Function Test, the court concluded that school officials were not state actors under any of the measures.

Contractual Due Process

The absence of state action means that the rights of students and employees are defined by the contracts they entered into with their educational institutions. Yet, even without a constitutional standard to govern their dealings with students and employees, courts expect officials in nonpublic educational institutions to demonstrate a modicum of fairness.

In evaluating whether institutional officials acted fairly, courts are ultimately influenced by constitutional due process as developed for public schools. An appellate court in Louisiana relied on this approach when officials expelled two high school students for violating a school rule prohibiting smoking within two blocks of the campus. Even though the rule called for a fine after the first offense and dismissal for subsequent transgressions, officials had not expelled any students for this offense prior to this suit. Nonetheless, the court upheld the expulsions, explaining:

> [w]e cannot say that such a penalty was beyond the scope of the disciplinary powers granted to the principal and acknowledged to be clearly within his authority and discretion. . . [B]oth young men were on notice of the result which would ensue upon their next violations of the smoking rule. When the specific dismissal precipitating violations did, indeed, occur, the young men were confronted by their accusers and the record offers no indication that these specific accusals [stet] were unjustly or erroneously made.[87]

Assessing the minimum safeguards needed by private schools, the court wrote that:

> [p]rivate institutions [such as the one in this case] have a near absolute right and power to control their own disciplinary procedure which, by its very nature, includes the right and power to dismiss students. This is not to say that due process safeguards can be cavalierly ignored or disregarded. But if there is color of due process that is enough.[88]

This case from Louisiana should be considered in conjunction with a dispute from Ohio in which a student was expelled for his involvement in an incident where someone threw a pie into a teacher's face. Upholding the student's expulsion pursuant to handbook language prohibiting "conduct detrimental to the reputation of the school" and "immorality in talk and action," the court observed:

---

[87] Flint v. St. Augustine High Sch., 323 So. 2d 229, 234-35 (La. Ct. App. 1976).
[88] *Id*. at 234-35.

> Although . . . a nonpublic school's disciplinary proceedings are not controlled by the due process clause, and accordingly such schools have broad discretion in making rules and setting up procedures for their enforcement, nevertheless, under its broad equitable powers a court will intervene where such discretion is abused or the proceedings do not comport with fundamental fairness.[89]

The very use of the concepts "color of due process" and "fundamental fairness" in the two preceding cases underscores the concept that courts look to what they know best in evaluating whether officials at private educational institutions have provided basic fairness, namely the considerable body of law developed in interpreting procedural due process in the public sector. Consequently, while officials in private schools have wide discretion in defining student and employee expectations of conduct, courts do require at the least that contract language provides sufficient notice of prohibited behavior and notice of the manner by which those accused of misconduct can present defenses.[90] In essence, this means three things.

First, persons charged with misconduct in private educational institutions are entitled at the minimum to challenge by objective measures whether they have actually violated institutional rules. Second, those accused of misconduct must receive the procedural rights associated with the color of due process. Third, the accused can challenge, by subjective measures, whether institutional officials exhibited good faith in interpreting and enforcing school rules. However, whether persons received appropriate measures of due process need not be complex analyses.

A case from the Supreme Court of Kentucky is the first of three illustrating how these principles play out. Reversing an earlier order to the contrary, the court thought that a student who was dismissed for possessing a knife on campus was not entitled to any further due process under his college's handbook. The court remarked that "where a student admits the charges against him there is no need to conduct further hearings or allow the student an opportunity to explain or to present his own version of the facts."[91]

In Mississippi, a former law student officials expelled for plagiarism failed in challenging his punishment on various grounds, including a charge that they violated his rights to due process.[92] Granting law school officials' motion for summary judgment, a federal trial court emphasized that insofar as the school was private, the student was not entitled to the same protections as those

---

[89] Geraci v. St. Xavier High Sch., 13 Ohio Op.3d 146, 149, 1978 WL 195016 at *3 (Ohio Ct. App. 1978).

[90] For a case recognizing the discretion of administrators to evaluate whether teachers had conditions that materially impaired their continued usefulness or ability to perform required services, see Bernard v. EDS Noland Episcopal Day Sch., 62 F. Supp.2d 535 [317 EDUC. L. REP. 629] (W.D. La. 2014) (partially allowing the case to proceed because issues of fact remained as to whether the teacher with an eating disorder was prejudiced by officials' failure to give her notice of her rights under the Family and Medical Leave Act, thereby precluding their motion for summary judgment on that claim).

[91] Centre Coll. v. Trzop, 127 S.W.3d 562, 568 [185 EDUC. L. REP. 1074] (Ky. 2004), *as modified on denial of reh'g* (2004).

[92] Beauchene v. Mississippi Coll., 986 F. Supp. 2d 755 [305 EDUC. L. REP. 877] (S.D. Miss. 2013).

enrolled in public schools. In addition, the court rejected the student's breach of contract claim under the theory that officials had not followed their own procedures as laid out in the handbook, specifying that the judiciary generally defers to school authorities in matters of academic discipline.

When a student in Ohio challenged his suspension from his private university due to sexual misconduct, a federal trial court rejected his motion for a temporary restraining order.[93] The court was of the opinion that university officials had the right to make their own regulations and that it would only intervene where the plaintiff could show that they abused their discretion and failed to follow the procedures set out in the handbook. Because the student could not show an abuse of discretion or a failure to follow procedures, the court declined to intervene in the actions of university officials in punishing the student.

Student/Employee Conduct and Violations of Contract

This section addresses two kinds of contract violation issues. The first type of violation concerns students and/or employees facing adverse action by officials in nonpublic educational institutions for conduct interpreted as violations of their educational contracts. The second kind of violation issues arise when educational institutions face lawsuits, generally for breach of contract,[94] fraud, or misrepresentation, for the manner by which educational officials interpreted and applied the terms of contracts. For purposes of this discussion, the term misconduct applies to both kinds of alleged contract violations. Whether violations of educational contracts have occurred presents three legal issues: whether the educational contracts expressly or impliedly prohibited the misconduct;[95] whether institutional officials followed their own procedures in addressing the misconduct; and whether institutional officials exhibited good faith and fairness in interpreting and enforcing their contract provisions.

Prohibited Conduct

Disciplining students or employees for alleged misconduct can be traumatizing and contentious experiences for those being chastised and for institutional

---

[93] Pierre v. Univ. of Dayton, 143 F. Supp. 3d 703 [330 EDUC. L. REP. 573] (S.D. Ohio 2015).

[94] For a case rejecting a breach of contract claim, see In re St. Thomas High Sch., 495 S.W.3d 500 [335 EDUC. L. REP. 455] (Tex. Ct. App. 2016) (rejecting a breach of contract claim where officials expelled a student in a dispute over grades as precluded by the ecclesiastical abstention doctrine). For another case involving the ecclesiastical abstention doctrine, see Flynn v. Estevez, 221 So. 3d 1241 [346 EDUC. L. REP. 653] (Fla. Dist. Ct. App. 2017) (applying the ecclesiastical abstention doctrine, which it noted is also called the church autonomy doctrine, to preclude judicial involvement in a religious controversy between a diocese and father over whether his son had to be immunized before being admitted to a school).

[95] For a case rejecting the claim that a contract contained an implied term expecting school officials to provide a safe learning environment, see Zelnick v. Morristown-Beard Sch., 137 A.3d 560 331 EDUC. L. REP. 1051 (N.J. Super. Ct. App. Div. 2015) (rejecting such a claim stemming from the alleged inappropriate sexual relationship that occurred between a former student and former teacher at the school when she was a minor).

officials. Still, the judiciary affords nonpublic institutions broad discretion in deciding what conduct is unacceptable.

In the first of five relevant cases, an appellate court in Ohio reviewed a dispute in which a student whose parents had paid his deposit for attendance at a school for his senior year claimed that his expulsion at the end of his junior year constituted a breach of contract. The court affirmed that pursuant to handbook language permitting expulsion for "conduct detrimental to the reputation of the school .... [and] immorality in talk or action," officials acted consistently in punishing him for his involvement in throwing a pie in a teacher's face. The court conceded that "no list of norms can cover every situation."[96]

An appellate court in Illinois upheld a student's expulsion under a catalog provision allowing college officials "to dismiss any student who in [their] judgment is undesirable and whose continuation in the school is detrimental to himself or his fellow students."[97] Reversing an earlier order to the contrary, the court agreed that the student could be disciplined because, after he was diagnosed as paranoid and a serious detriment to herself and others, he refused to cooperate with remedial efforts designed to help him adjust.

In a dispute from Vermont, the federal trial court reached mixed results. The court first rejected the student's claim that his being accused with "disrespect of persons," language mirroring that in his handbook requiring all on campus "to respect the dignity, freedom, and rights of others," was not so vague as to be unenforceable regarding a charge of sexual impropriety.[98] At the same time, the court was convinced that officials breached their contractual duty to inform the student of disciplinary charges against him, with particularity when charging him with rape, without informing him that even if his conduct did not amount to rape, it could still have been found to violate the student handbook provision prohibiting disrespect of persons.

The federal court in Massachusetts denied a private college's motion for summary judgment on a contract claim involving its student handbook policy on sexual harassment and sexual assault.[99] The dispute arose because officials changed the definition of sexual consent in the handbook between the time the alleged misconduct occurred and when the student was punished. Explaining that a jury could have agreed that the plaintiff obtained consent to engage in sexual relations under the old standard, his breach of contract claim could proceed.

Compliance with Procedures

Courts have upheld the dismissals of teachers who failed to follow established procedures,[100] as well as for carrying on an extramarital affair in

---

[96] Geraci v. St. Xavier High Sch., 13 Ohio Op.3d 146, 1978 WL 195016 at *3 (Ohio Ct. App. 1978).

[97] Aronson v. North Park Coll., 418 N.E.2d 776, 781 (Ill. App. Ct. 1981), reh'g denied (1981).

[98] Fellheimer v. Middlebury Coll., 869 F. Supp. 238 [96 Educ. L. Rep. 419] (D. Vt. 1994).

[99] Doe v. Western New England Univ., 228 F. Supp. 3d 154 (D. Mass. 2016).

[100] Odem v. Pace Acad., 510 S.E.2d 326 [132 Educ. L. Rep. 544] (Ga. Ct. App. 1998) (the teacher's unsatisfactory professional performance included not notifying the school of his absence, failing to attend class, and failing to secure a substitute).

violation of church doctrine.[101] In another case, an appellate court in Texas affirmed that there was good cause to dismiss a teacher who had knowledge of a serious student violation in the form of drunkenness, but failed to report it in light of a clear policy prohibiting such misbehavior.[102]

A case from Louisiana exemplifies a situation wherein officials in a faith-based school made clear their expectations for teachers. Officials terminated the teacher's contract because she lied on her employment application, in that the record revealed she drank four or five beers to celebrate her new contract on the day after she was hired. Reversing an earlier order in favor of the teacher, an appellate court was of the view that since the plaintiff's answer to a question on her application, namely that she did not consume alcoholic beverages, resulted in officials' hiring her by causing them to believe she possessed principles she lacked, her drinking vitiated their consent. The court concluded that the parties had not entered into a valid contract because there was no meeting of the minds.[103]

Employers in religious schools can expect their staff members to be familiar with the religious doctrines underpinning their belief systems. In a case from Ohio, an appellate court affirmed that officials of a Catholic diocese had no duty to notify an elementary teacher that she would be dismissed if she did not obtain an annulment of her previous marriage before she remarried.[104] Similarly, an appellate court in California affirmed an order dismissing a teacher in a religious school who was living with, but not married to, her boyfriend. The court agreed that school officials had the authority to fire the teacher because her behavior violated church teachings.[105]

Where employees of religious educational institutions are disciplined for violations of religious beliefs, courts generally do not intrude into the merits of the alleged misconduct for fear of violating the Establishment or Free Exercise clauses. In such a case, an appellate court in Wisconsin affirmed a bishop's dismissal of a principal during the term of his contract due to discord and disunity in the diocese. The court agreed that the principal lacked a breach of contract action for the balance of his salary because "it would infringe on

---

[101] Gosche v. Calvert High Sch., 997 F. Supp. 867 [126 EDUC. L. REP. 219] (N.D. Ohio 1998), *aff'd per curiam*, 181 F.3d 101 (6th Cir. 1999).

[102] Watts v. St. Mary's Hall, 662 S.W.2d 55 [15 EDUC. L. REP. 601] (Tex. Ct. App. 1983).

[103] LaCross v. Cornerstone Christian Acad., 896 So.2d 105 [197 EDUC. L. REP. 451] (La. Ct. App. 2004).

[104] Manno v. St. Felicitas Elem. Sch., 831 N.E.2d 1071 [200 EDUC. L. REP. 349] (Ohio Ct. App. 2005).

[105] Henry v. Red Hill Evangelical Lutheran Church of Tustin, 134 Cal.Rptr.3d 15 [274 EDUC. L. REP. 631] (Cal. Ct. App. 2011).

ecclesiastical authority to deny the Bishop authority to dismiss the church school principal in order to end a schism in the congregation."[106]

In the first of two cases from higher education, the Circuit Court for the District of Columbia affirmed the dismissal of claims filed by a nun who taught canon law when she was denied tenure.[107] The court agreed that insofar as the teaching of canon law was essentially religious in nature and was vital to spiritual and pastoral mission of the Roman Catholic Church, it could not intervene due to First Amendment concerns.

A similar dispute involving a faculty member at a Roman Catholic seminary arose in Indiana. When the faculty member was discharged after protesting Pope John Paul II's refusal to ordain women priests, an appellate court affirmed that she failed to present a viable breach of contract claim. The court pointed to language in the faculty handbook referencing academic freedom and responsibility as among the terms of her appointment as broad enough to include religious doctrine and ecclesiastical law, such that it lacked jurisdiction over the dispute under the Establishment Clause.[108]

Courts do not intervene when school officials advance religious reasons supporting their employment actions. Even so, courts might intervene in employment actions if proffered religious reasons are pretexts for some form of discrimination. For instance, employees have succeeded in litigation against their religious employers if they can demonstrate that the adverse employment actions they experienced had nothing to do with religion, such as when they file claims of age discrimination.[109]

As a practical matter, then, if officials in faith-based schools want courts to take their religious teachings seriously, they must enforce them consistently

---

[106] Black v. St. Bernadette Congregation of Appleton, 360 N.W.2d 550, 553 [22 Educ. L. Rep. 434] (Wis. Ct. App. 1984), relying on Serbian Eastern Orthodox Diocese for the United States of America and Canada v. Milivojevich, 426 U.S. 696, 721-22 (1976) (invalidating the actions of civil authorities where the church defrocked a bishop and created three new dioceses because under the First and Fourteenth amendments, state courts must defer to the authority of church officials), treating the removal of the plaintiff as ecclesiastical rather than secular in nature. Pursuant to *Milivojevich*, civil courts have no authority to consider whether religious bodies have authority under their religious law to resolve religious disputes. *See also* Ballaban v. Bloomington Jewish Cmty., 928 N.E.2d 329 (Ind. Ct. App. 2013) (upholding a grant of summary judgment in favor of a Jewish congregation that fired its rabbi who claimed it was for reporting child abuse, but was dismissed due to inappropriate behavior, including being angry and hostile, plus jeopardizing the congregation's tax-exempt status; the court declined to consider whether the First Amendment's ministerial exception applied).

[107] E.E.O.C. v. Catholic Univ. of Am., 83 F.3d 455 [109 Educ. L. Rep. 568] (D.C. Cir.1996). For a commentary on this case, see Charles J. Russo, *The Camel's Nose In the Tent: Judicial Intervention in Tenure Disputes at Catholic Universities,*" 117 Educ. L. Rep. 813 (1997).

[108] McEnroy v. St. Meinard Sch. of Theology, 713 N.E.2d 334 [136 Educ. L. Rep. 541] (Ind. Ct. App. 1999).

[109] For cases allowing age discrimination claims to proceed against religious employers, *see, e.g.,* DeMarco v. Holy Cross High Sch., 4 F.3d 166 [85 Educ. L. Rep. 674] (2d Cir. 1993); Guinan v. Roman Catholic Archdiocese of Indianapolis, 42 F. Supp.2d 849 [134 Educ. L. Rep. 900] (S.D. Ind. 1998); Tomic v. Catholic Diocese of Peoria, 442 F.3d 1036 (7th Cir. 2006), *cert. denied,* 549 U.S. 881 (2006). *But see* McGuire-Welch v. House of the Good Shepherd, 219 F. Supp.3d 330 (N.D.N.Y. 2016) (rejecting an age discrimination claim where an employee was dismissed due to poor job performance).

and continuously. The upshot is that any differential applications of religious employment terms may be sufficient to allow employees to present viable claims of mixed motives regarding adverse employment actions.

Adherence to Contract Terms

Contractual documents of nonpublic educational institutions become important when they impact the status of students and/or employees. In discipline situations, institutional documents generally contain language about the notice and hearing rights of students and employees; employees who fail to comply with the terms of their contracts may face adverse employment actions.

The general rule is that courts do not intervene in disciplinary actions as long as the processes accorded conform to the published rules and regulations of nonpublic educational institutions.[110] While some courts have suggested that substantial compliance with published procedures is sufficient,[111] a determination of such compliance may be left up to the trier of fact.[112] For instance, when a student in Indiana was expelled for violating his school handbook's conduct requirements in the second semester of the academic year, an appellate court granted officials' motion for summary judgment, refusing to override the contract between them and his parents by ordering his readmission.[113]

At the same time, as illustrated by a case from Vermont discussed earlier, the failure of officials in nonpublic educational institutions to provide adequate notice of violations can lead to their having to conduct new hearings.[114] The federal trial court invalidated a disciplinary action against a student for not respecting the dignity, freedom, and rights of others because college officials violated their contract with him by not providing him with notice of this charge. Although officials notified the student of the rape charge, of which he was cleared, the court determined that the "disrespect of persons" charge, of which he was guilty, sufficiently different so as to require them to provide him with

---

[110] *See* Galiani v. Hofstra Univ., 499 N.Y.S.2d 182 [30 EDUC. L. REP. 1247] (N.Y. App. Div. 1986).

[111] *See* Fraad-Wolf v. Vassar Coll., 932 F. Supp. 88 [111 EDUC. L. REP. 815] (S.D.N.Y. 1996) (rejecting a constructive discharge claim where a student withdrew from college while being investigated for sexual harassment, instead posting that officials substantially complied with the investigation procedures in the student handbook); Clayton v. Trs. of Princeton Univ., 608 F. Supp. 413 [25 EDUC. L. REP. 234] (D.N.J. 1985) (refusing to treat the loss of Honor Committee records as a substantial violation of a student's rights when he was suspended for one year for cheating, because this did not adversely impact him in any way). *But see* Tedeschi v. Wagner Coll., 427 N.Y.S.2d 760, 764 (N.Y. 1980) (ordering the reinstatement of a student who was suspended for disrupting a class pending his appearance before the Student-Faculty Hearing Board with an appeal to the President, as called for in the college's guidelines, because a hearing body composed of faculty and students might have view the alleged infraction differently than the dean).

[112] *See* Harvey v. Palmer Coll. of Chiropractic, 363 N.W.2d 443, 444 [23 EDUC. L. REP. 667] (Iowa Ct. App. 1984) (reversing in favor of a student who was suspended, observing that the "requirements imposed by the common law on private universities parallel those imposed by the Due Process Clause on public universities").

[113] *See* Jones v. Howe Military Sch., 604 F. Supp. 122 [24 EDUC. L. REP. 76] (D. Ind. 1984). For cases with similar outcomes, see Hutcheson v. Grace Lutheran Sch., 517 N.Y.S.2d 760, [40 EDUC. L. REP. 934] (N.Y. App. Div. 1987); Spell v. Bible Baptist Church, 303 S.E.2d 156 [11 EDUC. L. REP. 728] (Ga. Ct. App. 1983).

[114] Fellheimer v. Middlebury Coll., 869 F. Supp. 238 [96 EDUC. L. REP. 419] (D. Vt. 1994).

separate notice of that charge. Reversing the guilty verdict as to the "disrespect of persons" charge, the court remanded for a new hearing.

Courts carefully scrutinize cases wherein one or more parties seek to introduce statements or policies external to their contracts to explain or justify their positions. In such a case, the Supreme Court of New Jersey ordered the reinstatement of two Roman Catholic nuns who lost their jobs due to concerns over their qualifications to teach the courses of their assigned classes.[115] The court rejected the university's attempt to invoke canon law because the contracts under which they were hired did not reference it. The court reasoned that university officials violated their contract with the nuns by failing to provide the notice and hearing required under the institution's handbook.

A case from Pennsylvania reached a different result. An appellate court affirmed a grant of summary judgment in favor of a private university when a student who failed her Ph.D. oral defense filed a breach of contract action alleging that her dissertation committee did not perform specified duties. The court commented that the student could not "point to a single provision of the written contract between the university and its students that sets forth the obligations of members of a dissertation committee."[116] In other words, complainants are not entitled to rewrite the contracts they enter with their educational institutions by setting forth expectations they believe are important.

A student who was compelled to withdraw from a nursing program for failing to lose weight pursuant to an ancillary weight-loss agreement college officials required her to sign prevailed in her breach of contract claim against the college. The First Circuit affirmed that the student abided by the school's disciplinary rules, paid tuition, and maintained good academic standards, in exchange for which the college provided her with an education until graduation, a contract that officials subsequently modified by including the weight-loss agreement.[117] In the initial round of litigation, a jury agreed with the student that insofar as she substantially performed her contract with the college, she was entitled to damages for its breach.

The record revealed that the student had attempted to comply with the weight-loss agreement by attending Weight Watchers' meetings, but could not lose enough to meet the college's requirements. Moreover, after being compelled to withdraw from the college, the student successfully completed a nursing program at another institution, but had to repeat her junior year due to failing grades she allegedly received in part because she could not lose weight.

As demonstrated in the first of two cases involving employees in nonpublic schools, an appellate court in Louisiana held that because a letter of intent asking a teacher whether she intended to return to work the following year lacked a specific offer from officials, it could not, and did not, create a binding contract.[118] Likewise, where an administrator in a nonpublic school sent a teacher a form contract, including words to the effect that he was planning for the next

---

[115] Welter v. Seton Hall Univ., 608 A.2d 206 [75 EDUC. L. REP. 822] (N.J. 1992).

[116] Swartley v. Hoffner, 734 A.2d 915, 919 [137 EDUC. L. REP. 301] (Pa. Super. Ct. 1999).

[117] Russell v. Salve Regina Coll., 938 F.2d 315 [68 EDUC. L. REP. 982] (1st Cir. 1991).

[118] Knipmeyer v. Diocese of Alexandria, 492 So. 2d 550 [34 EDUC. L. REP. 332] (La. Ct. App. 1986).

year, an appellate court in North Carolina affirmed that it was unenforceable because it lacked the specificity characterized by an employment contract.[119]

Commitments that school officials make to students pursuant to documents from their educational institutions can serve as the bases of breach of contract actions if educators fail to honor those promises. In such a case from Pennsylvania, a student filed suit after he received life experience credits when he enrolled, but officials later revoked them, delaying his graduation. An appellate court ruled that the student presented a viable breach of contract claim. In its analysis of the relationship between educational institutions and students, the court noted:

> [A]n institution may make a contractual obligation to a student which it is not free to later ignore. The economic reality is that colleges and universities are competing to attract non-traditional age students and many of those institutions have designed programs to cater to them. Through advertising and recruitment campaigns, an increasing number of colleges and universities are promising students who wish to return to school, flexible schedules, evening and weekend classes, and academic credit for life experience.... Where an individual is induced to enroll in a university or college based upon an award of certain life experience credits, the institution cannot then, after the student's enrollment, revoke those credits.[120]

Beyond breach of contract claims as such, courts have considered whether contractual relationships between parties can give rise to duties under tort.[121] In an illustrative case, when university officials in Oregon offered a one-year visiting faculty member a tenure-track position, he asked the dean whether the poor evaluations he received during the spring semester of the one-year contract would have been a problem during the tenure process. The dean responded that it would not, but when the faculty member continued to receive poor student evaluations, officials offered him a terminal year contract at the end of his first tenure-track year, relying in part on past poor evaluations.

Even where the university's handbook required officials to provide employees with information pertaining to their job performance and career advancement, the Supreme Court of Oregon affirmed that this provision created neither a contractual obligation nor tort duty to further the interests of the faculty member.[122] The court was persuaded that since both parties acted for their own benefit in negotiating the contract, they had not created a special relationship such that the faculty member had no right to rely on university officials to achieve a particular outcome on his behalf.

The rationale of the Supreme Court of Oregon seems sound as to faculty members who may have some measure of bargaining power with their employ-

---

[119] Braun v. Glade Valley Sch., 334 S.E.2d 404 [27 Educ. L. Rep. 971] (N.C. Ct. App. 1985).

[120] Britt v. Chestnut Hill Coll., 632 A.2d 557, 560 [86 Educ. L. Rep. 905] (Pa. Super. Ct. 1993).

[121] For a case rejecting tort, breach of contract, and discrimination claims, *see* Benjamin v. Sparks, 173 F. Supp.3d 272 [335 Educ. L. Rep. 813] (E.D.N.C. 2016) (dismissing a case wherein the plaintiff claimed he was fired because of his Jewish faith).

[122] Conway v. Pacific Univ., 924 P.2d 818 [113 Educ. L. Rep. 942] (Or. 1996).

ers, but not as to students who have little choice but to rely on institutional claims in handbooks or promotional materials. As such, courts have supported negligent misrepresentation claims based on promotional statements where students[123] or faculty members[124] can establish that they justifiably relied on the statements, to their detriment.

A case from the Supreme Court of Alabama highlights that the failure of officials in a private school to deliver services as promised can result in claims for both breach of contract and fraud. The court found that parents had a viable cause of action for breach of contract and fraud where they paid a pre-registration fee but officials told them on the last day of school, without giving a reason why, that their sons would not be permitted to return the next year.

The court in Alabama explained that officials' returning the pre-registration fees to the parents did not necessarily refute "an inference that upon acceptance of the [the family's] registration, the school impliedly contracted to educate [their sons] for the upcoming school term in exchange for the [the family's] payment of preregistration fees and continued compliance with the schools' rules and registrations."[125] The court observed that while the handbook identified disciplinary reasons for removing students from the school, the boys seemed to be model students not subject to discipline. The court pointed out that once school officials accepted the registration fee, they had an implied contract to provide the education for which the parents contracted.

Similarly, the Supreme Court of Nevada was convinced that parents whose son had been enrolled in a private school for four years presented viable claims for both breach of contract and misrepresentation.[126] The dispute arose because school officials agreed, but failed, to provide specified services to the child such as appropriate, individualized reading instruction and adequate diagnostic and remediation services, should reading problems have developed. In addition, the parents alleged that the principal made specific representations in response to their questions about their son's potential reading problems and had sent progress reports, which negligently or knowingly misrepresented that the child was not having academic difficulties.

---

[123] *See, e.g.,* Troknya v. Cleveland Chiropractic Clinic, 280 F.3d 1200 [161 EDUC. L. REP. 782] (8th Cir. 2002) (upholding a judgment for compensatory damages for students who relied on misrepresentations about the institution's responsibility to provide patients in the clinical program); Idrees v. Am. Univ. of the Caribbean, 546 F. Supp. 1342 [6 EDUC. L. REP. 653] (S.D.N.Y. 1982) (allowing a plaintiff to recover damages for fraudulent misrepresentation where a medical school brochure advertised its library facilities, classroom microscopes and skeletons, and student slides and names of faculty, but they were not ready when classes began and officials failed to inform incoming students of the changed circumstances). *But see* Andre v. Pace Univ., 655 N.Y.S.2d 777 [117 EDUC. L. REP. 273] (N.Y. App. Div. 1996) (rejecting students' misrepresentation claim that school personnel advised them that their backgrounds in mathematics would be sufficient for a computer programming course as nonactionable, because it amounted to a claim of educational malpractice).

[124] *But see* Nugent v. Diocese of Rockville Centre, 26 N.Y.S.2d 556 [327 EDUC. L. REP. 878] (N.Y. App. Div. 2016) (rejecting a fired teacher's claims of unspecified incidents of negligent representation).

[125] Van Loock v. Curran, 489 So. 2d 525, 529 [32 EDUC. L. REP. 1313] (Ala. 1985).

[126] Squires v. Sierra Educ. Found., 823 P.2d 256 [72 EDUC. L. REP. 405] (Nev. 1991).

At the same time, the failure of educational officials to deliver services has been insufficient to support claims for malpractice. To this end, most courts have rejected, on public policy grounds, claims for alleged failures in the quality of the educational process,[127] as well as educational malpractice defenses to school actions to recover unpaid tuition.[128]

The Supreme Court of Iowa, though, came perilously close to recognizing an educational malpractice claim where a school counselor failed to advise a student-athlete adequately about an acceptable course to satisfy NCAA requirements for freshman eligibility for financial aid and participation in post-secondary athletics.[129] In dicta, the court identified a variety of areas raised as educational malpractice that are not justiciable: classroom methodologies or theories of education;[130] poor academic performance by students or their lack of expected skills;[131] the internal operations, curricular, or academic decisions of educational institutions, or assigned functions of schools under state law;[132] and interference with legislative standards and policies of competency.[133] The court's analysis notwithstanding, the difference between these educational malpractice claims and the one at issue in Iowa was thin.

---

[127] *See, e.g., id.* (permitting breach of contract and misrepresentation claims to proceed but not a charge of educational malpractice); Key v. Coryell, 185 S.W.3d 98 [207 EDUC. L. REP. 450] (Ark. Ct. App. 2004) (rejecting a variety of claims over a faith-based school's alleged failure to meet special education needs of an elementary school child).

[128] Sisters of the Holy Child Jesus at Old Westbury v. Corwin, 29 N.Y.S.3d 736 [329 EDUC. L. REP. 1036] (N.Y. App. Div. 2016) (upholding the liquidated damages clause in a registration contract obligating parents to pay tuition and fees for the full year after they withdrew their daughter from the school as not an impermissible penalty).

[129] Sain v. Cedar Rapids Cmty Sch. Dist., 626 N.W.2d 115 [153 EDUC. L. REP. 778] (Iowa 2001).

[130] *See, e.g.,* Salter v. Natchitoches Chiropractic Clinic, 274 So. 2d 490 (La. Ct. App. 1973); Moore v. Vanderloo, 386 N.W.2d 108 [31 EDUC. L. REP. 1263] (Iowa 1986); Helm v. Prof'l Children's Sch., 431 N.Y.S.2d 246 (N.Y. Sup. Ct. 1980).

[131] *See, e.g.,* Cavaliere v. Duff's Bus. Inst., 605 A.2d 397 [73 EDUC. L. REP. 1053] (Pa. Super. Ct. 1992); Peter W. v. S.F. Unified Sch. Dist., 131 Cal.Rptr. 854 (Cal. Ct. App. 1976). *See also* Ross v. Creighton Univ., 740 F. Supp. 1319, 1327 [62 EDUC. L. REP. 85] (N.D. Ill. 1990), *rev'd in part on other grounds,* 957 F.2d 410 [73 EDUC. L. REP. 352] (7th Cir. 1992).

[132] *See, e.g.,* Houston v. Mile High Adventist Acad., 872 F. Supp. 829 [97 EDUC. L. REP. 239] (D. Colo. 1994) (rejecting claims that the academy did not operate in conformity with its religious teaching, that teachers made offensive remarks, used inappropriate teaching materials, gave unwarranted grades, and one teacher allowed students to use his home for sexual relations); Sirohi v. Lee, 634 N.Y.S.2d 119 [105 EDUC. L. REP. 255] (N.Y. App. Div. 1995) (denying claims that a university failed to provide the quality educational environment promised and made false representations about its atmosphere and disciplinary process); Swidryk v. St. Michael's Med. Ctr., 493 A.2d 641[25 EDUC. L. REP. 814] N.J. Super. Ct. 1985) (rejecting a claim by a doctor, who was sued for medical malpractice in the delivery of a baby, that the director or residents failed to provide appropriate supervision); Paladino v. Adephi Univ., 454 N.Y.S.2d 868 [7 EDUC. L. REP. 190] (N.Y. App. Div. 1982) (denying the claim that officials failed to provide a quality education to a student enrolled in a private university).

[133] See *Sain,* 626 N.W.2d at 122; Smith v. Alameda County Soc. Agency, 153 Cal.Rptr. 712 (Cal. Ct. App. 1979) (refusing to fashion a new cause of action creating liability of a public adoption agency for negligent failure to find an infant an adoptive home). *But see* Nunn v. State, 187 Cal.Rptr. 315 [7 EDUC. L. REP. 647] (Cal. Ct. App. 1982) (permitting the administrator of the estate of a security guard who was beaten to death to go to trial on a negligence claim that the community college officials failed to provide information on state regulations about licensing of security guards to carry weapons).

Perhaps the best rationale for not permitting educational malpractice claims to proceed is in a case from higher education. After a college basketball player with the overall academic skills of a fourth-grader used up his four years of eligibility, he had accumulated only 96 of 128 credits needed to graduate. Although rejecting the former player's claim for educational malpractice, the Seventh Circuit allowed his breach of contract claim for the university's failure to provide a tutor as promised to move forward.[134] According to the court:

> Courts have identified several policy concerns that counsel against allowing claims for educational malpractice. First, there is the lack of a satisfactory standard of care by which to evaluate an educator. Theories of education are not uniform, and different but acceptable scientific methods of academic training make it unfeasible to formulate a standard by which to judge the conduct of those delivering the services. Second, inherent uncertainties exist in this type of case about the cause and nature of damages. Factors such as the student's attitude, motivation, temperament, past experience, and home environment may all play an essential and immeasurable role in learning.... A third reason for denying this cause of action is the potential it presents for a flood of litigation against schools.... A final reason courts have cited for denying this cause of action is that it threatens to embroil the courts into overseeing the day-to-day operations of schools. This oversight might be particularly troubling in the university setting where it necessarily implicates considerations of academic freedom and autonomy.[135]

One of the most difficult issues involving enforcement of contract terms concerns whether parents are obligated to pay tuition after educational officials expelled their children during school years. Contractual language ordinarily prevails, so that parents are not entitled to refunds unless the contracts are very specific and parents removed their children for reasons other than those identified in school handbooks.[136] However, actions by school officials to recover tuition parents owe may be subject to limitations that are part of normal con-

---

[134] Ross v. Creighton Univ., 740 F. Supp. 1319, 414-15 [62 Educ. L. Rep. 85] (N.D. Ill. 1990), rev'd in part on other grounds, 957 F.2d 410 [73 Educ. L. Rep. 352] (7th Cir. 1992).

[135] Id. at 957 F.2d 1319, 414-15.

[136] See Barrie Sch. v. Patch, 933 A.2d 382 [225 Educ. L. Rep. 973] (Md. 2007) (refusing to require educational officials to mitigate damages where parents breached their contract by removing their daughter from the school); Princeton Montessori Soc'y v. Leff, 591 A.2d 685 [68 Educ. L. Rep. 85] (N.J. Super. Ct. App. Div. 1991) (allowing educational officials to recover the balance of tuition where a father removed his child from school in October even though they did not mitigate damages because they made all of preparations necessary to educate the child for the school year); Moyse v. Runnels Sch., 457 So.2d 767 [20 Educ. L. Rep. 1280] (La. Ct. App. 1984) (affirming that parents were responsible for the balance of a year's tuition on withdrawing their son from the school where their reason for doing so was not one of the three reasons listed in the contract).

tractual negotiations.[137] Courts may choose to enforce oral modifications that school officials make to existing written refund policies where consideration for such changes exists.[138]

More problematic may be judicial orders that nonpublic schools do not need to mitigate damages in tuition refund cases where the plain language of contract does not allow for refunds.[139] Even more troublesome may be student withdrawal cases where the tuition payments parents owe are treated as liquidated damages, either as to their having to pay the balance of tuition owed or that school officials do not need to refund excess tuition paid.[140]

Courts have demonstrated a surprising tendency to treat student tuition or faculty salaries as permissible liquidated damages owed schools where parents withdraw their children or officials expel them during academic years,[141] or where faculty members resign in an untimely manner.[142] Even so, some courts have limited the effects of contractual liquidated damage clauses by refusing

---

[137] *See, e.g.,* Dr. Perkins Sch. v. Freeman, 741 F.2d 1503 [19 Educ. L. Rep. 881] (7th Cir. 1984) (permitting school officials to recover tuition based on oral promise, but not retroactive tuition increases where the parents had no notice of such increases; also entitling the parents to recover for breach of the school's contractual obligation to seek reimbursement from the state for special education costs associated with educating their daughter). *But see* Bishop v. Westminster Schs., 397 S.E.2d 143 [63 Educ. L. Rep. 643] (Ga. Ct. App. 1990) (rejecting school officials' motion for summary judgment on a father's oral promise to pay his daughter's tuition where he placed conditions on this promise).

[138] *See* Brenner v. Little Red Sch. House, 295 S.E.2d 607 [6 Educ. L. Rep. 1134] (N.C. Ct. App. 1982) (allowing a father to a tuition refund based on the principal's oral promise to make such a payment, even though written school policy apparently would not have authorized such an action).

[139] *See* Princeton Montessori Soc'y v. Leff, 591 A.2d 685, 687 [68 Educ. L. Rep. 85] (N.J. Super. Ct. App. Div. 1991) ("where the contract expressly provides that no deduction or refund will be made, the entire tuition is payable despite the fact that the student withdraws from the school . . .[and] [i]n these circumstances, the educational institution has no duty to mitigate damages").

[140] *See* Moyse v. Runnels Sch., 457 So. 2d 767, 769 [20 Educ. L. Rep. 1280] (La. Ct. App. 1984) (observing that "we have found no authority for the application of the doctrine of mitigation of damages to defeat the plain terms of an otherwise enforceable agreement which provides for liquidated damages.")

[141] *See* Lake Ridge Acad. v. Carney, 613 N.E.2d 183, 187 [82 Educ. L. Rep. 1181] (Ohio 1993) (treating the cut-off date of August 1 for withdrawal of a student as an option contract for liquidated damages purposes, such that the parental failure to exercise the option in a timely manner meant that "the option may not be exercised after that time has passed"); Thomas Jefferson Sch. v. Dapros, 728 S.W.2d 315 [39 Educ. L. Rep. 385] (Mo. Ct. App. 1987) (allowing educational officials to recover the balance of tuition owed where the student was expelled in October for violating the school's "no fighting" provision).

[142] Parizek v. Roncalli Catholic High Sch. of Omaha, 655 N.W.2d 404 [172 Educ. L. Rep. 968] (Neb. Ct. App. 2002) (upholding a liquidated damages clause as applied to a teacher while refusing to inquire into the contract's alleged unconscionability where asking such questions would have violated the First Amendment). *See generally* Ralph Mawdsley, *Liquidated Damages in Educational Contracts*, 186 Educ. L. Rep. 587 (2004) (discussing cases where both student tuition and faculty salaries have been treated as liquidated damages).

to require payments for services where institutions would not experience out-of-pocket expense,[143] or where officials had already located replacements.[144]

Fundamental Fairness

Courts grant considerable discretion to officials in nonpublic educational institutions to interpret and enforce their employee and student contracts. Still, courts expect interpretation and enforcement to be fair and in good faith while not being arbitrary or capricious. It is worth noting that while concepts of good faith and fair dealing are generally implied covenants in all contractual dealings, they cannot be used to subvert the parties' clear intentions.

In an illustrative case, an administrator in a faith-based school challenged the nonrenewal of her one-year contract. An appellate court in California decided that the plaintiff was not entitled to use her long service as an administrator in the school, coupled with the lack of negative evaluations, as a basis to require officials to employ her indefinitely, absent good cause for not renewing their employment relationship. In other words, where a term contract expires at the end of one year and neither party is required to renew it, the court rejected the claim that "an implied covenant of good faith and fair dealing [can be used] to transmute this unequivocal agreement to one terminable only upon a finding of good cause."[145]

As indicated, courts ordinarily grant broad discretion to school officials in interpreting contractual language. In such a case, an appellate court in Ohio upheld the expulsion of two students from a religious elementary school because of their parents' confrontational tactics and unwillingness to follow the dispute resolution process in the school handbook. Absent "a clear abuse of discretion by the school in the enforcement of its policies and regulations,"[146] the court refused to interfere with the action of school officials.

An appellate court in Illinois upheld the plaintiff's dismissal from a graduate social work program where officials had a rational basis for acting, namely

---

[143] *See* Perez v. Aerospace Acad., 546 So. 2d 1139 [55 EDUC. L. REP. 335] (Fla. Dist. Ct. App. 1989) (obligating parents to pay for the balance of the school year's tuition after their daughter was expelled for rule violations, but not board charges related to food that she would not be able to consume and officials had not yet purchased); O'Brian v. Langley Sch., 507 S.E.2d. 363 [130 EDUC. L. REP. 1358] (Va. 1998) (allowing parents to proceed to discovery over whether the liquidated damages clause requiring them to pay tuition for a full year after removing their daughter from school in an untimely manner was an unenforceable penalty).

[144] *See* Weisfeld v. Peterseil, 623 So. 2d 515 [85 EDUC. L. REP. 954] (Fla. Dist. Ct. App. 1993) (refusing to permit an administrator in a private school who was unwilling to release a teacher under contract to leave and take a job in a public school after the academic year started to enforce the liquidated damages clause of two months' wages where he had hired a replacement and denied the teacher the opportunity to honor her contract with the nonpublic school).

[145] Tollefson v. Roman Catholic Bishop of San Diego, 268 Cal.Rptr. 550, 556 [59 EDUC. L. REP. 803] Cal. Ct. App. 1990); disapproved of, but not overruled by Scott v. Pacific Gas & Electric Co., 46 Cal.Rptr.2d 427 (Cal. 1995) (specifying that an implied-in-fact agreement to demote only for good cause did not violate public policy).

[146] Allan v. Caspar, 622 N.E.2d 367, 371 [86 EDUC. L. REP. 959] (Ohio Ct. App. 1993).

that she failed to complete her field instruction successfully.[147] Likewise, in a case from Connecticut, an appellate court upheld a student's dismissal from a seminary program where officials had not made any promises permitting her to stay as long as necessary to complete her degree.[148] As demonstrated by the three preceding cases, the burden of proof is on those challenging school officials' actions to produce evidence of a lack of good faith.[149]

In a dispute in New York, a trial court overturned the dismissal of a student who failed four courses during her first year when three others, some with more failures and weaker excuses, were allowed to stay in school.[150] On further review, an appellate panel reversed in favor of the student because she acted in good faith on the basis of an exercise of sound academic judgment. Although based on subjective judgment, the court reasoned that "the college's action did not demonstrate bad faith, arbitrariness, or irrationality."[151] The court's observation that this case involved "the professional and academic milieu" is worth keeping in mind, because the judiciary generally grants broad discretion to educational officials addressing academic matters.[152]

Absent express or implied contractual provisions that a party or parties violated, courts are unlikely to treat institutional decisions as exhibiting bad faith simply because the outcomes required the exercise of discretion. Consequently, courts have assiduously avoided addressing questions about

---

[147] Raethz v. Aurora Univ., 805 N.E.2d 696 [186 EDUC. L. REP. 935] (Ill. App. Ct. 2004).

[148] Little v. Yale Univ., 884 A.2d 427 [203 EDUC. L. REP. 267] (Conn. Ct. App. 2005).

[149] *See* Raethz v. Aurora Univ., 805 N.E.2d at 699 ("The burden of establishing arbitrary or capricious conduct is a heavy one.... The plaintiff must show that her dismissal was 'without any discernible rational basis.'").

[150] Heisler v. New York Med. Coll., 449 N.Y.S.2d 834 [4 EDUC. L. REP. 240] (N.Y. Sup. Ct. 1982).

[151] Patti Ann H. v. New York Med. Coll., 453 N.Y.S.2d 196, 199 [5 EDUC. L. REP. 1233] (N.Y. App. Div. 1982).

[152] *See* Board of Curators of Univ. of Mo. v. Horowitz, 435 U.S. 78, 90, 92 (1978) (in upholding the dismissal of a medical student in her last semester of medical school, commenting that "[t]he determination whether to dismiss a student for academic reasons requires an expert evaluation of cumulative information and is not readily adapted to the procedural tools of judicial or administrative decision making.... Courts are particularly ill-equipped to evaluate academic performance."). For a discussion of the differences between judicial approaches to academic and disciplinary misconduct, see Ralph D. Mawdsley, ACADEMIC MISCONDUCT: CHEATING AND PLAGIARISM 45-52 (1994).

the dismissal of students for poor academic performance,[153] faculty grading practices,[154] or the severity of penalties when compared with past offenses.[155]

On a different matter involving fundamental fairness, a former administrator at a religious school who was dismissed filed a breach of contract claim against its officials under her employment contract. The contract stipulated that "[t]his contract may be terminated by the School upon a determination by the School, in its sole discretion that a reasonable cause exists to terminate the contract."[156] The dismissal language left the plaintiff particularly vulnerable. Officials terminated the plaintiff's contract after parents objected vehemently to her failure to have adult supervision at a dance conducted at the school. The facts did reveal that the plaintiff arranged for her 19-year-old son, his 18-year-old girlfriend, a student's 17-year-old older sister, and the sister's 18-year-old boyfriend to chaperone the dance that about eighty students from the sixth, seventh, and eighth grades were expected to attend

The court recognized that only notice the plaintiff was entitled to under her contract was post-termination, and even though a difference of opinion existed as to whether she received it, the court still held as a matter of law that no breach had occurred. As the court intimated, persons are unlikely to ever have a justiciable claim where notice would do nothing more than declare what is already an obvious *fait accompli* in the case at bar, namely that the administrator's employment was terminated.

In addition to suing the school for breach of contract, the administrator sued the parents for what she perceived as tortious interference with her contract. The plaintiff failed in both of her claims; there was no breach of contract because the board had complete discretion in dismissing her, and she lacked a tortious interference with contract claim because officials had not breached her contract. In sum, the court upheld the broad discretion the school officials had given themselves in ascertaining whether the administrator's contract should have been nonrenewed.

---

[153] *See* Shields v. The Sch. of Law, Hofstra Univ., 431 N.Y.S.2d 60 (N.Y. App. Div. 1980) (refusing to treat the actions of law school officials as arbitrary, capricious, and in bad faith in not counting summer school grades from another law school in her GPA, where no such provision existed in the school's catalog).

[154] *See* Susan M. v. New York Law Sch., 557 N.Y.S.2d 297, 300 [61 Educ. L. Rep.. 716] (N.Y. 1989) (upholding the dismissal of a student who received a failing grade absent evidence that the faculty member's reason for acting "demonstrated bad faith, arbitrariness, capriciousness, irrationality or a constitutional or statutory violation [observing that] the student's challenge to a particular grade or other academic determination relating to a genuine substantive evaluation of the student's academic capabilities, [was] beyond the scope of judicial review.").

[155] *See* Napolitano v. Princeton Univ., 453 A.2d 263, 275 [8 Educ. L. Rep. 74] (N.J. Super. Ct. App. Div. 1999) (upholding the one-year delay in awarding a baccalaureate degree to a senior who plagiarized because even though she was the first student whose diploma was delayed, "if the regulations concerned are reasonable; if they are known to the student or should have been; if the proceedings are before the appropriate persons with authority to act, to find facts, or to make recommendations; and if procedural due process was accorded the student, then the findings when supported by substantial evidence must be accorded some presumption of correctness.").

[156] Gatto v. St. Richard Sch., 774 N.E.2d 914, 920 [169 Educ. L. Rep. 371] (Ind. Ct. App. 2002).

At the same time, courts intervened where academic actions violated the terms of an educational institution's contract. In an usual case, a trial court in New York ordered officials at a private college to confer a baccalaureate degree on a student because in refusing to accept transfer credits from another institution, they invoked a newly added provision in the catalog that was not to take effect until the year after his scheduled graduation.[157] Further, officials relied differentially on only one part of the catalog, when other portions made conflicting statements. As in this case, when the actions of school officials are in direct conflict with published standards, discretion is no longer an issue, such that promissory estoppel becomes an appropriate concept to correct violations of the express terms of contracts.

Institutional actions may be arbitrary, capricious, and lacking in good faith where they violate public policy. In such a case from Illinois, a bankruptcy court invalidated the efforts of officials at a private college to collect past-due obligations by denying admission to students and refusing to send out their official transcripts after they arranged for Chapter 13 repayment plans. Although state action is ordinarily required before private institutions are affected by the nonretaliation protection of debtors' plans, the court asserted that "[w]here the actions of a private institution such as withholding a transcript, are really tools to collect a discharged debt or a debt provided for under a plan, debtors are denied the fresh start contemplated by Congress in enacting the Bankruptcy Code."[158] Still, as reflected by a case from New Jersey, private universities do not violate the Bankruptcy Code's stay-put requirement by withholding the transcripts of students who defaulted on loans not dischargeable under Chapter 13.[159]

Most case law involves allegations that school officials have exhibited bad faith in interpreting or applying contract language. As could have been expected, bad faith is not solely limited to employers. For example, as reflected in a case from Louisiana, faculty members can fail in their claims if they have not demonstrated good faith. The dispute arose when officials in a faith-based school cancelled the contract of a new religion teacher who was not honest on his job application. On the form the plaintiff checked off "Practicing Catholic: Yes" and under "Marital Status" had checked "Married." What the teacher failed to reveal, though, despite the fact that it had not come up during the interview, was that he had a prior marriage and divorce.

In light of an unpublished policy of not permitting divorced persons to teach religion, an appellate court in Louisiana affirmed the dismissal of the teacher's breach of contract claim.[160] The court acknowledged that since the teacher had spent six years in a Catholic seminary and was familiar with Church

---

[157] Blank v. Board of Higher Educ. of City of N.Y., 273 N.Y.S.2d 796 (N.Y. Sup. Ct. 1966).

[158] In re Parkman, 27 B.R. 460, 462 [9 EDUC. L. REP. 558] (N.D. Ill. 1983). The Bankruptcy Code imposes an automatic stay on retaliation against debtors who petition for protection under its provisions, prohibiting a broad range of collection efforts, but does not apply to such areas as alimony, paternity, and family support. *See* 11 U.S.C. §§ 362 (a), (b).

[159] In re Billingsley, 276 B.R. 48 [164 EDUC. L. REP. 289] (D.N.J. 2002).

[160] Bischoff v. Brothers of the Sacred Heart, 416 So. 2d 348, 351 [5 EDUC. L. REP. 334] (La. Ct. App. 1982), *reh'g denied* (1982).

teachings on marriage, his reluctance to reveal his marital history was likely because he knew that if he told the truth, the administration would not have been offered him the job. In light of the circumstances, the court considered the teacher's silence to be evidence of bad faith, thereby rendering his contract "void *ab initio*."[161]

The preceding case is a close call; without the teacher's admission against interest, the courts might have reached a different outcome. What this case does underscore is that employers in faith-based institutions need to make important employment information known explicitly to job applicants, preferably in published form, to avoid confusion about the specific requirements of their positions.

Recommendations

The following suggestions reflect the discussions in this chapter on constitutional and contractual relationships in nonpublic educational institutions.

1. Parties to employment contracts need to discuss general or ambiguous terms such as "other assigned duties." While employers may assume that such inquiries should the responsibilities of the new employees, the goal of effective administrators should be to eliminate surprises and the stress that can come from inadequate notice of the full scale of employment expectations. If "other assigned duties" routinely includes such matters as coaching, lunchroom duty, locker room or playground supervision, supervising after-school detention, or attendance at school activities, administrators have the duty to provide the most complete picture possible of the full scope of the employment relationship.

2. Officials must spell out service obligations or conduct standards clearly in faculty/staff and student handbooks. While such handbooks generally are part of employment contracts, documents must state these connections clearly. Employment contracts must contain language incorporated by reference handbooks and other documents setting forth employment requirements.

3. Students themselves generally do not sign contracts, but must be given copies of their handbooks and, where possible, orientation sessions explaining institutional expectations. While school officials can assume that students are able to read the handbooks, officials need to explain some provisions, such as harassment, bullying, plagiarism, and cheating, for which severe punishments may be imposed. Because school officials invest a considerable amount of time, energy, and expense in recruiting students, and conceding that a complete understanding of expectations

---

[161] *Id*. at 351. For another case where a teacher was dismissed for lying on an application for a job at a faith-based school, *see* LaCross v. Cornerstone Christian Acad., 896 So.2d 105 [197 Educ. L. Rep. 451] (La. Ct. App. 2004) (allowing school officials to invalidate a contract where a job applicant lied about whether she consumed alcoholic beverages).

may not always prevent problems, educators can forestall complaints about unfair or unreasonable interpretations of school rules in the future.

4. Educational institutions must reserve the authority to change handbook language as the need arises. As necessary as change is, school officials need to weigh carefully whether some changes, such as restricting the list of acceptable clothing or accessories, can wait until the beginning of the next school year. Even if officials have authority to make changes at any time during academic years, perceived decreases in the benefits enjoyed by students or employees are likely to have negative impacts on morale.

5. Where educational institutions hire at-will employees, officials should provide some written record of such identifications, even if in letters memorializing their employment relationships.

6. Both student and employee handbooks should state institutional discipline policies, including prohibited forms of conduct and the process for addressing alleged violations.

7. Officials should review institutional materials—including applications, promotional materials, and handbooks—annually to reconcile conflicts or contradictions between and among policies. Where possible, these reviews should involve the advice of their attorneys to assure compliance with federal and state law.

Conclusion

Not surprisingly, as in the public sector, litigation has ensued in faith-based institutions, whether in elementary and secondary education or higher education, when disputes arise between and among parents, students, school officials, and faculty members over the terms of the contracts the parties entered. While the litigants in these cases from nonpublic institutions do not have the same level of due process protection as their counterparts in the public sector, the courts have sought to ensure that fundamental fairness, however broadly the judiciary construes this term, is present to provide some protection for the rights of aggrieved parties. At the bottom line, then, in an attempt to engage in preventive school law, institutional officials should strive to make contract language as clear as they can, while students, parents, and faculty members should read their contracts carefully so that both parties have a true meeting of the minds as they begin their legal relationship.

Discussion Questions

1. Explain whether you think the courts should treat officials of faith-based institutions as having engaged in state action, especially when they receive substantial amounts of public aid, whether from federal or state governments.

2. How would you define "fundamental fairness" in employment or registration contracts in terms of the level and/or amount of due process to which aggrieved employees, students, and their parents are entitled in contract disputes?

3. What specific language would you recommend that school officials put in enrollment contracts identifying the permissible circumstances under which parents can remove their children from faith-based schools, and outlining the liquidated damages they can face if they breach their contracts?

4. In light of question 3, what do you think about enforcing liquidated damages clauses against teachers in faith-based schools who ask to be relieved of their contracts so they can take better-paying jobs to support themselves and their families? If it were up to you, would you enforce such a provision? What kind of exceptions might you suggest?

Key Words

Breach of contract
Constitutional constraints
Contract
Contractual rights
Fundamental fairness
Remedies
State action
Tenure

Governing Board
Responsibilities and Liability

Cristiana Ritchie-Carter

Contents

Introduction / 69
Board Structures / 70
Board Responsibilities / 73
       Defining and Maintaining the Missions of Religious Schools / 75
       Fiduciary Relationship / 80
       Standard of Care / 81
Liability / 83
       Use of Public Funds / 86
       Conflict of Interest / 87
       Vicarious Liability / 88
       Indemnification / 88
       Liability Insurance / 90
Conclusion / 90
Discussion Questions / 91
Key Words / 91

Introduction

Governing boards in nonpublic, faith-based, and/or religiously affiliated[1] schools, which vary in their structures, operate to ensure the promulgation of policies and plans consistent with the missions of their institutions. Boards in nonpublic schools differ from their counterparts in the public sector both in the scope of their duties[2] and as to how their members are elected or selected. Regardless, when individuals serve as members of boards in faith-based schools, they must commit to significant levels of engagement and may be accountable if they fail to carry out their duties.

---

[1] Unless otherwise noted, this chapter uses the terms nonpublic, faith-based, and religiously affiliated schools interchangeably.

[2] For a good, if slightly dated, examination of these differences at the secondary level, see David Baker, Mei Han, Charles T. Keil, *How Different, How Similar? Comparing Key Organizational Qualities of American Public and Private Secondary Schools*, National Center for Education Statistics, October 1996, available at https://nces.ed.gov/pubs/96322.pdf.

As discussed below, board models in nonpublic schools fall into one of three categories: advisory, consultative, or limited jurisdiction.[3] Boards with limited jurisdiction are also referred to as boards of trustees, policy-making boards, and/or governing boards.

Regardless of the models school boards employ, organizational constitutions and bylaws are critical elements in outlining the roles, duties, and responsibilities of their members as they delineate how to conduct business, by whom, and under which sets of circumstances. Fortunately—from their perspective—unlike their counterparts in public education, school boards in nonpublic schools have faced fewer instances of litigation despite the considerable responsibilities of their members. Accordingly, this chapter addresses legal issues that school boards and their members in nonpublic schools are likely to encounter.

Board Structures

Accountability, responsibility, and liability, along with minor variations in school board functions, are based on their legal structures as delineated in their articles of incorporation, bylaws, and perhaps external sources of power. In Catholic schools, for instance, the largest single denomination of nonpublic schools in the United States,[4] wherein the Code of Canon Law is explicitly part of Church teaching, it cannot be superseded by the articles of incorporation or bylaws.[5] Instead, the Code mandates who is the ultimate governing authority within the Catholic school system and in individual schools. Other centralized systems of religious schools may have to defer to doctrinal matters of their denominational structures.

In Catholic schools, civil law and church law commingle, sometimes creating tension.[6] According to Canon 803, "Catholic school is understood as one which a competent authority or a public ecclesiastical juridic person directs or which an ecclesiastical authority recognizes as such through a written document."[7] In Roman Catholic dioceses, bishops are the ecclesiastical authorities who consult with and delegate the operational functions of their school

---

[3] *Breathing New Life into Catholic Schools: An Exploration of Catholic School Governance Models* at 23-24, Foundations and Donors Interested in Catholic Activities, December 2014, available at www.fadica.org.

[4] *See* Statistics About Nonpublic Education in the United States, U.S. Department of Education, Office of Nonpublic Education (ONEP), available at https://www2.ed.gov/about/offices/list/oii/nonpublic/statistics.html (reporting on data as of Fall 2013). *See also* Private School Enrollment, National Center for Educational Statistics, https://nces.ed.gov/programs/coe/indicator_cgc.asp (last updated January 2018).

[5] THE CODE OF CANON LAW: A TEXT AND COMMENTARY (James A. Coriden, Thomas J. Green, Donald E. Heintschel, Eds. 1985).

[6] For a discussion of this issue, see Charles J. Russo (2009). *Canon Law, American Law, and Governance of Catholic Schools: A Healthy Partnership.* 13 CATHOLIC EDUC.: A J. OF INQUIRY AND PRACTICE 185 (2009).

[7] Code of Canon Law, 1983 § 1.

systems to their superintendents. Bishops, essentially acting as chief executive officers, ordinarily seek and rely on the expertise of their superintendents and central office staffs. At the parish level, pastors represent the ecclesiastical authority which similarly consults with and delegates educational authority to the principal, and perhaps a board.

The Catholic school "system," which is essentially a loosely coupled collection of largely independent schools, operates three types of schools: parish or parochial, diocesan, and private.[8] At the elementary level, the most common types are parish or parochial schools. These schools are affiliated with local parishes, drawing students from those church communities and perhaps the surrounding local areas and nearby parishes lacking schools. In these schools, governance resides in local parishes, where, according to Canon Law, pastors are the ultimate authorities who delegate educational responsibilities to the principals they hire. Pastors, again under Canon Law, retain responsibility for ensuring that schools are indeed Catholic, that faculty members who teach religion are competent, and that the religious curriculum is doctrinally sound. Pastors usually delegate day-to-day school operations to principals. A small, declining number of parishes also operate high schools.

Many dioceses operate high schools with the bishop, also known as an ordinary, as the school's juridic person. Bishops, usually in consultation with nominating committees of school boards, appoint new members, with the superintendents often serving as their delegates on the boards. Boards then adopt their own bylaws setting forth their functions regarding finance, strategic planning, and development, among many other areas. However, unlike in public schools, key decisions, such as hiring presidents of high schools or principals of elementary schools, are made in consultation with the bishop and superintendent.

The juridic person in Catholic schools can also be a member of the religious order that operates it, or can be a separately incorporated by a group of people. Juridic persons are really a group of people who act in concert, recognized by canonical authority as having the authority to proceed, and are entrusted with the task of carrying out the missions of their schools. As such, schools operated by religious orders are private schools wherein representatives of the religious orders sit on the boards participating in their decision making. In many instances, private schools with boards of trustees have bylaws that describe the mandatory duties of their juridic persons while acknowledging the discretionary powers of their boards.

Under Canon 803, §3, local bishops have the ultimate authority for designating the Catholicity of schools. In other words, no one person or organization may unilaterally establish a "Catholic" school in a diocese, without the express

---

[8] *See also* THE CATHOLIC HIGH SCHOOL, A NATIONAL PORTRAIT, National Catholic Educational Association 1985. The U.S. Department of Education, Office of Non-public Education (ONEP), identifies Roman Catholic schools as consisting of these same three categories. Statistics About Nonpublic Education in the United States, U.S. Department of Education, available at https://www2.ed.gov/about/offices/list/oii/nonpublic/statistics.html (reporting on data as of Fall 2013).

permission and approval of the bishop. Consequently, schools are Catholic if their bishop agrees they are, and if those operating them recognize the authority of their bishops regarding the proper religious training of students and staff.[9]

The governance model most commonly relied on in Catholic and many other faith-based schools is the advisory board. Advisory boards are responsible for formulating and recommending policy to the persons with authority to enact their provisions. In the parish school model, policies do not become effective unless their pastors, the authority under Canon Law, agree. If pastors agree, they usually delegate authority for enacting policies to the school principals.[10]

The consultative board structure differs only slightly from an advisory board, insofar as the person in authority is required to consult with the board before making decisions in designated areas. These boards typically consult in such areas as development, strategic planning, and finance. When operating pursuant to this model, the authority figure is only bound to seek advice, but does not have to follow a board's suggestions.

Boards of limited jurisdiction are sometimes called boards of trustees, or policy-making boards. Religious leaders have granted these boards the authority to make and enact policy in specified areas as articulated in their constitutions and bylaws. In independent nonpublic schools, the roles and responsibilities of members, and how they are selected or elected,[11] vary depending on their constitutions and bylaws. Boards of limited jurisdiction are often engaged in resolving grievances and addressing day-to-day operations of their schools on such matters as curricula, student discipline, and/or personnel matters.

In Catholic and many other faith-based schools, their boards may be charged with overseeing budgets, strategic planning, and policy development. In Catholic schools, though, the bylaws delineate powers through which the bishop is responsible for the Catholic identity and religious education of students, as well as to "appoint or approve teachers of religion and even to remove them and demand that they be removed if a reason of religion and morals requires it."[12]

Boards of limited jurisdiction have become prevalent in Roman Catholic schools as dioceses have begun experimenting with various structures to ensure better participation and greater accountability. For instance, in 2008, the Diocese of Brooklyn shifted from the parish school model, which included

---

[9] *Id.*

[10] Philip J. Brown, *Structuring Catholic schools: Creative imagination meets canon law*, 65-116 in DESIGN FOR SUCCESS: NEW CONFIGURATIONS IN CATHOLIC SCHOOLS (Regina Haney & Joseph M. O'Keefe Eds.) 2009.

[11] For an older case establishing this principle, see Minnesota Baptist Convention v. Pillsbury Acad., 74 N.W.2d 286 (Min. 1955) (holding that insofar as a constitutional amendment prohibiting the state legislature from enacting special or private laws respecting grants of corporate powers or privileges or granting special and exclusive franchises was only prospective in operation, it did not prohibit the amendment of corporate charters granted prior thereto, and special laws subsequently enacted granting the Convention the exclusive right to elect trustees to the Pillsbury Academy).

[12] THE CODE OF CANON LAW, *supra*, note 5.

combining schools regionally to what are now described as academies. Under the academy model in the Brooklyn Diocese, governing responsibilities fall under a two-tiered board system.[13] At the first level is the Board of Members, consisting of local pastors, the bishop, and the superintendent, who appoint laypeople with requisite skill sets to monitor and assist with budgeting, strategic planning, and policy formation. This Board maintains jurisdiction over the schools to ensure their Catholic identities. The second group, Boards of Directors, have limited jurisdiction over school governance. The intent of the academy model is to ensure that pastors have the opportunities to carry out their pastoral responsibilities while involving the laity more fully in their governance.

Regardless of the nature of schools, their boards are typically corporate bodies whose articles of incorporation must be registered in their states. Boards must take this step in order to obtain their Section 501(c)(3) tax status, which allows them to conduct business by opening bank accounts and engaging in other activities as tax-exempt, not-for-profit corporations.[14] Depending on the jurisdiction, nonpublic schools may also have to be incorporated separately under state law.

Board Responsibilities

In a manner similar to the way in which state laws establish the duties of public school boards, the articles of incorporation and bylaws of nonpublic educational institutions typically identify the two types of power boards possess. Mandatory, or ministerial, duties are those responsibilities boards are obligated to perform. Such duties include, but are not necessarily limited to, setting tuition rates and other fees; identifying who owns the property on which schools are housed; who has the authority to employ legal counsel; who hires the heads of schools, while approving other employment actions; establishing policies for disciplining students and employees; and how funds are disbursed.

On the other hand, discretionary powers identify tasks which boards are not legally obligated to carry out, but may engage in if they wish to do so. For example, boards may recommend policies such as whether students should wear uniforms and whether schools should offer advanced placement classes or extracurricular activities.

Boards of nonpublic school, regardless of the type of governance models they have adopted, share basic responsibilities such that their alleged, or actual, failure to carry out their duties can be cause for legal actions. Unfortunately, all

---

[13] Thomas Chadzutko, Lecture on Legal Issues in the Diocese of Brooklyn, April 25, 2018 (copy on file with author). *See also* Breathing New Life into Catholic Schools: An Exploration of Catholic School Governance Models (2014) available at http://www.usccb.org/beliefs-and-teachings/how-we-teach/catholic-education/k-12/upload/FADICA-Catholic-Schools-Governance-Paper-2015.pdf

[14] See 26 U.S.C. § 501(c) (identifying the types of not-for-profit organizations exempt from selected federal taxes). The criteria for earning such status are described in 26 U.S.C. §§ 501-503.

too often board members tend to leave bylaws on the proverbial shelf, where they are neglected, until disputes arise. Consequently, providing regular professional development sessions for board members is essential. Such sessions can keep board members apprised of their duties, along with updating them about legal and educational developments that are important for their schools.

During professional development sessions, board articles of incorporation and bylaws are a good place to begin introducing members to standard operating procedures and to the missions of their schools because, as noted, these documents outline duties and responsibilities, whether mandatory or discretionary. Moreover, in the event of litigation, courts often scrutinize the language of institutional articles of incorporation and/or bylaws when determining whether boards should be liable.

A case from Texas—albeit involving a university rather than an elementary or secondary school—illustrates the kind of contract issues boards in K-12 schools may face in terms of supervising their financial investments. When university officials hired a money manager to handle its large endowment and the firm he selected liquidated securities at his discretion, the Board of Regents tried to avoid having to reimburse the firm for the half-million-dollar loss it incurred when the securities were sold on the open market.

Rejecting the claim of the Board of Regents that the employee exceeded his authority, an appellate court acknowledged both that it had the ability to hire an investment firm and that it could delegate its authority to one of its employees to invest in the securities. Observing that the board later ratified the employee's actions, the court denied its claim for relief, instead granting the company's request for attorney fees.[15] This case is noteworthy because the court resolved it by applying the law of contracts, concluding that once the board delegated its authority to its money manager, it could not then try to recoup its losses by claiming that the employee exceeded his authority, because oversight of financial matters statements is a basic board function.

The case against the university suggests that board members in all educational institutions should meet their specified minimum legal responsibilities. These minimum responsibilities for board members are to attend and participate actively in board and committee meetings; to examine financial statements of the institutions; to review financial documents; to be familiar with all legal documents, such as articles of incorporation, constitution and bylaws, and institutional policies; to acquire working knowledge of institutional policies; to make inquiries about what is happening in their schools; and to discharge their duties in a reasonable, prudent, and informed manner.

Whether boards are advisory or of limited jurisdiction, reviewing operational vitality is fundamental to ensuring the health and integrity of their institutions. As indicated, in order to operate as tax-exempt, not-for-profit entities, boards must incorporate. Moreover, it is not unprecedented for state

---

[15] Bache Halsey Stuart v. Univ. of Houston, 638 S.W.2d 920 [6 EDUC. L. REP.] (Tex. Ct. App. 1982).

attorneys general to shut organizations down because their boards are failing to adhere to, or carry out, functions articulated in their articles of incorporation and/or bylaws. Because of the day-to-day operation of schools, though, coupled with the close relationships board members share with their schools, having the state order nonpublic schools to cease operations is not as common as it is for other not-for-profit organizations. However, board members may be liable for failing to fulfill their obligations.

Defining and Maintaining the Missions of Religious Schools

Challenges associated with procuring access to financial benefits have given focus to the responsibility of governing boards of faith-based schools to define and maintain their institutional religious missions. While preserving institutional religious identity may result in schools' being denied some financial benefits,[16] the issues are really more systemic than just about eligibility for public funds. For educational institutions with church affiliations, boards of trustees must first determine what degree of church control best serves their overall institutional interests, while considering the financial implications of their actions.

Where church-controlled schools may have difficulty in accessing many forms of public funds, church control may nonetheless offer benefits that might be attractive to some schools or their employees. For example, church-controlled organizations are generally exempt from participation under state unemployment compensation statutes,[17] as well as Social Security[18] and The Employee Retirement Income Security Act of 1974, commonly referred to as

---

[16] *See* Bob Jones Univ. v. U.S., 461 U.S. 574 [10 Educ. L. Rep. 918] (1983) (upholding the loss of the university's tax-exempt status for its refusal to eliminate religion-based rules prohibiting interracial dating and marriage); Bob Jones Univ. v. Johnson, 396 F. Supp. 597 (D.S.C. 1974) (upholding loss of veterans benefits due to racially discriminatory rules). *But see* Trinity Lutheran Church of Columbia v. Comer, 137 S. Ct. 2012 (ruling that religious organizations or individuals cannot be denied generally available benefits solely because they are religious).

[17] *See, e.g.,* Ohio Rev. Code Ann. § 4141.01(B)(3)(h)(i) (exempt employees "in the employ of a church or convention or association of churches, or an organization which is operated primarily for religious purposes and which is operated, supervised, controlled, primarily supported by a church, convention, or association of churches"); Bleich v. Maimonides Sch., 849 N.E..2d 185 [209 Educ. L. Rep. 413] (Mass. 2006) (holding that a Jewish school, while not controlled by a hierarchal religious organization, was exempt from unemployment compensation because although it was self-governing, its teachings were grounded in the Jewish faith and it derived substantial support from area synagogues and other Jewish organizations). *But see* Unity Christian Sch. of Fulton, Ill. v. Rowell, 6 N.E.3d 845 (Ill. App. Ct. 2014) (deciding that officials failed to prove that the school was operated, supervised, controlled, or principally supported by a church so as to be exempt from making compulsory contributions to the unemployment system); Mid-Vermont Christian Sch. v. Dep't of Employment and Training, 885 A.2d 1210 [203 Educ. L. Rep. 771] (Vt. 2005) (an independent religious school not affiliated with a church was not exempt from unemployment tax).

[18] 42 U.S.C. § 410(a)(8)(B) ("Service performed in the employ of a church or qualified church-controlled organization," provided an exemption has been filed with the IRS, is exempt from coverage under the Social Security Act).

ERISA,[19] a federal law which establishes minimum standards for most voluntarily adopted pension and health plans in the private sector to protection participants in these plans.

An illustrative case arose in Louisiana where a worker in a faith-based school unsuccessfully sued to recover for injuries he suffered in its gymnasium.[20] This case demonstrates that if church officials maintain control over school property, they may be able to limit institutional liability.

Rejecting the employee's negligence claim, an appellate court pointed out a variety of factors supporting its judgment that the church was not liable. The court recognized that even though the school and church were incorporated separately, church officials preserved their control over the school; the name of the school's chief administrator appeared in the church bulletin as a member of its pastoral staff; school board members had to be members of, and be elected by, the church community; and all of the property used by the school was under the control of church trustees. The court explained that this was important because insofar as state law forbade employees from suing their employers in negligence, the plaintiff's only remedy was under workers' compensation. In light of the church's control over the school, the court asserted that the plaintiff's only form of redress was limited to workers' compensation because he worked for the church and not the school.

At the same time, the pressure for school boards may be in the direction of severing, or at least diluting, church control, either to distance themselves from political denominational dissension or to gain access to financial benefits. Nonetheless, the alternative to these concerns may be even more troublesome for religious schools. Absence of church control may mean an increased likelihood that the National Labor Relations Board (NLRB) could reverse course[21] and assert jurisdiction over faith-based educational institutions.[22]

---

[19] 29 U.S.C. §§ 1002(33)(A); 1321(b)(3);26 U.S.C. § 414(e)(3)(B) (church benefit plans exempt from reporting and disclosure requirements of an Employee Retirement Income Security Program for "a church or ... a convention or association of churches [and] an employee of an organization ... which is controlled by or associated with a church or a convention or association of churches." Under § 414(e), a church or convention or association of churches is one "which is exempt from tax under section 501.").

[20] Morris v. State Farm Ins., 649 So. 2d 58 [97 EDUC. L. REP. 600] (La. Ct. App. 1994).

[21] See NLRB v. Catholic Bishop of Chicago, 440 U.S. 490 (1979) (affirming that the NLRB lacked jurisdiction to mandate collective bargaining between teachers and their employers in their faith-based secondary school). For a commentary on this case, see Charles J. Russo, *NLRB v. Catholic Bishop of Chicago: Collective Bargaining in Roman Catholic Secondary Schools Ten Years Later*, 57 EDUC. L. REP. 1113 (1989).

[22] See, e.g., Hill-Murray Fed'n of Teachers, St. Paul, Minn. v. Hill-Murray High Sch., Maplewood, Minn., 487 N.W.2d 857 [76 EDUC. L. REP. 864] (Minn. 1992); NLRB v. Hanna Boys Ctr., 940 F.2d 1295 (9th Cir. 1991) (subjecting labor disputes in faith-based schools to labor relations boards); Catholic High Sch. Ass'n of Archdiocese of N.Y. v. Culvert, 753 F.2d 1161 [22 EDUC. L. REP. 1117] (2d Cir. 1985) (the state labor relations board had jurisdiction over lay teachers). *But see* Central Catholic Educ. Ass'n v. Archdiocese of Portland, 891 P.2d 1318 [98 EDUC. L. REP. 1069] (Or. Ct. App. 1995) (affirming that the state Employment Relations Board lack jurisdiction in a labor dispute in a faith-based school)

Even more ominous is the possibility that faith-based schools might lose their protections under the religious exemptions in Title VII that permit hiring preferences and employment actions based on religion. For instance, in *EEOC v. Kamehameha Schools/Bishop Estate (Kamehameha)*,[23] the Ninth Circuit decided that the lack of church control meant that the schools were not entitled to protection under Title VII's religious exemptions. The schools in *Kamehameha* were established in 1896 pursuant to a bequest that required teachers to be Protestant. When a non-Protestant was denied a position as a substitute French teacher, she filed a complaint with the Equal Employment Opportunities Commission (EEOC), which ultimately sued the schools under Title VII. The attorneys for the schools responded that they were entitled to deny the applicant a job because of her religion.

On further review of an order in favor of the schools, the Ninth Circuit reversed on behalf of the EEOC and job applicant. The court rebuffed the schools' reliance on the Title VII religious exemption based on the facts that the schools were not supported or controlled by a religious organization, and the schools were not affiliated with "any denomination of Protestants or with any organization or with any association of religious schools."[24] At the same time, the schools were part of the Bishop Estate, "a large and overwhelmingly secular business,"[25] making no mention of religion in its annual reports. Moreover, faculty members, while nominally Protestant, were not required to maintain membership in a church and did not have to subscribe to a set of beliefs.

The Ninth Circuit added that the chaplain, who taught religious education and was pastor of the Bishop Memorial Church, had no authority over the curriculum;[26] religious affiliation was not taken into consideration for the 3000 boarding and day students and the more than 36,000 other students served through off-campus and outreach programs;[27] the wide variety of student activities did not differ appreciably from public and private schools across the nation;[28] and the curriculum, while incorporating some religious songs, prayer, and religious courses, lacked any "effort to instruct students in Protestant doctrine ...[and] disavowed any effort to convert non-Protestant students"'[29]

The application of *Kamehameha* in other litigation remains difficult to predict. There is wide variation among religious non-church-controlled schools

---

[23] 780 F. Supp. 1317 [72 EDUC. L. REP. 218] (D. Haw. 1991), *rev'd* 990 F.2d 458 [82 EDUC. L. REP. 303] (9th Cir. 1993), *cert. denied*, 510 U.S. 963 (1993).

[24] *Kamehameha*, 990 F.2d at 461 (the court considered it important that the Bishop Memorial Church, which was controlled by the schools, was a member of the Hawaii Conference of the United Church of Christ, but the schools themselves were not).

[25] *Id.*

[26] *Id.* at 462.

[27] *Id.* (fewer than one-third of the on-campus students were Protestant).

[28] *Id.* (the court noted that some of the activities, such as Bible studies and prayer before athletics, can be found in public schools; in addition, major events such as Founder's Day and Baccalaureate incorporated celebrations of both religion and Hawaiian culture).

[29] *Id.* at 463 (the court seemed to consider important a curricular change that no longer made a religious course mandatory).

as to the religious requirements imposed on students and employees. Elaborate religious requirements that at one time might have included having employees attend and participate in religious services on campus, in addition to having to attend church off campus, may well have, over the years, been made voluntary and finally eliminated.

After *Kamehameha*, non-church-controlled schools may learn that courts scrutinize not only the nature of the religious influences in their schools, but also the extent to which the religious influences have increased or decreased. In *Kamehameha*, the court examined school publications which revealed that "the purpose and emphasis of the [s]chools had shifted over the years from providing religious instruction to equipping students with ethical principles that will enable them to make their own moral judgments."[30]

The court in *Kamehameha* was of the opinion that a variety of factors resulted in the diminution of religious influences in the schools. In particular, the court acknowledged the decrease in the number of students who participated in religious services;[31] the reduction of required religion courses to the extent that they were only mandatory for first-year students;[32] and changes in course content from emphasis on Protestantism to the comparative study of religions and local Hawaiian culture.[33] Thus, non-church-controlled educational institutions could face judicial examinations in two linear directions: the nature of religious requirements imposed on faculty, students, and the curriculum, along with the extent to which current religious obligations were diluted over the years.

Given the narrow set of facts of *Kamehameha*, it seems to have little application to many religious educational institutions which, although not church-affiliated or church-controlled, nonetheless have maintained significant cores of religious content. The Ninth Circuit, though, suggested that the history of Title VII litigation warranted a broad interpretation of its order. The court found "no case holding the [Title VII] exemption to be applicable where the [educational] institution was not wholly or partially owned by a church."[34] The court also relied on a statement from a member of Congress that the Title VII exemptions were "limited to church affiliated colleges and universities, part of whose mission ... is to propagate the belief of the denomination that is supporting the educational institution."[35]

Whether the precedential value of *Kamehameha* is to be limited to its facts remains uncertain. Regardless, the Ninth Circuit clearly sent some cautionary signals that non-church-controlled religious schools may be viewed differently from church-controlled schools in terms of protection under Title VII. For governing boards, the difficult balancing task is to determine whether any

---

[30] *Id.* at 462.
[31] *Id.* at 462-63.
[32] *Id.* note 10.
[33] *Id.* at 464-65.
[34] *Id.* at 461, note 7.
[35] *Id.* at 464, quoting from Representative Purcell, 110 Cong. Rec. 2585-86 (Feb. 8, 1964).

advantages coming to their schools as a result of church control may be offset by political dissension and lack of access to financial resources. The factors on both sides need to be weighed carefully because once school boards diminish their church control and dilute their religious influences, it is doubtful that they school can ever return to the auspices of their faiths.

Against this background, it is worth noting that the Supreme Court unanimously upheld the constitutionality of the ministerial exception—albeit as it was extended under the Americans with Disabilities Act (ADA), rather than Title VII—in *Hosanna-Tabor Evangelical Lutheran Church and School v. Equal Employment Opportunities Commission* (*Hosanna-Tabor*).[36] Pursuant to the ministerial exception in Title VII, "a religious corporation, association, educational institution, or society with respect to the employment of individuals of a particular religion to perform work connected with the carrying on by such corporation, association, educational institution, or society of its activities."[37]

The ministerial exception places the burden of proof of the necessity of bona fide occupational qualifications on employers, even if individuals are not ordained. In order to apply this exception, officials in religious institutions must be able to prove that staff members' teaching or other activities are so integrally related to furthering their spiritual and pastoral missions that their duties may be treated as ministerial.

The underlying issue in *Hosanna Tabor* addressed whether officials at a Lutheran elementary school in Michigan could dismiss a contract teacher who was also a commissioned minister in the church. A unanimous Court held that despite the teacher's allegation that her primary duties were secular, the ministerial exception, which is rooted in the First Amendment, precluded her ADA claim.

Conceding that the First Amendment prevents the government from overriding the actions of church officials as to who can serve as ministers, in *Hosanna-Tabor* the Court held that the exception barred the teacher's claim even though she spent more than six hours of her seven-hour day teaching secular subjects, using secular textbooks, and not incorporating religion into her instruction. The Court added that teachers at the school were not required to be "called" or members of the Lutheran faith in order to conduct job-related religious activities, and that the job duties of contract teachers were identical to those lacking the title of minister.

In a post-*Hosanna Tabor* case from New York, the Second Circuit viewed a Roman Catholic elementary school as a "religious organization" for the purposes of the ministerial exception. The court thus affirmed the archdiocese's motion for summary judgment in response to charges a former principal filed when her contract was not renewed.[38] The court rejected the plaintiff's gender

---

[36] 563 U.S. 903 (2011), *rev'g,* 597 F.3d 769 [254 Educ. L. Rep. 520] (6th Cir. 2010), *reh'g and reh'g en banc denied* (2010).

[37] 42 U.S.C.A. § 2000e-1.

[38] Fratello v. Roman Catholic Archdiocese of N.Y., 863 F.3d 190 (2d Cir. 2017).

discrimination and retaliation claims because she was a "minister" for the purposes of Title VII.

Chapter 10, Federal Anti-Discrimination Legislation, discusses this exception more fully, addressing the important role it plays where the religious functions persons perform are the primary reasons for their employment. Because persons such as chaplains and pastors have unique roles to play, this uniqueness is what gives definition to religious institutions seeking protection under Title VII.

Fiduciary Relationship

Because board membership is a fiduciary relationship, courts examine business dealings between board members and their institutions with the greatest scrutiny. The allegations from the plaintiff's complaint in an older case from South Carolina illustrate the type of dealings between board members and their institution that can result in their being voidable at the option of institutional officers, minority board members, or even institutional employees.[39]

Five key elements in this case resulted in the court's setting aside a sale of institutional property to a board member. First, the court remarked on the purchasing member's attendance and activity at the meeting where the board discussed the transaction. Second, the court considered the potential profit to the board member and possible or actual present or future loss to the institution. Third, the court posited that the consideration, or price, the member offered for the property was less than two-thirds of its fair market value. Fourth, the court wrote that the transaction was authorized at an irregular board meeting, with ratification occurring at a subsequent meeting advocated by the purchasing board member. Fifth, the court indicated that the parties failed to satisfy the notice requirement imposed by the corporation's constitution.[40]

Even absent "actual fraud or fraudulent intent,"[41] the court set aside the board member's purchase because "his conduct failed to measure up to the high standard required by the law of one in his fiduciary relation . . . ."[42] While board members are certainly not prevented from dealing with their not-for-profit organizations, they bear the burden of proof of making full disclosures about purchases, paying full value, and not imposing any burdens on their institutions. The court concluded that this doctrine is firmly established that "a

---

[39] Gilbert v. McLeod Infirmary, 64 S.E.2d 524 (S.C. 1951).

[40] *Id.* at 527, 531.

[41] *Id.* at 531.

[42] *Id.*

person occupying a place of trust should not put himself in a position in which self-interest conflicts with any duty he owes to those for whom he acts."[43]

Whether a fiduciary relationship exists depends on the facts of each situation. In such a case, the Supreme Court of New Hampshire refused to find that a fiduciary relationship existed between a college board and its alumni who challenged the institution's elimination of single-sex fraternity and sorority houses.[44] The court reasoned that even if the board had concealed its intention to eliminate the houses prior to and during a fundraising campaign involving alumni donors, the plaintiffs failed to present evidence they "stood in a submissive, inferior or dependent position with respect to the college in the capital campaign so as to support the existence of a fiduciary relationship."[45]

In a second case from New Hampshire, the federal trial court clarified the circumstances under which institutions or individuals owe fiduciary duties. [46] The court, referencing an opinion of the state's highest court, "drew a distinction between the *fiduciary duty* that a *post-secondary* school owes its students to protect them from sexual harassment by faculty, and the *duty of care* that *a primary or secondary school* owes its students."[47] Rejecting a mother's complaint that officials breached their fiduciary to her daughter by dismissing her because of an eating disorder, the court observed that in order to establish the presence of a unique relationship supporting a fiduciary duty, there must be more than a dependent relationship such as between the mother and her daughter.

Standard of Care

The general rule for standard of care seems to be that governing boards of religious institutions must meet corporate, rather than charitable trust, principles.[48] In such a case, the Supreme Court of Georgia observed that decisions by a college's board of directors, flowing from its merger with a university, were to be resolved by applying corporate principles.

Due to declining enrollments, college officials entered into a merger agreement with a university, with the latter agreeing to "make a good faith

---

[43] *Id.* at 530. *See also* In re Beychok, 495 So.2d 1278 [35 Educ. L. Rep. 892] (La. 1986) (setting aside a board contract for advertising space where it the company was owned by a board member); Smith v. Dorsey, 599 So. 2d 529 [75 Educ. L. Rep. 692] (Miss. 1992) (finding that board issuance of contracts to consultants to promote and campaign for a tax referendum violated state law such that the board could recover the $51,775 paid to consultants from board members who voted for the contracts); Waller v. Moore, 604 So. 2d 265 [77 Educ. L. Rep. 1029] (Miss. 1992) (requiring a board member who voted to issue a contract to his wife, and his wife who received $18,055 under it, to repay that amount plus interest).

[44] Brzica v. Trustees of Dartmouth Coll., 791 A.2d 990 [162 Educ. L. Rep. 853] (N.H. 2002).

[45] *Id.* at 995.

[46] Franchi v. New Hampton Sch., 656 F. Supp. 2d 252 [252 Educ. L. Rep. 139] (D.N.H. 2009).

[47] *Id.* at 263.

[48] State laws are likely to set standards of care for board members. See, e.g., N.Y. Not-For-Profit Corp. Law §§ 717 Standards of directors and officers: (a) Directors and officers shall discharge the duties of their respective positions in good faith and with the care an ordinarily prudent person in a like position would exercise under similar circumstances. .

effort to operate [the college] at its … present … [but to hold as paramount] the preservation of an entity bearing the [former's] name for the education of women in a Christian context . . . . "[49] When the university's board of directors voted to close the college's campus, the plaintiffs sought to vacate the merger on the ground that the college's board of directors failed to exercise a standard of care compatible with trust principles.

Upholding the merger, the court entered a judgment on behalf of the board of directors:

> The formalities of trust law are inappropriate to the administra-
> tion of colleges and universities which, in this era, operate as
> businesses. These institutions hold a variety of assets, and those
> persons responsible for the operation of the institutions need the
> administrative flexibility to make the many day-to-day decisions
> affecting the operation of the institutions, including those decisions
> involving the acquisition and sale of assets.[50]

Earlier, the federal trial court in South Carolina, responding to the plain-tiff's breach of duty claims of mismanagement and self-dealing, made a more detailed analysis as to what legal standard of care ought to apply to board members.[51] The court distinguished between trustees who manage charitable trusts and directors who manage charitable corporations:

> Both trustees and corporate directors are liable for losses occasioned by
> their negligent mismanagement of investments. However, the degree of care
> required appears to differ in many jurisdictions. A trustee is uniformly held to
> a high standard of care and will be held liable for simple negligence, while a
> director must often have committed "gross negligence" or otherwise be guilty
> of more than mere mistakes of judgment.[52]

Even if board members of not-for-profit institutions are "held to the less stringent corporate standard of care … and are required to exercise ordinary and reasonable care in the performance of their duties, exhibiting honesty and good faith,"[53] the court in South Carolina identified three important principles about their responsibilities. Members of boards of educational institutions would be wise to heed the court's advice.

According to the court, a corporate board member can delegate investment decisions to committees "so long as all directors assume the responsibility for supervising such committees by periodically scrutinizing their work."[54] Second, the court thought that one who fails to supervise or even attend board

---

[49] Corporation of Mercer Univ. v. Smith, 371 S.E.2d 858, 860 [49 Educ. L. Rep. 446](Ga. 1988), *abrogated on other grounds*, Warren v. Bd. of Regents of Univ. Sys. of Ga., 527 S.E.2d 563 (Ga. 2000).

[50] *Id.* at 860-61.

[51] Stern v. Webb Hays Nat'l Training Sch. for Deaconesses and Missionaries, 381 F. Supp. 1003 (D.S.C. 1974).

[52] *Id.* at 1013 (D.S.C. 1974).

[53] *Id.* 1013.

[54] *Id.*

meetings "has violated his fiduciary duty to the corporation."[55] Third, the court declared that a member "should not only disclose his interlocking responsibilities but also refrain from voting on or otherwise influencing a corporate decision to transact business with a company in which he has a significant interest or control."[56]

Although the court dismissed the underlying complaint against the defendant financial institutions, rejected all claims of conspiracy, and refused to cancel the disputed mortgage, it explained that the board members breached their duties of care and loyalty to the hospital. The court thus ordered the board to enact and implement appropriate policies to prevent future conflicts.

Liability

Sources of litigation for both public and nonpublic schools typically stem from cases about negligence, student discipline, and personnel matters. In cases involving faith-based schools, parties also typically name bishops, pastors, other religious leaders, religious organizations, superintendents, and school leaders; plaintiffs less frequently name individual teachers and board members.

As reflected by a dispute from New Hampshire, insofar as boards can be sued, it is important to prepare members to understand their roles and duties. This was apparently the first case in which a group of religious women sued the Roman Catholic Church, also causing the court to reflect on judicial involvement in contracts and the nature of the ministerial exemption. The dispute arose when, after three nuns received a letter from the local bishop informing them that their employment contracts were not to be renewed, they sued the school board for allegedly violating its own policy by denying their request for a hearing.[57]

Without reaching the merits of the claims, the Supreme Court of New Hampshire ultimately ruled that it did have jurisdiction over the dispute because it involved a contractual claim rather than Church doctrine. Remanding the dispute for a trial that apparently never occurred, likely because the parties reached a settlement agreement, the court was careful to separate doctrinal matters from the contract issue. The court stipulated that while it would not entangle itself in matters of Church doctrine, neither would it waive its responsibility for taking up the civil case of the sisters' employment contracts. Courts continue to make such careful distinctions, such as where they allowed claims of age discrimination to proceed against faith-based schools[58] as long

---

[55] *Id.* at 1014.

[56] *Id.*

[57] Reardon v. Lemoyne, 454 A.2d 428, 8 Educ. L. Rep. 714 (N.H. 1982). *But see* Berthiaume v. McCormack, 891 A.2d 539 (N.H. 2006).

[58] DeMarco v. Holy Cross High Sch., 4 F.3d 166 [85 Educ. L. Rep. 674] (2d Cir. 1993); Guinan v. Roman Catholic Archdiocese of Indianapolis, 42 F. Supp.2d 849 [134 Educ. L. Rep. 900] (S.D. Ind. 1998); Tomic v. Catholic Diocese of Peoria, 442 F.3d 1036 (7th Cir. 2006), *cert. denied*, 549 U.S. 881 (2006).

as the employees did not fulfill duties that were largely religious or ministerial in nature.[59]

When nonpublic schools are independent of church structures and incorporate separately, they and their board members may still face liability because
they can be sued corporately and individually. In a case involving sexual abuse,
plaintiffs sued a nonpublic school in New York City along with its board, as
well as current and past administrators.[60]

The plaintiffs alleged that when they complained that the former football
coach, who died by the time the case came to trial, sexually abused them, the
defendants failed to take corrective action, while attempting to conceal both
his conduct and their knowledge of his misbehavior. Although it rejected the
plaintiffs' Racketeer Influenced and Corrupt Organizations Act (RICO) claims,
a federal trial court did rule decide that the dismissal of plaintiffs' negligent
retention or supervision claims based on the statute of limitations was unwarranted. In light of the court's willingness to permit the case to proceed to trial,
the parties negotiated a settlement agreement.[61]

Some faith-based groups have created separately incorporated entities
in the hope of escaping liability in litigation. Still, courts have consistently
rejected structural separation of not-for-profit organizations such as schools,
a concept also known as ascending liability;[62] this concept has proven more
successful in the corporate world and appears to be more difficult to apply in
the realm of not-for-profit organizations. Because not-for-profit organizations
such as schools share common missions, especially in church entities, it is
more difficult to demonstrate clear separations between units.[63] Even so, as
discussed more fully in Chapter 5, Torts, charitable immunity often applies to
shield faith-based schools from liability.[64]

---

[59] Ciurleo v. St. Regis Parish, 214 F. Supp.3d 647 [342 Educ. L. Rep. 185] (E.D. Mich. 2016);
Coulee Catholic Schs. v. Labor and Industry Review Comm'n, Dep't of Workforce Dev., 768
N.W.2d 868 (Wis. 2009).

[60] Zimmerman v. Poly Prep Country Day Sch., 888 F. Supp. 2d 317 [289 Educ. L. Rep. 152]
(E.D.N.Y. 2012).

[61] Secret, Mosi, *Suit Settled Over Claims of Abuse at Poly Prep*, New York Times, Dec 27, 2012,
available at https://www.nytimes.com/2012/12/28/nyregion/sexual-abuse-case-at-poly-prep-in-
brooklyn-is-settled.html.

[62] For a comprehensive review of this issue, see W. Cole Durham and Robert Smith, 2 Religious
Organizations and the Law § 18:8 (March 2017 update). See also Mark E. Chopko, *Ascending
Liability of Religious Entities for the Actions of Others*, 17 Am. J. Trial Advoc. 289 (Fall, 1994).

[63] Edward McGlynn Gafney, Jr. & Philip C. Sorenson (1984), Overview of Non-Profit Ascending
Liability Case Law. In Howard R. Griffin (Ed.) Ascending Liability in Religious and Other
Non-Profit Organizations (6-13) Macon, GA: Mercer Univ. Press.

[64] J.K. v. UMS-Wright Corp., 7 So.3d 300 [244 Educ. L. Rep. 861] (Ala. 2008) (rejecting a
father's allegations that school trustees demonstrated wanton conduct in expelling his children
as failing to overcome their statutory immunity). *See also* S.B. v. Saint James Sch., 959 So.
2d 72 [222 Educ. L. Rep. 444] (Ala. 2006) (affirming that volunteer immunity protected the
chairman of a not-for-profit school's board of trustees from claims filed by parents and their
daughters when the latter were expelled after photographs depicting them in the nude, in lewd
poses, circulated in the school).

A good example of a case illustrating ascending liability involved a class-action suit filed by almost 2000 residents of retirement communities operated in Arizona, California, and Hawaii against Pacific Homes and the United Methodist Church.[65] Because the defendant organization, a separately incorporated not-for-profit company, could no longer fulfill its continuing-care agreement with the residents, it sought relief under Chapter 11 bankruptcy. Although Pacific Homes claimed that it was connected to the United Methodist Church, the Methodist Conference contended that because it was an unincorporated and loosely affiliated entity, it did not bear legal responsibility.

An appellate court in California rejected the Conference's attempted defense because the United Methodist Church had a hierarchical structure and mission, in addition to the fact that Pacific Homes advertised its focus on the Church's mission. In so deciding, the court recognized that literature Pacific Homes distributed announced its sponsorship by the Southern California and Arizona Methodist Conference and its willingness to assist a limited number of Methodists. The court also commented that the Conference appointed board members of Pacific Homes, including lay Methodist members and pastors.

Brushing aside First Amendment religious issues,[66] the court was convinced that Pacific Homes was a subunit connected to the Methodist Church's "common purpose" because they "functioned under a common name"[67] within the Church's hierarchical structure, with its Bishop and Conference, coupled with the Conference's role in appointing board members of Pacific Homes. The court wrote that "[i]n summary, UMC is a highly organized religious body working through specific agencies to accomplish laudable goals."[68] The court also cited the state's Code of Civil procedure and noted that any organization, regardless of whether it is incorporated, can sue or be sued in the name by which it is known or has assumed.

The lesson from this case is that board members and officers of not-for-profit organizations can be responsible for unfulfilled obligations resulting from the failure of other, related entities. Thus, where the beneficiaries of services share common purposes with organizations such as churches, they may be unable to elude legal responsibility simply by contracting those services to a third party. If anything, an even stronger argument can be made for church liability where religious schools are parts of churches. Under this case, parents and students who are dissatisfied with educational services provided by schools still face uphill battles if they wish to sue the churches and their affiliated

---

[65] Barr v. United Methodist Church, 153 Cal.Rptr. 322 (Cal. Ct. App. 1979), *cert. denied*, 444 U.S. 973 (1979).

[66] *Id.* at 332-33.

[67] *Id.* at 328.

[68] *Id.* at 270.

schools about the quality of education they provide because the judiciary is reluctant to recognize claims premised on educational malpractice.[69]

Religious leaders may be able to avoid liability if they incorporate their schools separately from the churches. Plaintiffs with judgments against religious schools normally can pierce the corporate veil and reach church assets only where fraud is involved or where churches are alter egos of their schools.[70] At the same time, one can argue that, even if not fraudulent, the separate incorporation of schools sharing both common purposes and names with host churches seems to serve no purpose where the leadership of schools must conform to the churches' religious beliefs and practices. Separate incorporation may be plausible where schools lack common factors with churches and they can operate in ways incompatible with the religious tenets of the churches or inconsistent with the churches' goals of religious homogeneity in all units of their organizations.

In the wake of the sex abuse scandal involving the clergy, some Roman Catholic dioceses explored the option of separately incorporating their schools as a means of protecting themselves from liability and financial loss.[71] Yet, as noted, such separation is difficult. Also, the growth of charter schools has fueled the interest in leaders of faith-based organizations. However, because charter schools are public schools funded by government dollars, state laws forbid religious organizations from obtaining charters based on concerns about violating the Establishment Clause.[72]

Use of Public Funds

As discussed in detail in Chapter 4, State Aid to Faith-Based Schools, many nonpublic schools receive federal funds from various programs with the monies controlled by state or local educational agencies. For example, when dealing with federal programs such as Title I, officials in state departments of education and/or local public school boards must approve expenditures.[73] These funds then go directly to parents[74] or service providers, rather than to

---

[69] *See, e.g.*, Sisters of the Holy Child Jesus at Old Westbury v. Corwin, 29 N.Y.S.3d 736 [329 EDUC. L. REP. 1036] (N.Y. App. Div. 2016) (rejecting a claim the court described as being akin to educational malpractice in a faith-based school as not cognizable in the state).

[70] *See, e.g.*, Loving Savior Church v. U.S., 728 F.2d 1085 (8th Cir. 1984) (finding that a tax judgment against a person could be levied against a church under both fraud and alter ego bases).

[71] For a discussion of this issue in Roman Catholic schools, see Charles J. Russo, *The Impact of Pedophile Priests on American Catholic Education: Reflections of a Cradle Catholic*." 37 REL. & EDUC. Vol. 37, *No. 2*, 97-113 (2010).

[72] For a discussion of this issue, see Charles J. Russo & Gerald M. Cattaro (2009). *Faith-Based Charter Schools: An Idea Whose Time is Unlikely to Come*, 36 REL. & EDUC. *No. 1*, 72-93 (2009).

[73] *See, e.g.*, Agostini v. Felton, 521 U.S. 203 (1997) (permitting the on-site delivery of educational services for poor students who attended religiously affiliated nonpublic schools).

[74] *See, e.g.*, Zelman v. Simmons–Harris, 536 U.S. 639 (2002) (noting that voucher funds went directly to parents rather than the faith-based schools their children attended, who used them to pay tuition).

the nonpublic schools in order to minimize the risk of having the resources diverted to, or used improperly for, religious purposes.

Even with safeguards in place, conflicts can arise between local school boards and officials in nonpublic schools regarding transparency and pupil allocations. Because the significant amount of funds that may be available from federal and state sources are designed to benefit students directly, boards and their members must be aware of their impact and the rules guiding their use in their schools.

Conflict of Interest

Litigation over conflicts of interest involving nonpublic school boards is uncommon. Still, school leaders and boards should be mindful of the threat of legal actions should such conflicts arise. At a minimum, then, boards and their leaders should ensure that they make ethical decisions in all of their transactions. To this end, boards should devise policies about nepotism, awareness of the fiduciary duties of members.[75] In so doing, boards should devise procedures for a variety of issues including hiring, admitting students, awarding contracts, accepting donations, and conducting business transactions.

More specifically, because nonpublic schools are often small, insular communities consisting of families with historical ties and long-standing relationships with businesses and school employees near where they live, conflicts of interest can become insidious forces such that board members and administrators must remain vigilant to avoid creating such problems. Moreover, because nonpublic schools are not exempt from having well-meaning intentions of board members backfire, policies should define and prevent nepotism, ensure appropriate oversight over personnel and other decisions, and avoid even the mere appearance of favoritism, because any and all of these can lead to conflict and litigation.

In sum, even if they are faith-based, nonpublic schools are not exempt from potential lack of oversight by their boards. Board failure to monitor expenditures and oversee how staff members are paid can quickly lead to the demise of schools. Transparency is a hallmark of well-run, ethical organizations. Once board action or inaction results in breaches of the trust placed in them, families remove their children from the schools and teachers leave, because ultimately they are the ones most adversely impacted by poor decision making.

Vicarious Liability

Litigation over conflicts of interest involving nonpublic school boards is uncommon. Even so, courts have rendered board members personally liable

---

[75] *See* Walters-Southland Inst. v. Walker, 232 S.W.2d 448 (Ark. 1950) (holding that the fiduciary relationship existing between a church school and a bishop—who, as president of its board of trustees, collected, deposited, and disbursed school funds, while dominating and controlling the board—imposed on him the duty to render a proper accounting of the funds he handled, especially as to matters in which he was personally interested).

in cases other than financial dealings. For instance, in an old case from the Supreme Court of Tennessee, members of the executive committee of a private university charged with supervision of an office building were liable to a person who was injured in the fall of an elevator in the building.[76] The court found the members liable because they permitted the elevator to be operated, even though they knew it was unsafe.

Occasionally plaintiffs sued board members of educational institutions for refusing to ratify, or for altering, employment contracts negotiated by school administrators. These suits are generally unsuccessful because persons negotiating employment arrangements with school administrators are presumed to know that contracts are not final until approved by the governing boards.[77] The dearth of litigation notwithstanding, educational leaders and boards should be mindful to engage in preventive school law by taking steps to avoid litigation through the development and consistent application of sound policies.

Indemnification

Because most board members of not-for-profit educational institutions generally consider their duties to be forms of charitable activities, they serve without compensation.[78] Consequently, institutions indemnify board members against liabilities incurred in the course of their official duties serving their organizations.[79] However, institutional charters and/or bylaws or separate agreements with board members may limit indemnification, subject in all instances to further possible restrictions established by the statutes, regulations, and case law in their jurisdictions.

Pursuant to the Model Business Corporation Act, "[a] corporation shall indemnify a director who was wholly successful, on the merits or otherwise, in the defense of any proceeding to which he was a party because he was a director of the corporation against reasonable expenses incurred by him in connection with the proceeding."[80]

The act also allows for permissible indemnification:

---

[76] Gamble v. Vanderbilt Univ., 200 S.W. 510 (Tenn. 1918).

[77] *See* Bruner v. Univ. of S. Miss., 501 So.2d 1113 (Miss. 1987); Pelotte v. Simmons, 152 S.E. 310 (Ga. Ct. App. 1930).

[78] *See, e.g.*, N.Y. NOT-FOR-PROFIT CORP. LAW § 720-a, Liability of directors, officers and trustees: "For purposes of this section, such a director, officer or trustee shall not be considered compensated solely by reason of payment of his or her actual expenses incurred in attending meetings or otherwise in the execution of such office."

[79] *See, e.g., id.* No person serving without compensation as a director, officer or trustee of a corporation, association, organization or trust described in section 501 (c)(3) of the United States Internal Revenue Code 1 shall be liable to any person other than such corporation, association, organization or trust based solely on his or her conduct in the execution of such office unless the conduct of such director, officer or trustee with respect to the person asserting liability constituted gross negligence or was intended to cause the resulting harm to the person asserting such liability.

[80] Model Business Corporation Act § 8.52, Mandatory Indemnification (2018).

(a) Except as otherwise provided in this section, a corporation may indemnify an individual who is a party to a proceeding because he is a director against liability incurred in the proceeding if:

(1) (i) he conducted himself in good faith; and

(ii) he reasonably believed:

(A) in the case of conduct in his official capacity, that his conduct was in the best interests of the corporation; and

(B) in all other cases, that his conduct was at least not opposed to the best interests of the corporation; and

(iii) in the case of any criminal proceeding, he had no reasonable cause to believe his conduct was unlawful; or

(2) he engaged in conduct for which broader indemnification has been made permissible or obligatory under a provision of the articles of incorporation (as authorized by section 2.02(b) (5)).[81]

However,

(d) Unless ordered by a court under section 8.54(a)(3), a corporation may not indemnify a director:

(1) in connection with a proceeding by or in the right of the corporation, except for reasonable expenses incurred in connection with the proceeding if it is determined that the director has met the relevant standard of conduct under subsection (a); or

(2) in connection with any proceeding with respect to conduct for which he was adjudged liable on the basis that he received a financial benefit to which he was not entitled, whether or not involving action in his official capacity.

Board members need to check statutes regulating not-for-profit corporations in their own jurisdictions carefully, because some states may have set limitations on the right of these organizations to indemnify board members that appear to be more restrictive than the Model Act.[82]

---

[81] Model Business Corporation Act § 8.51, Permissible Indemnification (2018).

[82] *See, e.g.*, N.Y. NOT-FOR-PROFIT CORP. LAW § 721. Nonexclusivity of statutory provisions for indemnification of directors and officers. Under this section no indemnification may be made to or on to or on behalf of any director or officer if a judgment or other final adjudication adverse to the director or officer establishes that his acts were committed in bad faith or were the result of active and deliberate dishonesty and were material to the cause of action so adjudicated, or that he personally gained in fact a financial profit or other advantage to which he was not legally entitled. .... *See also* VA. CODE ANN. § 13.1-877. Mandatory indemnification ("Unless limited by its articles of incorporation, a corporation shall indemnify a director who entirely prevails in the defense of any proceeding to which he was a party because he is or was a director of the corporation against reasonable expenses incurred by him in connection with the proceeding.").

Liability Insurance

In a topic closely related to indemnification, consistent with the growing practice in public education,[83] it is likely that most not-for-profit educational corporations have purchased liability insurance to protect board members against personal liability. Further, such coverage is typically as broad as is necessary—in dollar amounts, and as applied to far-reaching activities, making it commensurate with the scope of their duties—as long as state laws allow boards to purchase coverage.[84] Yet, insurance protection may not apply to situations where state law prohibits indemnification, and it is questionable whether officials of not-for-profit educational institutions can authorize and properly expend funds to provide insurance protection for those areas beyond which they lack the authority to indemnify their members.

Finally, it is worth noting that some states have legislated that uncompensated directors of not-for-profit organizations are immune from lawsuits.[85] Clearly, leaders and boards of all not-for-profit educational institutions need to review their own insurance coverage carefully in light of applicable state law, and adopt policies best designed to protect themselves from liability.

Conclusion

Because board members may often underestimate the value of their presence and the need for well-informed oversight, it is essential for them to develop clear and cogent bylaws buttressed by ongoing professional development activities. Moreover, school board members, regardless of the governance model under which they operate, have legal and ethical responsibilities to be well-informed about their duties as outlined in their articles of incorporation, bylaws, and handbooks.

Effective boards and educational administrators can have a dramatic impact on the culture and well-being of the nonpublic schools they serve, especially when individual board members were selected because of their expertise in such areas as finance, law, facilities management, and leadership. Energetic and well-prepared board members bring a wealth of experience and wisdom to the table, but first must buy into the missions of their schools and

---

[83] *See, e.g.*, Magana v. Charlotte-Mecklenburg Bd. of Educ., 645 S.E.2d 91 [220 Educ. L. Rep. 938] (N.C. Ct. App. 2007); Yarbrough v. East Wake First Charter Sch., 108 F. Supp.3d 331 [325 Educ. L. Rep. 248] (E.D.N.C. 2015) (agreeing that when a board and educators at a charter school, respectively, purchased liability insurance, they did not waive their governmental immunity).

[84] *See e.g.*, N.Y. Not-For-Profit Corp. Law § 726. Insurance for indemnification of directors and officers.

[85] *See, e.g.* Del. Code Ann. tit. 10 § 8133, Limitation from civil liability for certain nonprofit organization volunteers ("(b) No volunteer of an organization shall be subject to suit directly, derivatively or by way of contribution for any civil damages under the laws of Delaware resulting from any negligent act or omission performed during or in connection with an activity of such organization.").

accept responsibility by working for the common good of all in their learning communities.

Discussion Questions

1. As you consider various governance structures, what are the potential areas for liability they may have in common? How do they differ? What are the strengths and weaknesses of each of these models?

2. What policies and procedures would you recommend mitigating potential board liability?

3. Considering the *Barr* case, cited in note 65, are there individuals or linked organizations (such as the home and school association, the finance committee, etc.) that could be held liable for actions or failure to carry out their duties? How would you go about protecting the organization from potential legal threats?

4. What are some of the implications for boards and their organizations if they choose to accept public funds?

5. Identify some key areas in which boards should receive training. How would you go about such an effort?

Key Words

Advisory boards
Ascending liability
Board of limited jurisdiction
Canon law
Conflict of interest
Consultative board
Discretionary powers
Fiduciary duty
Juridic person
Limited jurisdiction
Mandatory duties
Ministerial duties
Ministerial exception
Nepotism

4

State Aid to Faith-based Schools

Charles J. Russo

Contents

Introduction / 93
State Aid to Faith-Based Schools / 96
      Setting the Stage / 96
      Types of State Aid / 97
            Overview / 97
            Transportation / 97
            Textbooks / 98
            Secular Services and Salary Supplements / 99
            Tuition Reimbursement to Parents / 100
            Reimbursements to Faith-based Schools for Testing / 100
            Income Tax Benefits / 101
            Instructional Materials / 102
            Support Services / 103
            Vouchers / 104
            Facially Neutral State Aid Programs / 106
Conclusion / 106
Discussion Questions / 107
Conclusion / 107

Introduction

The two topics generating the most education-related litigation reaching the Supreme Court have arisen under the First Amendment religion clauses. These cases address the status of aid to faith-based schools, the topic of this chapter, and the place of religious activities such as prayer and Bible reading in public schools, a discussion beyond the scope of this chapter. Added to the Constitution in 1791 as part of the Bill of Rights, according to the sixteen words of the religion clauses of the First Amendment: "Congress shall make no law respecting an establishment of religion, or prohibiting the free exercise thereof."

As significant as issues involving religion have become, the Supreme Court did not resolve a case involving religion and public education under the First Amendment until 1947 in *Everson v. Board of Education* (*Everson*).[1] Earlier,

---

The material in this chapter is adapted from Charles J. Russo, THE LAW OF PUBLIC EDUCATION, 10TH EDITION published by Foundation Press (2018).
[1] 330 U.S. 1 (1947), *reh'g denied*, 330 U.S. 855 (1947).

recognizing that the First Amendment expressly forbids only Congress from making laws establishing religion, in *Cantwell v. Connecticut* (*Cantwell*)[2] the Supreme Court applied the First Amendment to the states through the Fourteenth Amendment. The *Cantwell* Court invalidated the convictions of Jehovah's Witnesses for violating a statute against the solicitation of funds for religious, charitable, or philanthropic purposes without prior approval of public officials. Consequently, individuals have the same rights when suing the federal and state governments over the establishment of religion.

When reviewing First Amendment religion cases, the Supreme Court has created confusion over the appropriate judicial test. The Justices initially enunciated a two-part test in *School District of Abington Township v. Schempp* and *Murray v. Curlett*[3] to review the constitutionality of prayer and Bible reading in public schools. Less than a decade later, the Court expanded this test into the tripartite Establishment Clause standard in *Lemon v. Kurtzman* (*Lemon*),[4] a dispute over governmental aid to religiously affiliated nonpublic schools.

When the Supreme Court applies the *Lemon* test in litigation addressing aid and religious activity, because of its inability to explain how, or why, it has morphed into a "one-size-fits-all" standard that leaves lower courts, lawyers, commentators, and educators seeking clarity. Under this test, when government and religion interact, "[f]irst, the statute must have a secular legislative purpose; second, its principal or primary effect must be one that neither advances nor inhibits religion; finally, the statute must not foster "an excessive government entanglement with religion."[5]

Confusion develops over the appropriate judicial test for addressing questions arising under the First Amendment. This confusion is present because the Justices fail to explain how the tripartite test—the first two prongs of which originated in companion cases on prayer and Bible reading, while, as discussed below, the third emerged in a dispute over tax exemptions for churches—work in tandem.

The lack of clarity with regard to cases arising under the Establishment Clause never seems to reach a clear resolution because, as membership on the Supreme Court changes, the views of the Justices on the status of state aid to nonpublic schools and religious activity in public schools is subject to modification. For example, in *Agostini v. Felton* (*Agostini*),[6] a case permitting the on-site delivery of educational services for poor students who attended religiously affiliated nonpublic schools, the Court modified the *Lemon* test. In *Agostini*, the Court only reviewed the first two parts, purpose and effect, while recasting

---

[2] 310 U.S. 296 (1940).

[3] 374 U.S. 203 (1963).

[4] 403 U.S. 602 (1971).

[5] *Id.* at 612–613.

[6] 521 U.S. 203 (1997). For a commentary on this case, see Allan G. Osborne & Charles J. Russo, *The Ghoul is Dead, Long Live the Ghoul: Agostini v. Felton and the Delivery of Title I Services in Nonpublic Schools*, 119 Educ. L. Rep. 781 (1997).

entanglement as one criterion in evaluating a statute's effect when the state provides aid to students who attend religiously affiliated nonpublic schools.

In addition to *Lemon*, the Supreme Court occasionally relies on two other tests involving religion and public education. In *Lee v. Weisman*,[7] Justice Kennedy enunciated the psychological coercion test in forbidding prayer at public school graduation ceremonies. Earlier, in *Lynch v. Donnelly*,[8] a non-school case about including a Nativity scene in a Christmas display on public property, Justice O'Connor's plurality opinion created the endorsement test. When using this test, the Court asks whether the purpose of a governmental action is to endorse or approve of a religion or religious activity. If an action endorses or approves of a religion, then it is unconstitutional.

The goal of this chapter is not to engage in a lengthy discussion of the different approaches to interpreting the Establishment Clause. Rather, for the purposes of this book, it is sufficient to acknowledge that two major camps emerged at the Supreme Court and throughout the judiciary with regard to the place of aid to students and their faith-based schools: separationists and accommodationists.

Separationists rely on the Jeffersonian[9] metaphor calling for a "wall of separation" between church and state, language not in the Constitution; this is the perspective most often associated with the Supreme Court since *Everson*, particularly with regard to prayer and religious activity in public schools. Accommodationists maintain that the U.S. Constitution[10] does not prohibit the federal and/or state governments from permitting some aid, serving the needs of children under the Child Benefit Test, or accommodating the religious preferences of parents who send their children to public schools.

Against this background, the remainder of this chapter reviews major Supreme Court cases involving aid to students and their religiously affiliated nonpublic schools. Other than in passing, the chapter does not address the myriad lower court cases on issues associated with aid and/or those not reaching the Supreme Court. The chapter also does not examine issues in higher education, because this is a topic beyond the scope of this volume. The chapter ends with a brief conclusion.

---

[7]   505 U.S. 577 (1992).

[8]   465 U.S. 668, 687 (1984).

[9]   Thomas Jefferson used the "wall of separation" metaphor in his letter of January 1, 1802, to Nehemiah Dodge, Ephraim Robbins, and Stephen S. Nelson, A Committee of the Danbury Baptist Association. 16 WRITINGS OF THOMAS JEFFERSON 281 (Andrew Adgate Lipscomb & Albert Ellery Bergh, eds. 1903). Jefferson wrote: "Believing with you that religion is a matter which lies solely between man and his God . . . act of the whole American people which declared that their legislature should 'make no law respecting an establishment of religion, or prohibiting the free exercise thereof,' thus building a wall of separation between church and state."

[10] State constitutions can be more restrictive about aid to faith-based institutions. In the most recent example of such a case, the Supreme Court rejected such a limit in Trinity Lutheran Church v. Comer, 137 S. Ct. 2012 (2017). For a discussion of this case, see *infra* note 54 and accompanying text.

State Aid to Faith-Based Schools

Setting the Stage

Pierce v. Society of Sisters of the Holy Names of Jesus and Mary[11] is generally accepted as the most far-reaching of the Supreme Court's three early cases on nonpublic schools. In *Pierce*, officials of a Roman Catholic elementary school and a secular school in Oregon, the Hill Military Academy, challenged a voter-approved initiative (enacted in 1922, intended to go into effect in 1926) resulting in a new compulsory attendance law. The law directed parents to send their children between the ages of 8 and 16, who had yet to complete the eighth grade, to public schools, apart from those who today would be identified as needing special education. The religious school officials challenged the law as presenting a threat to the continued existence of their schools.

After a federal trial court enjoined enforcement of the statute, the Supreme Court unanimously affirmed that the law would have seriously limited, if not destroyed, the profitability of the schools, while diminishing the value of their property. Although recognizing the power of the state "reasonably to regulate all schools, to inspect, supervise, and examine them, their teachers and pupils ...,"[12] the Court focused on the schools' property rights under the Fourteenth Amendment.

The *Pierce* Court ruled that school officials were entitled to protection from unreasonable interference with their students and the destruction of their businesses and properties. The Justices also decided that while states may oversee such important features as health and safety relating to the operation of nonpublic schools, they could not do so to an extent greater than they did for public schools. Further, in often-cited language recognizing the crucial role of parents, the Court declared that "[t]he child is not the mere creature of the state; those who nurture him and direct his destiny have the right, coupled with the high duty, to recognize and prepare him for additional obligations."[13]

In *Farrington v. Tokushige (Farrington)*,[14] decided less than two years after *Pierce*, the Supreme Court reasserted the right of parents to satisfy a compulsory attendance law by sending their children to the nonpublic schools of their choice. The Justices rejected attempts by public officials to regulate foreign language schools in Hawaii, most of which were Japanese; the other schools provided instruction in Chinese or Korean. The Court rejected state attempts at regulating the curricula at issue as infringing on the rights of the parents and the school owners.

Cochran v. Louisiana State Board of Education (Cochran)[15] involved a state law providing free textbooks for all students in the state regardless of

---

[11] 268 U.S. 510 (1925).
[12] *Id.* at 534.
[13] *Id.* at 535.
[14] 273 U.S. 284 (1927).
[15] 281 U.S. 370 (1930).

where they attended school. A taxpayer unsuccessfully challenged the law as violating the Fourteenth Amendment by taking private property through taxation for a nonpublic purpose. As in *Pierce*, the Supreme Court resolved the dispute based on the Due Process Clause of the Fourteenth Amendment, rather than the Establishment Clause. Unanimously affirming the judgment of the Supreme Court of Louisiana that insofar as the students, rather than their schools, were the beneficiaries of the law, the Court agreed that the statute had valid secular purpose, thereby anticipating the Child Benefit Test.

Types of State Aid

Overview

The Supreme Court's Establishment Clause perspective on state aid to K-12 education, sometimes referred to as parochiaid, evolved through three phases. During the first stage, beginning with *Everson v. Board of Education*[16] in 1947 and ending with *Board of Education of Central School District No. 1 v. Allen*[17] in 1968, the Court created the Child Benefit Test; this allows selected forms of publicly funded aid on the grounds that it helps children, rather than their faith-based schools.

The span between *Lemon v. Kurtzman*[18] in 1971, the leading case on the Establishment Clause in educational settings, and *Aguilar v. Felton*[19] in 1985 was the nadir from the perspective of supporters of the Child Benefit Test. This period marked the low point of the Child Benefit Test, because during this time the Court largely refused to move beyond the limits it set in *Everson* and *Allen*. In *Zobrest v. Catalina Foothills School District*,[20] the Court resurrected the Child Benefit Test, allowing it to enter a phase that extends through the present in which more forms of aid have been permissible. Given this history, the remaining sections of this chapter examine major cases involving state aid to faith-based schools and their students, essentially in the order in which they made their way to the Supreme Court.

Transportation

Everson v. Board of Education[21] involved a law from New Jersey permitting local school boards to enter into contracts for student transportation. After a local board reimbursed parents for the costs of bus fare sending their children to primarily Roman Catholic schools, a taxpayer challenged the statute

---

[16] 330 U.S. 1 (1947), *reh'g denied*, 330 U.S. 855 (1947).

[17] 392 U.S. 236 (1968).

[18] 403 U.S. 602 (1971). For a representative commentary on this case, see, e.g., Timothy V. Franklin, *Squeezing the Juice out of the Lemon Test*, 72 Educ. L. Rep. 1 (1992).

[19] 473 U.S. 402 (1985).

[20] 509 U.S. 1 (1993). For representative commentary on this case, see Allan G. Osborne, *Providing Special Education and Related Services to Parochial School Students in the Wake of Zelman*, 87 Educ. L. Rep. 329 (1994); Ralph D. Mawdsley & Cynthia Dieterich, *Limiting Services to Parochial School Students: What Does Zobrest now Mean?* 112 Educ. L. Rep. 555 (1996).

[21] 330 U.S. 1 (1947), *reh'g denied*, 330 U.S. 855 (1947).

as unconstitutional in two respects. First, in an approach similar to *Cochran*, the plaintiff failed in alleging that the law authorized the state to tax some citizens and bestow their money on others for the private purpose of supporting nonpublic schools, in violation of the Fourteenth Amendment. Second, the taxpayer charged that the statute was one "respecting an establishment of religion" because it forced him to contribute to support church schools, in violation of the First Amendment.

The Supreme Court rejected the Fourteenth Amendment claim, interpreting the law as having a public purpose, adding that the First Amendment did not prohibit the state from extending general benefits to all of its citizens without regard to their religious beliefs. The *Everson* Court thereby treated student transportation as another category of public services such as police, fire, and health protection.

Everson was the first case in which the Supreme Court, in an opinion by Justice Blackmun, introduced the Jeffersonian metaphor into its First Amendment analysis. He wrote that "[t]he First Amendment has erected a wall between church and state. That wall must be kept high and impregnable. We could not approve the slightest breach."[22]

In *Wolman v. Walter* (*Wolman*),[23] the Supreme Court considered whether public funds could be used to provide transportation for field trips for children who attended faith-based schools in Ohio. The Court rejected this practice as unconstitutional because insofar as field trips were curriculum-oriented, they were in the category of instruction rather than non-ideological secular services such as transportation to and from school.

Textbooks

Board of Education of Central School District No. 1 v. Allen (*Allen*)[24] was the first case involving textbooks that the Supreme Court resolved under the Establishment Clause. The Court basically followed its precedent from *Cochran* in affirming the constitutionality of a statute from New York that required local school boards to loan books to children in grades seven to twelve who attended nonpublic schools. The law did not mandate that the books had to be the same as those used in the public schools, but did require local board officials to approve the titles before educators in the religious schools could adopt the texts. Relying largely on the Child Benefit Test, the Court observed that the statute's purpose was not to aid religion or nonpublic schools, and that its primary effect was to improve the quality of education for all children.

Other than for the delivery of special education services to individual students, as in *Zobrest v. Catalina Foothills School District*,[25] *Allen* represented the outer limit of the Child Benefit Test prior to the Supreme Court's ruling

---

[22] *Id.*
[23] 433 U.S. 229 (1977).
[24] 392 U.S. 236 (1968).
[25] 509 U.S. 1 (1993).

in *Agostini v. Felton*,[26] discussed below. The Justices upheld the same type of textbook provisions in *Meek v. Pittenger*[27] and *Wolman v. Walter*,[28] both of which are also examined in more detail below.

Secular Services and Salary Supplements

The Supreme Court's most important case involving the Establishment Clause and education was *Lemon v. Kurtzman*, from Pennsylvania, heard along with the companion case of *Earley v. DiCenso*, from Rhode Island.[29] In *Lemon*, the Court invalidated a statute from Pennsylvania calling for the purchase of secular services, and a law from Rhode Island designed to provide salary supplements for teachers in nonpublic schools, most of which were Roman Catholic.

The Pennsylvania law directed the superintendent of education to purchase specified secular educational services from nonpublic schools. Officials directly reimbursed the nonpublic schools for their actual expenditures for teacher salaries, textbooks, and instructional materials. The superintendent had to approve the textbooks and materials for use in the subject areas of mathematics, modern foreign languages, physical science, and physical education.

In Rhode Island, officials could supplement the salaries of certificated teachers of secular subjects in nonpublic elementary schools by directly paying them up to 15% of their current annual salaries. The overall salaries of teachers could not exceed the maximum paid to public school teachers.

Invalidating both laws, the Supreme Court enunciated the three-part test known as the *Lemon* test. In creating this measure, the Court added a third prong to the two-part test it created in *School District of Abington Township v. Schempp* and *Murray v. Curlett*,[30] companion cases dealing with prayer and Bible reading in public schools. In *Walz v. Tax Commission of New York City*,[31] source of the third prong, the Court upheld New York State's practice of providing state property tax exemptions for church property used in worship services.

According to the *Lemon* test:

> Every analysis in this area must begin with consideration of the cumulative criteria developed by the Court over many years. Three such tests may be gleaned from our cases. First, the statute must have a secular legislative purpose; second, its principal or primary effect must be one that neither advances nor inhibits religion; finally, the statute must not foster "an excessive government entanglement with religion.[32]

---

[26] 521 U.S. 203 (1997). For a discussion of this case, see *infra* note 43 and accompanying text.
[27] 421 U.S. 349 (1975).
[28] 433 U.S. 229 (1977).
[29] 403 U.S. 602 (1971).
[30] 374 U.S. 203 (1963).
[31] 397 U.S. 664 (1970).
[32] 403 U.S. 602, 612-613 (1971).

As to entanglement and state aid to faith-based schools, the Court identified three additional factors: "we must examine the character and purposes of the institutions that are benefitted, the nature of the aid that the State provides, and the resulting relationship between the government and religious authority."[33]

In *Lemon*, the Supreme Court treated aid for teachers' salaries as different from secular, neutral, or non-ideological services, facilities, or materials. Reflecting on *Allen*, the Court remarked that teachers have a substantially different ideological character than books. The Court feared that while public school administrators and boards can recognize the content of textbooks, they are unable to know how teachers in faith-based schools cover subject matter absent observing them constantly, a form of excessive entanglement. The Court viewed the safeguards necessary to ensure that teachers avoid non-ideological perspectives as giving rise to impermissible entanglement.

Tuition Reimbursement to Parents

Two months after *Lemon*, the Pennsylvania legislature enacted a statute that allowed parents whose children attended nonpublic schools to request tuition reimbursement. The same parent as in *Lemon* challenged the new law as having the primary effect of advancing religion.

In *Sloan v. Lemon*,[34] the Supreme Court affirmed that the law impermissibly singled out a class of citizens for a special economic benefit. The Justices viewed this as unlike the "indirect" and "incidental" benefits that flowed to religious schools from programs aiding all parents by supplying bus transportation and secular textbooks for children. The Court determined that transportation and textbooks were carefully restricted to the purely secular side of church-affiliated schools and did not provide special aid to their students.

The Supreme Court expanded on *Sloan* in another case from New York, *Committee for Public Education and Religious Liberty v. Nyquist (Nyquist)*.[35] The Court ruled that even though the grants went to parents rather than to school officials, this did not necessitate a different outcome. The Court explained that because parents would have used the money to pay for tuition, and the law failed to separate secular from religious uses, the aid's effect would have provided the desired financial support for nonpublic schools. The Court pointed out that even if public officials offered the grants as incentives so parents could send their children to religious schools, the law violated the Establishment Clause regardless of whether the money made its way into the coffers of the religious institutions.

Reimbursements to Faith-Based Schools for Testing

On the same day that it handed down *Nyquist*, in a second case from New York, the Supreme Court largely used the same rationale in *Levitt v. Committee*

---

[33] *Id.* at 615.

[34] 413 U.S. 825 (1973).

[35] 413 U.S. 756 (1973).

for Public Education and Religious Liberty[36] in invalidating a law allowing the state to reimburse nonpublic schools for expenses incurred while administering and reporting test results, as well as other records. Absent restrictions on the use of the funds, such that teacher-prepared tests on religious topics were seemingly reimbursable, the Court viewed the aid as having the primary effect of advancing religious education because there were insufficient safeguards in place to regulate how officials in the faith-based schools spent the monies.

Seven years later, after the New York State remedied the deficiencies the Court identified in *Levitt*, it upheld the revised law in *Public Education and Religious Liberty v. Regan.*[37] The Court found that the legislature took adequate steps to avoid violating the Establishment Clause.

Wolman v. Walter,[38] a case from Ohio, saw the Supreme Court upholding a law permitting reimbursement for religious schools where officials used standardized tests and scoring services to evaluate student progress. The Justices distinguished these tests from the ones in *Levitt* because educators in nonpublic schools neither put the tests together nor scored the completed examinations. The Court also reasoned that the law did not authorize payments to church-sponsored schools for costs associated with administering the tests.

Income Tax Benefits

Another section of the same New York statute in *Nyquist* assisted parents via income tax benefits. Under the law, parents of children who attended nonpublic schools were entitled to income tax deductions as long as they did not receive tuition reimbursements under the other part of the statute. The Supreme Court invalidated the provision at issue in observing that in practical terms there was little difference, for purposes of evaluating whether such aid had the effect of advancing religion, between a tax benefit and a tuition grant. The Court thought that under both programs, parents received the same form of encouragement and reward for sending their children to nonpublic schools.

In *Mueller v. Allen,*[39] the Supreme Court upheld a statute from Minnesota that granted all parents state income tax deductions for the actual costs of tuition, textbooks, and transportation associated with sending their children to K-12 schools. The law afforded all parents deductions of $500 for children in grades K-6 and $700 for those in grades 7-12.

The Justices distinguished *Mueller* from *Nyquist* primarily because the tax benefit was available to all parents, not only those whose children were in nonpublic schools. The Supreme Court also recognized that the deduction was one among many rather than a single, favored type of taxpayer expense. Recognizing the legislature's latitude to create classifications and distinctions in tax statutes, and that the state could have been considered as gaining a benefit

---

[36] 413 U.S. 472 (1973).

[37] 444 U.S. 646 (1980).

[38] 433 U.S. 229 (1977).

[39] 463 U.S. 388 (1983). For a commentary on this case, see Leslie Gerstman, *Supreme Court Upholds Minnesota's Deduction for Educational Expenses*, 12 Educ. L. Rep. 203 (1983).

from the scheme because it promoted an educated citizenry while reducing the costs of public education, the Court was satisfied that the law met all three of *Lemon's* prongs.

Instructional Materials

In *Meek v. Pittenger*,[40] the Supreme Court examined the constitutionality of loans of instructional materials, including textbooks and equipment, to faith-based schools in Pennsylvania. Although the Court upheld the loan of textbooks, it struck down parts of the law on periodicals, films, recordings, and laboratory equipment, as well as equipment for recording and projecting, because the statute had the primary effect of advancing religion due to the predominantly religious character of participating schools.

The *Meek* Court was concerned that insofar as the only statutory requirement imposed on the schools to qualify for the loans was having their curricula offer the subjects and activities mandated by the commonwealth's board of education. The Court indicated that because the church-related schools were the primary beneficiaries, the aid to their educational function resulted in assistance to their sectarian enterprises as a whole.

Two years later, the Supreme Court reached similar results in *Wolman v. Walter*,[41] upholding a statute from Ohio which specified that textbook loans were to be made to students or their parents, rather than directly to their nonpublic schools. The Justices struck down a provision that would have allowed loans of instructional equipment including projectors, tape recorders, record players, maps and globes, and science kits. Like *Meek*, the Court invalidated the statute's authorizing the loans given its concern that insofar as it would have been impossible to separate the secular and sectarian functions for which these items were being used, the aid inevitably provided support for the religious roles of the schools.

Mitchell v. Helms,[42] a Supreme Court case from Louisiana, expanded the categories of permissible aid to faith-based schools. A plurality upheld the constitutionality of Chapter 2 of Title I, now Title VI, of the Elementary and Secondary Education Act, a federal law that permits the loans of instructional materials including library books, computers, television sets, tape recorders, and maps to nonpublic schools.

In *Helms*, the Supreme Court relied on the modified *Lemon* test enunciated in *Agostini v. Felton*,[43] discussed below, by reviewing only its first two parts, while recasting entanglement as one criterion in evaluating a statute's effect. Insofar as the purpose part of the test was not challenged, the plurality

---

[40] 421 U.S. 349 (1975).

[41] 433 U.S. 229 (1977).

[42] 530 U.S. 793 (2000), *on remand sub nom.* Helms v. Picard, 229 F.3d 467 (5th Cir. 2000). For a commentary on this case, see Julie F. Mead & Julie K. Underwood, *Lemon Distilled with Four Votes for Vouchers: An Examination of* Mitchell v. Helms *and its Implications*, 149 Educ. L. Rep. 639 (2001).

[43] 521 U.S. 203 (1997).

only considered Chapter 2's effect, finding that it did not foster impermissible indoctrination because aid was allocated pursuant to neutral secular criteria that neither favored nor disfavored religion and was available to all schools based on secular, nondiscriminatory grounds. The plurality explicitly reversed those parts of *Meek* and *Wolman* that were inconsistent with its analysis on loans of instructional materials.

Support Services

In *Meek v. Pittenger*,[44] the Supreme Court invalidated a law from Pennsylvania permitting public school personnel to provide auxiliary services on-site in faith-based schools. The Court also forbade the delivery of remedial and accelerated instructional programs, guidance counseling and testing, and services for children who were educationally disadvantaged. According to the Court, it was immaterial that the students would have received remedial, rather than advanced, work because the surveillance needed to ensure the absence of ideology would have given rise to excessive entanglement between church and state.

Wolman v. Walter[45] saw the Supreme Court reach mixed results on aid. In addition to upholding the textbook loan program, the Court allowed Ohio to supply nonpublic schools with state-mandated tests, while allowing public school employees to go on-site to perform diagnostic tests to evaluate whether students needed speech, hearing, and psychological services. In addition, the Court allowed public funds to be used to provide therapeutic services to students from nonpublic schools, as long as they were delivered off-site. The Court forbade state officials from loaning instructional materials and equipment to schools or, as noted above, from using funds to pay for field trips for students in nonpublic schools.

Zobrest v. Catalina Foothills School District[46] signaled a sea change as to the Supreme Court's Establishment Clause jurisprudence with regard to aid to students in faith-based schools. At issue was a school board in Arizona's refusal to provide a sign-language interpreter for a student who was deaf, under the Individuals with Disabilities Education Act, after he transferred into to a Roman Catholic high school. In a suit filed as the student entered high school, but which was resolved shortly after he graduated, the Court found that an interpreter provided neutral aid to him without offering financial benefits to his parents or school, and there was no governmental participation in the instruction because the interpreter was only a conduit to effectuate his communications.[47]

---

[44] 421 U.S. 349 (1975).

[45] 433 U.S. 229 (1977).

[46] 509 U.S. 1 (1993).

[47] *See also* Board of Educ. of Kiryas Joel Village Sch. Dist. v. Grumet, 512 U.S. 687 (1994) (invalidating a statute creating a school district with the same boundaries as an Orthodox Jewish community). For a commentary on this case, see David Schimmel, *Kiryas Joel Village School District v. Grumet: The Establishment Clause Controversy Continues*, 94 EDUC. L. REP. 685 (1994).

In *Aguilar v. Felton*,[48] the Justices considered whether public school teachers in New York City could provide remedial instruction under Title I of the Elementary and Secondary Education Act of 1965. Title I of the Act was designed for specifically targeted children who were educationally disadvantaged, on-site in their faith-based schools.[49] The Supreme Court affirmed that the program permitting the on-site delivery of services to children in their religiously affiliated nonpublic schools, most of which were Roman Catholic, was unconstitutional.

The Court invalidated the program at issue, even though the New York City Board of Education (NYCBOE) developed safeguards to insure that public funds were not spent for religious purposes. The Court feared that if a monitoring system were put in place to have avoided the creation of an impermissible relationship between church and state, doing so might have resulted in excessive entanglement under the third prong of the *Lemon* test.

Twelve years later, in *Agostini v. Felton*,[50] the Supreme Court took the unusual step of dissolving the injunction that it upheld in *Aguilar*. The Court reasoned that the Title I program did not violate the *Lemon* test because there was no governmental indoctrination, there were no differences between recipients based on religion, and there was no excessive entanglement. The Court thus ruled that a federally funded program providing supplemental, remedial instruction and counseling services to disadvantaged children on a neutral basis did not violate the First Amendment when the aid was provided on-site in faith-based schools, as part of a program using safeguards such as those the NYCBOE implemented. Perhaps the most important aspect of *Agostini* was the Court's having modified the *Lemon* test by reviewing only its first two prongs, purpose and effect, while recasting entanglement as one element in evaluating a law's effect.

Vouchers

Considerable controversy has arisen over the use of vouchers, with courts reaching mixed results in disputes over their constitutionality. The only Supreme Court case on vouchers arose when the Ohio General Assembly, acting pursuant to a desegregation order, enacted the Ohio Pilot Project Scholarship Program (OPPSP) to assist children in Cleveland's failing public schools. The primary purpose of the OPPSP was to permit an equal number of students to receive vouchers and tutorial assistance grants while attending regular public schools. Another part of the law provided greater choices to parents and children via the creation of community, or charter, schools and magnet schools, while a third section provided tutorial assistance.

The Supreme Court of Ohio upheld the OPPSP, but severed the part of the law affording priority to parents who belonged to a religious group sup-

---

[48] 473 U.S. 402 (1985).

[49] On the same day as *Aguilar*, the Court invalidated a program that allowed teachers from faith-based schools to work part time in public schools. Grand Rapids v. Ball, 473 U.S. 373 (1985).

[50] 521 U.S. 203 (1997).

porting a sectarian institution.[51] Yet, in finding that the OPPSP violated the state constitutional requirement that every statute have only one subject, the court struck it down. When the court stayed enforcement of its order to avoid disrupting the then-current school year, the Ohio General Assembly passed a revised statute.

After lower federal courts, relying largely on *Nyquist* (1973), enjoined the operation of the revised statute as a violation of the Establishment Clause, the Supreme Court agreed to hear an appeal. In *Zelman v. Simmons-Harris*,[52] the Court reversed the judgment of the Sixth Circuit and upheld the constitutionality of the OPPSP.

Relying on *Agostini*, the *Zelman* Court began by conceding the lack of a dispute over the program's valid secular purpose in delivering instructional programming for poor children in a failing school system. The Court thus examined whether the OPPSP had the impermissible effect of advancing or inhibiting religion. The Court upheld the voucher program because insofar as it was part of the state's far-reaching attempt to provide greater educational opportunities to students in a failing school system, the law allocated aid on the basis of neutral secular criteria neither favoring nor disfavoring religion. Moreover, the Court pointed out that the aid was available to both religious and secular beneficiaries on a nondiscriminatory basis, while offering assistance directly to a broad class of citizens who directed the aid to religious schools based entirely on their own genuine, independent, private choices.

The *Zelman* Court was not concerned by the fact that most of the participating schools were faith-based, since parents chose to send their children to them because surrounding public schools refused to take part in the program. If anything, the Court acknowledged that most of the children went to faith-based schools, most of which were Roman Catholic, not as a matter of law, but because they were unwelcome in the public schools. The Court concluded that insofar as it was following an unbroken line of its own precedent supporting true private, parental choice that provided benefits directly to a wide range of needy private individuals, its only choice was to uphold the voucher program. Lower courts continue to reach mixed results over vouchers.[53]

---

[51] Simmons–Harris v. Goff, 711 N.E.2d 203 (Ohio) 1999.

[52] 536 U.S. 639 (2002). For representative commentary on this case, see Martha M. McCarthy, *Zelman v. Simmons–Harris: A Victory for School Vouchers*, 171 Educ. L. Rep. 1 (2003); Charles J. Russo & Ralph D. Mawdsley, *Equal Educational Opportunities and Parental Choice: The Supreme Court Upholds the Cleveland Voucher Program*, 169 Educ. L. Rep. 485 (2002).

[53] For cases upholding voucher programs, see, e.g., Meredith v. Pence, 984 N.E.2d 1213 [290 Educ. L. Rep. 998] (Ind. 2013); Hart v. State of N. C., 774 S.E.2d 281 [320 Educ. L. Rep. 465] (N.C. 2015); Oliver v. Hofmeister, 368 P.3d 1270 [329 Educ. L. Rep. 1270] (Okla. 2016). For cases invalidating voucher programs, see, e.g., Owens v. Colorado Cong. of Parents, Teachers and Students, 92 P.3d 933 [189 Educ. L. Rep. 395] (Colo. 2004); Eulitt ex rel. Eulitt v. Maine, Dep't of Educ., 386 F.3d 344 [192 Educ. L. Rep. 651] (1st Cir. 2004). For a commentary on vouchers, see Richard Fossey & Robert LeBlanc, *Vouchers for Sectarian Schools After Zelman: Will The First Circuit Expose Anti–Catholic Bigotry In The Massachusetts Constitution?* 193 Educ. L. Rep. 343 (2005).

Facially Neutral State Aid Programs

Trinity Lutheran Church v. Comer[54] arose when the church's year-around preschool and daycare center, which served approximately ninety children, was denied a grant that would have allowed it to participate in Missouri's Scrap Tire Program. The program, operated by the state's Department of Natural Resources (DNS), offered limited numbers of grants designed to reduce the volume of used tires in landfills and dump sites. More specifically, center officials sought to participate in the program so they could be reimbursed for the cost of replacing the surface of their playground with softer, safer material so that children who fell would have less chance of being injured.

Officials of the DNS rejected the center's request in light of a policy, based on state law, forbidding aid to churches, sects, or other religious entities. After a federal trial court and the Eighth Circuit upheld the denial, and even though the governor rescinded the policy a week before oral arguments, the Supreme Court refused to treat the case as moot and agreed to intervene.

Reversing in favor of the center, the Supreme Court appears to have ushered in a new day in its First Amendment jurisprudence with regard to aid to faith-based institutions. The Court ruled that except if doing so would violate the Establishment Clause, the Free Exercise Clause prohibits public officials from conferring or denying benefits to faith-based institutions, or individuals, solely due to their religious beliefs. As evidence of *Trinity Lutheran's* impact, a day after it handed down its judgment, the Court disposed of two cases involving the exclusions of religious schools from school choice programs by granting certiorari, vacating the judgments, and remanding both for further proceedings in light of its order.[55]

Conclusion

As noted in the introduction, this chapter was limited to cases litigated before the Supreme Court, generally not addressing the many disputes in the lower courts on over aid to faith-based schools and their students. In light of *Trinity Lutheran Church v. Comer*, it bears watching to see whether the Court continues to expand the boundaries of permissible aid under the First Amendment to faith-based schools and their students, thereby allowing them to play a significant role in the marketplace of ideas known as education.

---

[54] For a commentary on this case, see William E. Thro & Charles J. Russo, *Odious to the Constitution: The Educational Implications of Trinity Lutheran Church v. Comer*, 346 EDUC. L. REP. 1 (2017).

[55] *See* Taxpayers for Pub. Educ. v. Douglas Cnty. Sch. Dist., 351 P.3d 461, 473–74 (Colo. 2015) (finding that Colorado's Establishment Clause precludes private religious schools from participating in a school choice program), *cert. granted, judgment vacated sub nom.* Colorado State Bd. of Educ. v. Taxpayers for Pub. Educ., 137 S. Ct. 2327 (2017); Moses v. Skandera, 367 P.3d 838, 846-49 (N.M. 2015) (interpreting New Mexico's Establishment Clause as prohibiting private religious schools from taking part in school choice programs). *cert. granted, judgment vacated sub nom.* New Mexico Ass'n of Non-public Schs. v. Moses, 137 S. Ct. 2325 (2017).

Discussion Questions

1. Do you think that the Wall of Separation metaphor is still apt? Should it be more of a chain link fence in light of how much aid is permissible?

2. What do you think of the Child Benefit Test? Is it still viable?

3. Whether served by Title I or the IDEA, children are identified based on their needs, not the religious beliefs they hold with their parents. As such, what do you think about the on-site delivery of Title I services in faith-based schools in light of *Agostini?* Should the IDEA and its regulations be revised to allow the on-site delivery of special education services to students in their faith-based schools?

4. What do you think about the use of vouchers, not unlike the practice in many Western European nations and Australia, to allow parents to send their children to faith-based schools? Can such vouchers pass constitutional muster?

5. Do you think that *Trinity Lutheran* will be as significant as some are suggesting?

Key Words

Accommodationists
Child benefit test
Establishment Clause
Facially neutral state aid programs
Faith-based schools
First Amendment
Instructional materials
Lemon test
Prayer
Religion
Secular services
Separationists
Support services
Textbooks
Transportation
Tuition reimbursement
Vouchers

5

Tort Liability

Charles J. Russo and Mary Angela Shaughnessy

Contents

Introduction / 110
Tort Theories / 110
Strict Liability / 110
Intentional Torts / 111
        Assault and Battery / 111
        Sexual Abuse / 112
        Corporal Punishment / 113
        Hazing and Bullying / 115
        Defamation / 116
        False Imprisonment / 118
        Intentional Infliction of Emotional Distress / 119
        Invasion of Privacy / 119
Negligence / 120
        Elements of Negligence / 121
            Duty / 121
            Supervision / 124
            Breach / 126
            Injury / 128
            Causation / 129
            Defenses / 130
                 Consent/Assumption of Risk / 130
                Contributory/Comparative Negligence / 132
                Charitable Immunity / 133
Special Topics / 135
        Insurance Coverage / 135
        Exculpatory Clauses / 137
        Negligent Hiring, Supervision, and Retention / 142
        Self-Defense and Restraint / 145
        Field Trips / 147
        Medical Needs / 150
        Child Abuse Reporting / 154
Conclusion / 157
Discussion Questions / 157
Key Words / 157
Appendices A, B, C, D / 158-161

Introduction

A major concern for educational leaders in faith-based and other nonpublic, or any, schools is how to keep students and staff safe while avoiding litigation, much of which focuses on tort claims.[1] Torts—derived from the old French and/or medieval Latin, meaning "twisted" or "injury"—are civil wrongs, other than breaches of contracts,[2] occurring when persons suffer losses or are harmed due to the improper conduct of others.

An important reality for school administrators to keep in mind is the old adage, "ignorance of the law is no excuse." Leaders of faith-based schools are rightly concerned with the religious identity of their schools. Yet, leaders must be mindful of the boundary that civil law draws around all of their activities and the exercise of their religious faith. Stepping outside of that boundary can result in losing all that is within it, namely, a school's very existence and its faith-based mission. The focus of this chapter, then, is on the most likely issues to emerge in faith-based and other nonpublic schools: intentional torts, negligence, and other special topics.

Tort Theories

It is well-settled law that "[s]chools are not insurers of safety... for they cannot reasonably be expected to continuously supervise and control all movements and activities of students."[3] In order to recover for injuries in tort, plaintiffs must present viable claims under one of three theories: strict liability, intentional torts, or negligence. Claims can fail for a variety of reasons. Still, the threshold requirement for all suits is that plaintiffs, the parties bearing the burden of proof, must produce evidence proving sufficient facts under one of the theories in order to have their claims survive motions for dismissal or summary judgment.

Strict Liability

Strict liability does not require proof of fault or a breach of a duty of care. As such, courts consistently refuse to impose strict liability on educational institutions. While strict liability can apply under a products liability theory as to dangerous items, courts have refrained from using this standard in disputes

---

[1] Because litigation involving nonpublic schools is not as voluminous as with public schools, this chapter relies primarily on cases involving nonpublic schools even if they are a bit less current. Where citations are unavailable from nonpublic schools, references are to cases involving public schools.

[2] *See* Speller v. Toledo Pub. Sch. Dist. Bd. of Educ., 38 N.E.3d 509, 520 [322 EDUC. L. REP. 466] (Ohio Ct. App. 2015) ("[i]t is not a tort to breach a contract, no matter how willful or malicious the breach.") (affirming the denial of a former principal's breach of contract claim) (internal citations omitted).

[3] Mirand v. City of N.Y., 598 N.Y.S.2d 464, 375 [83 EDUC. L. REP. 372 (N.Y. App. Div. 1993).

involving schools. Even if courts consider items in schools, such as science laboratories, to be dangerous, they are more likely to elevate the standard of care requirements in order to ease recovery under negligence, rather than impose strict liability.

Intentional Torts

Officials and boards in nonpublic schools can be liable under state and federal statutes for the intentional actions of employees and/or students. Educators may also be liable for injuries resulting from the most commonly alleged intentional torts inflicted on students, such as assault and battery, intentional infliction of emotional distress, invasion of privacy, false imprisonment, and, increasingly, defamation.

An important matter emerges between intentional torts and negligence as to attorney fees. Because attorneys representing injured parties in negligence actions ordinarily work on the basis of contingency fees, they typically receive no payments unless or until they achieve either favorable settlements for their clients or prevail in judicial actions. Conversely, in intentional tort actions, attorneys usually charge fees up front before initiating actions.

Assault and Battery

Assault and battery are common law intentional torts. Because confusion can arise, due to these terms also being used in criminal law, educators should be careful to distinguish between the two in policies and handbooks—what may be statutorily defined as criminal battery in one jurisdiction is criminal assault in another, and vice-versa. For example, in the following subsections, school boards and teachers face civil or criminal liability for assault and/or battery in cases involving sexual misconduct and corporal punishment involving students.

Assault is placing someone in the immediate fear of an unwanted touching of which one is aware.[4] Battery is the actual contact. As such, if a student ducks when he sees a teacher throw a piece of chalk or an eraser at him that misses him but hits a classmate who was not paying attention, the educator may be liable for having assaulted the first child and battering the second. This outcome results because one need not be aware that a touch is about to occur. School boards and educators can be liable for assault[5] and battery[6] involving students if they failed to provide adequate supervision.

---

[4] Spacek v. Charles, 928 S.W.2d 88 [112 Educ. L. Rep. 525] (Tex. Ct. App. 1996).

[5] Scott v. Mid-Del Sch. Bd. of Educ., 229 F.Supp.3d 1254 [344 Educ. L. Rep. 1018] (W.D. Okla. 2017), aff'd in part rev'd in part, __ Fed.App'x __, 2018 WL 898590 (10th Cir. 2018) (affirming that a teacher could be personally liable for assaulting and bullying a middle school student because he yelled at, cursed at, and intimidated him in front of his peers in the classroom).

[6] See, e.g., Doe v. Archbishop Stepinac High Sch., 729 N.Y.S.2d 538 [156 Educ. L. Rep. 665] (N.Y. App. Div. 2001) (allowing charges filed by students alleging that they were assaulted by peers on an overseas trip to proceed, but rejecting claims for negligent infliction of emotional distress). For a similar outcome, see McClyde v. Archdiocese of Indianapolis, 752 N.E.2d 229 [155 Educ. L. Rep. 1336] (Ind. Ct. App. 2001).

A case involving assault and battery arose in Missouri, where a federal trial court rejected some of the various intentional tort claims students filed against their faith-based boarding school.[7] Because genuine issues of material fact existed as to whether school employees threw a student to the ground and/or poked her, while other staff members encouraged or incited those present to touch her offensively, the court rejected the defendants' motion for summary judgment.

The court also rejected the students' battery claim because they failed to make a case for it under state law, based on the allegation that employees surreptitiously gave them antipsychotic drugs. The court rejected this claim because the students either did not identify any of the defendants as having ever given a student medication, food, drink, or other items to ingest and/or did not provide expert testimony to link their claimed symptoms to the alleged administration of Thorazine. Finally, the court rejected the students' false imprisonment claims because they were minors while enrolled in the school, with the consent of their parents.

Sexual Abuse

Sexual abuse is a particular kind of assault and battery. In recent years a significant number of charges and suits have arisen against faith-based institutions, particularly the Roman Catholic Church and some of its schools.[8] While all such instances are legally and ethically inexcusable, the fact that abuse allegedly occurred did not mean that the religious bodies were always liable.

When litigating claims for sexual abuse in schools, courts often apply *Gebser v. Lago Vista Independent School District* (Gebser).[9] In *Gebser*, the Supreme Court affirmed that a board could not be liable under Title IX for a teacher's misconduct unless an official with the authority to institute corrective measures had actual notice of, and was deliberately indifferent to, a teacher's sexual misconduct. The Justices ruled that because the board behaved appropriately, by acting promptly and decisively in punishing the teacher, the student and her mother could not proceed with their claim. Similarly, in *Davis v. Monroe County Board of Education*,[10] the Court addressed peer-to-peer sexual harassment, but the Justices relied on an actual notice standard, among other elements, in evaluating liability by school officials.

---

[7] Woods v. Wills, 400 F. Supp.2d 1145 [205 Educ. L. Rep. 350] (E.D. Mo. 2015).

[8] For a discussion of this issue in Roman Catholic schools, see Charles J. Russo, *The Impact of Pedophile Priests on American Catholic Education: Reflections of a Cradle Catholic*, 37 Rel. & Educ. Vol. 37, No. 2, 97-113 (2010).

[9] 524 U.S. 274 [125 Educ. L. Rep. 1055] (1998).

[10] 526 U.S. 629, 646, 650 [134 Educ. L. Rep. 477] (1999).

Religious organizations sometimes avoid liability[11] due to the expiration of the statute of limitations.[12] Even so, nonpublic schools[13] and their individual employees are often liable for sexual misconduct involving their students.

Corporal Punishment

The extent to which corporal punishment is used in nonpublic schools is difficult to assess. Due to legal questions associated with intentional tort and child abuse complaints, educators in nonpublic schools should consider using corporal punishment judiciously, if at all. School policies should identify the precise circumstances when it can be used, who may impose it, and limitations on its use.

Generally viewed as a form of discipline, sometimes referred to as paddling, corporal punishment in its broadest meaning includes physical contact between educators and students.[14] Generally, though, corporal punishment means swats administered to punish students for misconduct. The Supreme Court refused to make corporal punishment a constitutional tort in *Ingraham v. Wright,*[15] such that aggrieved students must pursue remedies under state civil and criminal laws. To date, all but nineteen states have banned the use of corporal punishment in public schools.[16]

On a related issue, courts have upheld the actions of teachers who used reasonable force to restrain students or in acts of self-defense. For instance, teachers were not liable when one restrained a child with Asperger's syndrome;[17] another grabbed the arm of a student who was attempting to retrieve a shirt

---

[11] For such a case, see Doe v. Brouillette, 906 N.E.2d 105 [244 Educ. L. Rep. 242] (Ill. App. Ct. 2009) (affirming that an archdiocese was not liable for abuse a student suffered at the hands of a counselor with a history of pedophilia because he was never in its care, the abuser was not one of its employees, and its officials lacked knowledge of the counselor's history of pedophilia as required for the claim of fraudulent concealment to proceed).

[12] For such a case, see State ex rel. Marianist Province of the U.S. v. Ross 258 S.W.3d 809 [235 Educ. L. Rep. 1164] (Mo. Banc 2008), *reh'g denied.*

[13] *See, e.g.,* Hardwicke v. American Boychoir Sch., 902 A.2d 900 [211 Educ. L Rep. 377] (N.J. 2006) (treating a private school as a person subject to passive abuse provision in state law in affirming that it could be vicariously liable for common-law claims based on child abuse committed by its employees).

[14] For an egregious case, see Neal v. Fulton Cnty. Bd. of Educ., 229 F.3d 1069 [148 Educ. L. Rep. 86] (11th Cir. 2000), *reh'g en banc denied,* 244 F.3d 143 (11th Cir. 2000) (treating the actions of a high school football coach as "conscience-shocking" where he struck a student with a metal weight lock, resulting in the loss of the use of his eye).

[15] 430 U.S. 651 (1977).

[16] *See* Tim Walker, *Why Are 19 States Still Allowing Corporal Punishment in Schools?,* NEA Today, Oct. 17, 2016, available at http://neatoday.org/2016/10/17/corporal-punishment-in-schools/

[17] Brown *ex rel.* Brown v. Ramsey, 121 F. Supp.2d 911 [149 Educ. L. Rep. 392] (E.D. Va. 2000), *aff'd without published opinion,* 10 Fed.Appx. 131 (4th Cir. 2001).

and pulled him toward a door;[18] and a third grabbed and twisted a child's wrist in an effort to have her give him a $20 bill she picked up from the floor.[19]

Civil or criminal liability for using corporal punishment depends on a variety of factors including its reasonableness;[20] the motives of the individuals inflicting it, such as anger;[21] the size of students;[22] evidence of physical injuries;[23] and instruments used.[24]

In a case from Ohio, an appellate court affirmed that because a childcare worker at a church caused severe traumatizing injuries to two children, it was liable for $2,871,431.87 in compensatory and punitive damages plus attorney fees.[25] This case stands out because church officials sought to conceal information from the parents about the physical injuries to their children, as well as the employee's lack of knowledge of the church's corporal punishment policy.

Officials in faith-based schools, in particular, who wish to employ corporal punishment need to consider the following five points: (1) whether education is a parental or school function; (2) whether the biblical mandates about its use are directed to parents or to schools; (3) whether schools have a legitimate interest in requiring parents to sign written consent forms delegating their authority to use corporal punishment, regardless of whether parents use it at home; (4) whether school policies requiring delegation or corporal punishment apply to all aspects of their operations; and (5) whether educators can perform educative functions without using corporal punishment.

Consent forms signed by parents are generally defenses to the use of corporal punishment. However, the forms are not adequate to defend against the unreasonable use of corporal punishment, weighing the factors highlighted in the preceding paragraph.

Another item for officials in nonpublic schools to consider is whether their liability insurers cover corporal punishment and, if not, whether riders

---

[18] Widdoes v. Detroit Pub. Schs., 619 N.W.2d 12 [148 Educ. L. Rep. 1039] (Mich. Ct. App. 2000), *appeal denied*, 625 N.W.2d 785 (Mich. 2001).

[19] Bisignano v. Harrison Cent. Sch. Dist., 113 F. Supp.2d 591 [147 Educ. L. Rep. 529] (S.D.N.Y. 2000).

[20] Nolan v. Memphis City Schs., 589 F.3d 257 [251 Educ. L. Rep. 533] (6th Cir. 2009) (affirming that a coach's use of paddling was not unreasonable corporal punishment because he acted based on reports from teachers about the student's in-class misconduct, such that the coach did not commit assault and battery). For another case upholding corporal punishment as reasonable under the circumstances, see Campbell v. Gahanna-Jefferson Bd. of Educ., 717 N.E.2d 347 [137 Educ. L. Rep. 1104] (Ohio Ct. App. 1998).

[21] *See* Tinkham v. Kole, 110 N.W.2d 258 (Iowa 1961) (imposing liability on a teacher who acted in anger, striking a student on the ear and bursting his eardrum, because the child had not obeyed a directive).

[22] *See, e.g.*, Frank v. Orleans Parish Sch. Bd., 195 So.2d 451 (La. 1967) (affirming liability by a board and teacher where the latter, a 230-pound, 6'2" physical education instructor squeezed a student who was 4'9" and weighed 101 pounds, breaking his arm).

[23] *Id.*

[24] *See* Neal v. Fulton Cnty. Bd. of Educ., 229 F.3d 1069 [148 Educ. L. Rep. 86] (11th Cir. 2000), *reh'g en banc denied*, 244 F.3d 143 (11th Cir. 2000).

[25] Faieta v. World Harvest Church, 891 N.E.2d 370 [234 Educ. L. Rep. 285] (Ohio Com. Pl. 2008), *aff'd*, 2008 WL 5423454 (Ohio Ct. App. 2008).

to their existing policies are possible. If riders are unavailable or would be too expensive, officials must consider whether they can afford to be self-insured, should parents sue and secure judgments. Appendix A offers suggestions for officials in nonpublic schools using corporal punishment.

Hazing and Bullying

Hazing and bullying are intentional torts that have witnessed increased legal interest in recent years. Hazing generally applies to physical or verbal intimidation involving student participation in activities, resulting in physical and/or emotional injuries, and is often associated with initiation into organizations.

Addressing hazing can be difficult, because even though most states have adopted laws punishing it and permitting civil actions for damages, it lacks a clear definition. For example, Ohio law defines hazing as "doing any act or coercing another, including the victim, to do any act of initiation into any student or other organization that causes or creates a substantial risk of causing mental or physical harm to any person."[26]

On the other hand, Pennsylvania law defines hazing more broadly as "any action or situation which recklessly or intentionally endangers the mental health or physical safety of a student, including, but not limited to, any brutality of a physical nature, such as whipping, beating, branding, forced calisthenics, exposure to the elements, or any other forced physical activity which adversely affects physical health and safety of the individual, and shall include any activity which would subject the individual to extreme mental stress, which could adversely affect the mental health or dignity of the individual."[27]

Both laws prevent physical or mental/emotional abuse or the infliction of harm on others, but they are far from clear in terms of the duties of school officials. Because hazing[28] and bullying are still relatively new claims, unless school officials are directly involved in hazing, their liability has tended to be framed under negligent supervision.

"Bullying is a persistent, pernicious problem in our schools—[that] can cause emotional and, at times, physical harm."[29] Bullying is a more general term referring to taunts and ridicule, as well as physical harms, resulting in student alienation. In public schools, common law tort liability typically depends on state governmental immunity statutes, while liability for constitutional tort

---

[26] Ohio Rev. Code Ann. § 2903.31(A).

[27] 24 Pa. Stat. Ann. § 5352.

[28] For two older cases, see Rupp v. Bryant, 417 So.2d 648 [5 Educ. L. Rep. 1309] (Fla. 1982) (ruling that university officials had a duty to control an initiation including hazing that took place off-campus because they had noticed hazing occurred in the past and was about to happen); Leahy v. Sch. Bd. of Hernando County, 450 So.2d 883 [17 Educ. L. Rep. 1282] (Fla. 1984) (deciding that questions of fact existed as to whether the injury a student suffered during football drills was the result of his coach's failure to provide adequate instruction and supervision).

[29] Cormier v. City of Lynn, 91 N.E.3d 662, 663 [352 Educ. L. Rep. 296] (2018).

under Section 1983 may hinge on the special relationship and state-created danger doctrines.[30]

To date, almost all states have enacted statutes requiring school officials to develop policies aimed at preventing bullying and harassment. Policies should identify consequences for violations, along with mechanisms for reporting and redressing incidents. Since nonpublic schools may not enjoy state immunity protection from common law torts[31] and may face liability based on negligent supervision,[32] officials would do well to develop both anti-hazing and anti-bullying policies. As reflected in a case from Louisiana involving a public school, educators are unlikely to be liable for injuries students sustained due to bullying if officials lacked notice that it occurred.[33]

Defamation

Litigation over defamation in nonpublic schools has largely arisen from disputes about recommendations for employees. Defamation is the "[m]alicious or groundless harm to the reputation or good name of another by the making of a false statement to a third person."[34] Spoken defamation is slander;[35] written defamation is libel. Depending on the jurisdiction, some courts require allegedly defamatory remarks to contain objectively verifiable assertions of fact rather than mere opinions.[36]

---

[30] L.R. ex rel. N.R. v. Sch. Dist. of Philadelphia, 836 F.3d 235 [336 EDUC. L. REP. 90] (3d Cir. 2016) (affirming that officials in Pennsylvania violated a kindergartner's rights, both under Section 1983 pursuant to the state-created danger theory and the Fourteenth Amendment, where a teacher allowed her to leave his class with an unidentified adult, by whom she was sexually assaulted).

[31] See, e.g., Brugger v. Joseph Acad., 781 N.E.2d 269 [172 EDUC. L. REP. 923] (Ill. App. Ct. 2002) (refusing to apply the state's immunity statute to a private, not-for-profit school for students with disabilities).

[32] See Bradley T. v. Cent. Catholic High Sch., 653 N.W.2d 813 [171 EDUC. L. REP. 936] (Neb. 2002) (affirming an award of $125,000 against a school where a student was sexually assaulted by a peer because officials delayed in addressing the problem).

[33] Bella v. Davis, 531 Fed.Appx. 457 [298 EDUC. L. REP. 740 (5th Cir. 2013). Courts are beginning to apply the standards in bullying and harassment cases from Davis v. Monroe Cnty. Bd. of Educ., 526 U.S. 629, 646, 650 [134 EDUC. L. REP. 477] (1999), wherein the Court addressed peer-to-to peer sexual harassment. Interpreting Title IX, the Court held that recipients of federal financial assistance are liable for damages in "circumstances wherein the recipient exercises substantial control over both the harasser and the context in which the known harassment occurs." The Court added that recipients "are properly held liable in damages only when they are deliberately indifferent to sexual harassment, of which they have actual knowledge, that is so severe, pervasive, and objectively offensive that it can be said to deprive the victims of access to the educational opportunities or benefits provided by the school."

[34] BLACK'S LAW DICTIONARY (10th ed. 2014).

[35] Taylor v. Calvary Baptist Church, 630 S.E.2d 604 [209 EDUC. L. REP. 914] (Ga. Ct. App. 2006) (affirming the denial of a former teacher's slander claim because vague statements or even derogatory comments do not reach the point of becoming slander when one cannot reasonably conclude from what is said that the comments are imputing a crime onto the plaintiff).

[36] See, e.g., Lifton v. Board of Educ. of City of Chicago, 416 F.3d 571 [200 EDUC. L. REP. 39] (7th Cir. 2005).

Individuals accused of defamation can rely on one of three defenses to avoid liability: truth, privilege, and opinion. If statements are true and do not invade persons' rights to privacy, they are not defamatory.[37] If there is a question of fact as to whether statements are true, an area overlapping with privilege, such matters are ordinarily questions of fact for juries.

In an overlap between privilege and opinion, educators are protected when they make statements in recommendations or evaluations offering their views to appropriate persons in the line of duty, as long as they are supported by some evidence.[38] If statements are clearly opinions, such as where parents and students criticized teachers[39] or school officials,[40] then they are unlikely to be liable for defamation.

Milkovich v. Lorain Journal Company,[41] wherein a high school wrestling coach sued a newspaper for defamation when an editorial suggested that he committed perjury, may be the most important public school case on opinions. The Supreme Court conceded that remarks about the coach in the newspaper were not opinions because they could have been proven to be true or false. According to the Court, "where a statement of 'opinion' on a matter of public concern reasonably implies false and defamatory facts regarding public figures or officials, those individuals [can recover damages if they] show that such statements were made with knowledge of their false implications or with reckless disregard of their truth."[42] Further, defamation claims may be denied if the nature of the comments are intertwined with a school's religious mission.[43]

Another element associated with defamation development addresses public figures. In educational contexts, courts typically treat board members[44] and

---

[37] Gatto v. St. Richard Sch., 774 N.E.2d 914 [169 Educ. L. Rep. 371] (Ind. Ct. App. 2002).

[38] *Id. See also* Crevlin v. Board of Educ. of City Sch. Dist. of City of Niagara Falls, 43 N.Y.S.3d 614, 615 [338 Educ. L. Rep. 497] (N.Y. App. Div. 2016) (asserting that board members "are absolutely immune for discretionary acts carried out in the course of official duties.").

[39] Ansorian v. Zimmerman, 627 N.Y.S.2d 706 [101 Educ. L. Rep. 366] (N.Y. App. Div. 1995).

[40] Nampa Charter Sch. v. DeLaPaz, 89 P.3d 863 [187 Educ. L. Rep. 1056] (Idaho 2004).

[41] 497 U.S. 1 [60 Educ. L. Rep. 1061] (1990)

[42] *Id.* at 20.

[43] *See, e.g.*, State ex rel Gaydos v. Blaeuer, 81 S.W.3d 186 (Mo. Ct. App. 2002) (rejecting the defamation claims filed by a former administrator in a Catholic school whose contract was not renewed because the reasons for her dismissal were intertwined with the school's religious mission).

[44] Peavy v. Harman, 37 F. Supp.2d 495 (N.D. Tex. 1999). *But see* Roberts v. Board of Educ., 25 F. Supp.2d 866 [131 Educ. L. Rep. 128] (N.D. Ill. 1998).

superintendents[45] as public figures, but are divided with regard to teachers,[46] principals,[47] and coaches.[48]

The key Supreme Court decision on public figures is *New York Times Co. v. Sullivan.*[49] The Court ruled that in order for public officials to succeed in defamation claims, they must prove that defendants acted with actual malice[50] in making harmful remarks known to be false, or that persons acted with reckless disregard for the truth. These standards can also apply to limited-purpose public figures, those who achieve fame or notoriety due to one specific incident or issue, such as someone who wins the lottery.

False Imprisonment

False imprisonment is "[t]he restraint of a person in a bounded area without legal authority, justification, or consent,"[51] even if the individual does not suffer harm. False imprisonment is uncommon and is rarely successful absent egregious behavior by educators, such as where a teacher in Kentucky chained a student with poor attendance to a tree for ninety minutes, claiming that he did so as a joke.[52]

To the extent that policies allow educators to keep children after school in detention if they misbehave, false imprisonment claims are likely to fail as long as the amount of time that officials retain students is reasonable. However, in order to make sure that children get home safely and do not miss their rides, officials in many schools no longer impose detention on the day students misbehave. Rather, they typically send notes home to parents informing them that students are to be punished by having to stay after school on a set day of the week, so parents can plan to get their children home safely.

---

[45] *See, e.g.*, Mitchell v. Pruden, 796 N.E.2d 77 [340 EDUC. L. REP. 505] (N.C. Ct. App. 2017) (rejecting a libel claim against a superintendent who criticized the owner of charter schools because he was a "public officer" under the state's official immunity law).

[46] For a case refusing to treat a teacher as a public official, see Dec v. Auburn Enlarged Sch. Dist., 672 N.Y.S.2d 591 [126 EDUC. L. REP. 365] (N.Y. App. Div. 1998). For cases recognizing teachers as public officials, see, e.g., Kelley v. Bonney, 606 A.2d 693 [74 EDUC. L. REP. 896] (Conn. 1992).

[47] For cases affirming that principals were not public officials, see, e.g., Ellerbee v. Mills, 422 S.E.2d 539 [78 EDUC. L. REP. 1104] (Ga. 1992), *cert. denied*, 507 U.S. 1025 (1993); Beeching v. Levee, 764 N.E.2d 669 [162 EDUC. L. REP. 938] (Ind. Ct. App. 2002). For cases affirming that although principals were public officials, defendants were not liable for defamation because they did not act with reckless disregard for the truth, see, e.g., Jordan v. World Pub. Co., 872 P.2d 946 [90 EDUC. L. REP. 1227] (Okla. Ct. App. 1994); Palmer v. Bennington Sch. Dist., 615 A.2d 498 [78 EDUC. L. REP. 881] (Vt. 1992).

[48] O'Connor v. Burningham, 165 P.3d 1214 (Utah 2007) (refusing to treat a basketball coach as a public figure).

[49] 376 U.S. 254 (1964).

[50] *See, e.g.*, Hustler Magazine v. Falwell, 485 U.S. 46 (1988) (rejecting a religious leader's defamation claim against the publisher of a magazine that printed a scatological cartoon of him, since he injected himself into the public spotlight through his media and political activities and could not prevail without proof of actual malice).

[51] BLACK'S LAW DICTIONARY (10th ed. 2014).

[52] Banks v. Fritsch, 39 S.W.3d 474 [152 EDUC. L. REP. 379] (Ky. Ct. App. 2001).

Intentional Infliction of Emotional Distress

As uncommon as false imprisonment, intentional infliction of emotional distress[53] is "[t]he tort of intentionally or recklessly causing another person severe emotional distress through one's extreme or outrageous acts."[54] In a case where a plaintiff succeeded, an appellate court in Florida affirmed that a teacher had a claim against students who participated in the production and distribution of a newsletter in which the author threatened to rape and kill her and all of her children.[55] The court agreed that the behavior at issue was so outrageous in character and extreme in degree that it exceeded all bounds of decency, thereby allowing the teacher's claim to proceed.

Invasion of Privacy

Invasion of privacy, "[a]n unjustified exploitation of one's personality or intrusion into one's personal activities, actionable under tort law and sometimes under constitutional law,"[56] is not recognized in all jurisdictions.[57] While truth is a defense in defamation, it is not so in invasion of privacy actions because they are based on intrusions into persons' expectations of privacy rather than the truth or falsity of what defendants have said or done. Invasion of privacy is actually four separate torts: intrusion upon a person's solitude;[58] appropria-

---

[53] The corresponding claim of negligent infliction of emotional distress, defined as "intentionally or recklessly causing another person severe emotional distress through one's extreme or outrageous acts" in BLACK's LAW DICTIONARY (10th ed. 2014), is so rarely successful that it is briefly identified here rather than under the main heading of negligence. In a case involving a nonpublic school, the highest court in the District of Columbia rejected the claim of a father who sued for intentional infliction of emotional distress after officials refused to permit his son to re-enroll after he had not paid his child's tuition. Sibley v. St. Albans Sch., 134 A.3d 789 [330 EDUC. L. REP. 193] (D.C. 2016).

[54] BLACK's LAW DICTIONARY (10th ed. 2014).

[55] Nims v. Harrison, 768 So. 2d 1198 [148 EDUC. L. REP. 518] (Fla. Dist. Ct. App. 2000).

[56] BLACK's LAW DICTIONARY (10th ed. 2014).

[57] See, e.g., Russell v. Salve Regina Coll., 890 F.2d 484 [57 EDUC. L. REP. 382] (1st Cir. 1989), (identifying invasion of privacy as a statutory right in New Hampshire); Anderson v. Strong Mem'l Hosp., 531 N.Y.S.2d 735 [48 EDUC. L. REP. 629] (N.Y. Sup. Ct. 1988), aff'd on other grounds, 542 N.Y.S.2d 96 [54 EDUC. L. REP. 589] (N.Y. App. Div. 1988) (conceding that invasion of privacy was not recognized as a common law tort under state law).

[58] See, e.g., S.B. v. St. James Sch., 959 So.2d 72 222 EDUC. L. REP. 444 [Ala. 2006] (rejecting a claim for invasion of privacy by intrusion into students' physical solitude where officials in a nonpublic school expelled them for circulating "sexted" pictures of themselves).

tion of a person's name or likeness;[59] public disclosure of private facts;[60] and putting a person in a false light.[61]

Generally, the standard in each of the four torts, as reflected in a case from Pennsylvania, is whether a disclosure "(a) would be highly offensive to a reasonable person, and (b) is not of legitimate concern to the public."[62] The court rejected the claim that two newspaper articles referring to the plaintiff-parents' son as having a learning disability constituted publicity into their child's private life where he was discussed at a school board meeting in the context of reimbursing his parents for the cost of an independent evaluation. The court reasoned that confidentiality under the Individuals with Disabilities Education Act (IDEA)[63] was offset here by the public's interest in knowing "that the school [board] was being asked to pay with tax dollars the cost of a privately retained psychologist."[64]

Negligence

The vast majority of suits brought against nonpublic institutions involve negligence, the failure to exercise "that degree of care which an ordinarily prudent person would exercise under the same or similar circumstances to avoid injury to another."[65] Whether liability exists for allegedly negligent acts very much depends on the facts of each case. Accordingly, as an introductory matter, it is worth acknowledging that due to the importance of specific facts in negligence and adequate supervision-of-student claims, many of the cases in this chapter can be cited for more than one element of negligence.

The one key similarity in all of these cases is that plaintiffs must satisfy the four elements of a negligence claim: a legal duty, breach of the duty, injury, and causation. The upshot is that it is fair to say that most negligence cases in schools boil down to questions of whether educators provided adequate supervision of students. Moreover, in order for plaintiffs to prevail, defendants must

---

[59] *See, e.g.*, Hart v. Electronic Arts, 717 F.3d 141 (3d Cir. 2013) (allowing a claim for the misappropriation of likeness and identity of football players for commercial purpose to proceed against a video game developer).

[60] *See, e.g.*, Doe v. Gonzaga Univ., 24 P.3d 390 [154 EDUC. L. REP. 963] (Wash. 2001), *rev'd on other grounds*, 536 U.S. 273 [165 EDUC. L. REP. 458] (2002) (upholding a $100,000 judgment for a state claim of invasion of privacy where university officials revealed information from a student's educational record to state personnel, resulting in his being denied teacher licensure).

[61] *See, e.g.*, Stead v. Unified Sch. Dist. No. 259, Sedgwick Cnty., Kan., 92 F. Supp.3d 1088 [322 EDUC. L. REP. 220] (D. Kan. 2015) (rejecting a former principal's false light invasion of privacy claims based on statements board officials made about her to the press after not renewing her contract because what they said was not false).

[62] Culver v. Port Allegany Reporter Argus, 598 A.2d 54, 55 [70 EDUC. L. REP. 869] (Pa. Super. Ct. 1991), *appeal denied*, 617 A.2d 1274 (Table) (Pa. 2000) (rejecting a parental invasion-of-privacy claim based on an accurate newspaper article reporting on a public school board meeting about their request for reimbursement of the cost to evaluate their son with a learning disability, who was asked to repeat the third grade).

[63] 20 U.S.C.A. §§ 1400 *et seq.*

[64] *Id.* at 56.

[65] Gossett v. Jackson, 457 S.E.2d 97, 100 (Va. 1995) (internal citations omitted).

be unable to assert defenses, namely consent/assumption of risk, contributory or comparative negligence, or charitable immunity.

Elements of Negligence

Duty

A duty is "[a] legal obligation that is owed or due to another and that needs to be satisfied."[66] Legal duties in schools are based on relationships, such as employment and/or enrollment contracts. The absence of legal duties is fatal to negligence claims.

Once the law recognizes the existence of legal relationships, educators have the duty to anticipate reasonably foreseeable risks to students or others in their care or custody and to try to protect them from harm. In such a case, an appellate court in Missouri affirmed that insofar as educators did not have physical custody and control over a high school student who was killed in an automobile accident while traveling to watch his school's softball team in its championship game, officials had no duty to supervise his safety.[67]

Conceding that foreseeability is a highly flexible concept that varies based on the age, maturity level, and physical condition of students, coupled with the degrees of danger inherent in situations, the law does not expect educators to foresee all possible harms. Instead, educators are responsible for only those mishaps they can reasonably foresee, or of which they are actually aware.

Foreseeability is an extremely fluid concept because it must be applied to a wide range of factual situations, such as whether school officials had prior notice of similar incidents;[68] the injuries or damages were intentionally inflicted;[69] school rules or state laws were specifically directed to the misconduct;[70] or students were engaging in voluntary activities outside of their

---

[66] BLACK'S LAW DICTIONARY (10th ed. 2014).

[67] *See, e.g.*, Davis v. Lutheran S. High Sch. Ass'n of St. Louis, 200 S.W.3d 163213 EDUC. L. REP. 296] (Mo. Ct. App. 2006).

[68] *See, e.g.*, Leo v. Mount St. Michael Acad., 708 N.Y.S.2d 372 [44 EDUC. L. REP. 626] (N.Y. App. Div. 2000) (affirming that school officials were not liable where they lacked actual or constructive notice of water on stairs in a building).

[69] *See, e.g.*, Daniels v. Fluette, 64 A.3d 302 [291 EDUC. L. REP. 821] (R.I. 2013) (affirming that a Catholic school was not liable for injuries a student sustained when a friend pushed him toward a window in a school restroom that he fell through, causing glass to shatter and lacerating his wrist, absent showing that there was a history of horseplay in the area or that others complained about the pushing student's conduct).

[70] *See, e.g.*, Wilson v. Darr, 553 N.W.2d 579 [113 EDUC. L. REP. 419] (Iowa 1996) (affirming a grant of summary judgment in favor of a priest where a former student sued him for failure to report physical and sexual abuse by her father, because the priest did not have a statutory duty to report child abuse). *But see* Scott v. Indep. Sch. Dist. No. 709, 256 N.W.2d 485 (Minn. 1977) (affirming a school's liability where a student's eye was injured when struck by an object after he removed goggles, because state law mandated that eye protection be worn in specified classes such as the industrial arts course he was taking).

school programs.[71] While foreseeability may be difficult to define, it is not a hindsight test permitting courts to second-guess the actions of school officials.[72]

A difficult threshold question associated with duty is determining whether school officials were obligated to act. Cases sometimes produce outcomes that were not readily obvious. For example, in the first of two cases from Florida, an appellate court affirmed that a faculty member and his college were not liable for the death of a student who was killed in a car accident as he was driving a group to a field trip.[73] The court agreed that the faculty member was not liable because he did not act in the scope of his employment when the accident happened; the trip occurred a day after the term ended, and the college had a policy that such activities could only occur during class time.

When a 17-year-old student who consumed alcohol at a private, non-school-related party, crashed his car into a tree, killing his passenger and rendering him a quadriplegic with a traumatic brain injury, his parents filed suit. On further review of a $12.95 million judgment entered on behalf of the plaintiffs, an appellate court in Florida reversed in favor of the school, its officials, and the diocese.[74] The court found that in light of a disclaimer in the school's handbook indicating that it would not be liable for nonsanctioned events, educators had no duty to inform the parents about the party their son attended.

On the other hand, an appellate court in Louisiana affirmed that a school board and various officials were liable when parents sued after their 327-pound, 16-year-old son collapsed and died during while playing basketball in a physical education class in a hot, poorly ventilated gymnasium. The court agreed that a substitute art teacher who supervised the class failed to exercise reasonable supervision that might have prevented the student's death.

If educators take reasonable precautions to keep students safe, but unforeseeable intervening acts occur, then they are unlikely to be liable. An example is where a student was injured during basketball practice when a peer who was supposed to be assisting the coach kicked him in the face. An appellate court in

---

[71] *See, e.g.*, Swanson v. Wabash Coll., 504 N.E.2d 327 [37 Educ. L. Rep. 916] (Ind. Ct. App. 1987) (affirming a grant of summary judgment in favor of a college when it was sued by a student who was injured while participating in a recreational baseball practice because he voluntarily did so, knowing no professional coaching assistance or supervision was available, based on the written guidelines he received).

[72] *See, e.g.*, Adams v. Cado Parish Sch. Bd., 631 So.2d 70, 73 [89 Educ. L. Rep. 330] (La. Ct. App. 1994), *writ denied*, 637 So. 2d 466 (La. 1994), *reconsideration denied*, 638 So.2d 224 (La. 1994) (refusing to impose liability on a board for failing to separate two female students as they sat in the office waiting to see an administrator, as no school personnel could recall a situation where a fight had ever broken out there; the court noted that "foreseeability cannot be measured through hindsight, and it is error to do so.")

[73] Fernandez v. Florida Nat'l Coll., 925 So.2d 1096 [208 Educ. L. Rep. 673] (Fla. Dist. Ct. App. 2006).

[74] Archbishop Coleman F. Carroll High Sch. v. Maynoldi, 30 So.3d 533 [255 Educ. L. Rep. 479] (Fla. Dist. Ct. App. 2010).

New York affirmed that since no amount of supervision could have prevented the unforeseeable, spontaneous attack, the school was not liable for the injury.[75]

Fashioning the legal duties where officials in nonpublic schools have duties to act is not easy because their responsibilities do not readily separate themselves into readily definable categories. Courts have essentially recognized five sometimes overlapping elements involving duties, namely, competent personnel,[76] adequate supervision,[77] adequate instruction,[78] furnishing and maintaining safe equipment and premises,[79] and making and enforcing adequate rules.[80]

Having special relationships with students can impact the duty of educators to exercise one or more of the five items just identified. Even so, where a player suffered a fatal heart attack during a lacrosse game, the Third Circuit rejected the claim that his college was liable for his death.[81] The court explained that decedent's having been recruited to play lacrosse did not create a special relationship requiring it to have athletic trainers present at all practices

[75] McCollin, Jr. v. Roman Catholic Archdiocese of N.Y., 846 N.Y.S. 2d 158 [226 EDUC. L. REP. 972] (2007).

[76] *See, e.g.*, Brugger v. Joseph Acad., 781 N.E.2d 269 [172 EDUC. L. REP. 923] (Ill. 2002) (affirming that where a teacher disregarded a medical note from a doctor and required a student to participate in a dodgeball game, neither the school nor the educator was entitled to immunity because the school was not a "local public entity,").

[77] While supervision can have a variety of meanings, the simplest and most effective is physical presence. For cases agreeing that educators failed to provide adequate supervision or allowed such claims to proceed, see, e.g., McClyde v. Archdiocese of Indianapolis, 752 N.E.2d 229 [155 EDUC. L. REP. 1336] (Ind. Ct. App. 2001); Doe v. Archbishop Stepinac High Sch., 729 N.Y.S.2d 538 [156 EDUC. L. REP. 665] (N.Y. App. Div. 2001); Traficienti v. Moore Catholic High Sch., 724 N.Y.S.2d 24 [153 EDUC. L. REP. 347] (N.Y. App. Div. 2001); Smith v. Archbishop of St. Louis, 632 S.W.2d 516 [4 EDUC. L. REP. 671] (Mo. Ct. App. 1982). *But see* Smith v. Roman Catholic Church of Archdiocese of New Orleans, 995 So.2d 1257 [239 EDUC. L. REP. 784] (La. Ct. App. 2008) (affirming that where a student tripped and fell over a book bag while carrying equipment for a teacher and sustained facial injuries, he could not recover because the teacher was reasonably supervising students when the plaintiff tripped).

[78] *See, e.g.*, Potter v. N.C. Sch. of the Arts, 245 S.E.2d 188 (N.C. Ct. App. 1978) (affirming that a student who was burned when a fog machine exploded backstage in a theater could recover for his injuries because the student operating it had been adequately instructed).

[79] For cases rejecting negligence claims where school officials lacked actual notice of conditions that caused injuries see, e.g., Leo v. Mount St. Michael Acad., 708 N.Y.S.2d 372 [144 EDUC. L. REP. 626] (N.Y. App. Div. 2000) (involving a wet stairway); Velez v. Our Lady of Victory Church, 486 N.Y.S.2d 302 [23 EDUC. L. REP. 993] (N.Y. App. Div. 1985) (involving defective desks).

[80] *See, e.g.*, Tollenaar v. Chino Valley Sch. Dist., 945 P.2d 1310, 1312 [121 EDUC. L. REP. 1154] (Ariz. Ct. App. 1997) (affirming that educators were not liable for failing to enforce a closed campus policy where the parents of students who were killed in a vehicle crash on leaving school during the day, failed to prove that they "undertook to provide a service that [they] recognized, or should have recognized, as necessary for the students' protection.").

[81] Kleinknecht v. Gettysburg Coll., 989 F.2d 1360 [82 EDUC. L. REP. 43] (3d Cir. 1993).

because it was not foreseeable that he would have suffered life-threatening injuries at practice.[82]

Special relationships can be significant in some cases, but require officials to have individualized knowledge about the needs of students or employees. For example, an appellate court in New York affirmed that educators and a board had a special relationship with students who were in the custody of officials when they were assaulted as they tried to leave school.[83]

At the same time, special relationships can be negated if students are no longer on school property or educators took steps to warn them of dangerous conditions. For instance, the Circuit Court for the District of Columbia affirmed the dismissal of a negligence claim against the board where a student was injured crossing a street on her way home from school.[84] The court agreed that simply because board officials placed a homeless mother and daughter in a shelter six miles from the school, they did not have a special duty to provide transportation to get her home safely.

Supervision

Because supervision is at the heart of just about all duties insofar as it represents the physical presence of personnel, especially classroom teachers, it is worthy of special consideration. Student supervision is a multifaceted concept involving the interplay of such questions as whether teachers' physical presences could have prevented student injuries;[85] whether teachers provided adequate instruction to students about safety hazards or dangerous situations;[86] and whether teachers made and enforced adequate safety rules.[87] Supervision also concerns whether adequate numbers of personnel were present,[88] and

---

[82] On special relationships and constitutional torts, see DeShaney v. Winnebago County Dep't of Soc. Servs., 489 U.S. 189 (1989) (affirming the absence of a special relationship where county social services employees placed a child back with his father, who severely beat his son).

[83] Mirand v. City of N.Y., 598 N.Y.S.2d 464, 460 [83 Educ. L. Rep. 372 (N.Y. App. Div. 1993).

[84] Powell v. District of Columbia, 634 A.2d 403 (D.C. Cir. 1993).

[85] For cases rejecting liability insofar as events were unforeseeable and so could not have been prevented by adequate supervision, see, e.g., McCollin v. Roman Catholic Archdiocese of N.Y., 846 N.Y.S.2d 158 [226 Educ. L. Rep. 972] (N.Y. App. Div. 2007); Luina v. Katharine Gibbs Sch. N.Y., 830 N.Y.S.2d 263 [216 Educ. L. Rep. 605] (N.Y. App. Div. 2007).

[86] See, e.g., Wells v. Harrisburg Area Sch. Dist., 884 A.2d 946 [203 Educ. L. Rep. 288] (Pa. Cmwlth. Ct. 2005) (affirming that a teacher engaged in negligent supervision where a student severely injured his hand during a woodshop class).

[87] See, e.g., Verkel v. Indep. Sch. Dist. No. 709, 359 N.W.2d 579 [22 Educ. L. Rep. 371] (Minn. 1984) (upholding judgments against a board where official failed to provide adequate instruction and supervision of a new cheerleader advisor).

[88] See, e.g., Collins v. Bossier Parish Sch. Bd., 480 So.2d 846, 848 [29 Educ. L. Rep. 887] (La. Ct. App. 1985) (observing that "[t]here is nothing in evidence to show that had there been more teachers on duty this unfortunate incident would not have still occurred.").

whether officials were aware of the dangers and risks in activities in need of supervision.[89]

Certainly, the greater the risk, the more important the role of teacher supervision, in that educators are expected to respond commensurately and appropriately to the level of risk in school activities. The failure of teachers to adjust their levels of supervision to increased dangers in instructional settings, even if the possible harms are of the educators' own makings, can result in liability for themselves and their boards. As such, an appellate court in Missouri affirmed a verdict of $1,250,000 in favor of a student in a faith-based school who suffered burns over 45% of her upper body when the candle a teacher lit in their classroom ignited the child's paper costume.[90]

The highest court in the District of Columbia affirmed an award of $250,976.00 to a fourth-grader who was lured from school and raped after a teacher left her in charge of a second-grade class on going to another area of the building for supplies.[91] On the other hand, an appellate court in Louisiana affirmed that a teacher who was alone supervising ninety students in an area the size of football field was not liable for the injuries a child suffered when she fell or was pushed off a tree stump in the playground.[92] The court pointed out both that the teacher warned the children not to play in the area where the tree stump was located, and she had no reason to expect that the child would fail to comply with her instructions.

If normal supervisory procedures are in place, it can be difficult for injured students to recover damages. For instance, an appellate court in New York affirmed that a teacher who was alone supervising students was not liable for the injuries a child suffered when she slipped or tripped on an allegedly defective condition on a concrete playground while playing "tag" during recess.[93] The court decided that neither the teacher nor administrators had actual or constructive notice of the allegedly dangerous condition.

The more teachers deviate from established rules or routines, the greater the likelihood of liability. To send students to neighboring stores or teachers' cars to pick up items for personal or school use are situations that would be difficult to justify in court. Of course, teachers often send students who are ill or injured to offices if school nurses or principals. Yet, one wonders how much thought educators give to whether students are following instructions. Boards should thus develop safety polices requiring teachers to have trustworthy

---

[89] *See, e.g.*, Fazzolari v. Portland Sch. Dist. No. IJ, 734 P.2d 1326 [38 Educ. L. Rep. 809] (Or. 1987) (reversing a directed verdict in favor of a board and remanding for a trial as to liability for the rape of a student where officials had notice that another rape occurred fifteen days earlier). *But see* Velez v. Our Lady of Victory Church, 486 N.Y.S.2d 302 [23 Educ. L. Rep. 993] (N.Y. App. Div. 1985) (upholding the dismissal of a suit for an injury to a student's hand when a desk toppled absent evidence officials had actual or constructive notice the desks were defective).

[90] Smith v. Archbishop of St. Louis, 632 S.W.2d 516 [4 Educ. L. Rep. 671] (Mo. Ct. App. 1982).

[91] District of Columbia v. Doe, 524 A.2d 30 [38 Educ. L. Rep. 1037] (D.C. Cir. 1987).

[92] Partin v. Vernon Parish Sch. Bd., 343 So.2d 417 (La. Ct. App. 1977).

[93] Walker v City of N.Y., 918 N.Y.S.2d 775 [265 Educ. L. Rep. 733] (N.Y. App. Div. 2011).

peers accompany students to the offices of the nurse or principal. Plus, in an age where almost all people have cell phones, perhaps policies should direct teachers to notify officials when students have left their classes.

Teachers who leave classrooms are at risk of litigation. Contrary to popular myth, though, schools and/or teachers are not strictly liable if educators leave classrooms unsupervised temporarily to deal with emergencies such as disturbances in halls, as long as they instruct students about how to behave before leaving. In such situations, one can treat teacher absences as being on a continuum from emergencies at one end to solely personal concerns at the other. The further teacher absences are toward the emergency end of the continuum, the less scrutiny courts typically apply to the instructions they gave their classes.

Of course, the higher the risk level represented by a class, such as a chemistry laboratory, the more likely that teachers should have established protocols for dealing with emergencies. As teacher absences move closer to the personal end of the continuum, the less likely their instructions are to exculpate liability. In Louisiana, an appellate court affirmed that an industrial arts teacher who frequently left to get scrap metal for class and to catch students smoking was negligent, along with his board, even though he provided a list of 200 instructions to students, among which was not to use power equipment in his absence.[94] The court remarked that the instructions the teacher provided failed to excuse or mitigate his absence where his being gone reflected both poor lesson planning and that he engaged in unnecessary policing functions during class time. Appendix B contains suggestions for teacher supervision.[95]

Breach

In addition to having to prove that educators owed them duties, plaintiffs must demonstrate that defendants breached their duties. When evaluating whether educators breached their duties of care, two important questions come into play. The first insofar as educators can breach their duties in one of two ways. Nonfeasance occurs when educators fail to act in light of duties to act. Nonfeasance occurs when educators fail to act properly.[96] If administrators fail to provide adequate supervision of school employees and/or lack adequate policies to this effect, they and their boards are likely to share in fault under what is referred to as joint and several liability, insofar as they have a duty to maintain safe educational settings.

The second major consideration under breach is the standard of care educators must provide. In evaluating whether individuals met the requisite

---

[94] Lawrence v. Grant Parish Sch. Bd., 409 So.2d 1316 [2 Educ. L. Rep. 1234] (La. Ct. App. 1982).

[95] *See also* Charles J. Russo, Allan G. Osborne, & C. Daniel Raisch, *Twelve Safety Tips for Avoiding Liability*, 257 Educ. L. Rep. 544 (2010); Suzanne E. Eckes, Janet R. Decker, & Emily N. Richardson, Trends in Court Opinions Involving Negligence in K–12 Schools: Considerations for Teachers and Administrators, 275 Educ. L Rep. 505 (2012).

[96] Where educators act improperly, or with evil intent, they commit malfeasance, a misdeed that is more properly an intentional tort. It is mentioned here because it sounds much like the names of the negligence torts and often arises in cases involving sexual misconduct with students.

level of care, courts have adopted the common law standard of reasonableness. In other words, courts ask whether hypothetical persons with the defendants' intelligence, physical attributes, perception and memory, and special skills should be responsible for student injuries. This is an attempt to devise objective standards defining the hypothetical characteristics of reasonable persons, a process involving examinations of the experience, ages, and skills of educators, whether teachers, administrators, and/or coaches, and the nature of venues such as classrooms, athletic fields and/or on field trips. In other words, courts are likely to expect reasonable educators to provide greater care than reasonable persons lacking the same education and training but not the same amount as reasonable parents.[97]

Without using the term reasonable educator per se, the highest courts of New York[98] and Nebraska,[99] in cases involving injuries to players on their teams, held football coaches to a standard below that of a reasonable parent. The court in Nebraska pointed out that the coaches had to meet the standard of reasonable person with a teaching certificate and coaching endorsement rather than the standard of the reasonable person lacking such credentials.

Trials examining both the knowledge and instructional skills of teachers in relation to the ages and experiences of students are time-consuming and enervating experiences. However, as reflected in a slightly older case from Louisiana, the court was of the opinion that a teacher had the duty to conduct his classes and other activities so as not to expose his students to unreasonable risks of injury, particularly potentially dangerous activities. The court did think that an educator's skill level for an activity, here as a wrestling coach, does not have to be based on formal instruction or coursework and can be based on practical experience.[100] The court concluded that even though the coach lacked formal training in wrestling, his instruction in, preparation for, and supervi-

---

[97] Courts have agreed that educators working with preschool students must meet the higher standard of the reasonable parent. *See*, *e.g.*, Milligan v. Harborfields Cent. Sch. Dist., 962 N.Y.S.2d 664 [291 Educ. L. Rep. 438] (N.Y. App. Div. 2013) (finding that a board was not liable because it met the reasonable parent standard when an 8-year-old was injured on well-maintained monkey bars); Diana G. v. Our Lady Queen of Martyrs Sch., 953 N.Y.S.2d 640 [286 Educ. L. Rep. 647] (N.Y. App. Div. 2012) (stating that educators had the duty to exercise the same degree of care toward students as reasonably prudent parents); Paragas v. Comsewogue Union Free Sch. Dist., 885 N.Y.S.2d 128 [248 Educ. L. Rep. 785] (N.Y. App. Div. 2009) (affirming that educators owed first-graders the same standard of care as reasonably prudent parents, but were not liable because they met their duty); Enright by Enright v. Busy Bee Playschool, 625 N.Y.S.2d 453 [99 Educ. L. Rep. 1073] (N.Y. Sup. Ct. 1995) (declaring that preschool officials owed children the duty of a prudent parent rather than ordinary reasonable care).

[98] Benitez v. New York City Bd. of Educ., 543 N.Y.S.2d 29 [54 Educ. L. Rep. 933] (N.Y. 1989) (refusing to expect a coach to provide the same level of care as a reasonable parent; insofar as the plaintiff was a 19-year-old football player, the court also applied assumption of risk).

[99] Cerny v. Cedar Bluffs Junior/Senior Pub. Sch., 628 N.W.2d 697 [155 Educ. L. Rep. 827] (Neb. 2001), *after remand*, 679 N.W.2d 198 [187 Educ. L. Rep. 783] (Neb. 2004). Following remand, the court affirmed that the coaches met the higher standard because they evaluated the player multiple times before letting him return to the game, and they understood concussion symptoms.

[100] Green v. Orleans Parish Sch. Bd., 365 So.2d 834 (La. Ct. App. 1978), *writ denied.*

sion of the drill in which a student was injured did not fall below locally or nationally accepted standards of care for teachers under similar circumstances.

While most cases involving injuries to students tend to focus on the reasonableness of the behavior of educators in terms of whether they met their duties, courts sometimes factor in the conduct of children in assessing the reasonable person standard. In an illustrative case from Maryland, an appellate court affirmed that a 16-year-old female who was seriously injured while playing in her first high school football scrimmage was not entitled to special warnings about possible physical injuries in football, because these should have been obvious.[101]

Courts may also take the ages of students into consideration in evaluating whether educators met or breached their duties to foresee manifestations of their behaviors. The Supreme Court of Texas affirmed that educators were liable for the injuries a 14-year-old suffered when he fell from a balcony while his friends encouraged him to jump from it into his school's swimming pool. The court noted that "[i]t is not uncommon for children of [plaintiff's] age to willingly or intentionally engage in conduct that, if left unsupervised, would be harmful. It is for this reason that the school has a duty to reasonably supervise its students."[102]

Injury

Persons can recover in negligence, like any other tort, only if they have real rather than imagined injuries for which compensation can be awarded. Unfortunately, as reflected by a case from Oregon, persons can have exaggerated perceptions of wrongs educators commit. An appellate court upheld a grant of summary judgment in favor of a school board and its teachers when they directed a student to use her given name in class rather than her nickname largely because it was associated with marijuana. The court wrote that "[w]e fail to see how a reasonable juror could find that such conduct constitutes an extraordinary transgression of the bounds of socially tolerable conduct."[103]

When injuries are cognizable, they do not need to be substantial or physical in order for plaintiffs to recover. For example, an appellate court in Louisiana affirmed a judgment in favor of a kindergarten-aged child who suffered emotional injuries when a physical education teacher told him that he hanged his friends with a jump rope. The court agreed that the family was entitled to financial damages because the facts revealed that the 5-year-old was normal before the teacher pretended to have hanged his friends with a jump rope, but who afterward "began to exhibit infantile behavior. He refused to go to the bathroom alone and refused to wipe himself. He was afraid that [the] Coach … would come out of the mirror in the bathroom and harm him. Justin would

---

[101] Hammond v. Bd. of Educ. of Carroll Cnty., 639 A.2d 223, 226 [90 Educ. L. Rep. 256] (Md. Ct. App. 1994).

[102] Univ. Preparatory Sch. v. Huitt, 941 S.W.2d 177, 181 [117 Educ. L. Rep. 367] (Tex. 1997).

[103] Phillips v. Lincoln Cnty. Sch. Dist., 984 P.2d 947, 951 [137 Educ. L. Rep. 1127] (Or. Ct. App. 1999).

no longer sleep in his own room. He became overly dependent on his mother and was not comfortable when she was out of sight."[104]

Causation

Causation is the logical and sequential connection between breach and duty, meaning they are closely related in time and space on one hand and the injury on the other. In order to establish causation, plaintiffs must produce evidence that injuries would not have occurred "but for" the breaches. Injuries must be the natural and probable results of breaches with no intervening causes.[105] Moreover, as reflected by many of the cases in this chapter, the failure of plaintiffs to establish causation results in the dismissals of their actions.

As illustrated by a case from New York, causation can have a spatial quality. After a school nurse denied treatment to a 14-year-old girl with asthma, she told her to return to class. Instead, the student left school, went home, and fell from her apartment window, sustaining serious injuries. Affirming the dismissal of the complaint, the court was satisfied that the nurse's conduct was not the cause of the student's injuries because once the child arrived home, she came under the control and protection of her mother.[106]

Cause also becomes an issue where schools have rules or policies that have not been enforced and plaintiffs claim that "but for" their failure to comply, their injuries would not have occurred. A tragic set of facts emerged in a case before the Supreme Court of Vermont. The court affirmed that school officials were not liable when a 15-year-old with a history of truancy and drug abuse was murdered in an intervening action after she left school without authorization.[107] The court agreed that educational officials were not liable because there was no causation between their actions and the student's death, insofar as she left school voluntarily and without permission.

Cause, as the vital connecting link between breach of duty and injury, is more likely to be present when duties are well recognized or the conduct of school officials appears unreasonably indifferent to possible injuries. As to the well-recognized duty of supervision, the Third Circuit affirmed that a kindergarten teacher and school officials in Pennsylvania were liable for the sexual assault a child suffered at the hands of the unidentified man to whom the educator released the student.[108] The court agreed that the risk of harm presented by releasing the student from classroom to the unidentified adult was so obvious that it rose to the level of deliberate indifference.

---

[104] Spears on Behalf of Spears v. Jefferson Parish Sch. Bd., 646 So.2d 1104, 1106 [96 EDUC. L. REP. 884] (La. Ct. App. 1994).

[105] *See* Greening v. Sch. Dist. of Millard, 393 N.W.2d 51, 53 [34 EDUC. L. REP. 1199] (Neb. 1981).

[106] Griffith v. City of N.Y., 507 N.Y.S.2d 445 [35 EDUC. L. REP. 507] (N.Y. App. Div. 1986).

[107] Edson v. Barre Supervisory Union #61, 933 A.2d 200 [225 EDUC. L. REP. 959] (Vt. 2007).

[108] L.R. ex rel. N.R. v. Sch. Dist. of Philadelphia, 836 F.3d 235 [336 EDUC. L. REP. 90] (3d Cir. 2016).

Defenses

Even if plaintiffs have proven the elements of negligence, defenses to tort liability diminish or eliminate liability. The defenses available to defendants in nonpublic schools are consent/assumption of risk, contributory/comparative negligence, and charitable immunity.

Defenses are premised on the notion that while educators have the duty to look after students and others, because they are not insurers of safety, they cannot be liable for all possible harms taking place in and around schools.

Consent/ Assumption of Risk

Consent and the closely related concept assumption of risk are popular defenses which courts frequently apply interchangeably when reviewing cases where plaintiffs who freely accepted risks suffered injuries associated with their activities. Although consent and assumption of risk can be included exculpatory language on forms, writing is not necessary because defenses can be applied without being based on persons' prior training and experience.

Defendants traditionally rely on consent in cases where written exculpatory language is present, while assumption of risk applies where no written language is present and the differences are no longer worth preserving. Thus, for purposes of this chapter, the two defenses are viewed interchangeably, even though only one of the terms is normally used in a given case.

An important element of these defenses is that plaintiffs must have known and appreciated the risks resulting in their injuries. Thus, assumption of risk (or consent) represents "[t]he principle that one who takes on the risk of loss, injury, or damage cannot maintain an action against a party that causes the loss, injury, or damage."[109] Knowledge and understanding of risks can be acquired in various ways. In some cases, the risks may be obvious—as in contact sports, such as where football players are injured making tackles[110]—while in others, understanding may be based on watching demonstrations, videos, and participating in training camps.

Neither consent nor assumption of risk apply if injuries are unforeseeable. In such a case from Pennsylvania, an appellate court affirmed a damages award in favor of a student who was hurt while firing a toy cannon at athletic events, even though he had already done so more than 200 times. Rejecting the assumption of risk defense, the court commented that "lax supervision over use of the cannon, compared with the tight controls the Academy exercised over use of firearms, would not alert someone to the fact that the cannon would injure a body part not within the range of the small flame."[111]

Assumption of risk is also inapplicable if it is used to attempt to discharge a duty requiring reasonable care to "exercise that degree of skill and care . . .

---

[109] BLACK'S LAW DICTIONARY 157-58 (10th ed. 2014).

[110] *See, e.g.*, Benitez v. New York City Bd. of Educ., 543 N.Y.S.2d 29 [54 EDUC. L. REP. 933] (N.Y. 1989).

[111] Struble v. Valley Forge Military Acad., 665 A.2d 4, 7 [103 EDUC. L. REP. 785] (Pa. Commw. Ct. 1995).

ordinarily employed by members of the profession under similar conditions and circumstances."[112] Nor is assumption of risk an appropriate defense where injured parties did not appreciate the nature of the risks.

In a case of this nature, the operators of a shelter sought further review of an order rejecting the assumption of risk defense where a 15-year-old student diagnosed with operational defiant disorder was injured after being run over by a fire truck while on a field trip. The facts revealed that the student attempted to jump onto the passenger side of the fire truck while it was backing up, despite a fireman's warning him to stay away. Affirming a grant of summary judgment precluding the shelter from relying on assumption of risk, the Supreme Court of South Carolina ruled that "[n]o evidence was presented to establish that [the student] appreciated the nature and extent of the danger of riding on the side of the fire truck. The evidence also does not show that [the student] in fact knew the condition was dangerous."[113]

Not surprisingly, courts have applied assumption of risk to athletes who were injured while voluntarily participating in baseball,[114] basketball,[115] cheerleading,[116] football,[117] gymnastics,[118] ice hockey,[119] lacrosse,[120] soccer,[121] softball,[122] swimming,[123] tennis,[124] and wrestling.[125] On the other hand, courts have refused to apply assumption of risk in cases where coaches failed to warn a student sufficiently about the dangers of diving into a pool,[126] lacked

---

[112] Hoeffner v. The Citadel, 429 S.E.2d 190, 194 [82 EDUC. L. REP. 692] (S.C. 1993).

[113] Cunningham v. Helping Hands, 575 S.E.2d 549, 552 (S.C. 2003).

[114] See, e.g., O'Connor v. Hewlett-Woodmere Union Free Sch. Dist., 959 N.Y.S.2d 750 [289 EDUC. L. REP. 870] (N.Y. App. Div. 2013).

[115] See, e.g., Perez v. New York City Dep't of Educ., 982 N.Y.S.2d 577 [302 EDUC. L. REP. 748] (N.Y. App. Div. 2014).

[116] See, e.g., Christian v. Eagles Landing Christian Acad., 692 S.E.2d 745 [256 EDUC. L. REP. 934] (Ga. Ct. App. 2010).

[117] See, e.g., Benitez v. New York City Bd. of Educ., 543 N.Y.S.2d 29 [54 EDUC. L. REP. 933] (N.Y. 1989).

[118] See, e.g., Weber v. William Floyd Sch. Dist., 707 N.Y.S.2d 231 [144 EDUC. L. REP. 610] (N.Y. App. Div. 2000).

[119] See, e.g., Litz v. Clinton Cent. Sch. Dist., 5 N.Y.S.3d 636 [316 EDUC. L. REP. 483] (N.Y. App. Div. 2015).

[120] See, e.g., Safon v. Bellmore-Merrick Cent. High Sch. Dist., 22 N.Y.S.3d 233 [325 EDUC. L. REP. 1000] (N.Y. App. Div. 2015).

[121] See, e.g., Ballou v. Ravena-Coeymans-Selkirk Sch., 898 N.Y.S.2d 358 [255 EDUC. L. REP. 948] (N.Y. App. Div. 2010).

[122] See, e.g., Kelly v. McCarrick, 841 A.2d 869 [185 EDUC. L. REP. 6620] (Md. Ct. Spec. App. 2004) (involving a Catholic high school).

[123] See, e.g., Aronson v. Horace Mann-Barnard Sch., 637 N.Y.S.2d 410 [106 EDUC. L. REP. 1281] (N.Y. App. Div. 1996), leave to appeal denied, 651 N.Y.S.2d 15 (N.Y. 1996).

[124] See, e.g., Bendig v. Bethpage Union Free Sch. Dist., 904 N.Y.S.2d 731 [258 EDUC. L. REP. 373] (N.Y. App. Div. 2010).

[125] See, e.g., Philippou v. Baldwin Union Free Sch. Dist., 963 N.Y.S.2d 701 [291 EDUC. L. REP. 847] (N.Y. App. Div. 2013).

[126] See, e.g., Kahn v. East Side Union High Sch. Dist., 4 Cal.Rptr.3d 103 [180 EDUC. L. REP. 312] (Cal. 2003).

experience to provide adequate supervision over cheerleaders[127] or a football practice.[128] Courts also refused to apply assumption of risk for injuries students experienced during activities in physical education classes because they are part of mandatory curricula.[129]

The viability of assumption of risk is in question in some states because it eliminates liability by defendants. Consequently, unless plaintiffs' assumptions of risks are clear as matters of law, courts increasingly submit cases to juries to assess the alleged risk factors under contributory negligence in determining liability, or under comparative negligence in setting damages.[130]

Contributory/Comparative Negligence

Historically, most states relied on contributory negligence wherein courts recognized that "[a] plaintiff's own negligence that played a part in causing the plaintiff's injury and that is significant enough (in a few jurisdictions) to bar the plaintiff from recovering damages."[131] Insofar as this approach resulted in plaintiffs' being denied redress if they contributed in any way to their injuries, most jurisdictions now apply comparative negligence, acknowledging that "[a] plaintiff's own negligence that proportionally reduces the damages recoverable from a defendant."[132]

Under comparative negligence, lack of care by plaintiffs lowers the amount of damages by apportioning a percentage of their own negligence in reducing awards, but does not prevent all recovery.[133] By way of illustration, if a jury decides that a plaintiff is entitled to an award of $100,000, but was 20%

---

[127] *See, e.g.*, Larson v. Cuba Rushford Cent. Sch. Dist., 912 N.Y.S.2d 827 [262 Educ. L. Rep. 584] (N.Y. App. Div. 2010).

[128] *See, e.g.*, Duffy v. Long Beach City Sch. Dist., 22 N.Y.S.3d 88 [325 Educ. L. Rep. 995] (N.Y. App. Div. 2015).

[129] *See, e.g.*, Godoy v. Cent. Islip Union Free Sch. Dist., 985 N.Y.S.2d 732 [304 Educ. L. Rep. 583] (N.Y. App. Div. 2014) (involving floor hockey); Muniz v. Warwick Sch. Dist., 743 N.Y.S.2d 113 [165 Educ. L. Rep. 731] (N.Y. App. Div. 2002) (involving softball).

[130] *See, e.g.*, Trustees of Trinity Coll. v. Ferris, 491 S.E.2d 909, 913 (Ga. Ct. App. 1997) ("[e]xcept in plain, palpable and undisputed cases where reasonable minds cannot differ as to the conclusions to be reached, questions of ... assumption of risk ... are for the jury.").

[131] BLACK'S LAW DICTIONARY (10th ed. 2014).

[132] *Id.*

[133] For a useful discussion of comparative and contributory negligence including listings of the jurisdictions into each of the categories, see Gary Wickert of Matthiesen, Wickert & Lehrer, S.C., August 2013, available at https://www.mwl-law.com/understanding-comparative-fault-contributory-negligence-and-joint-and-several-liability/

negligent, the amount must be reduced by $20,000.[134] In addition, comparative negligence apportions fault damages among defendants.[135]

In states relying on comparative negligence, courts carefully scrutinize the apportionment of damages involving small children.[136] As noted, in noncomparative negligence states, even the smallest percentage of contributory negligence results in jury awards being set aside. However, noncomparative negligence states can mitigate some of the harshness of disallowing recovery by treating plaintiffs as too young to be contributorily negligent. In such a case from South Carolina, an appellate court affirmed that a substantial issue of fact existed as to whether a 9-year-old who was injured as she crossed a road to return to her bus was capable of contributory negligence, precluding a bus company's motion for summary judgment.[137]

Charitable Immunity

Charitable institutions include a wide range of nonpublic organizations engaged in educational, medical, religious, and/or other charitable functions. Introduced in 1876 in the United States,[138] charitable immunity was a common law method of eliminating or reducing liability for the actions of employees and/or board members of nonpublic institutions dedicated to the common good, because the imposition of liability would have been unfair insofar as the organizations received no financial benefits from their works.[139]

Most courts abolished charitable immunity, agreeing that organizations may be liable to individuals who are hurt due to the actions of their board

---

[134] For case applying comparative negligence, see, e.g., Williams v. Junior Coll. Dist. of Cent. Southwest Mo., 906 S.W.2d 400 [103 EDUC. L. REP. 871] (Mo. Ct. App. 1995) (affirming a 20% reduction in a negligence award by the percent the jury apportioned to the plaintiff who slipped on liquid on concrete floor); Lockett v. Bd. of Educ. for Sch. Dist. No. 189, 555 N.E.2d 1055 [61 EDUC. L. REP. 212] (Ill. App. Ct. 1990) (affirming a 20% reduction in a negligence award by the percent the jury apportioned to the plaintiff who was injured on lowering a bus window below the stop-line in violation of state rules).

[135] See Williams v. Cahill, 629 N.E.2d 1175 [89 EDUC. L. REP. 922] (Ill. App. Ct. 1994) (in a negligence claim by a student on a school bus that was struck by a truck, the jury found the bus driver 60% negligent and the truck driver 40% negligent, but insofar as the bus driver settled prior to the verdict for $60,000, the truck driver was totally responsible for the $293,000 award, minus the $60,000; had the settlement not occurred, each defendant would have had to pay their full percentage).

[136] See, e.g., Branch v. Stehr, 461 N.Y.S.2d 346 [10 EDUC. L. REP. 708] (N.Y. App. Div. 1990) (upholding an order for a new trial where a jury apportioned 90% of fault to a 6-year-old child who was injured in a traffic accident and 10% on the part of the village which assumed the duty of assigning a school crossing guard to the intersection in question).

[137] Sharpe v. Quality Educ., 296 S.E.2d 661 [7 EDUC. L. REP. 459] (N.C. Ct. App. 1982). See also Simmons ex rel. Simmons v. Columbus Cnty. Bd. of Educ., 615 S.E.2d 69, 76 [199 EDUC. L. REP. 955] (N.C. Ct. App. 2005) (declaring that "[i]n North Carolina, children between the ages of seven and fourteen are presumed to be incapable of contributory negligence.")

[138] For the first charitable immunity case in the United States, see McDonald v. Mass. Gen'l Hosp., 120 Mass. 432, 1876 WL 10813 (Mass. 1876) (holding that the funds of a charity, in this case a hospital, were in trust, the diversion of which it would not permit).

[139] See Cox v. DeJarnette, 123 S.E.2d 16, 22 (Ga. Ct. App. 1961) (decreeing that charitable immunity preserves "eleemosynary funds as to enable the charity to carry out its beneficent purposes.")

members, volunteers, and/or employees under *respondeat superior*.[140] With the demise of charitable immunity, courts now apply *respondeat superior* to render organizations liable for the wrongdoings of those acting on their behalf. In general, injured parties must produce evidence as to three elements common to suits under *respondeat superior*: injuries caused by the negligence of directors, volunteers, or employees; institutional-director/ employee/volunteer relationships; and directors/employees/volunteers acting within the scope of their duties.

With the prominence of medical malpractice, charitable immunity for hospitals eroded quickly under the rationale that hospitals are now businesses operating in a competitive market. However, this business rationale extended to other kinds of charitable institutions.

States still recognizing charitable immunity wrestle with the implications of their statutory protection in light of sex abuse scandals involving religious and educational institutions. In such a case, the Supreme Court of New Jersey suggested an end run around its charitable immunity statute by asserting that a man who was denied ordination as a priest had an implied breach of contract claim against his diocese when he was subjected to unwanted homosexual advances.[141] Such an approach would permit plaintiffs to recover for injuries while sidestepping the fiction in some jurisdictions of treating charitable immunity as a rule of property, whereby the doctrine, although not prohibiting the filing of tort claims, does prevent prevailing parties from levying the assets of the charitable institution.[142]

Judicial pressure to abolish charitable immunity has led some state legislatures to limit the liability of charitable institutions.[143] In a more esoteric vein, choice of law conflicts between states that eliminated charitable immunity and those recognizing it have involved loss-distributing interest analysis of the states with the greater contacts. In the case of states allowing charitable immunity, this means injured parties have aligned themselves with the laws of jurisdictions whose underlying policies are "to encourage the growth of charitable work within its borders."[144]

In today's litigious society, one should not be surprised to learn that courts encourage officials in educational institutions to purchase liability insurance

---

[140] For cases abolishing charitable immunity, see, e.g., Fitzer v. Greater Greenville S.C. YMCA, 282 S.E.2d 230 (S.C. 1981); Albritton v. Neighborhood Ctrs. Ass'n for Child Dev., 466 N.E.2d 867 (Ohio 1989); Myers v. Drozda, 141 N.W.2d 852, 853 (Neb. 1966); Hungerford v. Portland Sanitarium and Benevolent Ass'n, 384 P.2d 1009, 1011 (Or. 1963); Pierce v. Yakima Valley Mem'l Hosp. Ass'n, 260 P.2d 765, 774 (Wash. 1953); Roman Catholic Church v. Kennan, 243 P.2d 455 (Ariz. 1952).

[141] McKelvey v. Pierce, 800 A.2d 840 [166 EDUC. L. REP. 673] (N.J. 2002).

[142] *See* Clayborn v. Bankers Standard Life Ins. Co., 75 S.W.3d 174, 179-180 (Ark. 2002) (distinguishing between immunity from suit and from liability).

[143] See ARK. CODE ANN. § 16-120-703; N.J. STAT. ANN. § 2A:53A-7.

[144] Schultz v. Boy Scouts of Am., 491 N.Y.S.2d 90 (N.Y. 1985) (affirming that a tort action against the Boy Scouts, charging it for negligently hiring and supervising troop leaders who sexually abused the plaintiffs' sons, was governed by New Jersey law where the parties were codomiciliaries and the tortious acts occurred in New York).

both for themselves and their school. Officials in nonpublic schools would be well advised to have their own liability insurance coverage, or at least have protection under the policies of their parent organizations.

Not being able to rely on charitable immunity as a defense, officials in nonpublic schools need to assess their risk factors, such as the age groups served, their total numbers of students, the sizes and states of repair of their facilities, the nature of high-risk activities, and whether they use corporal punishment. While many parents have medical insurance to provide care if their children are injured, this does not prevent them from wanting to reach the liability insurance coverage of their schools, especially where their own coverage includes a dollar cap. Reviewing liability insurance coverage should be careful, collaborative efforts involving school boards, their administrators, attorneys, and insurance agents.

Special Topics

Insurance Coverage

Even with liability insurance, nonpublic schools should be aware that insurers only protect areas covered by their policies, typically excluding claims for sexual misconduct. In such a case from Virginia, an insurance company sought a declaratory judgment that it had no duty to defend or indemnify a faith-based school and various officials in a suit a mother filed on behalf of her 11-year-old daughter. The suit alleged assault and battery, intentional and negligent infliction of emotional distress, and negligent improper sexual conduct as a result of a teacher's having supposedly touched the student in a sexual manner. A federal trial court held that insofar as the plaintiffs did not allege that the child suffered a bodily injury, the negligence claim fell outside scope of policy's comprehensive general liability coverage, so the insurer had no duty to defend the school and its officials.[145]

On the other hand, an appellate court in Indiana, in a dispute involving contractual language virtually identical to what was present in Virginia, reached a different outcome. The court rejected the insurance company's claim that it had no duty to defend a public school board because under state law, emotional damage arising from a principal's sexual molestation of a student constituted a "bodily injury."[146]

---

[145] Am. and Foreign Ins. Co. v. Church Schs. of Diocese of Va., 645 F. Supp. 628 [35 EDUC. L. REP. 676] (E.D. Va. 1986). *See also* D.M.A. v. Hungerford, 488 S.W.3d 683 [331 EDUC. L. REP. 1165] (Mo. Ct. App. 2016) (conceding that a board did not have to indemnify teachers who engaged in sexual misconduct with students because doing so was outside of the scope of their employment).

[146] Wayne Twp. of Sch. Comm's v. Indiana Ins. Co., 650 N.E.2d 1205 [100 EDUC. L. REP. 1123] (Ind. Ct. App. 1995). For an unreported case from Kentucky reaching the same outcome, see Ky. Sch. Bds. Ins. Trust v. Bd. of Educ. of Woodford Cnty., 2003 WL 22520018 (Ky. Ct. App. 2003).

Self-insured schools and boards present unique legal issues. In a case from Louisiana, when a high school teacher severely beat a student, the latter sued the teacher, his professional insurer, and the self-insured school board. An appellate court affirmed that the teacher was not entitled to a defense or indemnification from his insurer, because his policy provided that "the insurance afforded by this policy is excess over any other valid and collective insurance, including self-insurance programs covering the insureds up to the limits of the taxing authority."[147] Because the $6000 in damages did not exceed what the court described as the taxing authority, it decided that the self-insured board was responsible for the full amount.

Securing liability insurance requires contacts with insurer and brokers or insurance agents. In order to be covered, officials in nonpublic schools must make sure they provided the information their insurers need. Accordingly, a case from Florida is worth considering.[148] An insurer successfully sued the insurance broker to whom a religious school sent premium payments. The insurer argued successfully that where the insurer informed the broker that it needed a new completed application form, the broker lacked the apparent authority to bind the insurer to a contract by failing to forward it to the insurer and then sending a bill to the school.

Reversing an earlier order to the contrary, and ruling in favor of the insurer, an appellate court was of the opinion that since the insurer had not received the information it sought, which could affect its deciding whether to issue a policy, the broker could not act as an agent in accepting the school's premium payment. From the school's perspective, sending in an insurance payment did not create an enforceable insurance contract, a distressing outcome because the insurance was to cover transportation of students by the school's buses. The lesson of this case is that while insurance brokers can commit insurance companies when acting as their agents, school officials need to be sure to address the insurers' requirements. Learning after the fact that communications with brokers have not created insurance contracts is an expensive lesson if intervening accidents leave schools without insurance coverage.

A common theme in many cases is sexual misconduct by school employees. These claims can be devastating for nonpublic schools if parents lose confidence in their leadership and withdraw their children. If, as reflected in the litigation, insurance companies aggressively seek to exclude coverage for such misconduct, schools would be doubly vulnerable, losing students and lacking coverage.

The insurance coverage alternative to the loss of charitable immunity may be a fragile option, so that school officials must seek legal advice about the extent of coverage. Further, officials in nonpublic schools need to do what they can to preempt litigation over employee misconduct by thoroughly

---

[147] Edwards v. Saul, 637 So.2d 1258, 1261 [91 EDUC. L. REP. 1275] (La. Ct. App. 1994).

[148] Nat'l Indem. Co. of the South v. Consolidated Ins. Servs., 778 So.2d 404 [152 EDUC. L. REP. 410] (Fla. Dist. Ct. App. 2001).

investigating applicants before hiring and by responding promptly to student complaints involving misconduct by their staff members.

Exculpatory Clauses[149]

Like their public counterparts, nonpublic educational institutions have responsibilities to those present on their premises, whether they are students, parents, guests, and/or delivery persons. This responsibility is referred to as the standard of care, a fluid concept which often requires educational officials to act preemptively to reduce, if not eliminate, liability for injuries resulting from breaches. To the extent that school officials can exculpate their institutions from liability prior to the occurrence of injuries, they may well have reduced the time and expense associated with litigation.

Exculpatory clauses are most frequently associated with contractual limitations on liability, generally referred to as release or consent forms. Even so, any means of reducing or eliminating liability broadly has exculpatory functions. While public schools in most states have varying degrees of statutory governmental immunity shielding them from some or all tort liability, this immunity does not apply to nonpublic schools.[150]

Past legislative efforts to extend governmental immunity to parents and other private parties who volunteer to transport children or serve as coaches or referees as a means of encouraging participation have been unsuccessful. This leaves public school boards in very much the same position of nonpublic schools in the sense that the efforts of both to protect volunteers is a matter of insurance coverage. However, some state laws limiting tort liability to gross negligence or willful conduct for public schools have extended this standard to nonpublic schools.[151] Further, some states with recreational use statutes have extended liability limitations to nonpublic schools.[152] For the most part, though, exculpation of liability for nonpublic schools is a matter of contract language associated with agreements not to sue.

The contractual nature of nonpublic educational institutions lends itself to efforts to reduce or eliminate liability resulting from breaches of standards of care. Attempts to exculpate liability by one-time releases, hold or save harmless clauses, or general contractual language are common in nonpublic schools and not uncommon in public ones. Still, exculpatory clauses or contracts to exempt parties from liability "place the norm of freedom of contract in tension with the

---

[149] *See* Donald H. Henderson, Eugene L. Golanda, Robert E. Lee, *The Use Of Exculpatory Clauses And Consent Forms By Educational Institutions*, 67 Educ. L. Rep. 13 (1991).

[150] *See, e.g.*, Brugger v. Joseph Acad., 781 N.E.2d 269 [172 Educ. L. Rep. 923] (Ill. 2002) (refusing to treat a private school as a "local public entity" under the state immunity law).

[151] *See id.* (ordering a trial as to whether school officials committed willful and wanton conduct in disregarding a physician note and forcing a student to play dodgeball, injuring her knee).

[152] *See, e.g.*, White v. City of Troy, 735 N.Y.S.2d 648 [160 Educ. L. Rep. 495] (N.Y. App. Div. 2002) (applying the state's recreational use statute to immunize a private school located next to a public park from ordinary negligence suits).

principle that actors should bear responsibility for their own actions."[153] The challenge is determining what circumstances permit exculpatory clauses to be enforceable without violating public policy. Courts are more likely to uphold exculpatory clauses involving voluntary activities, such as sports.

Litigation dealing with exculpatory contractual language has in common the element of informed consent, "[a] voluntary yielding to what another proposes or desires; agreement, approval, or permission regarding some act or purpose, esp[ecially] given voluntarily by a competent person; legally effective assent."[154] Informed consent, which must be present if exculpatory language is to be enforceable, incorporates three aspects of cognition: knowledge of the elements of the activities in persons wishing to participate; comprehension of the risks of injury associated with participation; and application of persons' understandings of risks to their choices to participate.[155]

An example of informed consent to students interested in football would look something like this: Students have knowledge about the elements associated with the sport such as blocking, kicking, running, tackling, hitting, and being hit by other participants. At the same time, the students must understand and articulate the risks of injuries associated with what they know about football including broken bones, dislocations, contusions, lacerations, internal damage, quadriplegia, and death. Finally, aware of this information, the students, and their parents, still consent to participation.[156]

Judicial response to exculpatory language depends on two variables, the ages of the participants and the levels of risk represented by their activities. The younger the participants and the higher the levels of risk, the more closely courts scrutinize exculpatory language. Although the Restatement of Law (Contracts) declares that "unless a statute provides otherwise, a natural person has the capacity to incur only voidable contractual duties until the beginning of the day before the person's eighteenth birthday,"[157] some courts

---

[153] Note, *Negligence – Exculpatory Clauses-School Districts Cannot Contract Out of Negligence Liability in Interscholastic Athletics-Wagenblast v. Odessa School District*, 110 Wash.2d 845, 758 P.2d 968 (1988), 102 HARV. L. REV. 729 at 729 (1989).

[154] BLACK'S LAW DICTIONARY (10th ed. 2014).

[155] For a similar test applied to assumption of risk, see Davenport v. Cotton Hope Plantation Horizontal Regime, 508 S.E.2d 565, 569 (S.C. 1998) ("(1) the plaintiff must have knowledge of the facts constituting a dangerous condition; (2) the plaintiff must know the condition is dangerous; (3) the plaintiff must appreciate the nature and extent of the danger; and (4) the plaintiff must voluntarily expose himself to the danger.").

[156] For a discussion of these aspects of understanding, see Hammond v. Bd. of Educ. of Carroll Cnty., 639 A.2d 223 [90 EDUC. L. REP. 256] (Md. Ct. App. 1994) (treating consent a defense where a female was injured in a football game because although she and her mother had knowledge of elements of the game and an understanding of at least some of the risks involved, they still consented in writing to her participation).

[157] RESTATEMENT (SECOND) OF CONTRACTS § 14 (1981).

allowed parents to consent on behalf of their minor children.[158] Other courts do not recognize parentally signed consent forms as exculpating liability for their minor children.[159] Even so, if parentally signed consent forms cannot exculpate liability for their children, they may extinguish any of their claims.[160]

Other than with minor children, consent forms may be suspect due to public policy considerations. In a case from Minnesota, the federal trial court refused to treat a general exculpatory clause in an enrollment contract as enforceable in the face of a negligence claim for a serious head injury a student suffered on being hit in the head by a golf ball during a physical education class. The court pointed out that the clause requiring the person "to agree to hold [the] School harmless from all damages arising from personal injury or property loss"[161] was too broad because it could be applied to intentional, willful, or wanton acts. The court also referred to the lack of bargaining power, questioning "whether a Taiwanese woman signing a pre-printed form written in English without the aid of a translator had much, if any, bargaining power with regard to the Enrollment Contract's terms."[162]

The public service aspect of public policy may have limited application to most nonpublic schools because it addresses "a business of a type generally thought suitable for public regulation."[163] Most release forms used in nonpublic schools, like their public counterparts, raise different kinds of questions because they generally are submitted on "take-it-or-leave-it bases," it remains to be seen to what extent the nature of the services offered and the relative bargaining powers of those signing the forms impact their validity and enforceability.

Because exculpatory clauses vary in specificity, courts must weigh how this factors into liability. Some courts refuse to treat releases as exculpatory unless they specifically reference the negligence of the entities providing services. For example, in the first of two cases from New York, an appellate court affirmed that a student who signed a general release and hold harmless

---

[158] *See, e.g.*, Zivich v. Mentor Soccer Club, 696 N.E.2d 201, 205 (Ohio 1998) (refusing to find a public policy violation where a 7-year-old plaintiff gave up his right to sue for the negligent acts of others). *See also* Aaris v. Las Virgenes Unified Sch., 75 Cal. Rptr.2d 801, 805 [126 Educ. L. Rep. 350] (Cal. Ct. App. 1998) (upholding a grant of summary judgment in favor of a board where a cheerleader was injured because "[i]t is well established that a parent may execute a release on behalf of his or her child.")

[159] *See, e.g.*, Meyer v. Naperville Manner, 634 N.E.2d 411, 415 (Ill. App. Ct. 1994) ("Since a parent generally may not release a minor child's cause of action after an injury, there is no compelling reason to conclude that a parent has the authority to release a child's cause of action prior to the injury.").

[160] *See, e.g.*, Simmons v. Parkette Nat'l Gymnastic Training Ctr., 670 F. Supp. 140 (E.D. Pa. 1987) (barring a mother's claim to recover for her daughter's injuries because she signed an exculpatory release, but allowing the child's claims to proceed); Childress v. Madison v. Madison Cnty., 777 S.W.2d 1 (Tenn. Ct. App. 1989) (treating a release form a mother signed as barring her claim, but allowing the negligence suit of her son, who was severely injured, to proceed).

[161] Wu v. Shattuck-St. Mary's Sch., 393 F. Supp. 2d 831, 837-38 [204 Educ. L. Rep. 99] (D. Minn. 2005).

[162] *Id*. at 838 note 1.

[163] Tunkl v. Regents of Univ. of Cal., 383 P.2d 441, 444 (Cal. 1963).

provision absolving operators and instructors of a skydiving school "from any and all manner of actions" did not bar his negligence action, because the release did not specifically mention the school's negligence, fault, or carelessness in instruction.[164]

Another appellate court in New York affirmed, but modified, an order positing that a release form signed by parents and their daughter prior to an overseas trip did not prevent their suit for her having been sexually assaulted by three male peers. The court commented that the release did "not clearly and unequivocally express the intention of the parties to relieve the appellants from liability for injuries sustained as the result of the [defendants'] negligence."[165]

In light of these illustrative cases, one must ask whether, if exculpatory clauses must contain the specific language envisioned by courts, any person would sign them with full disclosure. Put another way, one must ask how likely are the exculpatory clauses educational institutions rely on in such areas as improperly instructing and/or supervising both employees and students, as well as improperly installing and maintaining equipment to protect them. If such specificity is required, then exculpatory clauses are probably doomed to failure, if for no other reason than that consumers are not likely to seek the educational services they offer.

As a practical matter, courts have upheld unambiguous releases, even where they lacked specificity about the acts of negligence subject to exculpation. In such a case, an appellate court in Florida noted as a matter of law that parents of a child who was killed on being struck by a bus at a crosswalk lacked a claim against their board because of a "Special Release" they executed. The court rejected the parental allegation that they never intended to release the board from all claims. Instead, the court treated the language in the release form as unambiguous: "…we do hereby release acquit and discharge the School … from all claims and demands, actions and causes of action, damages, costs, loss of services, expenses and compensation … and any and all known and unknown, foreseen and unforeseen damages and the consequences thereof…."[166]

A case with a like outcome arose in Louisiana, where a federal trial court rejected the claims parents filed against officials in a Catholic school for children with mental impairments, alleging that they failed to provide proper medical care after their son's appendix burst, rendering him comatose. The court was of the view that the application and release form the parents signed absolved the school from liability because it excused the school "from any and all liability of every nature, kind and description as a result of any injuries, hurt or damage sustained by the child herein described."[167]

---

[164] Sivaslian v. Rawlins, 451 N.Y.S.2d 307, 308 (N.Y. App. Div. 1982).
[165] Doe v. Archbishop Stepinac High Sch., 729 N.Y.S.2d 538, 539 [156 Educ. L. Rep. 665] (N.Y. App. Div. 2001).
[166] Bellefonte Ins. Co. v. Queen, 431 So.2d 1039, 1040 [11 Educ. L. Rep. 751] (Fla. Dist. Ct. App. 1983).
[167] Battig v. Hartford Accident and Indem. Co., 482 F. Supp. 338 (W.D. La. 1977).

On the other hand, the federal trial court in Connecticut voided a release form from a nonpublic boarding school as violating public policy, even though it had an unambiguous waiver of negligence liability, when a student became seriously ill with an insect-borne disease while on a school trip to China.[168] On being transferred to a state venue, the Supreme Court of Connecticut chose not to interpret public policy as precluding the imposition of liability and so refused to disturb an award of $41.5 million to the student, of which $31.5 million was for pain and suffering.[169]

One needs to query whether judicial determinations such as in the preceding cases that the exculpatory clauses were not ambiguous means they were sufficiently specific. As a practical matter, the lack of ambiguity appears to have little to do with the kind of specific language some courts believe is necessary. Arguably, the emphasis on the lack of ambiguity has more to do with students and parents understanding that they agree not to sue entities providing services than it does with the specificity of circumstances leading to injuries. Ultimately, though, the reliability of exculpatory clauses in eliminating tort liability is a poor substitute for meeting the standard of care expectations discussed under the legal requirements for tort liability.

Educators in nonpublic schools should not rely solely on exculpatory language in applications, handbooks, and release forms as substitutes for adequate instruction and supervision and/or safe equipment and premises. Nonetheless, the process of considering the efficacy of using exculpatory language can perform a worthwhile analytical function for educational leaders and their lawyers. Three important considerations come into play.

First, officials in nonpublic schools need to find out whether exculpatory clauses are enforceable in their jurisdictions. If exculpatory language is suspect, school officials should change the emphasis from removing liability to informing students and parents adequately about the risks of injury in various activities.

Second, school leaders must consider the effect of exculpatory language on their clientele. Officials in schools treating exculpatory clauses as enforceable need to think about whether they should be able to enforce their contracts against parents to recover tuition while eliminating their duty to keep the same children safe. Indeed, if officials treat exculpatory provisions as contractual in nature, it is unclear whether they want parents negotiating changes in these provisions in exchange for gifts of money or services.

Third, school officials need to be aware of the different levels of awareness between parents and their children in understanding the meaning of exculpation. Even if parents understand exculpation, it is doubtful many students will grasp the concept as fully. To rely on the ability of parents to exculpate the claims of their children ignores the underlying importance of schools dedicat-

---

[168] Munn v. Hotchkiss Sch., 933 F. Supp.2d 343 [296 EDUC. L. REP. 889] (D. Conn. 2013), *adhered to*, 24 F. Supp.3d 155 (D. Conn. 2014), *question certified by* 795 F.3d 324 [320 EDUC. L. REP. 616] (2d Cir. 2015).

[169] Munn v. Hotchkiss Sch., 165 A.3d 1167 [347 EDUC. L. REP. 401] (Conn. 2017).

ing their efforts to providing safe educational environments while eliminating supervisory concerns that can form the bases for negligence claims.

On the other hand, despite the cautionary language in the preceding paragraphs, exculpatory provisions may still be useful and helpful for schools for four reasons. First, depending on their jurisdictions, releases may protect institutions from liability. In other words, school officials would be unwise to refrain from using release forms simply because they might avoid liability. Whatever can be said about the appropriateness of using exculpatory language, educational officials have the duty to act responsibly to protect their resources for their schools.

Second, releases may place older high school- and higher education-aged students on notice about their obligations to act responsibly. Older students should have every reason to report circumstances that might result in injuries, such as lack of supervision or unsafe equipment. Third, awareness by students and parents that they signed release forms may prevent them from filing essentially frivolous suits designed to provide leverage in seeking negotiated settlements. Fourth, releases can bolster assumption of risk defenses by helping signers think about what they are doing when they agree to participate in activities involving risks of injuries.

Negligent Hiring, Supervision, and Retention

The tort, or combination of torts, associated with negligent hiring, supervision, and retention has become increasingly popular in suits filed by parents of injured students, especially when they learn that teachers engaged in similar conduct at previous jobs. Virtually all of the cases concerning negligent hiring, supervision, and retention involve sexual misconduct by employees with students. As a threshold issue, claims under these combined torts focus on three important employment actions: investigating the records of employees prior to their being hired; providing adequate supervision of individuals on the job; and dismissing those who engaged in misconduct, sexual or otherwise.

It all but goes without saying that the beginning of any good employment process is a thorough background check. In an illustrative case from Alabama, a mother, acting on behalf of her 12-year-old son, unsuccessfully sued officials at his boarding school after a teacher sexually molested him over a six-month period.[170] As often happens in such cases, the student did not notify school officials promptly about the abuse, such that the teacher's supervisor failed to learn of the misconduct until well over a year after it ended.

Affirming a grant of summary judgment in favor of the school, the court found, in effect, that officials, particularly the teacher's supervisor, did everything correctly. The court noted that the supervisor conducted a thorough background check on the teacher. Moreover, because the institution was a boarding school, the court acknowledged that the supervisor had daily contact

---

[170] Anonymous v. Lyman Ward Military Acad., 701 So.2d 25 [122 EDUC. L. REP. 352] (Ala. Civ. Ct. App. 1997).

with the teacher and students and accompanied the teacher and students on school-related field trips. Further, when the supervisor confronted the teacher on first learning of the sexual abuse of another student, he doubted the teacher's vehement denial, so requested and received an immediate resignation. The court thus concluded that the plaintiffs failed to produce substantial evidence of negligent supervision supporting liability based on *respondeat superior*.

Employment processes are only as good as the information educators receive about applicants. Hiring decisions based on inaccurate, incomplete, misleading, and/or dishonest information can become the grist of negligent hiring claims if employees later harm students.

The Supreme Court of California resolved the leading case that helped reshape the landscape of negligent hiring. The court held that school boards can be liable for providing good recommendations to individuals who did not deserve them and went on to harm students on their next jobs.[171] The dispute arose when board officials allowed an administrator who allegedly sexually molested a student to resign in exchange for a positive letter of recommendation. Based on the positive letter, the administrator went to work in another district where he allegedly engaged in sexual misconduct with a second student. The court allowed the second student's claim against the first board to proceed because its having given the administrator the good letter of reference meant that he was in a position to have harmed her

In a similar situation, the Supreme Court of Illinois affirmed that the suit filed by elementary school students and their parents could proceed against school officials, who wrote an unwarranted positive reference letter for the teacher who sexually abused the students.[172] The court also observed that educators in the district the teacher left did not fill out an employment verification honestly and failed to document or investigate complaints parents made about the abuse he committed, even after they stripped him of classroom duties.

Citing the case from California, the court observed that when officials in the hiring district requested a completed form from the first board, their doing so gave rise to a duty to provide factually accurate and honest information. The court allowed the case to proceed insofar as the failure of the officials in the sending district to perform their duty in honestly stating the teacher's record created the risk of harm that resulted in his having sexually abused the students in the case at bar.

While the preceding cases suggest the possibility of negligent misrepresentation claims when hiring boards rely on positive recommendations, what constitutes misrepresentation is not clear. In such a situation, an appellate court in Washington affirmed that actionable misrepresentation did not occur when the individual who wrote a letter of recommendation for a former school custodian failed to mention that the man was charged with child molestation

---

[171] Randi W. v. Muroc Joint Unified Sch. Dist., 60 Cal.Rptr.2d 263 [115 Educ. L. Rep. 502] (Cal. 1997).

[172] Jane Doe-3 v. McLean Cnty. Unit Dist. No. 5 Bd. of Dirs., 973 N.E.2d 880 [283 Educ. L. Rep. 1118] (Ill. 2012).

and reprimanded for making inappropriate comments to students. The court agreed that since a police investigation failed to confirm the charges, and an administrator in the district the custodian left treated the charges as baseless, no reasonable person would have foreseen that an employee with the custodian's record would pose a risk of harm to students.[173]

At best, case law is unclear about the viability of permitting employees who allegedly engaged in sexual misconduct to resign quietly rather than face discharge proceedings. Of course, no school official wants to hire employees who have molested or abused students. As such, the cases from California and Illinois expose the difficulties in hiring where personnel actions may hinge on information that is neither complete nor accurate.

Even if school officials do not have a legal duty to reveal unsolicited information about misconduct by former employees, they should have an obligation to provide accurate references about these individuals if requested. In not directly addressing charges against employees, officials place themselves in difficult positions when others request information. Some boards and schools have taken the position that they provide only employment verification data such as dates employed, subjects taught, and salary. While this approach may arguably be defensible, one must ask how fair it is to former employees with good work records who may have difficulty being hired without qualitative comments about their performances. On the other hand, providing only brief descriptive statements would not be satisfactory if officials have duties to respond to queries about sexual misconduct of former employees.[174]

In most cases, school officials can, and likely do, provide excellent references for deserving employees who have not faced charges or allegations of impropriety. However, deliberating whether to report allegations or charges of impropriety depends on what actions officials have taken to investigate the claims. A case from Ohio is instructive.

The Supreme Court of Ohio affirmed that the statutory duty to report abuse of a child does not run solely to the identified abused child, meaning that a board may be liable if the failure of officials to report a teacher's sexual abuse of a student results in the same person harming another child in the future.[175] Consequently, officials are likely better served by reporting all allegations of abuse to social services agencies and letting them investigate. If confidential investigations fail to uncover abuse, then the matters are over and no references to the charge of abuse in a letters of recommendation would be necessary.

Conversely, if investigations by social services agencies discover abuse, they would likely be followed by some form of discipline which then could be reflected in teachers' records. Regardless of whether school officials have confidence in the effectiveness of investigations by social services agencies, these

---

[173] Richland Sch. Dist. v. Mabton Sch. Dist., 45 P.3d 580 [164 EDUC. L. REP. 476] (Wash. Ct. App. 2002).

[174] *Id.* (refusing to impose liability on an official in a sending district, in part because he did not receive a specific request about a custodian's alleged prior misconduct).

[175] Yates v. Mansfield Bd. of Educ., 808 N.E.2d 861 [187 EDUC. L. REP. 1005] (Ohio 2004).

procedures bring measures of closure to charges of impropriety. Without this element of closure, the revelation of allegations in letters of recommendation brings the possibility of defamation or invasion-of-privacy claims by current or former employees for whom the disclosure of charges without appropriate investigations carries the stigma of guilt.

In light of the uncertainty about the reliability of recommendations from former employers, those responsible for hiring new employees in nonpublic schools must design hiring policies and practices in conjunction with attorneys knowledgeable about state employment law. Key features of hiring policies should include background checks, recommendations, and/or contact persons in all prior schools where individuals worked. Once on the job, policies should include clear prohibitions against sexual and other identified forms of misconduct, in both physical and verbal contact between employees and students. It is important to spell out processes for investigating, documenting, and coming to closure on all charges or complaints of sexual misconduct. Finally, policies should include penalties for employees who engage in sexual misconduct, ranging from letters of reprimand, suspensions, and dismissal, with possible referrals to appropriate police agencies.

Self-Defense and Restraint

Self-defense and restraint present issues for school personnel and students not only out of concern for their own safety, but also due to the possibility they might be sued by those they restrained or against whom they used self-defense. The number of suits resulting from self-defense or use of restraint is low, perhaps reflecting judicious actions by school personnel. The subject of self-defense presents the three issues of deadly force, retreat, and retaliation.

The concept of deadly force does not mean that someone has died. Instead, deadly force indicates power in action, regardless of whether attackers used instruments or death occurred.[176] The essential elements of self-defense—that the person has not provoked the attack and that convenient or reasonable means of escape did not exist—must be considered in the context of the ages of both the aggressors and those attacked, the nature of the attacks, and the actions of the persons attacked after the attacks ceased.[177] The recommended policy of retreating from impending harm before using self-defense may make sense in some social settings, but is hardly applicable in schools where teachers and administrators have a legal duty to supervise students.

---

[176] BLACK'S LAW DICTIONARY (10th ed. 2014) defines deadly force as "[v]iolent action known to create a substantial risk of causing death or serious bodily harm."

[177] See, e.g., McDonald v. Terebonne Parish Sch. Bd., 253 So. 2d 558 (La. Ct. App. 1971) (affirming that where a smaller student threw a broom at a larger special education peer who aggressively pursued him, knocking out the aggressor's eye, he exercised reasonable self-defense not constituting excessive violence).

While school personnel have a duty to supervise students, their duty to protect students from harm is generally limited.[178] Still, some states have codified the use of reasonable force:

Persons employed or engaged as teachers, principals, or administrators in a school, whether public or private, and nonlicensed school employees and school bus drivers may, within the scope of their employment, use and apply such amount of force and restraint as is reasonable and necessary to quell a disturbance threatening physical injury to others, to obtain possession of weapons or other dangerous objects upon the person or within the control of the pupil, for the purpose of self-defense, or for the protection of persons or property.[179]

As discussed in Chapter 6 (School Safety), in a post-Columbine era when educators are more conscious of safety within schools, the general rule, as reflected by the statute cited in the prior paragraph, is that defensive force may be used commensurate with the force of an attack. Moreover, the use of self-defense does not require proof that force was necessary to protect one's self or others from imminent personal injury, only that its necessity was real and apparent.[180]

Mere belief of the person attacked is not sufficient to justify the use of force.[181]

Teachers are expected to exercise reasonable judgment in responding to student disturbances, ranging from voice commands to the use of force. Still,

---

[178] *See, e.g.*, Ramirez v. Genovese, 986 N.Y.S.2d 220 [305 EDUC. L. REP. 379] (N.Y. App. Div. 2014) (refusing to impose liability on the security service college officials hired to protect students where a cab driver was injured in a fight with students over a fare); Dabbs v. Aron Security, 784 N.Y.S.2d 601 [193 EDUC. L. REP. 579] (N.Y. App. Div. 2004) (rejecting the claim that the security service a board hired had a common law or contractual duty to protect students who were attacked by their peers); Ruegsegger v. Jefferson Cnty. Sch. Dist. R-1, 187 F. Supp. 2d 1284, 1287 [162 EDUC. L. REP. 796] (D. Colo. 2001) (in a case stemming from the tragedy at Columbine High School, rejecting claims filed by a student who was seriously injured because "Colorado's common law imposes no duty to protect others from harm by third parties."). *But see* Frugis v. Bracigliano, 827 A.2d 1040 [178 EDUC. L. REP. 845] (N.J. 2003) (imposing a duty on a board to protect students from foreseeable harm from teachers); T.K. v. Simpson Cnty. Sch. Dist., 846 So.2d 312 [177 EDUC. L. REP. 703] (Miss. Ct. App. 2003) (affirming that a board had the duty to protect a female student who was raped by two male peers under the ordinary care standard).

[179] *See, e.g.*, OHIO REV. CODE § 3319.41(C).

[180] *See, e.g.*, Landry v. Ascension Parish Sch. Bd., 415 So.2d 473 [4 EDUC. L. REP. 1361] (La. Ct. App. 1982) (affirming that a tenured teacher's dismissal was arbitrary and unreasonable where it was based on his displaying a gun in an attempt to defend himself from being physically attacked by a student with a 30-inch, two-by-four board).

[181] *See, e.g.*, Johnson v. Newburgh Enlarged Sch. Dist., 239 F.3d 246 (2d Cir. 2001) (rejecting a teacher's claim for qualified immunity where he assaulted a student who threw a baseball at him, but missed, as exceeding the bounds of legitimate self-defense); Parham v. Raleigh Cnty. Bd. of Educ., 453 S.E.2d 374 [97 EDUC. L. REP. 536] (W. Va. 1994) (affirming that a teacher could be suspended for ten days because in striking a student to keep him quiet and get his attention, he did not act in self-defense).

school personnel are not required to jeopardize their own physical safety in addressing aggressive student behaviors by waiting until they are attacked before responding.[182] As reflected by a case from New Mexico, in assessing reasonableness, courts consider "the need for the application of force, the relationship between the need and the amount of force that was used, the extent of injury inflicted or the reasonably foreseeable risk of serious bodily injury, and whether the force was applied in a good faith effort to maintain or restore discipline or maliciously and sadistically for the purpose of causing harm."[183] Once attackers are disarmed or neutralized, further aggressive actions by teachers are likely to result in liability.

Field Trips

Field trips have always raised legal concerns for educators because issues ordinarily associated with the relatively closed environments of schools are exacerbated by applying school rules in different settings. In their broadest definitions, field trips are sponsored excursions outside of schools including not only the usual range of academic-related trips such as museums, concerts, plays, and nature sites, but also extracurricular non-academic-related events including athletic events, class trips, music events, and picnics.

As a preliminary matter, organizers must address three issues when students go on school-sponsored activities: providing information, supervision, and emergencies. The most frequently used method of informing students and parents about field trips is consent forms signed by parents and returned to supervising teachers. Consent forms need to provide comprehensive information in sufficient detail, leaving parents with three options. First, parents can sign the forms as they are, with assurances that their children are to receive the same degree of reasonable care as if they were in school. Second, parents can refuse to sign the forms due to their opposition to some aspect of trips, such as their destinations. Third, parents can make further inquiries and perhaps request alterations, such as accommodations for the needs of their children.

As is evident from the form in the Appendix C, one cannot treat suggested permission slips for field trips as one-size-fits-all. Accordingly, school officials should not allow blanket approvals and should require separate forms for each trip or activity. The goal is to provide enjoyable and safe outings for participants. Thus, contacting officials at the places groups intend to visit is a prerequisite for organizers of field trips so those devising consent forms have the necessary information to develop appropriate documents.

---

[182] *See, e.g.,* Wallace v. Batavia Sch. Dist., 68 F.3d 1010 [104 EDUC. L. REP. 132] (7th Cir. 1995) (affirming that a teacher and board were not liable for the alleged injury to a student's elbow after she was twice asked to stop screaming at a peer and then grabbed by the elbow as the teacher directed her to the door).

[183] Gonzales v. Passino, 222 F. Supp. 2d 1277, 1282 [170 EDUC. L. REP. 705] (D.N.M. 2002) (affirming that a teacher's striking a student on the arm with a plastic bat after being insulted was not excessive force, because the plaintiff did not suffer a serious bodily injury).

Pivotal to safe and enjoyable trips is supervision, meaning the number of adult chaperones or supervisors present. Parents often act as chaperones, but their effectiveness depends on how well they follow instructions. While there is no magic number as to how many chaperones are required, a good rule of thumb is that the younger the students are, the greater the amount, and degree, of supervision needed. Moreover, children with special needs require greater supervision.[184] Organizers also need to take the nature of venues, such as amusement parks, as opposed to small contained locations such as movie theaters, into consideration.

New York's highest court reviewed a dispute wherein the a sixth-grade student sued her school board for injuries she sustained when an acquaintance raped her after they left the park where her class field trip gathered. The student did not return to the park by the designated departure time, or within the time the teacher searched for her, and went home rather than returning to school. While the teacher contacted the child's mother, he did not disclose the incident to school officials. The court affirmed that the board was liable because the rape was a foreseeable result of the danger created by the failure of educators to provide adequate supervision of the outing.[185]

A case from Illinois highlights the importance of the nature of venues. An appellate court affirmed that museum officials and two teachers who were supervising fifty children were not liable for injuries a 12-year-old student sustained on being assaulted there. The court agreed that insofar as the risk of being assaulted in the museum while unsupervised was minimal, to reach any other judgment "would well discourage schools and teachers from affording opportunities to children to enjoy many extracurricular activities."[186]

Conversely, an appellate court in New York affirmed the denial of a nonpublic school's motion for summary judgment in a case where peers assaulted a student while they were all on an overseas field trip.[187] The court agreed that material issues of fact precluded the board's motion for summary judgment as to whether educators were liable due to negligent supervision.

The ratio of supervisors to students is a more problematic concern. For instance, an appellate court in Louisiana affirmed that having one teacher accompanying eleven students with developmental delays from a school to a gymnasium three blocks away was inadequate after one of them was struck by a car and killed while crossing a street.[188]

In an earlier case involving supervision, a mother sued her school board on behalf of her daughter for injuries the child suffered when her wrist was slashed and her purse stolen at a school-sponsored showing of a documentary

---

[184] For an article on point, see Ralph D. Mawdsley, *Supervisory Standard of Care for Students with Disabilities*, 80 Educ. L. Rep. 779 (1993).

[185] Bell v. Board of Educ. of the City of N.Y., 665 N.Y.S.2d 42 [122 Educ. L. Rep. 1031] (N.Y. 1997), *on remand*, 671 N.Y.S.2d 499 (N.Y. App. Div. 1998).

[186] Mancha v. Field Museum of Natural History, 283 N.E.2d 899, 902 (Ill. App. Ct. 1972).

[187] Archbishop Stepinac High Sch., 729 N.Y.S.2d 538 [156 Educ. L. Rep. 665] (N.Y. App. Div. 2001).

[188] Foster v. Houston General Ins. Co., 407 So.2d 759 [1 Educ. L. Rep. 1402 (La. Ct. App. 1981).

film which she was compelled to attend. Affirming a judgment in favor of the plaintiffs, the Supreme Court of Minnesota agreed that while the board was not liable for the sudden, unanticipated misconduct of students, it was at fault because such behavior that probably could have been prevented if enough teachers were present.[189] Without setting a number that would have provided adequate supervision, the court rejected a ratio of one teacher to thirty-five students as inadequate, but did not identify what an acceptable ratio might have been.

A case from New York reveals that boards are not liable for all injuries students sustain on field trips. An appellate court ruled that a board was not liable when a kindergarten student who was on a field trip was hurt on being thrown from a hayride that hit a bump in the road.[190] The court pointed out that because the forty children on the ride were accompanied by twelve adults, one of whom was sitting right next to the child who tossed from the hayride, the board did not breach its duty of supervision in light of the unexpected, and unforeseeable, event.

School personnel responsible for organizing field trips must understandably be concerned about liability, knowing that courts engage in some second-guessing about trip preparations. Sometimes organizers take anticipatory steps for field trips which may not have prevented injuries, appear to reflect well on planning.

A tragic case involved a student's drowning while on a senior field trip. Before approving the field trip, the principal told the seniors that they could go swimming only if they furnished their own lifeguard. A physical education instructor, an excellent swimmer, accepted an invitation as one of three adults to join the outing to a beach without lifeguards at which a sign was posted, "Swim At Your Own risk." The student, while in the company of two peers, drowned as he swam toward a diving tank about forty yards from shore, on which was attached a sign reading "Off Limits," before the teacher could reach his location.

The Supreme Court of Kentucky affirmed that because the principal gave appropriate instructions, setting forth the conditions under which students could go on the class outing, he was not negligent with respect to the high school student's drowning, on the theory that harm was foreseeable.[191] The court was likely influenced by the principal's having directed the students to take someone along as a lifeguard.

A persistent issue for all schools is transporting students on field trips. Clearly, school buses or common carriers are the preferred choice if they have adequate insurance. When engaged in the risky proposition of having faculty members or parents transport participants in their vehicles, questions arise about whether the drivers are agents of the school. Creation of agency relationships depends on such variables as whether drivers used private cars

---

[189] Raleigh v. Indep. Sch. Dist. No. 625, 275 N.W.2d 572 (Minn. 1978).

[190] David v. City of N.Y., 835 N.Y.S.2d 377 [220 Educ. L. Rep. 792] (N.Y. App. Div. 2007).

[191] Cox v. Barnes, 469 S.W.2d 61 (Ky. 1971).

with the permission of and for the convenience of the schools; whether such use was standard school practice; and whether the schools reimbursed the driver for expenses.

In an illustrative case from Minnesota, the Eighth Circuit affirmed a grant of summary judgment in favor of two school boards that cosponsored a football team where a participant driving his own car to a practice at the other school struck a car, injuring the driver.[192] The court reasoned that insofar as the cosponsoring agreement created no special relationships for a higher degree of supervision than under the usual ordinary care negligence standard, the boards were not responsible for an injury that supervision would not have prevented.

For nonpublic educational institutions that lease or rent vehicles, often using untrained volunteers as drivers, a case from Louisiana provides a cautionary warning. A husband recovered on behalf of himself and his son for the death of his wife, a nursing student, when she was killed while on a mandatory field trip for all students for which she received academic credit. The woman died when the rented van she was riding in was in an accident. Affirming in favor of the husband, the court predicated liability on the failure of school officials to meet their "duty . . . to provide a driver qualified and trained in transporting a large group of students over a long distance on a heavily traveled interstate highway."[193]

Field trips can be rewarding for all participants. Yet, those in charge of trips should expect emergencies to arise. Simply because incidents are emergencies do not mean that they cannot be anticipated and plans of action prepared. Students on field trips can violate rules just like they can at school.

Prior to leaving for field trips, parent and students should have consented in writing to conduct guidelines, paralleling school guidelines, including specified disciplinary provisions. Forms should also include statements indicating that students can be sent home early on public carriers at the parents' expense. Of course, educators should exercise care in selecting modes of transportation and notify parents before sending students home.[194] Organizers should also be mindful of the venues of field trips, so as to be able to pay attention to safety details such as including trained lifeguards on trips to swimming activities; snake-bite kits on hikes to rocky or marshy areas; and/or stretchers, splints, and accomplished guides on hikes.

Medical Needs

Officials in nonpublic schools can expect to have children with medical needs in their student bodies. Chapters 8, on special education, and 10, on federal antidiscrimination statutes, review the IDEA and other important

---

[192] Gylten v. Swalboski, 246 F.3d 1139 [153 EDUC. L. REP. 35] (8th Cir. 2001).

[193] Whittington v. Sowela Tech. Instit., 438 So.2d 236, 247 [13 EDUC. L. REP. 1184] (La. Ct. App. 1983).

[194] Ette v. Linn-Mar Cmty. Sch. Dist., 656 N.W.2d 62 [173 EDUC. L. REP. 662] (Iowa 2002) (chiding officials for sending a misbehaving ninth-grader home alone from a band trip via an 1100-mile, cross-country bus trip).

laws impacting the medical needs of children in nonpublic schools, such as Section 504 of the Rehabilitation Act[195] and the Americans with Disabilities Act,[196] in greater detail.

Apart from the laws addressing the needs of students with disabilities, the responsibilities of officials in nonpublic schools are similar to those of their public school counterparts. Basically, officials are expected to act as reasonable and prudent persons who contact medical personnel for assistance when students need attention or, in some situations, anticipate medical needs and have appropriate staff or equipment available. Unless specifically educated to do so, school officials are not expected to administer assistance for which they are not trained or licensed and can be liable if untrained persons attempt to provide assistance and aggravate injuries.

Concerns about the proliferation of drug use in and around schools have led to policies requiring students to store their prescription drugs in school offices.[197] If school officials forbid students from carrying their medications and store them in controlled-temperature environments, educators need to devise policies and procedures for the safekeeping of these substances in school, along with parent consent forms for their administration.[198]

The extent to which officials in nonpublic schools can set restrictions on students with medications is questionable. In California, a federal trial court granted the request of parents of a child with asthma that officials in a Montessori school rescind their policy of neither providing medication to children nor administering inhalation medication to those in need. Enjoining the policy, the court decided that the child would have suffered an irreparable injury because his name would have gone on a waiting list at another school thereby delaying his "opportunity to get a head start on his education, and learn and play with other children his same age."[199] The court added that the parents were likely to prevail on the merits of the claim that the policy violated Title III of the ADA because preschools are places of public accommodation. Because Title III of the ADA exempts religious schools from its coverage,[200] this case should be of interest to educators in nonsectarian private schools.

A different medication administration issue is whether school officials have duties to students if their policies call for leaving their medications stored in school offices. This can be crucial because many nonpublic schools lack full-time nurses, thus administration of medications becomes the responsibility of principals, secretaries, and/or teachers.

---

[195] 29 U.S.C.A. § 794(a).

[196] 42 U.S.C.A. §§ 12101 et seq.

[197] For an article on point, see Charles J. Russo, Allan G. Osborne, & Pamela C. Young, *Guidelines for Safe Administration of Medications in Schools*, 317 Educ. L. Rep. 6 (2015).

[198] Appendix D is a Rhode Island regulation containing essential elements of a medication dispensation policy.

[199] Alvarez v. Fountainhead, 55 F. Supp.2d 1048, 1051 [137 Educ. L. Rep. 592] (N.D. Cal. 1999).

[200] 28 C.F.R. § 36.102(c) ("This part does not apply... to any religious entity....").

In light of the many questions that can emerge over dispensing prescription medications to students in nonpublic schools, it is imperative for officials to develop policies and review them annually to ensure that they are up-to-date with developments in state and federal law, as well as medical regimens. The following two paragraphs address the kinds of prescription medication-related questions that can come up in schools.

The first question concerns whether officials in nonpublic schools are responsible for assuring that students take only the prescribed amounts of their medications. Related questions address what happens if students fail to appear for their medications, whether educators have the duty to track them down and, if so, whether they use a means of communication preserving the confidential nature of the medication use. Another concern is what happens if students fail to appear and refuse to take their medications. This raises the question about the duties of school officials to notify parents in a timely manner.

An additional question is what happens if students are ready to take their medications, but no one who is qualified to supervise them is present to dispense them. A related issue ensues if students return to class without having taken their medications and forget to return.

Finally, if parents call school officials verbally seeking to change medication regimens for their children, educators should refuse to do so unless they have such requests in writing.

The more substantive question is the extent to which school control of medications imposes affirmative duties on educators to act. While school personnel can place exculpatory provisions in medication forms placing complete responsibility on students, a cogent argument can be made that possession imposes an obligation to act, one that would not be present if children were permitted to carry their own medications. After all, students are not storing their medications in school offices voluntarily. The better course of action is that school officials who wish to oversee what students do with their medications have a duty to act reasonably and contact students who fail to appear.

Procedures and the administration of medicines are usually governed by state laws concerning the practice of nursing and medicine.[201] Whether identified procedures must be performed by persons with specific licenses or training depends on state statutes or regulations.[202]

In a case involving a student with disabilities, *Cedar Rapids Community School District v. Garret F.*,[203] the Supreme Court observed that school officials should be able to provide related services that are medical in nature if they are

---

[201] *See, e.g.*, VA. CODE ANN. §§ 54.1-290A.26 [nor preventing] [a]ny employee of a school board, authorized by a prescriber and trained in the administration of insulin and glucagon, when, upon the authorization of a prescriber and the written request of the parents ..., assisting with the administration of insulin or administrating glucagon to a student diagnosed as having diabetes and who requires insulin injections during the school day or for whom glucagon has been prescribed for the emergency treatment of hypoglycemia;....

[202] *See, e.g.*, R.I. ADMIN. CODE 14-3-175:1.8C.1.

[203] 526 U.S. 66, 70 [132 EDUC. L. REP. 40] (1999) (noting that the child's parents performed various medical services during the school day).

performed by parents or members of the child's family. While lower courts may address the issue of medical licensure, it has not prevented the judiciary from imposing the duty to perform services on school personnel.[204] Despite concerns by nurses to limit non-nursing staff to functions not requiring nursing judgments where results are predictable, where safety is not an issue, and where improper performance is not life-threatening, the licensure issue of personnel performing medical/nursing functions has received scant judicial attention.

This discussion brings an important question to mind about the standard of care school officials must be provided if non-medically licensed personnel provide nursing or medical-type services. In such a case from Louisiana, an appellate court held that a biology instructor at a university who drew samples from students for blood-type analysis had to meet a medical standard of care. The instructor permitted students to take blood samples from each other while they were sitting on a stool. After a student had her blood sample extracted, she fell forward, breaking six teeth. The court commented that the instructor "owe[d] a duty to the volunteer patient or blood donor to see that the same precautions are taken for the safety and well-being of that patient as would be taken by licensed medical doctors in that locality." [205]

Courts have rarely suggested that non-medical personnel might be subject to the medical standard of care.[206] Still, educators should ensure that all persons responsible for caring for those with injuries or disabilities have received appropriate training on a continuing basis.

School officials have had one of three responses to the distribution or use of generic, nonprescription medications, such as aspirin: (1) prohibiting their distribution by school staff; (2) dispensing pills as requested by students; and (3) dispensing pills as permitted and/or requested by parents in writing. A broader question arises if students distribute these items.[207] Any good that might be done for students by dispensing generic, nonprescription pills such as aspirin or cough drops has been replaced by the zero-tolerance approach taken in many schools.

Officials in nonpublic schools have the opportunity to impose an element of common sense into what has become in many public schools a rigid, inflexible practice of no-distribution rules. While the rules against distribution

---

[204] *See, e.g.*, Irving Indep. Sch. Dist. v. Tatro, 486 U.S. 883 [18 EDUC. L. REP. 138] (1984) (allowing non-medically licensed personnel to perform clean intermittent catheterizations).

[205] Butler v. La. Bd. of Educ., 331 So.2d 192, 196 (La. Ct. App. 1976). *See also* Hebert v. LaRocca, 704 So.2d 331 [123 EDUC. L. REP. 416] (La. Ct. App. 1997) (affirming that a physician in a fellowship program met the standard requiring those in such positions to follow the instructions and directions of teaching physicians, perform tasks as assigned, and report anything which appears improper).

[206] *See, e.g.*, Orr v. Brigham Young Univ., 108 F.3d. 388 (D. Utah 1997) (refusing to treat football trainers who allegedly provided inadequate care as subject to the medical practice standard).

[207] Zero tolerance began as a national enforcement policy in 1980s to interdict the flow of illegal drugs into the United States. While courts were originally generally supportive of these policies, they became less so. *See* Charles J. Russo, *Has Time Expired for Zero Tolerance Policies?* SCH. BUS. AFFAIRS, June 2013 at 33-36 (2013).

of illegal substances are clearly vital concerns for schools, one must question the merits of implementing zero-tolerance policies that punish students for giving pain relief tablets to peers.[208] At the very least, officials in nonpublic schools have the chance to treat students as individuals and not confuse acts of kindness with illegality.

Child Abuse Reporting

All states have statutes requiring school personnel and other to report suspected child abuse.[209] In some states, reporting is required for all professionals associated with schools, while other jurisdictions identify specific categories of individuals who must report, such as principals, teachers, coaches, nurses, and counselors.

Perhaps the most significant change affecting reporting in nonpublic schools, largely in response to the sexual abuse cases in the Catholic Church, has been the increase in the number of states requiring clergy to report child abuse.[210] At least twenty-three states specifically identify clergy among those required to report child abuse; clergy are not named as mandated reporters, but may be included with the "any person" designation in another seven jurisdictions, while two states identify neither clergy nor "any person" as mandated reporters.[211]

The standard for reporting child abuse is normally a low threshold, something akin to "reason to believe" that an offense has occurred, without which individuals are not required to make reports. In such a case, an appellate court in Oregon affirmed that a counselor was entitled to have her job back because her board improperly fired her, insofar as she lacked "reasonable cause"[212] under state law to report suspected sexual abuse of a 17-year-old student.

As evidenced by a case from Arkansas, statutorily mandated reporters who fail to report suspected incidents of child abuse can be charged with criminal violations. An appellate court affirmed that a teacher's failure to make an immediate report about an inappropriate sexual relationship between an colleague and a student that began when the latter was 16 could be charged with a criminal violation of the law.[213] The court concluded that the student's

---

[208] *See* Safford Unified Sch. Dist. No. 1 v. Redding, 557 U.S. 364 (2009) (invalidating a strip search of a student for what was known to be over-the-counter medications).

[209] For a comprehensive list through 2015, see Child Welfare Information Gateway. Mandatory reporters of child abuse and neglect. Washington, D.C.: U.S. Department of Health and Human Services, Children's Bureau, 2016, available at https://www.childwelfare.gov/pubPDFs/manda.pdf

[210] Child Welfare Information Gateway. Clergy as mandatory reporters of child abuse and neglect. Washington, D.C.: U.S. Department of Health and Human Services, Children's Bureau, 2016, available at https://childwelfare.gov/topics/systemwide/laws-policies/statutes/manda/

[211] *See id.* at 3 for the lists of states.

[212] *See, e.g.*, Meier v. Salem-Keizer Sch. Dist., 392 P.3d 796, 789 (Or. Ct. App. 2017).

[213] Griffin v. Arkansas, 454 S.W.3d 262 (Ark Ct. App. 2015).

having turned 18 before the teacher learned of the relationship did not relieve her of her duty. [214]

Even if individuals who fail to report suspected child abuse avoid criminal sanctions, they may lose their jobs. In such a case from Arkansas, an appellate court affirmed that a school board had just and reasonable cause to dismiss a principal when for failing to report suspected abuse.[215]

Once officials of appropriate agencies receive reports of child abuse, their personnel must conduct investigations within set time periods.[216] As highlighted by a case from North Carolina, though, if agency officials overstep their boundaries, they can be subject to civil suits for damages. A federal trial court refused to dismiss constitutional claims that church leaders and members of their congregation filed against officials from the county's department of social services for allegedly violating their rights under the Establishment and Free Exercise clauses, as well as to free speech and association, plus a civil rights conspiracy grounded in religious animus.[217]

In an intrusive, long-term investigation into alleged child abuse that agency officials conducted over religious practices at the church, its officials proposed an agreement that would have limited parents and church members as to how they could pray for and with their children. The court refused to dismiss the plaintiffs' requests for declaratory judgment and injunctive relief.

Other statutory provisions attendant to reporting child abuse also come into play.

Disclosure of the names of those who report child abuse can be,[218] but is not always,[219] a criminal violation of the law. Further, state laws permitting

---

[214] For earlier cases, see, e.g. State v. Brown, 140 S.E.3d 51, 53 (Mo. 2004); State v. Motherwell, 788 P.2d 1066 (Wash. 1990). A search on Westlaw revealed that a significant number of these cases are not reported.

[215] Struble v. Blytheville Sch. Dist., 516 S.W.3d 269 [343 Educ. L. Rep. 1133] (Ark. Ct. App. 2017). For a like outcome, see Crenshaw v. Columbus City Sch. Dist. Bd. of Educ.2008 WL 802708 (Ohio Ct. App. 2008), *appeal not allowed*, 893 N.E.2d 516 (Ohio 2008). *But see* Taylor v. Bd. of Educ. of City of Chicago, 10 N.E.3d 383 (Ill. App, Ct. 2014) (remanding the claims of a former elementary school assistant principal who was retaliated against after reporting an alleged act of abuse a teacher perpetrated on a student; a new trial was necessary because as an at-will employee, it was unclear what damages the plaintiff suffered).

[216] See, e.g., N.Y. Civil. Serv. § 415. Reporting procedure: noting that "[o]ral reports shall be followed by a report in writing within forty-eight hours after such oral report;" Ohio Rev. Code Ann. § 2151.421(G)(1) Persons required to report injury or neglect; procedures on receipt of report (mandating an investigation within twenty-four hours of when a report is received).

[217] Words of Faith Fellowship v. Rutherford Cnty. Dep't of Social Servs., 329 F. Supp.2d 675 (W.D.N.C. 2004).

[218] *See* State v. Polashek, 646 N.W.2d 330 [166 Educ. L. Rep. 312] (Wis. 2002) (holding that disclosure of confidential information regarding the name of a person reporting child abuse is a strict liability offense, but the state has the burden of proving that the recipient of the information had no prior knowledge of it).

[219] *See* Golian v. New York City Admin. for Children Servs, 282 F. Supp.3d 718 [352 Educ. L. Rep. 160) (S.D.N.Y. 2017) (dismissing the claim of a teacher, as a mandated reporter of child abuse, that when officials of the city's administration for children services allegedly disclosed her identity, they violated her Fourteenth Amendment right to substantive due process).

public officials to investigate child abuse by interviewing children without parental notice or consent are usually not violations of parental rights to familial privacy.[220]

Jurisdictions in which clergy are mandatory reporters of child abuse may not have to reveal their records about counseling persons who are later charged with crimes if the information they obtained is protected by their states' clergy-penitent communications privilege.[221] Child abuse reporting statutes protect good faith reports from claims such as malicious prosecution, defamation, or negligence.[222] Laws do not provide immunity for child abuse reports made in bad faith.[223]

Whether failure to report can be the basis for a civil action for damages depends on the facts. A former student in a Catholic school whose father allegedly sexually and physically abused her sued the church that operated it, a priest, and a guidance counselor. The Supreme Court of Iowa affirmed a grant of summary judgment in favor of the priest because, even though there had been a factual basis as to whether the student told him specifically about the abuse, he was not required to report.[224] Although the statute required a "counselor" to make a report, it did not apply to the priest because his professional practice was that of a clergyman, not a counselor. As to the counselor, even though his job was identified among required reporters, the court agreed he was not civilly liable because absent evidence the student informed him about the abuse, he lacked a reasonable belief that it occurred.

On a different issue, a mother in Washington sued a school board and various officials after her daughter had a sexual relationship with one of the district's security guards. The court affirmed that the mother had an implied cause of action against the board to recover for her own injuries because she was hurt by knowing that the failure of officials to report the suspected abuse lead to the harm her daughter suffered.[225]

---

[220] *See* R.S. v. State, 459 N.W.2d 680 (Minn. 1990) (interpreting the state's interest in protecting victims of child abuse as outweighing a parental interest in familial privacy).

[221] *See, e.g.*, Nussbaumer v. State, 882 So.2d 1067 (Fla. Dist. Ct. App. 2004); Doe v. Corp. of the President of the Church of Latter Day Saints, 90 P.3d 1147 (Wash. Ct. App. 2004). *But see* State v. Glenn, 62 P.3d 921 (Wash. Ct. App. 2003) (commenting in dicta that the clergy-penitent privilege does not prevent pastors from voluntarily reporting child abuse); In re S.D., 66 P.3d 462 (Okla. Civ. App. 2002) (abrogating the privilege to the extent it conflicted with mandatory reporting of child abuse).

[222] *See, e.g.*, OHIO REV. CODE ANN. § 2151.421(H)(1) Persons required to report injury or neglect. See also O'Heron v. Blaney, 583 S.E.2d 834 (Ga. 2003); Liedtke v. Carrington, 763 N.E.2d 213 [161 EDUC. L. REP. 958] (Ohio Ct. App. 2001).

[223] *See, e.g.*, COLO. REV. STAT. ANN. § 19-3-309 Immunity from liability--persons reporting ("Any person... participating in good faith in the making of a report, ... shall be immune from any liability, civil or criminal, or termination of employment that otherwise might result by reason of such acts of participation, unless a court of competent jurisdiction determines that such person's behavior was willful, wanton, and malicious.").

[224] Wilson v. Darr, 553 N.W.2d 579 [113 EDUC. L. REP. 419] (Iowa 1996).

[225] Evans v. Tacoma Sch. Dist. No. 10, 380 P.3d 553 [335 EDUC. L. REP. 1143] (Or. Ct. App. 2016), *review denied*, 385 P.3d 124 (Wash. 2016).

Conclusion

Compliance with the rules of tort law does not guarantee that educational leaders in nonpublic schools can avoid all legal liability. However, the more carefully educational leaders, working in conjunction with their attorneys and boards, impress the need to follow these directions on teachers and other staff members by providing ongoing professional development activities and modeling legally sound behaviors and practices, then the more likely they are to avoid costly litigation, while keeping all members of their school communities safer.

Discussion Questions

1. What do you think are the most significant differences between intentional torts and negligence?

2. In light of the material discussed in this chapter, how effective are your school's policies with regard to
    A. Assault and battery, particularly as the deal with the use or prohibition of corporal punishment and/or touching children so as to avoid allegations of sexual misconduct with students.
    B. Defamation, especially with regard to letters of recommendation.
        1) More specifically, can anyone write letters of recommendation for colleagues who are pursuing other job opportunities either because their contracts were not renewed or they are leaving of their own accord?
        2) Should there be limits on who can write letters or recommendation? Please explain why you answered as you did.
        3) Student supervision? Have you ever had a professional development session on the rules of negligence and adequate supervision? If not, should such sessions be offered at your school?

3. Did you receive instruction on the legal dimensions of torts, including negligence and adequate supervision, as a pre-service teacher? If not, do you recommend the adoption of such a course at the institution you attended?

Key Words

Assumption of risk
Charitable immunity
Consent
Contributory negligence
Comparative negligence
Defenses
Field trips
Intentional torts
Negligence
Strict liability

Appendix A

Guidelines for officials in nonpublic schools using corporal punishment:
1. Provide notice to students and parents of the kinds of conduct that may result in corporal punishment along with notice to parents when paddling is to be administered.
2. Use corporal punishment as a last resort. Instead, emphasize alternative means of modifying student behavior, including perhaps some of the behavior-modification strategies used for children with behavioral disabilities.
3. Investigate denials of fault prior to administering corporal punishment.
4. Designate only one person in the school to administer corporal punishment.
5. Have a witness present when administering corporal punishment.
6. Limit punishment to not more than three swats on the buttocks.
7. Do not paddle children in daycare, preschool, or kindergarten programs or in grades where students do not understand the relationship between physical punishment and their (mis)behavior.
8. Notify parents after the third time their children have been subjected to corporal punishment and set up a meeting with students' teacher, an administrator, a counselor, and the parent(s). If children are old enough to understand why the meetings are taking place, they may be invited to attend.

Appendix B

Suggestions to increase the safety awareness of teachers
1. Schools should hold at least one faculty and staff in-service day at the beginning of each school year to help develop a preventive rather than a reactive approach to student safety.
2. School administrators should encourage teachers to establish partnerships with adjoining teachers to help watch classes during the emergency absence of a teacher.
3. Teachers in high-risk equipment areas should test each student on each piece of equipment and have each student sign a set of course safety rules before being permitted to use the equipment.
4. Teachers should provide periodic oral refresher instructions to students regarding safety equipment.
5. Teachers should instruct students to report safety hazards and dangerous situations such as water on the floor, broken stair treads, glass or sharp objects on the playground, malfunctioning equipment, and strangers in the building.

6. Schools should permit teachers and other staff to supervise activities only if their qualifications are appropriate for the level of risk of the subject area being supervised.

7. Schools should require that all teachers have a published protocol regarding class expectations whenever an emergency occurs, practicing that protocol at least once each semester.

Appendix C

Suggested permission slip for a field trip

1. Description of Field Trip (identify place to be visited, method of transport, type and time of supervision, time and place of departure and return).

2. Objectives of Field Trip (if academic-related, describe objectives and how they may relate to coursework in school: tour factory and observe automation, assembly line for history class; hike along river [identify name of river and approximate location on river] or in mountains [identify mountain and approximate location on mountain] or along seashore [describe name and location] to observe flowers, erosion, birds, fish, soil for science class); view a play [identify name of play and venue]). (if extracurricular/ non-academic related, identify purpose of trip and location: volleyball game [identify venue]; class picnic [identify location]).

3. Provisions Needed (The list will depend on the venue and the nature of the activity, but may include lunch, special items of clothing, student items necessary for participation such as musical instruments or uniforms, text or note books, money, medications, insect repellent, sun block.)

4. Instructions to be given to students by Parent and Teachers
a) Emphasis on safety/security, such as students staying with the group and reporting dangerous or hazardous situations to a supervisor.
b) Information provided by the venue to be visited, which can include maps, location of important features such as restrooms, and special rules unique to that venue, such as in the case of a nature site, staying on the walk ways.
c) Applicability of school rules/policies which can include, on one hand, reinforcement that certain rules will apply the same to field trips as to school such as use of alcohol, drugs, tobacco, profanity, and, on the other hand, rules for which modifications might be made such as the dress code.
d) Other instructions teachers wish to include.

5. By signing the form, I (parent or guardian; please circle one)
    certify that I request and give my permission for my child
    _____ (please print the child's name) to go
    on this field trip. I have read the instructions above and release
    the teacher, principal, and school from all liability and waive any
    claims against them.

_____

Please print the parent's name

_____

Parent Signature   Date

Appendix D

Regulation containing essential elements of a medication dispensation
policy
    R.I. Admin. Code 14-3-175:1.8C.1

C. Medication Administration
    1. Prescribed and non-prescribed (over the counter) medication is not
    administered to a child without:
        a. written permission from the parent/guardian; and
        b. a written order from a licensed physician, physician's assistant,
        or nurse practitioner (which may include the label on the medi-
        cation) indicating that the medicine is for a specified child. The
        medication must be in the original container.
            (1) The written order includes the name of the child, the name of
            the medication, circumstances under which it may be adminis-
            tered, route, dosage, and frequency of administration.
    2. The Child Care or School Age Administrator or designee dispenses
    all medications
    3. A daily log is maintained of every medication administered. This
    record includes the:
        a. child's name;
        b. name and dosage of medication administered;
        c. date and time administered;
        d. name and signature of the person who administered the medica-
        tion; and
        e. name of the licensed physician, physician's assistant, or nurse
        practitioner prescribing the medication.
    4. The medication log is transported with the child to the emergency
    treatment facility in the event of an emergency.

5. The first dose of a medication must be administered by the parent/guardian.

6. Medications are stored:

    a. in clearly labeled original containers;

    b. in spaces secured with child safety locks that are separate from any items that attract children; and

    c. in a way that does not contaminate play surfaces or food preparation areas.

6

School Safety

R. Stewart Mayers

Contents

Introduction / 164
State and Local Safety Codes / 165
     Religious Land Use and Institutionalized Persons Act / 167
     Zoning Codes / 167
Higher Education Crime Reporting / 168
Crisis Management Plans / 171
Persistently Dangerous Schools / 173
     School Safety and the Every Student Succeeds Act / 174
Student Searches / 175
     Generally / 175
     Defining Contraband / 176
     T.L.O. Reasonableness Standard / 176
     Contractual Language Authorizing Searches / 177
     Suspicionless Searches / 178
     Zero Tolerance Policies / 178
     Source of Information / 179
     Scope of Search / 180
          Intrusiveness / 180
          Age and Sex / 181
          Nature of Infraction / 182
     Special Types of Searches / 183
          Field Trips/Activities Outside of Schools / 183
          Car/Vehicle Searches / 186
          Metal Detectors / 187
          Sniff Dogs / 188
          Strip Searches / 189
          Breath Analysis / 191
          Cell Phone Searches / 191
          Cyber Speech / 192
Recommendations for Practice / 193
Drug Testing / 194
     Drug Testing Policies / 195
Employee Searches and Drug Testing / 198
     Employee Searches / 198
     Electronic Surveillance / 199

Suspicionless Searches / 200
Searches of Employee Computers / 200
Guidelines for Employee Searches / 200
Employee Drug Testing / 201
Conclusion / 202
Discussion Questions / 203
Key Words / 204

Introduction

According to a 2015 survey of ninth- to twelfth-graders conducted by the Centers for Disease Control, 7.8% of students reported having been in physical fights on school grounds, 6% said they were threatened or harmed by some type of weapon, and 20.2% responded that they were bullied on school property. Another 15.5% of students reported being cyberbullied.[1] While accurate numbers of school shootings on PK-20 campuses can be difficult to locate, one site reports that 146 such incidents occurred between 2000 and March 2018, including the tragedy at Parkland (Florida) High School, resulting in 158 deaths and 246 injuries.[2] Moreover, a recent study reveals that the majority of teenagers fear that shootings can occur at their schools.[3]

School safety also involves compliance with building, health, and safety codes. Today, a key duty of school officials is to design emergency evacuation plans, as well as to engage in both individualized suspicion and suspicionless searches of students on school property and possibly in school-sponsored extra-curricular activities. Consequently, much of this chapter discusses the roles of educational officials in the difficult and highly litigious area of school searches.

Most of the litigation involving school safety focuses on students. Even so, school officials have an equal responsibility to protect employees. One obvious difference between students and employees is that school emergency plans require the active participation of employees in lockdown or evacuation situations.

Risk factors in schools also relate to such items as compliance with electrical and building codes. At the same time, risk factors increase in direct proportion to the amount of time school officials have custody of students. When parents entrust their children to the care of educators, or when individuals who reached their age of majority enroll in institutions of higher learning,

---

[1] Center for Disease Control, Understanding School Violence Fact Sheet 2016. Retrieved from https://www.cdc.gov/violenceprevention/pdf/school_violence_fact_sheet-a.pdf

[2] Statistic Brain Research Institute Mass Shooting Statistics. Retrieved from https://www.statisticbrain.com/school-shooting-statistics/

[3] See Nikki Graf, *A majority of U.S. teens fear a shooting could happen at their school, and most parents share their concern*, Pew Research Center, April 18, 2018, Retrieved from http://www.pewresearch.org/fact-tank/2018/04/18/a-majority-of-u-s-teens-fear-a-shooting-could-happen-at-their-school-and-most-parents-share-their-concern/?utm_source=Pew+Research+Center&utm_campaign=04bca95fdf-EMAIL_CAMPAIGN_2018_04_18&utm_medium=email&utm_term=0_3e953b9b70-04bca95fdf-400258905.

they expect officials in charge to have anticipated potential risks and either eliminated them or, if that is not possible, minimized them while providing appropriate notices. Certainly, while school officials cannot ever guarantee that their educational institutions are 100% safe, they should be able to anticipate problems and act preemptively to reduce the likelihood that the accompanying risks will result in injuries to students and/or employees.

State and Local Safety Codes

All states and municipalities have zoning and building codes applicable not only to the construction of physical structures, but also to the location and installation of electrical, plumbing, heating, air conditioning, and other services. Code requirements vary considerably among jurisdictions, but invariably apply to both new construction and renovations. Generally, these codes obligate school officials and/or builders to secure permits prior to new construction and alterations, along with inspections during and at the completion of those changes. The permits mandate payments of fees and the involvement of inspectors who are generally paid, as well as employed, by municipalities, counties, and/or states.

In many nonpublic schools, parents and perhaps even students have service commitments to perform construction and/or alteration tasks so schools can save money by not incurring the expense of paying outside contractors. Having volunteers perform these tasks cannot substitute for satisfying permit and inspection requirements. Work not meeting code standards represents risks to students and employees, while injuries resulting from such unapproved modifications can subject school officials to civil and even criminal sanctions.

Some localities exempt religious schools from selected code requirements, resulting in constitutional challenges. In a case from Maryland that reached the Fourth Circuit, homeowners challenged whether a county building code exception for schools located on land owned or leased by churches or religious organizations violated the Establishment Clause. For nonreligious educational institutions, the code mandated the filing of petitions containing specified information, including a statement explaining "in detail how the special exception is proposed to be operated"[4] and supported by a plat, drawings, and a site plan for the proposed construction.

Under state law, officials could only have granted the petition after public notice and a hearing at which residents could testify. The Board of Appeals could grant special-exception petitions only if it decided that uses by private schools would not constitute nuisances and that the changes would be "housed in buildings architecturally compatible with other buildings in the surrounding neighborhood." In addition, the Board had to be convinced that the exception would not "affect adversely or change the present character or future develop-

---

[4] Ehlers-Renzi v. Connelly Sch. of the Holy Child, 224 F.3d 283, 286 [148 Educ. L. Rep. 574] (4th Cir. 2000).

ment of the surrounding residential community," and that it "can and will be developed in conformity with" various specified requirements.[5]

On further review of an order invalidating the code as violating the Establishment Clause, the Fourth Circuit relied heavily on *Amos v. Corporation of the Presiding Bishop*[6] in ruling that the code did not violate the tripartite *Lemon v. Kurtzman*[7] test. As the court observed in citing *Amos*, "the government is entitled to accommodate religion without violating the Establishment Clause, and at times the government must do so."[8] In fact, the court's acknowledgment of the code's secular purpose under the first prong of the *Lemon* test is worth noting:

> The exemption from the special exception requirement relieves Connelly School from having to justify its religious or religion-related needs before civil authorities and convince those authorities that the school's renovations and additions satisfy such subjective requirements as, for example, "architectural[ ] compatib[ility]" or conformity with "the present character ... of the community." Would a cross on a building offend citizens in the neighborhood? Would Gothic windows offend a neighborhood that was determined to maintain an American colonial style? Would a chapel or chapel bell or chapel organ offend? The exemption also extricates Montgomery County from the resolution of disputes that could have a religious underpinning. Would citizen challenges actually be cloaking anti-religion or anti-denomination animosity? In short, the low threshold of this first Lemon prong is readily cleared by the Zoning Ordinance's plausible purpose of extricating Montgomery County from these involvements in religion.[9] ... In sum, building codes providing exemptions for private schools on religiously owned land do not violate the Establishment Clause where their effect is "simply allowing a religious school to "better ... advance [their] purposes."[10]

---

[5] *Id.* at 286 (county building code sections omitted).

[6] 483 U.S. 327 (1987) (upholding a change to Title VII expanding its protection for religious exemptions to "activities" as opposed to "religious activities.")

[7] 403 U.S. 602, 612-13 (1973) (invalidating state statutes providing pay supplements to teachers in nonpublic schools who taught secular subjects using a three-part test; under this test, governmental action must "[first] have a secular legislative purpose; second, its principal or primary effect must be one that neither advances nor inhibits religion; finally, the statute must not foster 'an excessive government entanglement with religion.'").

[8] *Ehlers-Renzi*, 224 F.3d at 287, citing to *Amos*, 483 U.S. at 338.

[9] *Id.* at 289.

[10] *Id.* at 291, quoting from *Amos*, 483 U.S. at 336.

Other courts have upheld building code distinctions between private and religious schools as not violating the Establishment Clause.[11]

Religious Land Use and Institutionalized Persons Act

Religious educational organizations have also challenged adverse zoning orders under the Religious Land Use and Institutionalized Persons Act (RLUIPA),[12] pursuant to which

> [n]o government shall impose or implement a land use regulation . . . that imposes a substantial burden on the religious exercise of a person, including a religious assembly or institution, unless the government demonstrates that imposition of the burden . . . (A) is in furtherance of a compelling governmental interest; and (B) is the least restrictive means of furthering that compelling governmental interest.[13]

The cases have met with mixed results, as religious institutions prevailed in some,[14] but not all, disputes.[15]

Zoning Codes

Litigation involving zoning requirements admittedly does not raise safety issues as dramatically as the topics discussed in the balance of this chapter. Even so, these disputes do reflect a climate regarding the treatment of nonpublic, especially religious, schools. Clearly, nonpublic schools should not be subjected to zoning and building safety requirements harsher than those applicable to other kinds of building requests.

Zoning codes accommodate the use of facilities in conformity with religious beliefs and practices, such as where religious schools are integral parts of houses of worship. Still, accommodations of this type should not undercut other code requirements dealing with fire and health that clearly address matters of safety. Whether in new construction or alterations of existing buildings,

---

[11] *See* Association of Zone A and B Homeowners' Subsidiary v. Zoning Bd., 749 N.Y.S.2d 68 [171 Educ. L. Rep. 329] (N.Y. App. Div. 2002); Forest Hills Early Learning Ctr. v. Grace Baptist Church, 846 F.2d 260 [46 Educ. L. Rep. 1123] (4th Cir. 1988); Creative Cnty. Day Sch. of Sandy Spring v. Montgomery Cnty. Bd. of Appeals. 219 A.2d 789 (Md. 1966). *See also* Jobe v. City of Orange, 105 Cal. Rptr. 2d 782 [152 Educ. L. Rep. 185] (Cal. Ct. App. 2001) (ruling that a religious school that prevailed in a challenge from a neighbor to changes to its property that were approved by city officials was not entitled to attorney fees under state law as the prevailing party).

[12] 42 U.S.C. §§ 2000cc – 2000cc-5.

[13] 42 U.S.C. §§ 2000cc(a)(1)(A), (B).

[14] For cases decided in favor of religious institutions, see, e.g., Grace Methodist Church v. City of Cheyenne, 235 F. Supp.2d 1186 (D. Wyo. 2002); Westchester Day Sch. v. Village of Mamaroneck, 504 F.3d 338 [226 Educ. L. Rep. 595] (2d Cir. 2007); Tree of Life Christian Schs. v. City of Upper Arlington, 823 F.3d 365 [332 Educ. L. Rep. 1] (6th Cir. 201), *reh'g denied.*

[15] For cases resolved in favor of public officials, see, e.g., Westchester Day Sch. v. Village of Mamaroneck, 386 F.3d 183 (2d Cir. 2004); Corporation of Presiding Bishop of Church of Jesus Christ of Latter Day Saints v. City of West Linn, 111 P.3d 1123 (Or. 2005).

officials in nonpublic schools can ill afford to compromise the safety of their students and staffs by having fire and safety practices that put their children at greater risk than their counterparts in public schools.

In its *Update on the Justice Department's Enforcement of the RLUIPA: 2010-2016*,[16] the United States Department of Justice (DOJ) reported that practitioners of minority faiths and Christian congregations comprised of racial minorities were particularly vulnerable to discrimination with regard to zoning issues. Moreover, since 2010, nearly half (49%) of all DOJ investigations have involved the disparate treatment of religious versus nonreligious groups.[17]

A case from Mississippi provides a good example of discrimination against a church. City officials informed church leaders who needed a larger meeting space for their congregation that they could not occupy the space they rented without the approval of at least 60% of property owners within a 1300-foot radius of their location, a condition inapplicable to nonreligious groups. Reversing the earlier denial of the church leaders' request for an injunction, the Fifth Circuit explained that the congregation established a prima facie case for unequal treatment under RLUIPA, and that it would have suffered irreparable harm had its request not been granted.[18]

Higher Education Crime Reporting

In 1990, Congress enacted the Crime Awareness and Campus Security Act, also known as the Clery Act.[19] This Act requires officials in institutions of higher learning to implement procedures for students and others to report crimes, programs to inform students about crime prevention, and to collect data about criminal offenses on campuses. Under this law, the duty to report crimes applies to officials on campuses and in facilities owned by institutions of higher learning, as well as to public property such as sidewalks, streets, and/or parking lots in reasonably contiguous areas.

Pursuant to the Clery Act, campus officials must report crimes including criminal homicides; murders and non-negligent manslaughters; negligent manslaughters; manslaughter; sex offenses, whether forcible or non-forcible; robberies; aggravated assaults; burglaries; motor vehicle thefts; arsons; and arrests of persons referred for disciplinary action involving liquor-law violations, drug-related violations, and weapons possession.[20] If institutions have more than one campus, reports must be made separately for each campus.[21] The Secretary of Education can fine officials, and their institutions of higher education, up to $25,000 for each violation or misrepresentation if they sub-

---

[16] Retrieved from https://www.justice.gov/crt/file/877931/download

[17] *Id*. at 6.

[18] Opulent Life Church v. City of Holly Springs, MS, 697 F.3d 279 (5th Cir. 2012).

[19] 20 U.S.C. § 1092(f). The act was named after Jeanne Clery, a college student who was raped and murdered by a peer in her residence dormitory in 1986.

[20] 20 U.S.C. § 1092a(f)(F)(1)(f)(i).

[21] 34 C.F.R. § 668.46(d).

stantially misrepresent the number, location, or nature of the crimes on which they must report.[22]

In 1994, Congress enacted the Campus Sex Crimes Prevention Act as part of the Violent Crime Control and Law Enforcement Act, effective in 1996.[23] The act obligates sex offenders to register under state laws and to report to appropriate state agencies, while notifying officials in institutions of higher education in which they work or attend as students; individuals must also report changes in their status. In response to these statutes, some states required that the names of sex offenders be posted on the Internet.[24] Moreover, Congress amended the Family Educational Rights and Privacy Act[25] to permit officials in postsecondary institutions to disclose information about registered sex offenders under state law.[26]

In *Smith v. Doe*,[27] the Supreme Court upheld a state law from Alaska requiring sex offenders to register and have their names placed in a registry on the Internet. In a companion case, *Connecticut Department of Public Safety v. Doe*,[28] the Court rejected the liberty clause due process claims a convicted sex offender raised when officials of a state agency posted his name on the Internet. Responding to the claimant's argument that he was no longer danger-ous, the Justices wrote that "the due process clause does not entitle [plaintiff] to establish a fact—that he is not currently dangerous—that is not material under the statute. [T]he law's requirements turn on an offender's conviction alone—a fact that a convicted offender has already had a procedurally safe-guarded opportunity to contest."[29]

One can argue that *Smith v. Doe* and *Connecticut Department of Public Safety v. Doe* have eliminated concerns about the privacy rights of persons who are past sex offenders. As such, where information about specific sex offenders is made public, institutional officials presumably now have a duty to make students aware of their presence on campuses.

The state laws at issue before the Supreme Court were enacted in response to opinions such as one handed down by New York's highest court. The court reversed the imposition of liability on a university whose officials admitted a convicted felon after he served his sentence, who later raped and murdered another student while in attendance.[30] The court sought to balance the benefits

---

[22] 20 U.S.C. § 1094(c)(3)(B).

[23] 42 U.S.C. § 170101.

[24] *See* Wayne Logan, *Megan's Laws as a Case Study in Political Stasis*, 61 Syracuse L. Rev. 371 (2010) (discussing the federal statutes requiring sex offenders to register). For a list of the statutes, see Julia T. Rickert, *Denying Defendants the Benefit of a Reasonable Doubt: Federal Rule of Evidence 609 and Past Sex Crime Convictions*, 100 J. Crim. L. & Criminology 213, 235, n. 106 (2010).

[25] 20 U.S.C. § 1232g (b)(7)(A)

[26] 42 U.S.C. §§ 14072 (e), (j).

[27] 538 U.S. 84 (2003).

[28] 538 U.S. 1 (2003).

[29] *Id*. at 7.

[30] Eiseman v. State, 518 N.Y.S.2d 608 [41 Educ. L. Rep. 275] (N.Y. 1987).

to the felon to pursue his education and the rights of other students to be free from harm. The court was of the view that insofar as allowing a released felon to attend the university constituted a discretionary function, entitling the institution to immunity, its officials had no duty to restrict his activities on campus or to warn other students.

President Barack Obama signed the Violence Against Women Reauthorization Act of 2013, amending the Clery Act through the Campus Sexual Violence Elimination Act of 2013 (or the Campus SaVE Act).[31] The SaVE Act covers students and employees of educational institutions while expanding the requirements for reporting sexual violence. Specifically, the SaVE Act added domestic violence, dating violence, and stalking to the list of criminal offenses that officials of institutions of higher education must report to appropriate state authorities.

According to federal law,

> [t]he term "domestic violence" includes felony or misdemeanor crimes of violence committed by a current or former spouse or intimate partner of the victim, by a person with whom the victim shares a child in common, by a person who is cohabitating with or has cohabited with the victim as a spouse or intimate partner, by a person similarly situated to a spouse of the victim under the domestic or family violence laws of the jurisdiction receiving grant monies, or by any other person against an adult or youth victim who is protected from that person's acts under the domestic or family violence laws of the jurisdiction.[32]

> Federal law further defines "[t]he term "dating violence" to mean violence committed by a person

> (A) who is or has been in a social relationship of a romantic or intimate nature with the victim; and

> (B) where the existence of such a relationship shall be determined based on a consideration of the following factors:

> (i) the length of the relationship,

> (ii) the type of relationship, and

> (iii) the frequency of interaction between the persons involved in the relationship.[33]

Additionally, the Campus SaVE Act amended the Higher Education Act of 1965 by adding sexual orientation and sexual identity to the list of protected

---

[31] 42 U.S.C. § 13925, now codified at 34 U.S.C. §§ 12291 *et seq.*

[32] 34 U.S.C. § 12291(a)(8).

[33] 34 U.S.C. § 12291(a)(10).

categories. Accordingly, institutional officials must offer primary prevention programs, including statements prohibiting

> larceny-theft, simple assault, intimidation, and destruction, damage, or vandalism of property, and of other crimes involving bodily injury to any person, in which the victim is intentionally selected because of the actual or perceived race, gender, religion, national origin, sexual orientation, gender identity, ethnicity, or disability of the victim that are reported to campus security authorities or local police agencies, which data shall be collected and reported according to category of prejudice;[34]

Crisis Management Plans

Nonpublic educational institutions are no different from their public counterparts in that they need to have operational plans in place for evacuations and/or lockdowns, as needed. Many states have enacted legislation obligating local school boards to adopt safety plans. Because not all state plans are comprehensive, though, educators need to devise policies for crisis intervention, as well as emergency management and responses.[35]

In some states, officials in both public and nonpublic schools must devise safety policies and plans. Even if not required to do so, officials in nonpublic schools would be wise to adopt safety plans like their public counterparts. Officials in nonpublic schools may want to consider the following suggestions in drafting or revising their crisis management plans:

1. Involve all teachers and support staff, plus the school's attorney, parents, as well as local police and first responders who have experience dealing with crises, in the design, implementation, and review of plans, including practice exercises.

2. Encourage a heightened awareness of suspicious persons on school premises, of packages or other objects at school, of threats by students or others, and of unauthorized vehicles in parking lots, mandating the reporting of these suspicions to school staff.

---

[34] 20 U.S.C. § 1092(F)(f)(ii).

[35] *See, e.g.,* CAL. EDUC. CODE § 32282.5 (disaster preparedness); GA. CODE ANN., § 20-2-1185; 105 ILCS 5/10-20.32 (school safety plans); KY. REV. STAT. § 158.163 (limited to tornados and earthquakes); MISS. CODE ANN. § 37-3-83 (school safety grant program); NEV. REV. STAT. §§ 388.229 et seq. (school crisis plans); N.Y. MCKINNEY'S EDUC. LAW § 2801-a (district wide safety plans); OHIO REV. CODE § 3313.536 (comprehensive emergency management plans); 70 OKLA. STAT. ANN. § 5-148 (school security drills); RHODE ISLAND STAT. § 16-21-23 (about school safety teams); UTAH CODE ANN. § 53A-3-40218)(a) (comprehensive emergency response plan); VA Code Ann. (§ 22.1-279.8 (school safety audits; school crisis, emergency management, and medical emergency response plans) required; WASH. REV. CODE ANN. § 28A.320.125 (safe school plans).

3. Designate persons to supervise high-density and high-traffic areas in schools, particularly before and after school in parking lots and bus areas, as well as during recess.

4. Control the entrances to schools, limiting entrances to one door.

5. Ask a school nurse and other medical professionals to assess the medical preparedness of the schools in order to determine what medical supplies and equipment needs to be stored.

6. Prepare emergency communication mechanisms including how to notify teachers; contacting law enforcement officers, fire, medical, and other first responder personnel; and informing parents.

7. Identify potentially dangerous or hazardous sites in each school—including electrical, gas, heating, ventilation, water supply and sewage system locations and shut-off valves, and storage areas for cleaning supplies and chemicals—and have them regularly checked by safety personnel.

8. Because crisis management plans need to include provisions for both lockdowns, in the event of external threats or intruders, as well as evacuation procedures, in the event of such catastrophes as fire, both need to be practiced regularly so staff and students know what to do and where to go in emergencies.

9. Include material on safety plans in faculty and student handbooks, as well as in materials sent home to parents and placed on school websites.

10. Educate students, staff, and parents about the importance of school safety, and provide appropriate training to all school personnel.

11. Create crisis management teams to review plans annually.

A pair of cases from Georgia illustrates the issues that can arise as to whether school officials met a state requirement to have a safety plan in place after a student was attacked on the premises. The court held that since the preparation of such a plan was a ministerial, or mandatory, function rather than discretionary, the board was liable.[36]

Two years later, though, the Supreme Court of Georgia reached the opposite result in treating safety plans as discretionary.[37] The court reasoned that the safety plans, reflecting the contributions of a community-wide management team, satisfied state law even though the board had not officially approved the final policy. The court treated the plans as falling within the broad requirements of state law, refusing to invalidate them because they were developed by third parties rather than by the board and the superintendent, inasmuch as it was a discretionary duty.

---

[36] Leake v. Murphy, 644 S.E.2d 328 [220 EDUC. L. REP. 377] (Ga. Ct. App. 2007).

[37] Murphy v. Bajjani, 647 S.E.2d 54 [221 EDUC. L. REP. 904] (Ga. 2007).

Persistently Dangerous Schools

On December 10, 2015, President Obama signed the Every Child Succeeds Act (ESSA)[38] into law, effectively ending the era of No Child Left Behind Act (NCLB). The ESSA, like the NCLB, requires officials in each state to report public schools that are "persistently dangerous."[39] While these reports must be filed with appropriate authorities in each state, the responsibility rests generally with officials of local boards to notify parents in "persistently dangerous" schools of their status and the right to transfer their children to safer learning environments.[40]

A shortcoming of the ESSA, like the NCLB, is that it leaves the definition of what constitutes "persistently dangerous" up to a wide array of state laws. States differ not only as to the crimes that count in determining "persistently dangerous," but also as to the length of time during which crimes occur before schools are so identified.[41] In Illinois, for example, a school is "persistently dangerous" only if it meets the following three requirements for two consecutive years:

1. [H]ave greater than 3% of the students enrolled in the school expelled for violence-related conduct;
2. [H]ave one or more students expelled for bringing a firearm to school ...; and
3. [H]ave at least 3% of the students enrolled in the school exercise the individual option to transfer schools ... [because they were] a victim of a violent crime ... that must have occurred on school grounds during regular school hours or during a school-sponsored event.[42]

Pursuant to the ESSA, students in schools identified as "persistently dangerous," or who are victims of "a violent criminal offense, as determined by State law, while in or on the grounds of a public elementary school or secondary school that the student attends, [must] be allowed to attend a safe public elementary school or secondary school within the local educational agency, including a public charter school."[43]

---

[38] 20 U.S.C.A. §§ 6301 *et seq.*

[39] 20 U.S.C. § 7912(a).

[40] *See, e.g.,* N.Y. EDUC. LAW § 2802(7)(c) (requiring notification by local board officials but not mandating parental notification if "there are no other public schools within the local educational agency at the same grade level or such transfer to a safe public school within the local educational agency is otherwise impossible.")

[41] *See, e.g.,* N.H. REV. STAT. ANN. § 193-G:1 (a school is "persistently dangerous" only if three of the specified acts occurred as separate incidents during the course of one school year for three consecutive years and during regular school hours, at school-sponsored activities, or while transported by the school, homicide, first, or second-degree assault, aggravated sexual felonious assault, arson, robbery as a class A felony, unlawful possession, or use of a firearm or other dangerous weapon.)

[42] 105 ILL. COMP. STAT. ANN. 5/10-21.3a(a)(1)-(3).

[43] 20 U.S.C. § 7912(a).

While state laws can provide the right to transfer, they can restrict the choices available to parents. For example, in Illinois, students cannot transfer to the following schools without changing their residences or securing special permission of their school boards under the following circumstances:

1. an attendance center that exceeds, or as a result of the transfer would exceed, its attendance capacity;

2. an attendance center for which the board has established academic criteria for enrollment if the student does not meet the criteria, provided that the transfer must be permitted if the attendance center is the only attendance center serving the student's grade that has not been identified for school improvement, corrective action, or restructuring under (20 U.S.C.C. Sec. 6316); and

3. any attendance center if the transfer would prevent the school district from meeting its obligations under a State or federal law, court order, or consent decree applicable to the school district.[44]

Another difficulty here is that it is not always clear how school officials can remove the "persistently dangerous" label. Yet, New Hampshire law provides that "[a]ny school which is designated a persistently dangerous school, which for 2 consecutive years has operated as a safe school, shall be decertified as a persistently dangerous school."[45]

In the event of litigation, courts must determine whether the failure of school officials to comply fully with the reporting requirements of state statutes supports private claims for damages. In such a case, the Supreme Court of Georgia was of the opinion that there was no indication that the state legislature intended to impose civil liability plus criminal sanctions for non-reporting of prohibited conduct. The court concluded that nothing in the statute created a private cause of action by victims purportedly harmed by violations of the penal law.[46]

The reporting requirement for "persistently dangerous" schools does not apply directly to nonpublic schools under NCLB. However, nonpublic schools may experience transfers of students from schools that have problems with crime and violence, regardless of whether the incidents in the public schools satisfy the "persistently dangerous" standard.

School Safety and the Every Student Succeeds Act

A major goal of ESSA was to roll back the intrusion of the federal government into the formation and operation of education policy by replacing the NCLB. For instance, the ESSA requires school boards to use a portion of their funding for "activities to support safe and healthy students."[47] Specific suggestions in the ESSA include drug and violence prevention activities; programs to educate students against the use of tobacco and alcohol, marijuana, smoke-

---

[44] 105 ILL. COMP. STAT. ANN. 5/10-21.3a (b).

[45] N.H. REV. STAT. ANN. § 193-G:3.

[46] Murphy v. Bajjani, 647 S.E.2d 54, 58 (Ga. 2007).

[47] *Id.* at § 7118.

less tobacco, and electronic cigarettes; professional development/training in identification, mentoring, and recovery support services for students who are already using illicit drugs; school-based mental health services; developing relationship-building skills for the prevention of coercion, violence or abuse; mentoring of students who are academically at risk, or at risk of involvement in criminal activities; and training school personnel in suicide prevention, crisis management, and conflict resolution strategies.[48]

Another section of the ESSA directs School Emergency Response to Violence programs to "carry out ... activities to improve students' safety and well-being, during and after the school day."[49] The ESSA also addresses "assurances" required when local educational agencies apply for funding, in which LEAs must prioritize funding for schools with the greatest needs, especially those that "are identified as persistently dangerous public elementary or secondary schools."[50]

Student Searches

Generally

As part of their commitment to security for students, educational officials in nonpublic need to engage in searches involving individuals' expectations of privacy and the degree to which educators can intrude on that privacy. The validity of searches invariably involves a balancing of this expectation of privacy and the reason for the searches.

The law on school searches relies largely on the Fourth Amendment's prohibition against unreasonable searches and seizures. The Fourth Amendment provides:

> The right of the people to be secure in their persons, houses, papers, and effects, against unreasonable searches and seizures, shall not be violated, and no Warrants shall issue, but upon probable cause, supported by Oath or affirmation, and particularly describing the place to be searched, and the persons or things to be seized.

Although the U.S. Constitution does not apply to nonpublic schools, it is worth remembering that precedent and emerging judicial guidelines addressing searches in public schools apply a reasonableness standard relevant for all schools, even though virtually all litigation on the Fourth Amendment has occurred in public schools. Officials in nonpublic schools would thus be wise to treat this material, as well as the other topics throughout this chapter, as akin to best practices designed to safeguard the rights of their students and staffs.

---

[48] *See id.* at 5(D).

[49] *Id.* at § 7281(a)(1)(B).

[50] *Id.* at § 7912(a).

Defining Contraband

The starting points for searches and seizures are schools' definition of contraband; this can be a broad range of items, many of which are identified by state law, while others are prohibited solely by school rules. In most situations, the list of prohibited items is contained in school handbooks and often can be fairly lengthy.

Examples of contraband can include, but are not necessarily limited to, items that are illegal for everyone to possess: (1) heroin, cocaine, and/or stolen goods; (2) items that are illegal for persons below specified ages to possess and use, such as alcohol and/or tobacco; (3) items that are dangerous but not illegal to possess and cannot be brought onto school property, such as guns, knives, and/or other weapons; (4) items that are permissible for students to use, but may be impermissible for students to have in their possession or distribute while in schools, such as prescription medications; and (5) items that educational officials identify as impermissible on school premises, even though not otherwise dangerous or unlawful to possess or use, such as cell phones and/or specified types of wearing apparel.

All searches involve looking for contraband as defined by school rules. Consequently, identifying what is contraband warrants careful attention. Composing a list of prohibited items presents the tension between the need to be specific enough so students and employees know what they cannot do, yet be broad enough to allow flexibility in addressing new issues. Because a list of prohibited items may change during school years, the most effective strategy involves frequent reminders of changes to staff members, students, and their parents. These reminders can include orientation sessions at the beginning of school years, as well as announcements in assemblies or via a public address system, and on board websites.

T.L.O. Reasonableness Standard

In many instances, students become suspects regarding contraband infractions because someone has provided information identifying them as such. Officials in nonpublic schools need to be aware of various legal issues when conducting student or employee searches based on tips received from informants.

The pivotal case involving student searches in the public schools is *New Jersey v. T.L.O.* (*T.L.O.*).[51] In *T.L.O.*, the Supreme Court upheld an assistant principal's (AP) search of a female student's purse under a "reasonable suspicion" standard after she denied smoking in a school restroom. The Court held that the privacy interests of students needed to be reconciled with the substantial interest of school officials in maintaining safe and orderly learning environments. Establishing reasonable suspicion as the standard for school searches, rather than probable cause, obligates educators to consider the amount

---

[51] 469 U.S. 325 [21 Educ. L. Rep. 1122] (1985).

of information they have in order to possess "sufficient probability," but not "absolute certainty,"[52] of violations of school rules or the law.

The *T.L.O.* reasonableness standard requires searches to be reasonable both at their inception and as to their scope. The inception of a search requires "reasonable grounds for suspecting that the search will turn up evidence that the student has violated or is violating either the law or the rules of the school."[53] In essence, this means that school officials must have specific and articulable facts about students, which, when taken with rational inferences from those facts, reasonably warrants intrusions. In *T.L.O.*, the search of the student's purse was reasonable at its inception because a teacher had reported T.L.O. smoking in the restroom, and, when questioned by the AP, she denied any smoking at all.

The scope of a search means it must be reasonably related to its purpose and not be excessively intrusive in light of the age and sex of a student. Scope can be viewed in three ways: first, in terms of sequence, where it refers to the order in which places are searched; second, in terms of priorities, where it refers to the first places to be searched; and third, in terms of breadth, where it refers to the authority of officials to continue a search regardless of whether the first place searched led to the discovery of evidence.

While the Supreme Court created *T.L.O.*'s reasonable suspicion standard under the Fourth Amendment, it can apply to nonpublic schools because it relies on reasonableness, a common concept broadly applicable to all educational institutions. Even with searches in nonpublic schools controlled by language in handbooks, courts are likely to overlay interpretations and applications of these contractual provisions with a reasonableness standard, at least to the extent that school officials cannot be arbitrary in the manner in which they conduct searches. To this end, officials in nonpublic schools should heed judicial interpretations of *T.L.O.*'s reasonable suspicion standard.

Contractual Language Authorizing Searches

Student life in nonpublic educational institutions is very much controlled by the language of their handbooks, which likely grants broad authority to school officials to conduct searches. However, the extent to which handbooks can supplant entirely the *T.L.O.* reasonable suspicion standard is not clear. Distinctions most likely can be drawn between searches of school-owned property, on one hand, and students and their personal property, on the other. While public schools are still subject to the constitutional reasonable suspicion limitation, even when searching their own property, officials in nonpublic institutions have no such limitations, at least if they include clear language in their handbooks expressing their right to conduct searches of their own property, such as lockers, at any time.

---

[52] Hill v. Cal., 401 U.S. 797, 804 (1971), quoted by *T.L.O.*, 469 U.S. at 346.

[53] *T.L.O.*, 346 U.S. at 341.

Searches of student items, such as book bags and jackets in lockers and desks, represent intrusiveness into private areas, but probably can be addressed contractually, provided again that handbooks clearly state that searches of lockers and desks can include students' personal items in those places. Searches of students or the personal items they carry with them, such as purses and wallets, are even more intrusive and more likely to be subject to judicial review under a reasonableness standard. Subjecting students to having to empty their pockets, pat-downs, or removing articles of clothing as part of personal searches, where school officials lack reasonable suspicion, invites litigation for invasion of privacy. The more intrusive searches in nonpublic schools are, the more likely courts are likely to require proof of reasonableness.

Suspicionless Searches

Reasonableness may have a part to play even as to suspicionless searches of school property. Suspicionless searches relate to those for which school officials have no reason to believe are likely to produce contraband. Examples can include school officials looking through all student lockers, using sniff dogs to examine lockers or automobiles in school parking lots, or using metal detectors at school entrances. A feature of suspicionless searches is generally that they apply to all students or student property, not to specific students.

School officials need to be aware that in crafting search policies not based on reasonable suspicion, their implementation may seem intimidating and even traumatizing for some students and their parents, particularly where suspicionless school property searches involve selected individuals. If officials in nonpublic schools wish to conduct suspicionless school property searches, they would do well to distinguish between those that are school-wide and those directed toward specific students. Individualized searches of school property without reasonable suspicion, even if authorized in handbooks, are difficult to justify. Selecting the lockers of specific students for periodic searches, without any reasons related to contraband, is even more problematic, and may be perceived as arbitrary and capricious.[54]

Zero Tolerance Policies

Zero tolerance policies were popular among public schools, and probably among nonpublic school as well.[55] The U.S. Department of Education defined a zero tolerance policy as "a school or school district policy that mandates predetermined and severe consequences or punishment for specific offenses."[56]

---

[54] *See* In re Adam, 697 N.E.2d 1100 [127 EDUC. L. REP. 1029] (Ohio Ct. App. 1997) (invalidating a state statute permitting locker searches without reasonable suspicion, but upholding the search at issue because reasonable suspicion was present; the law has been amended to correct this defect).

[55] For a discussion of issues related to zero tolerance policies, see Robert Cloud, *Due Process and Zero Tolerance*, 178 EDUC. L. REP. 1 (2003). *See also* Charles J. Russo, *Has Time Expired for Zero Tolerance Policies?* SCHOOL BUSINESS AFFAIRS, VOL. 79, No. 6, 33-36 (2013).

[56] For the citation, *see id.* at 1.

While such policies send a strong message about the commitment of school officials to student safety, they have been subject to litigation.

Courts were initially supportive of zero tolerance policies,[57] but are increasingly critical of the lack of good judgment in enforcing them.[58] Because the creation and enforcement of zero tolerance policies requires "a balance between being strong and being fair," school leaders need to "initiate a dialog on values related to personal responsibility and safety."[59]

Source of Information

In light of the protective responsibility of officials in public schools for their students when acting *in loco parentis*, courts have granted them broad latitude in responding to information about contraband. This is especially true if it is illegal, such as weapons and/or drugs, and its presence would represent risk to students and others in schools.[60]

School officials can receive information about contraband from a variety of sources, including employees, students, and/or parents. While educators may often know individuals providing the information, some comes from anonymous or unidentified sources. The judiciary often upholds searches conducted based on anonymous or unidentified sources, however, some courts have required school officials to evaluate whether anonymous tips are reliable, or whether identified sources may have had animus against the persons reported.[61]

The lesson for today is that all school officials need to act judiciously in responding to reports of contraband. Courts are much less likely to heavily scrutinize responses to tips about weapons at school, but may subject searches for other kinds of contraband, even drugs, to a reasonableness analysis. While officials in nonpublic schools who respond to informants are unlikely to be subject to constitutionally grounded reasonableness tests, they may learn that similar analyses can occur in invasion of privacy suits by students and their

---

[57] *See, e.g.*, South Gibson Sch. Bd. v. Sollman, 768 N.E.2d 437 [165 Educ. L. Rep. 316] (Ind. 2002) (upholding a school's denial of credit, but refusing to permit a suspension to carry over into the next school year).

[58] *See, e.g.*, Ette v. Linn-Mar Cmty. Sch. Dist., 656 N.W.2d 62 [173 Educ. L. Rep. 662] (Iowa 2002) (reversing on governmental immunity as to a negligent endangerment claim against educators who, after discovering a 15-year-old student smoking in violation of zero tolerance policy while on a school trip, sent him home alone 1100 miles on a bus); Seal v. Morgan, 229 F.3d 567 [148 Educ. L. Rep. 34] (6th Cir. 2000) (reversing the expulsion of a student who had a knife in his truck, directing the board to conduct a hearing as to whether he knew it was there).

[59] Robert Cloud, *Due Process and Zero Tolerance*, 178 Educ. L. Rep. at 11 (containing useful guidelines for creating zero tolerance policies.)

[60] *See, e.g.*, Williams v. Cambridge Bd. of Educ., 370 F.3d 630 [188 Educ. L. Rep. 131] (6th Cir. 2004) (affirming a grant of summary judgment in favor of school officials and police officers who searched students who stated they were planning to bring weapons to school).

[61] *See* Fewless v. Bd. of Educ. of Wayland, 208 F. Supp.2d 806 [167 Educ. L. Rep. 153] (W.D. Mich. 2002) (invalidating the search of a student's pockets and a strip search in response to four student informants' claims that he possessed marijuana, where the school administrator failed to question the clearly ulterior motives of the informants, three of four of whom were to serve detention and pay restitution for destroying the student's school project).

parents where searches are allegedly unreasonable because they were too intrusive.[62] As such, courts are likely to treat searches of student book bags or purses rooted in anonymous tips as reasonable, but are unlikely to view strip searches in the same manner.

Scope of Search

Intrusiveness

The scope of searches means they must be reasonably related to their purposes and not be excessively intrusive in light of the age and sex of the student and the nature of the infractions. From the perspective of intrusiveness, a search continuum from least to most intrusive includes school lockers, student vehicles, student book bags and/or purses/wallets, emptying of pockets, pat-downs, strip searches, and body cavity searches. While some might rearrange the locations of some of the places subject to searches on the continuum, most are likely to agree on the outer limits of the least intrusive such as school locker and the most intrusive in the form of body cavity searches.

A multidimensional concept, the scope of searches can, as noted above, be interpreted in three ways. First, scope can mean simply the order in which places are searched. In *T.L.O.*, the AP only looked in one place, the student's purse, even though his actions involved a sequence of searches, meaning that he continued to look for the other items he discovered after he saw the cigarettes in plain view. If school officials receive information that students have contraband, searches of a number of places are not uncommon. In this way, searches could progress from lockers to book bags to having students empty their pockets. The fact that officials search a number of places is not in itself a significant legal concern, as long as all of the locations could reasonably have contained the contraband that was the subject of the search.

The second way to view scope is the priority of searches, a notion applicable to the selection of the first place to be searched. Not surprisingly, information about contraband does not often come with identified places. For example, because the AP in *T.L.O.* did not have a location, he began with the student's purse. In the continuum of places searched, purses are arguably more intrusive to students' privacy than their lockers. In *T.L.O.*, the Supreme Court did not require the AP, nor have lower courts obligated educators to begin searches in the least-intrusive places before moving to more-intrusive locations.

As long as contraband could reasonably be located in the places where searches begin, courts are unlikely to second-guess their sequences.[63] In some cases, when information provided to school officials reveals specific locations,

---

[62] *See* Brousseau v. Town of Westerly, 11 F. Supp.2d 177 [128 Educ. L. Rep. 1069] (D.R.I. 1998) (rejecting a sixth-grade female student's motion for summary judgment in response to a pat-down around her pockets in search of a missing cafeteria knife, because officials did not invade her privacy insofar as the search was based on reasonable suspicion).

[63] *See* Wilcher v. State, 876 S.W.2d 466 [91 Educ. L. Rep. 719] (Tex. Ct. App. 1994) (upholding a student's conviction for marijuana possession after he emptied his pockets, even though a pat-down should have occurred first because the official was responding to a report of a weapon).

the question becomes whether searches must begin at the identified places.[64] Generally, though, school officials do not need to begin searches in the places identified as long as the first place searched falls within the parameters of reasonableness.

The third way to think about the scope of searches is their breadth, the authority to continue searches, and whether the first place examined produced evidence of contraband. In *T.L.O.*, when the AP removed the cigarettes, he saw the other items including a pipe, rolling paper, and a list of names that justified his second search. The difficult question that the Supreme Court did not answer in *T.L.O.* is whether educators can continue to search after locating the contraband for which they may be looking.

Case law in public schools is sparse, but suggests that searches continuing beyond the discovery of the sought contraband may be unreasonable because officials exceeded the scope of their searches.[65] Whether officials in nonpublic schools would be subject to this restriction in conducting searches is uncertain. This much is clear: Searches should not be fishing expeditions, giving license to extended intrusions into student privacy, serving only to satisfy officials' curiosity with no relationship to the safety of students or schools.

Age and Sex

Courts typically uphold searches, whether beginning at less-intrusive or more-intrusive places, as long as they do not become excessively intrusive, considering the age and sex of the students.[66] Although courts often address the reasonableness of searches based on those two considerations, cases involving the most intrusive and offensive of searches, strip searches, hardly ever seem to turn just on these factors.

An illustrative case arose in South Dakota. When school officials who strip searched two eighth-grade girls looking for a missing $200, the federal trial court rejected educators' motions for summary judgment because they lacked reasonable suspicion to extend it to the students' bras and underwear after failing to located the money in their pockets, shoes, or socks.[67]

---

[64] *See* Commonwealth v. Snyder, 597 N.E.2d 1363, 1368 (Mass. 1992) (upholding a locker search where marijuana was discovered in a book bag in the student's locker, despite information that it was in a videocassette case, because the locker was not only a less-intrusive search but also represented a reasonable judgment); Commonwealth v. J.B., 719 A.2d 1058 (Pa. Super. Ct. 1998) (upholding a search based on a student's slurred speech wherein he emptied his pockets and a police officer shook the cuff of his pants, resulting in a bag of marijuana falling out).

[65] *See* In Interest of Dumas, 515 A.2d 984 (Pa. Commw. Ct. 1994) (affirming the invalidity of the search of a locker where marijuana was discovered because the administrator seized cigarettes from the student's hand that were the basis for the original search).

[66] *See* Rinker v. Sipler, 264 F. Supp.2d 181 [178 EDUC. L. REP. 730] (M.D. Pa. 2003) (granting a parental motion for summary judgment where a search for marijuana that began with emptying their son's pockets, then patting him down, before asking him to remove his socks and lower his pants to his knees, and finally looking in his book bag and locker, all of which produced no marijuana, and finally directing him to produce a urine sample that was negative).

[67] Konop v. Northwestern Sch. Dist., 26 F. Supp.2d 1189[131 EDUC. L. REP. 201] (D.S.D. 1998).

Cases upholding strip searches, based on their reasonableness at inception and having appropriate scope, indicated that the legality of searches in general, and strip searches in particular, were very much governed by the facts of each case, rather than gender and age.[68] Factors such as whether students are required to remove their underwear, whether officials made physical contact with students, and whether educators made threats if students failed to obey, seem to be the controlling factors, rather than age and sex. In light of *Safford Unified School District No. 1 v. Redding*,[69] because educators who strip search students run the risk of personal liability, they should avoid such searches at all costs.

Nature of Infraction

In addition to the age and sex of students, in *T.L.O.* the Supreme Court observed that

> another factor to consider in evaluating whether searches are reasonable is "the nature of the infraction."[70] School handbooks contain rules prohibiting a wide range of behaviors, some of which are impermissible because they are identical to provisions in criminal codes, such as possessing weapons and/or drugs on campuses. Other rules prohibit conduct related to disrupting safe and orderly learning environments; examples include wearing apparel, using appropriate stairways, and following guidelines on the amount of money students can bring to school. The reasonableness issue deals with evaluating which of these rule violations justifies searches of students and/or their possessions.

In *T.L.O.*, the assistant principal based his search of the student's purse on her denial that she was smoking, in violation of a school rule. While possession of cigarettes would not, in itself, have proven that T.L.O. was smoking, it would have corroborated the report that she was smoking while undermining her defense to the charge of smoking. The relevance of T.L.O.'s possession of cigarettes to the question of whether she was smoking, and to the credibility of her denial that she smoked at all, supplied the necessary nexus between the item searched and the infraction under investigation.

---

[68] For cases upholding fairly invasive strip searches, see, e.g., Jenkins v. Talladega City Bd. of Educ., 115 F.3d 821 [118 Educ. L. Rep. 867] (11th Cir. 1997) (granting a school nurse and a teacher immunity for searching two 8-year-old elementary students in attempt to locate $7 stolen from a classmate, because the law had not clearly established that their conduct violated the Fourth Amendment); Williams v. Ellington, 936 F.2d 881 [68 Educ. L. Rep. 302] (6th Cir. 1991) (upholding immunity for the search of a female high school student involving her being required to remove her shirt, lower her jeans to her knees, and take off her shoes and socks in the presence of two female employees, because this was not a custom or practice at the school); Cornfield v. Consol. High Sch., 991 F.2d 1316 [82 Educ. L. Rep. 379] (7th Cir. 1993) (upholding the strip search of a high school male thought to be "crotching" drugs, where he was taken to a locker room and asked to remove his school clothes and put on his gym clothes in the presence of two male employees).

[69] 557 U.S. 364 [245 Educ. L. Rep. 626] (2009).

[70] *T.L.O.*, 469 U.S. at 342.

The following guidelines relating searches to the nature of the infraction may be helpful:

1. All searches need reasonable ties between alleged infractions and evidence that might be secured.

2. When officials conduct searches due to rules infractions, they must have some reason to believe their actions are going to produce evidence of the ultimate fact at issue, such as T.L.O.'s smoking, even if the searches fail to produce evidence of such infractions.

3. Searches are not unreasonable at their inception simply because officials fail to locate evidence of rule violations. However, searches may be invalidated as unreasonable if they become excessively intrusive in scope.

4. Not all rule infractions can, or should, result in searches. For example, a student running in the hallway may be violating school rules, but officials would be hard-pressed trying to justify a search of the child's locker after such an incident. Absent additional evidence that students possess contraband, or represent a danger to themselves or others, searches of running students would not produce additional evidence of wrongdoing that was not already plainly evident.

5. Persons conducting individualized suspicion searches, such as in *T.L.O.*, must establish connections between the rules and their infractions. For example, an appropriate question in *T.L.O.* prior to the search of her purse would have been, "Were you smoking in the restroom?" Such a question serves to provide notice to the student of the objectionable conduct under investigation, and to obviate the need for a search if she admits to the conduct and produces the evidence of her infraction.

Special Types of Searches

Field Trips/Activities Outside of Schools

Because field trips and external activities are integral parts of education, when students participate in off-campus activities they are subject to school rules.[71] There is scant reported litigation addressing searches of students while away from school; however, in a classic case, a federal trial court in New York upheld the authority of educators to search student rooms during a field trip.[72] Even though officials conducted the search because they had reasonable suspicion of wrongdoing, rather than written consent forms, this case serves as a template of how to prepare students and parents for field trips.

The underlying dispute involved a senior field trip to Disney World, which required school officials to provide parents and students with three pieces of

---

[71] For more information on the law related to field trips, see Russo & Mawdsley, Searches, Seizures and Drug Testing Procedures: Balancing Rights and School Safety 2d Ed. 45-50 (LRP 2008).

[72] Rhodes v. Guarricino, 54 F. Supp.2d 186 [137 Educ. L. Rep. 258] (S.D.N.Y. 1999).

information. First, each parent and student had to sign a permission slip that provided in part:

> We understand that responsible behavior is imperative to a successful and safe trip. We accept the financial responsibility of our son/daughter coming home early through separate travel accommodations if the coordinator and chaperones deem that the student's individual behavior is in violation of school policy, standards, and/ or civil law....
>
> WE UNDERSTAND THE ABSOLUTE FORBIDDEN USE OF ANY ALCOHOL OR DRUGS BY OUR SON/DAUGHTER, AND THAT PARTAKING IN SUCH SUBSTANCES WOULD SUBJECT HIM/HER TO EARLY DEPARTURE AND SCHOOL DISCIPLINE POLICIES UPON RETURN.[73]

Second, each parent and student signed a "Drug, Alcohol and Incident Free Pledge" that stated in relevant part:

> It is imperative that students understand that this is an earned privilege and a school sanctioned activity that can be enjoyed without improper behavior or incidents of drug and alcohol use. This most unique O'NEILL occasion must not be tainted in any way by poor individual judgment and choice. Direct involvement or implication by association can result in school levied consequences for such action....
>
> As a participating O'NEILL student, I pledge and personally guarantee, with the support of my parent/guardian, that: (1) I will participate in the '98 senior trip without the use of any drugs, alcohol, or any illegal substance; (2) My behavior will be respectful of people and property. I understand that violation of this guarantee will result in my disqualification from senior activities and graduation ceremonies. My signature and that of my parent/guardian will serve as verification of my understanding of the behavioral terms.[74]

Third, school officials gave all students a brochure specifically notifying them that they would be subject to "room checks." The brochure also advised students that "behavior discrepancies, either direct or by close association, will be dealt with through 'School Disciplinary Codes and Procedures.'"[75]

Despite this preparation, a school official smelled marijuana and saw a large group of students outside of one specific room. After securing a passkey from hotel staff,[76] the official discovered a bottle of alcohol in one room and

---

[73] *Id.* at 188.

[74] *Id.* at 190.

[75] *Id.* at 188.

[76] The hotel had a policy of permitting chaperones to enter the rooms of students in groups, certainly a policy that would be well to know about prior to engaging a hotel.

marijuana in another. After officials promptly sent the students home and suspended them, their parents sued unsuccessfully.

This case provides four key insights concerning field trips and off-campus activities. First, even the best-crafted permission slips signed by parents do not prevent them from suing when officials enforce the language on the forms against their children. While school officials cannot prevent parents from suing, they can make certain that students and parents have clear notice of the rules and their enforcement.

Second, permission slips need to state clearly that student rooms are subject to searches. In the case from New York, the parents had argued that notice about "room checks" did not include a search, confusion that could easily have been cleared up by adding appropriate language to the materials sent to parents and students.

Third, in the case from New York, students were not present when officials searched their rooms, even though their checks were limited to the hotel's furnishings rather than personal bags. As such, although searches of rooms only, not student luggage, are easier to defend, no case to date suggests that students must be present for searches. The practical arguments about having students present weigh both ways. On one hand, the presence of students is some protection against charges of missing or damaged goods. On the other hand, notice to students to be in their rooms because searches are being conducting provides opportunities for those who are not the first to be searched to dispose of contraband prior to their searches.

Fourth, courts have reached mixed results in disputes from public schools as to whether permission slips allow searches of student luggage prior to or during trips without reasonable suspicion. In a pre-*T.L.O.* case, the Supreme Court of Washington invalidated a band director's search of luggage prior to a trip outside of the United States because officials feared that a search of luggage by border guards might find illegal contraband.[77] The court held that the reasonable suspicion standard required particularized suspicion that officials would locate contraband for each student searched. The court did not think that officials met this standard by the mandated submission to an across-the-board search of each student's luggage as a condition to of participating in the concert tour.

On the other hand, an appellate court in New Jersey, in a post-*T.L.O.* case, reached a different result. The court upheld the search of all student hand luggage prior to a seventh-grade field trip because it was convinced that school officials voiced a legitimate interest in preventing them from taking contraband on the field trip.[78]

Nonpublic schools can probably handle searches contractually as part of the consent forms students and their parents sign. Alternatively, the Sixth Circuit, in a case Tennessee, reached the same outcome as the court in New York by relying on *in loco parentis*. The court noted that when parents are

---

[77] Kuehn v. Renton Sch. Dist., 694 P.2d 1078 [22 Educ. L. Rep. 1297] (Wash. 1985).

[78] Desilets v. Clearview Bd. of Educ., 627 A.2d 667 [84 Educ. L. Rep. 329] (N.J. Super. Ct. 1993).

not present and have given consent for trips, they would be reluctant to allow their children to participate if "the accompanying school officials' authority to impose supervision were subject to the same Fourth Amendment limitations as apply to local police forces."[79]

Car/Vehicle Searches

Searches of student vehicles normally require reasonable suspicion in public schools.

This suspicion can be based on student or faculty tips relating to contraband in vehicles, or suspicionless searches of vehicles in parking lots by drug-sniffing dogs where positive alerts provide reasonable suspicion for searches.[80]

Officials in many public schools attempt to circumvent reasonable suspicion by using implied consent forms whereby driving vehicles to and parking at school is treated as a privilege, thereby permitting searches without reasonable suspicion. The implied consent argument has plausibility as applied to student vehicles. While students have a right under state law to attend public schools, this typically does not include driving to school. To date, though, the constitutional limits of such implied consent in the public sector have yet to be tested.[81] Whether school officials can essentially have students waive whatever constitutional rights they might have to privacy in their vehicles is not clear.

On the other hand, officials in nonpublic schools should have less difficulty in using implied consent forms. Such forms have a contractual quid pro quo quality to them paralleling the broader contractual provisions of nonpublic education. Since nonpublic schools can prohibit all student vehicles on school property, officials could specify in handbooks that the exchange for permitting student vehicles on school grounds is that they can be subject to searches at any time.

At the same time, school officials need to distinguish suspicionless vehicle searches from those based on individual suspicion. If all vehicles are searched as part of sweeps of parking lots, the searches probably do not need reasonable suspicion. Without using sniff dogs, though, a suspicionless search of the inside of all vehicles would probably take more time than it is worth. Any other kind of vehicle search would involve some form of individualized

---

[79] Webb v. McCullough, 828 F.2d 1151, 1157 [41 Educ. L. Rep. 851] (6th Cir. 1987).

[80] *See* James v. Unified Sch. Dist. No. 512, 959 F. Supp. 1407 [118 Educ. L. Rep. 161] (D. Kan. 1997) (upholding a student's expulsion where police received an anonymous tip that he had a gun in a truck in the school parking lot); F.S.E. v. State, 993 P.2d 771 [141 Educ. L. Rep. 1176] (Okla. Ct. Crim. App. 1999) (upholding the search of a student's car resulting in the discovery of marijuana based on the smell of it on his person coupled with his explanation that a stranger smoked marijuana in his car); Covington County v. G.W., 767 So. 2d 187 (Miss. 2000) (upholding the suspension of a student based on corroborated statements that he had been drinking alcohol on school property, his admission that he had beer in his truck, and an educator seeing empty beer cans in the back of the truck).

[81] *See* Anders v. Ft. Wayne Cmty. Schs., 124 F. Supp.2d 618 (N.D. Ind. 2000) (ruling in favor of school officials where a board policy included an implied consent provision resulting in the search of car based on reasonable suspicion the student had been smoking in the vehicle).

suspicion; in such a case, nonpublic school officials would need to be cautious in carrying out a search where the basis for selecting only one or two vehicles is not rooted in reasonable suspicion. Because student vehicles, like their book bags and jackets, are not school property, these searches are much easier to defend where they lose the appearance of being arbitrary if they are based on reasonable suspicion. [82]

Metal Detectors

Many public schools use metal detectors, but most nonpublic schools choose not to use them, either because of the expense or the impression created in the minds of parents regarding school safety. Because violence involving students with weapons does occur in nonpublic schools, it is appropriate to offer guidelines regarding the use of metal detectors.[83] Educational leaders and their lawyers in nonpublic schools would be wise to consider the following:

1. Formulate rationales for using metal detectors, even if only general statements to protect students. In most instances, the emphasis in nonpublic schools is on preemptive rather than corrective action.

2. Designate a person in a school who can authorize the use of metal detectors.

3. Determine whether the school will purchase metal detectors or contract with private agencies to provide services.

4. Designate in writing—preferably in the student handbook and materials sent home to parents, as well as on the school website—the range of penalties for bringing weapons to school, indicating whether evidence of violations may be turned over to the police.

5. Note whether those individuals tasked with operating metal detectors have the discretion to decide how frequently to use them or whether, as an alternative, detectors are used randomly on the basis of an acceptable sampling technique.

6. Limit access to the school building to only one entrance.

7. Even if contractors conduct searches by metal detector, a school administrator must be present.[84]

---

[82] For more information on the law related to car/vehicle searches, see RUSSO & MAWDSLEY, SEARCHES, SEIZURES AND DRUG TESTING PROCEDURES: BALANCING RIGHTS AND SCHOOL SAFETY 2D ED. 42-45 (LRP 2008).

[83] For a more complete discussion of metal detector searches, see CHARLES RUSSO & RALPH MAWDSLEY, SEARCHES, SEIZURES AND DRUG TESTING PROCEDURES: BALANCING RIGHTS AND SCHOOL SAFETY 2D ED. 50-57 (LRP 2008).

[84] See In re F.B., 726 A.2d 361 [133 EDUC. L. REP. 528] (Pa. 1999) (affirming a conviction for juvenile delinquency for possession of a weapon located as a result of scanning a student as he entered school, because it took place pursuant to a published policy).

Sniff Dogs

As with the use of metal detectors, most nonpublic schools are unlikely to employ sniff dogs for searches on school property. Dogs are typically used for drugs, though some canines have been trained to detect other substances such as alcohol, tobacco, and explosive materials. The use of these dogs is fairly common in public schools, thereby raising issues about whether the dogs are used to search the students themselves, or their property located in lockers, desks, and/or vehicles.

In an early case from Texas, the Fifth Circuit reached mixed results.[85] The court held that because using sniff dogs for inanimate objects such as lockers and vehicles did not constitute searches, they did not invoke reasonable suspicion.[86] The court explained that all that was necessary was an inquiry into the reliability of the dogs. At the same time, the court decided that using sniff dogs to search students did constitute searches and required individualized suspicion.

Similarly, in a case from California, the Ninth Circuit maintained that insofar as the use of dogs to sniff students constituted a search, reasonable suspicion was necessary.[87] Another way to understand this case is that using dogs on suspicionless bases, even if their noses do not touch students, is excessively intrusive on their expectations of privacy. This was particularly true here because the searches were sudden and unannounced, with student participation completely involuntary.

If officials in nonpublic schools intend to use sniff dogs, then students and parents need to be notified of such in student handbooks and in other materials. As with other types of searches, using dogs to sniff students should be distinguished from sniffing lockers or vehicles. Although sniff dogs, like metal detectors, can be used preemptively to prevent or discourage problems before they occur, either kind of search is likely to invoke concerns among parents.

If school officials receive information about drugs on campus, sniff dogs are an efficient way of conducting searches of school property and student vehicles quickly, with minimal inconvenience. When handlers are working with dogs, students need to stay in their classrooms. After searches, officials should send notes home to parents, explaining the reason(s) for using the dogs, emphasizing that student safety is their primary concern. School officials interested in the use of sniff dogs should contact their local police or sheriff department for information.[88]

---

[85] Horton v. Goose Creek Indep. Sch. Dist., 690 F.2d 470 [6 EDUC. L. REP. 950] (5th Cir. 1982), *cert. denied*, 463 U.S. 1207 (1983).

[86] *But see* Doe v. Renfrow, 631 F.2d 91 (7th Cir. 1980) (in a largely ignored outcome, rejecting the claim that using a dog to sniff 2780 high school students constituted a search).

[87] B.C. v. Plumas Unified Sch. Dist., 192 F.3d 1260 [138 EDUC. L. REP. 1003] (9th Cir. 1999).

[88] For more information on the law related to sniff dogs, see RUSSO & MAWDSLEY, SEARCHES, SEIZURES AND DRUG TESTING PROCEDURES: BALANCING RIGHTS AND SCHOOL SAFETY 2D ED. 57-62 (LRP 2008).

Strip Searches

Litigation over strip searches has been more common than one would, or should, expect.[89] Virtually all strip searches involve money and drugs. Following *T.L.O.*, some,[90] but not all,[91] courts invalidated strip searches for personal items rather than drugs or other contraband. While courts demonstrated some initial reluctance to render public school officials liable for strip searches under a constitutional tort theory, such reluctance should not be viewed as judicial tolerance for strip searches. Instead, the reluctance represents only a recognition that no well-established constitutional standard against such searches existed at the time.[92]

Courts now generally view strip searches as excessively intrusive. As such, courts require school officials to have both individualized suspicion and to demonstrate that the objects of the searches represent dangers to student safety.[93]

In *Safford Unified School District No. 1 v. Redding* (*Safford*),[94] the Supreme Court addressed a Fourth Amendment challenge to the strip search of a female middle school student in Arizona, who had to expose her body to a search for prescription and over-the-counter drugs that she allegedly brought to school. After an AP ordered a school nurse and an administrative assistant to search under the girl's bra and underwear, without locating the drugs, the student filed suit under Section 1983, alleging constitutional violations.

A majority of the *Safford* Court refused to treat strip searches generally as violations of the Fourth Amendment. Yet, the Court did invalidate the search at issue because the AP failed to meet the reasonableness standard enunciated in *T.L.O.*; this was due to his lacking a level of suspicion matching the degree of intrusion when he ordered it, because the nurse and assistant were looking for

---

[89] For more information on the law related to strip searches, see Russo & Mawdsley, Searches, Seizures and Drug Testing Procedures: Balancing Rights and School Safety 2d Ed. 62-66 (LRP 2008).

[90] *See, e.g.,* Thomas ex rel. Thomas v. Roberts, 261 F.3d 1160 [156 Educ. L. Rep. 508] (11th Cir. 2001); State ex rel. Galford v. Mark Anthony B., 433 S.E.2d 41 [84 Educ. L. Rep. 1138] (W. Va. 1993).

[91] *See, e.g.,* Williams ex rel. Williams v. Ellington, 936 F.2d 881 [68 Educ. L. Rep. 302] (6th Cir. 1991); Cornfield by Lewis v. Consolidated High Sch. Dist. No. 230, 991 F.2d 1316 [82 Educ. L. Rep. 379] (7th Cir. 1993); Jenkins by Hall v. Talladega City Bd. of Educ., 115 F.3d 821 [118 Educ. L. Rep. 867] (11th Cir. 1997), *cert. denied sub nom.* Jenkins by Hall v. Herring, 522 U.S. 966 (1997).

[92] *See* Thomas v. Clayton Sch. Dist., 323 F.3d 950 [174 Educ. L. Rep. 874] (11th Cir. 2003) (on remand from the Supreme Court to reconsider in light of Hope v. Pelzer, 536 U.S. 730 (2002) that for purposes of qualified immunity public officials can still be on notice of a constitutional standard where novel circumstances are involved, the Eleventh Circuit in *Thomas* held that individual school officials are entitled to immunity because federal case law at the time the search occurred in 1996 did not provide school defendants and police with "fair warning" that a strip search of an elementary school class for missing money would be unconstitutional under the Fourth Amendment.)

[93] *See, e.g.,* Fewless v. Bd. of Educ. of Wayland Union Schs., 208 F. Supp.2d 806 [167 Educ. L. Rep. 153] (W.D. Mich. 2002) (invalidating a strip search where the AP failed to check on the reliability of the informants and the student's permission for the search was involuntary).

[94] 557 U.S. 364 [245 Educ. L. Rep. 626] (2009).

what he knew were over-the-counter medications. The Justices pointed out that henceforth, educators would need a heightened level of reasonableness due to the intrusiveness of strip searches. Moreover, the Court was of the opinion that the AP who ordered the search was protected by qualified immunity because the law was unclear at that time.

Safford laid the groundwork for search and seizure liability. Not only has the Supreme Court raised the level of reasonable suspicion but, as evidenced by a case from Kentucky that reached the Sixth Circuit,[95] school administrators, and those they instruct to conduct strip searches, may not be entitled to qualified immunity protection in the future. The impact of no qualified immunity means individual school personnel could be personally liable for damages.[96]

While personnel in private schools, as non-state actors, cannot be liable for damages under the Constitution, they may be sued under state invasion of privacy theories. As suggested in the discussion of invasion of privacy earlier in this chapter, liability can be premised under an invasion of privacy tort claim based on students' expectations of privacy. Even if officials in nonpublic schools cannot be liable for violating the Fourth Amendment, they should be aware that courts may superimpose *Safford*'s constitutional standard for intrusive searches on state law tests of intrusiveness under their torts of invasion of privacy.

Any requests officials make for students to remove articles of clothing, other than their jackets, are likely to be treated as strip searches. While these searches represent the outer limit on a continuum—from removing socks and shoes, to taking off shirts and/or blouses, to removing slacks and/or dresses, and finally, underwear—the difference is one of degree, not definition. Officials in nonpublic schools need to know that even if they are not subject to the Fourth Amendment's reasonable suspicion standard, students may have state tort claims under theories such as battery, invasion of privacy, or infliction of emotional distress.[97]

The least-defensible strip searches are those for missing money where school personnel lack individualized suspicion and, instead, may be directing their searches toward entire classes or portions of classes. In a case of this nature, the federal trial court in South Dakota invalidated a strip search of eighth-grade girls who were made to remove all of their clothes except for their pants and bras in a search for $200 missing from cheerleading sales. In rejecting their motion for qualified immunity, the court emphasized that "school

---

[95] Knisley v. Pike Cnty. Joint Vocational Sch. Dist., 604 F.3d 977 [256 Educ. L. Rep. 535] (6th Cir. 2010), *cert. denied*, 562 U.S. 962 (2010) (rejecting a motion for qualified immunity because the law was clear).

[96] *See* Ralph D. Mawdsley and Allan G. Osborne, *Strip Searches: What is Their Constitutional Viability After the Supreme Court's Redding Decision?*, 252 Educ. L. Rep. 21 (2010).

[97] *See, e.g.*, Oliver v. McClung, 919 F. Supp. 1206 [108 Educ. L. Rep. 619] (N.D. Ind. 1995) (rejecting the unlawful imprisonment claim of a student in a physical education class who, in being searched for a missing $4.50, included having her remove her shoes, socks, her shirt and bra, plus checking the waistline of her underwear, but allowing her charges of battery and negligent infliction of emotional distress).

officials were not looking for weapons or drugs or anything else posing even a possible threat to students or others."[98]

Breath Analysis

Most instances of breath analysis are imposed by law enforcement officers in conjunction with the operation of motor vehicles. Even so, a limited number of cases involving schools have arisen.

In Oregon, the federal trial court refused to invalidate Breathalyzer tests a police officer administered to seventy-three students on a senior field trip.[99] The record revealed that the student who filed suit had a blood-alcohol level of .033 and was suspended for three days, denying him the opportunity of participating in his school's senior awards ceremony. Due to the involvement of police, the court determined that the appropriate constitutional standard was probable cause, which the police had in light of a report the principal received regarding drinking, coupled with his smelling alcohol on the student's breath.[100]

More recently, in a case from Florida, the Eleventh Circuit affirmed that a board and school officials did not violate the Fourth Amendment by searching a bus and detaining students in order to require them to take a breathalyzer test before they could enter their prom.[101] The court acknowledged that insofar as the students had no actual or reasonable expectations of privacy on the bus, the officials were entitled to qualified immunity.[102]

Cell Phone Searches

To date, the few reported cell phone searches in schools that reached the federal courts have yielded mixed results. In the earlier of two cases resolved in favor of school officials, a dispute arose in Tennessee when educators confiscated a middle school student's cell phone because it rang in class, subjecting her to a one-day, in-school suspension. Recognizing the authority of educational officials to enforce school rules, the Sixth Circuit determined that they did not violate the student's due process rights because she was allowed to remain in school and complete her classwork.[103]

The Supreme Court of Arkansas affirmed the rejection of claims that school officials engaged in conversion and trespass to chattels when they confiscated a

---

[98] *See* Konop v. Northwestern Sch. Dist., 26 F. Supp.2d 1189, 1203 (D.S.D. 1998).

[99] Juran v. Independence Cent. Sch. Dist. 13J,, 898 F. Supp. 728 [103 Educ. L. Rep. 1068] (D. Or. 1995).

[100] For an earlier case relying on reasonable suspicion, see Anable v. Ford, 663 F. Supp. 149 [40 Educ. L. Rep. 1175] (W.D. Ark. 1985) (upholding a breath test but, because the student's submission to a urinalysis was involuntary, granting his request for injunctive relief against the retention of the urinalysis record and denying school officials' motion for immunity).

[101] Ziegler v. Martin Cnty. Sch. Dist., 831 F.3d 1309 [335 Educ. L. Rep. 1] (11th Cir. 2016).

[102] For more information on the law related to breath analysis, see Russo & Mawdsley, Searches, Seizures and Drug Testing Procedures: Balancing Rights and School Safety 2d Ed. 66-70 (LRP 2008).

[103] Laney v. Farley, 501 F.3d 577 [225 Educ. L. Rep. 93] (6th Cir. 2007).

student's cell phone and returned it to his parents via certified mail.[104] The court agreed that school officials could select the most appropriate punishments in enforcing a policy preventing students from having cell phones in classrooms.

On the other hand, in the first of three orders in favor of students, the Sixth Circuit invalidated a search where educators acted on knowledge that a year-and-a-half earlier, a high school student in Kentucky had suicidal thoughts, admitted to smoking marijuana, and violated a policy against using cell phones in school when he sent text messages while in class.[105] The court determined that school officials' generalized knowledge of the student's behavior did not amount to reasonable suspicion to search his phone.

A federal trial court in Pennsylvania ruled in favor of a student when school officials confiscated his cell phone, called his friends named in its directory, accessed his text messages and voice mail, and had an instant messaging conversation with his brother, without identifying themselves.[106] The court was satisfied that the student presented claims for an unreasonable search and seizure against the board and officials in their individual capacities.

In Virginia, a federal trial court mostly upheld the search of a student who was suspected of possessing marijuana. The court did reject an associate principal's motion for qualified immunity in the face of the claim she violated the Fourth Amendment in searching his cell phone, because it was not reasonable for her to have expected to discover marijuana hidden in the device.[107]

Cyber Speech

Along with cell phones, the internet has presented new challenges for school officials. In public schools, officials must wrestle with search and seizure and free speech concerns in seeking to punish students who create offensive websites at home and who use their cell phones at school to share offensive information. Student web-based cyber speech presents multi-layered constitutional issues. At the very core of these issues is the protected privacy right of students to express their views in websites, almost invariably created off school premises. Courts have reached divergent outcomes in cases from public schools, entering judgments in favor of students[108] and school officials.[109]

---

[104] Koch v. Adams, 361 S.W.3d 817 [278 Educ. L. Rep. 1167] (Ark. 2010).

[105] G.C. v. Owensboro Pub. Sch., 711 F.3d 623 [290 Educ. L. Rep. 527] (6th Cir. 2013).

[106] Klump v. Nazareth Area Sch. Dist., 425 F. Supp.2d 622 [209 Educ. L. Rep. 82] (E.D. Pa. 2006).

[107] Gallimore v. Henrico Cnty. Sch. Bd., 38 F. Supp.3d 721 [313 Educ. L. Rep. 634] (E.D. Va. 2014).

[108] For cases in favor of students, see, e.g., Layshock v. Heritage Sch. Dist., 593 F.3d 249 [253 Educ. L. Rep. 31] (3d Cir. 2010), cert. denied, 565 U.S. 1156 (2012); J.S. ex rel. Snyder v. Blue Mountain Sch. Dist., 650 F.3d 915 (3d Cir. 2011), cert. denied, 565 U.S. 1156 (2012); Burge ex rel. Burge v. Colton Sch. Dist. 53, 100 F. Supp.3d 1057 [323 Educ. L. Rep. 854] (D. Or. 2015).

[109] For cases in favor of school officials, see, e.g., Kowalski v. Berkeley Cnty. Schs., 652 F.3d 565 [271 Educ. L. Rep. 707] (4th Cir. 2011), cert. denied, 565 U.S. 1173 (2012); D.J.M. ex rel. D.M. v. Hannibal Pub. Sch. Dist. No. 60, 647 F.3d 754 [270 Educ. L. Rep. 465] (8th Cir. 2011); A.N. ex rel. Niziolek v. Upper Perkiomen Sch. Dist., 228 F. Supp.3d 391 [344 Educ. L. Rep. 907] (E.D. Pa. 2017).

One issue of significance for school safety addresses is whether postings on the internet by the latter are "true threats" justifying their being disciplined. In disputes of this nature, courts generally enter judgments in favor of school officials[110] rather than students[111] The strange odyssey of a case from Mississippi serves as a good illustration of the challenge facing school personnel when evaluating what constitutes a true threat.

A high school student in Mississippi wrote, produced, and uploaded to YouTube and Facebook a rap song accusing two coaches at his school of inappropriately touching female students. On learning of the song, officials suspended the student. A federal trial court entered a judgment in favor of educators, but the Fifth Circuit reversed on behalf of the student.[112] Subsequently, an en banc panel reinstated the suspension because there was "no genuine dispute of material fact that [the student] threatened, harassed, and intimidated the coaches by intentionally directing his rap recording at the school community."[113] The court concluded that insofar as the student's speech created a material and substantial disruption, it was unnecessary to resolve whether it constituted a true threat.

Recommendations for Practice

1. Officials in nonpublic schools need policies authorizing searches of lockers, vehicles, students and/or their possessions, preferably distinguishing between searches of inanimate places and the persons of students. Searches of students should meet the individualized reasonable suspicion standard, even if this is not specified in school handbooks.

2. Searches of students should be conducted by at least two persons of the same gender and should avoid physical contact, except where those being searched engage in threatening behavior.

3. In light of how common cell phones with cameras are, officials should consider making videos of all searches of students, their lockers, and/ or their property.

4. All school personnel need to be taught about conducting searches, including assessing evidence that suffices for reasonable suspicion, determining how to balance the reasons for searches with the objects

---

[110] For cases in favor of school officials, see, e.g., J.S. v. Bethlehem Area Sch. Dist., 807 A.2d 847 [170 Educ. L. Rep. 302] (Pa. 2002); Riehm v. Engelking, 538 F.3d 952 [236 Educ. L. Rep. 65] (8th Cir. 2008); Lovell v. Poway Unified Sch. Dist., 90 F.3d 367 [111 Educ. Law Rep. 116] (9th Cir. 1996); Bradford v. Norwich City Sch. Dist., 54 F. Supp.3d 177 [315 Educ. L. Rep. 819] (N.D.N.Y. 2014); R.L. v. Central York Sch. Dist., 183 F.3d 625 [337 Educ. L. Rep. 625] (M.D. Pa. 2016).

[111] For a case in favor of students, see, e.g., Burge ex rel. Burge v. Colton Sch. Dist. 53, 100 F. Supp.3d 1057 [323 Educ. L. Rep. 854] (D. Or. 2015).

[112] Bell v. Itawamba Cnty Bd. of Educ., 774 F.3d 280 (5th Cir. 2015), *cert denied*, ___ U.S. ___, 136 S. Ct. 1166 (2016).

[113] Bell v. Itawamba Cnty Bd. of Educ., 799 F.3d 379, 397 (5th Cir. 2015) (en banc).

being sought to assess intrusiveness, and how to conduct actual searches.

5. If officials seek the assistance of law enforcement officers, an educator needs to be present.[114] School policy should designate which school officials should either conduct searches or must be present when searches are conducted.

6. Searches of student cellphones should be limited to the minimum the school official needs to see to determine whether violations of school rules occurred. If officials exceed this limit, they risk liability for violating the rights of students.

Drug Testing

In light of *Vernonia School District 47J v. Acton*[115] and *Board of Education of Independent School District No. 92 of Pottawatomie County v. Earls*,[116] wherein the policies were primarily rehabilitative rather than punitive, the law is well settled that suspicionless universal and random drug tests for extracurricular activities do not violate the Fourth Amendment. Moreover, it appears that extending such drug testing to all students would probably violate the Fourth Amendment.[117]

At the same time, courts disagree about whether mandatory drug testing based on student behavior is constitutional,[118] even as officials in some public schools extended testing to students who drive vehicles to school.[119] In addi-

---

[114] Although not involving a search, in J.D.B. v. North Carolina, 564 U.S. 261 (2011), the Supreme Court ruled that when police officers question students in custodial school settings about their possible involvement in criminal activities, then law enforcement officials must take their ages into consideration in evaluating whether to provide them with *Miranda* warnings.

[115] 515 U.S. 646 [101 EDUC. L. REP. 37] (1995) (upholding universal and random drug testing for high school athletes when officials responded to a crisis in drug use where athletes were leaders in the drug culture.)

[116] 536 U.S. 822 [166 EDUC. L. REP. 79] (2002) (upholding universal and random drug testing for students in extracurricular activities where officials acted to prevent drug use in voluntary activities operated pursuant to rules inapplicable to students at large). For a commentary on this case, see David Schimmel, *Supreme Court Expands Random Drug Testing: Does the Fourth Amendment Still Protect Students?*, 170 EDUC. L. REP. 15 (2002).

[117] *See* Tannahill v. Lockney Indep. Sch. Dist., 133 F. Supp.2d 919 [152 EDUC. L. REP. 549] (N.D. Tex. 2001) (invalidating a drug-testing policy applicable to all students as a violation of the Fourth Amendment).

[118] *See* Willis v. Anderson Cmty. Sch. Corp., 158 F.3d 415 [130 EDUC. L. REP. 89] (7th Cir. 1998) (invalidating a school policy mandating drug testing for students suspended for fighting). *But see* Gardiner v. Tulia Indep. Sch. Dist., 2002 WL 32172310 (N.D. Tex. 2002) (upholding drug testing when teachers have reasonable suspicions that students are under the influence of alcohol or inhalants, or are using tobacco products).

[119] *See* Todd v. Rush County Schs., 133 F.3d 984 [125 EDUC. L. REP. 18] (7th Cir. 2000) (upholding a policy that included random drug testing for students who drove to school); Linke v. N.W. Sch. Corp., 763 N.E.2d 972 [162 EDUC. L. REP. 525] (Ind. 2002) (upholding random drug testing for students wishing to drive themselves to and from school).

tion, drug testing, even if permissible under the federal Constitution, can still be challenged under state constitutional provisions.[120] Drug-testing policies typically test for illegal drugs, while some have also tried to check for alcohol and tobacco.[121]

Clearly, officials in nonpublic schools could use drug testing for the same student populations for which it is permissible in the public sector, as long as it clearly stipulated in their handbooks. In addition, officials in nonpublic schools could probably go beyond testing students in extracurricular activities to test all students, again as long as their policies are stated clearly in school handbooks. However, as noted in the following guidelines, the most significant factor in determining whether school policies employ random drug testing is the cost.

Drug Testing Policies[122]

Drug-testing policies should include the following elements:

1. Provide rationales for testing. Officials can articulate a variety of reasons in school handbooks to justify universal or random drug testing. Key reasons justifying tests are addressing student behaviors during school days or at school activities that exhibit characteristics of drug use; preventing substances that could impair student performance from getting into school; eliminating drug use that could have an adverse effect on student safety; and assuring that student leaders in extracurricular activities are effective role models. As in *Acton* and *Earls,* officials would be wise to emphasize that testing is primarily rehabilitative, to identify students who are abusing substances and get them help, rather than merely punitive in nature.

2. Identify the substances sought in tests. Generally, drug testing policies test for illegal drugs such as cocaine, opiates, PCP, and marijuana, plus misused prescription drugs such as amphetamines, barbiturates, benzodiazepines, including Valium and Librium. Banning alcohol should not be a problem, but school officials should consider how this might impact student discipline. If officials want to include tobacco, they should check with their attorneys to determine whether testing for it meets state privacy laws. The two general methods of testing are the enzyme multiplied immunoassay technique (EMIT) and gas chromatography (CG-MS), with the EMIT being the more commonly used; the cost for

---

[120] For a case invalidating drug testing under the state constitution, see Trinidad Sch. Dist. v. Lopez, 963 P.2d 1095 [129 Educ. L. Rep. 812] (Colo. 1998). *But see* Linke v. Northwestern Sch. Corp., 763 N.E.2d 972 [162 Educ. L. Rep. 525] (Ind. 2002) (upholding random drug testing for students in extracurricular activities under the state constitution).

[121] *See* Joy v. Penn-Harris-Madison Sch. Corp., 212 F.3d 1052 [144 Educ. L. Rep. 866] (7th Cir. 2000) (upholding suspicionless random drug testing for drugs and alcohol, but invalidating it as to nicotine).

[122] These guidelines are discussed in greater detail in, and adapted from Ralph D. Mawdsley, *Random Drug Testing for Extracurricular Activities: Has the Supreme Court Opened Pandora's Box for Public Schools,* 2003 B.Y.U. Educ. and L. J. 587, 606-620.

a basic EMIT test can run as high as $50, with additional expense for testing alcohol, nicotine, LSD, and anabolic steroids. In public schools, boards typically bear the cost of testing. However, officials in nonpublic schools have the option of assessing students separate testing fees or increasing the general school fee to include testing.

3. Designate the activities covered by testing. Policies could cover some, or all, extracurricular activities, but can also be extended to students driving to school. Policies could be extended to cover co-curricular activities in which part of students' grades are based on their performances; testing for extracurricular performances is problematic in public schools, unless students who refuse to consent to drug testing for the co-curricular parts of courses are offered alternative assignments.[123]

4. Create consent forms. Unless signed by students and their parents, individuals should be rendered ineligible to participate in designated activities. Further, consent forms serve three purposes: to provide notice that random drug testing is to occur; to authorize school officials to administer drug tests; and to serve as written indicia of the voluntary choices of students to participate in the designated activities.

5. Identify procedures for selecting students to be tested. Selection procedures must be random according to criteria related to the frequency of testing and the number of students to be tested; school officials can select their own random procedures or use a private testing firm with a random procedure.

6. Collecting samples. Since student privacy is an important issue, school officials can wait outside of closed stalls while students provide urine samples, and then test the samples by performing temperature tests. Both students and those supervising testing need to sign chain-of-custody forms, which, in turn, are signed by all who handle samples. School officials should send the samples to laboratories performing the testing, unless the test is performed by a private company, in which case its personnel are responsible for collecting and forwarding all samples. If schools use different types of testing, such as hair, then officials should begin with the second sentence under this item.

7. Testing samples. Technicians in the laboratories with whom school officials have contracted perform the test analysis for the substances authorized. Urine samples should be divided into three portions to permit re-tests on second samples in case of positive results, and then leaving third samples if they wish to have test analyses performed at other facilities at their own expense. Substances tested cannot exceed

---

[123] *See, e.g.,* Penn-Harris-Madison Sch. Corp. v. Joy, 768 N.E.2d 940, 942 [165 EDUC. L. REP. 323] (Ind. Ct. App. 2002) (noting language in a drug testing policy specifically stating that "[e]xtracurricular activities for testing purposes do not include activities where the student receives a grade.")

the authorization, and, if school officials request analyses for substances or conditions not authorized, students may have invasion of privacy claims.[124]

8. Reporting positive test results. Positive test results can be shared with those with legitimate needs to know, such as the school administrator responsible for discipline, activities advisors/coaches and, if students are in special education placements, members of their IEP teams.[125]

9. Defenses to positive tests. Students who have not done so can provide medications lists, meaning naming prescriptions they may be taking which might generate positive results, to be placed in sealed envelopes and attached with their samples, possibly to be used for parental requests for re-tests of remaining samples.[126]

10. Penalties for positive test results. Penalties are generally progressive, involving removal from extracurricular activities for progressively longer periods of time, depending on the number of violations and whether students complied with attendance at drug-assessment programs.[127] In public schools, removal penalties are limited to extracurricular activities and have not been extended to removals from school; however, if the latter, they may represent violations, if not of the Fourth Amendment's prohibition against unlawful searches, then at least of the right to an education under most state constitutions. Even so, officials in nonpublic schools are likely not prohibited from including removals from school among the list of penalties in their handbooks.

---

[124] *See* Doe v. High-Tech Inst., 972 P.2d 1060 [132 Educ. L. Rep. 989] (Colo. Ct. App. 1998) (deciding that a student who consented to a rubella test had an invasion of privacy claim where a school official instructed the testing agency to test for HIV, as well).

[125] *See* Theodore v. Delaware Valley Sch. Dist., 836 A.2d 76, 80 [183 Educ. L. Rep. 174] (Pa. 2003) (upholding a procedure identifying right to know as including "the guidance counselor, the student's coach and/or advisor, the designated substance abuse professional, and the Student Assistance Team"); Penn-Harris-Madison Sch. Corp. v. Joy, 768 N.E.2d 940, 943 (Ind. Ct. App. 2002) (affirming the validity of a policy under which school staff received information "on a need-to-know basis only and may not divulge test results to anyone other than the student and parent except under court order.")

[126] Other defenses are presumably possible. *See* Brennan v. Bd. of Trs. for Univ. of La. Sys., 691 So.2d 324 [117 Educ. L. Rep. 803] (La. Ct. App. 1997) (where a student who tested positive for anabolic steroid testosterone unsuccessfully argued that his high level of testosterone was due to sexual activity the night before the test).

[127] Policies have described the progressive nature of penalties variously. *See, e.g.*, Linke v. Northwestern Sch. Corp., 763 N.E.2d 972 [162 Educ. L. Rep. 525] (Ind. 2002); Miller v. Wilkes, 172 F.3d 574 [133 Educ. L. Rep. 765] (8th Cir. 1999); Schaill v. Tippicanoe County Sch. Corp., 864 F.2d 1309 [45 Educ. L. Rep. 651] (7th Cir. 1988).

Employee Searches and Drug Testing

Employee Searches

The leading Supreme Court case on employee searches, *O'Connor v. Ortega (Ortega)*,[128] relied largely on *T.L.O.*, but did not involve a school setting. The Supreme Court has yet to address a school employee search case comparable to student searches in *T.L.O.*

The search in *Ortega* involved two hospital officials who entered the locked personal office of a medical doctor in charge of residents, ostensibly looking for evidence of alleged sexual harassment and suspected coercion of past residents to donate money for his computer. The two officials did not discover any evidence supporting either allegation, but did look through the doctor's personal possessions. Ultimately, although the officials claimed that they were also conducting an inventory of the materials in the doctor's office, they placed his personal possessions, along with hospital property, in boxes.

Ortega represented an incredible odyssey through the federal court system, giving definition to the notion that justice moves with leaden speed. After being dismissed in 1981, the doctor filed suit in a federal trial in California in 1982, alleging that the officials violated his Fourth Amendment rights in searching and seizing some of his property. On further review of a grant of summary judgment in favor of the defendants, the Ninth Circuit affirmed on their behalf.[129]

In 1987, the Supreme Court reversed in favor of the doctor, remanding to the Ninth Circuit, which remanded to the trial court.[130] In 1993, the trial court upheld its initial order treating the search as reasonable in light of the Supreme Court's judgment.[131] However, in 1995 the Ninth Circuit reversed in part, again remanding.[132] At trial in 1996, a jury found that the two hospital officials conducted an unconstitutional search and seizure, awarding the doctor $376,000 in compensatory damages plus $25,000 in punitive damages against one official and $35,000 against the other. The Ninth Circuit affirmed in favor of the doctor in 1998,[133] who finally prevailed sixteen years after filing suit.

The *Ortega* Court's discussion is useful, but not very helpful in terms of trying to distill acceptable guidelines for search and seizure involving employees. Applying the *T.L.O.* reasonable suspicion rationale, the Justices held that employee workplace searches must be reasonable both as to their inception and scope. The Justices added that employees' expectations of privacy are influenced by the amount of access other persons have to the workplace, which in this case involved a doctor who had a personal, locked office. The Court suggested that the workplace applies only to the area over which employers exert control—such as hallways, break room, desks, file cabinets, and class-

---

[128] 480 U.S. 709 (1987).
[129] 764 F.2d 703 (9th Cir. 1985).
[130] 817 F.2d 1408 (9th Cir. 1987).
[131] 1993 WL 87804 (N.D. Cal. 1993).
[132] 50 F.3d 778 (9th Cir. 1985).
[133] 146 F.3d 1149 (9th Cir. 1998).

rooms—but does not extend to the personal property of the employees in their offices in the form of personal luggage, handbags, briefcases, and the like.

The *Ortega* Court identified three reasons explaining why entering employees' workplaces would be facially reasonable: to take inventories pursuant to established policies, such as when individuals announce they are leaving their jobs; to investigate claims of wrongdoing, which the officials disingenuously alleged in *Ortega*; and to locate records, reports, or files belonging to the employers. An inference from the listing of these three reasons is that all other bases for conducting searches of employee offices need individualized suspicion. Another inference seems to be that searches of employees' personal property also need individualized suspicion. While the doctor was not present during the search of his office, the Court's analysis sheds no light on how his presence would have affected the outcome.

In a post-*Ortega* case, the Second Circuit[134] provides some insight about handling of the property of departing employees. Here, officials in New York gave a public school teacher who was dismissed for misconduct two opportunities to remove his personal property from his classroom. Although the former teacher removed some of his property, he did not take it all, leading school administrators to have the lock on the classroom file cabinet drilled out and have the remaining materials placed in boxes. When the teacher picked up the boxes, he alleged that a number of personal items were missing.

In assessing the teacher's expectation of privacy, the Second Circuit held that once the teacher surrendered his room keys and had an opportunity to pick up his personal items, he no longer had an expectation of privacy. Of some note is that the Second Circuit's definition of expectation of privacy differed from that of the trial court, which would not have granted the former teacher any privacy expectation because his room was accessible by others, such as teachers, custodians, students, and administrators. The Second Circuit's opinion, in effect, suggests that teachers have expectations of privacy until they act, or fail to act, in response to collecting personal materials, to divest the indicia of control in the form of the room key. While the trial court's definition of privacy would be much easier for educators to manage, the Second Circuit's rationale imposes a measure of continuing responsibility on building administrators.

Electronic Surveillance

An order of an appellate court in Ohio offers some insight into the appropriate use of surveillance. When a principal suspected third-shift custodians of taking unauthorized breaks, he had a hidden video camera installed in the break room. The videotape revealed evidence of unauthorized breaks, and, in response to being disciplined, the custodians filed suit challenging the use of the videotape as an unlawful search.

---

[134] Shaul v. Cherry Valley-Springfield Cent. Sch. Dist., 363 F.3d 177 [186 EDUC. L. REP. 604] (2d Cir. 2004).

Upholding the principal's action, an appellate court agreed that custodians could not have an expectation of privacy in a break room accessible to all employees.[135] The court observed that the search was reasonable at its inception because the principal had reasonable suspicion about the unauthorized breaks. Most importantly, though, in terms of the reasonableness of scope, the court determined that the search was less intrusive than it could have been because the principal turned off the sound and recorded only the visual images it portrayed.

Suspicionless Searches

Suspicionless searches of teachers very closely follows the laws applicable to students. Courts have upheld policies allowing dog sniffing of vehicles in a school parking lot,[136] including teachers' vehicles.[137] Presumably, school employees could also be subject to having to pass through metal detectors on entry to school buildings due to concerns for safety. In public schools, some management prerogatives in conducting employee searches may be affected by the negotiated terms of collective bargaining agreements, a limitation not as likely to exist in nonpublic schools.

Searches of Employee Computers

In evaluating whether employees have expectations of privacy in their work computers, courts have looked to *Ortega* for guidance. Although some federal circuit courts agreed that employees have reasonable expectations of privacy in the contents of their office computers,[138] the courts have permitted employers to alter expectations in light of their "office practices, procedures, or regulations."[139]

Guidelines for Employee Searches

Officials in nonpublic schools are unlikely to be subjected to the Fourth Amendment arguments that dominate searches in public schools. Even so,

---

[135] Brannen v. Kings Local Sch. Dist. Bd. of Educ., 761 N.E.2d 84 [160 EDUC. L. REP. 535] (Ohio Ct. App. 2001).

[136] *See, e.g.*, Marner v. Eufala City Sch. Bd., 204 F. Supp.2d 1318 [166 EDUC. L. REP. 224] (M.D. Ala. 2002) (upholding the search of a student's car that led to the discovery of a knife, pursuant to a dog alert to narcotics that were not found).

[137] *See, e.g.*, Hearn v. Bd. of Pub. Educ., 191 F.3d 1329 [138 EDUC. L. REP. 662] (11th Cir. 1999), *cert. denied*, 529 U.S. 1109 (2000) (upholding the dismissal of a teacher who refused to comply with a board policy to submit to a drug test within two hours of the discovery of drugs in her car after a dog alerted officials as to the presence of contraband).

[138] *See* United States v. Slanina, 359 F.3d 356 (5th Cir. 2004), *reh'g and reh'g en banc denied*, 99 Fed.Appx. 564 (2994), *cert. denied*, 543 U.S. 845 (2004) (upholding the defendant's conviction for possession of child pornography on a work computer despite his reasonable expectation of privacy as to his files because the *Ortega* exception to warrant a requirement applied). For other cases upholding searches, see Muick v. Glenayre Electronics, 280 F.3d 741 (7th Cir. 2002); Leventhal v. Knalek, 266 F.3d 64 (2d Cir. 2001); United States v. Simons, 206 F.3d 392 (4th Cir. 2000), *aff'd after remand*, 2001 WL 265182 (4th Cir. 2001).

[139] United States v. Simons, *Id.* at 398.

officials in nonpublic schools can benefit from the following factors applicable in public schools.

1. Create comprehensive search policies for employees comparable to those for students. If officials wish to have unlimited, suspicionless access to employee work areas to look through school-owned desks, cabinets, file cabinets, and the like, their policies should state this explicitly.

2. Searches of the personal property of an employee, such as luggage, purses, and briefcases, should only be based on individualized reasonable suspicion.

3. Base policies limiting suspicionless access to employee work spaces to the three reasons enunciated in *Ortega* and have lists of items that are the objects of the search. While having such lists is not mentioned in *Ortega*, it does provide credibility if challenges arise to the inception or scope of the searches.

4. Provide any teachers who have been dismissed, or their contracts not renewed, mutually acceptable times to remove personal items. Policies can and should allow a board representative to ensure that individuals do not inadvertently take school materials.

Employee Drug Testing

Drug testing for public school employees generally is a matter of collective bargaining negotiations. In many school systems, teachers must submit to drug testing prior to being hired, but after that, drug testing tends to be limited to individualized suspicion.

The Sixth Circuit was the federal appellate court to uphold mandatory random drug testing for teachers and other school employees such as principals, traveling teachers, teacher aides, substitute teachers, secretaries, and school bus drivers in Tennessee. The court allowed testing to continue because these educators had "safety-sensitive" positions[140] comparable to other safety positions, such as railroad crews after being involved in accidents[141] and customs agents engaged in drug interdiction.[142] The court reasoned that school personnel were safety-sensitive because they were responsible for the safety and security of children and, since education is a highly regulated field, similar to railroads and customs.[143]

---

[140] Knox Cnty. Educ. Ass'n v. Knox Cty. Bd. of Educ., 158 F.3d 361 [130 Educ. L. Rep. 62] (6th Cir. 1998). For a commentary on this case, see Charles J. Russo & Ralph D. Mawdsley, *Drug Testing of Teachers: Student Safety v. Teacher Rights or An Overreaching School Board?* 134 Educ. L. Rep. 661 (1999).

[141] Skinner v. R.R. Labor Executives Ass'n, 489 U.S. 602 (1989).

[142] National Treasury Employees Union v. Von Raab, 489 U.S. 656 (1989).

[143] *But see* American Fed'n of Teachers-West Va. AFL-CIO v. Kanawha Cnty. Bd. of Educ., 592 F. Supp.2d 883 [241 Educ. L. Rep. 570] (S.D. W.Va. 2009); Jones v. Graham Cnty. Bd. of Educ., 677 S.E.2d 171 [245 Educ. L. Rep. 497] (N.C. Ct. App. 2009) (invalidating suspicionless drug testing policies premised on the safety-sensitive nature of teaching).

Courts have upheld suspicionless drug testing of other educational employees such as school bus attendants;[144] a mechanic's helper;[145] bus drivers (following accidents resulting in bodily injury or $1000 in property damage, except where buses were hit when parked legally);[146] and custodians, as well as other safety-sensitive school personnel in an elementary school.[147] In these cases the courts agreed that the safety-sensitive nature of the job functions involved outweighed the expectation of privacy of school employees.

Because officials in nonpublic schools are not subject to the constitutional concerns of the safety-sensitive nature of their employees, they have almost complete freedom to impose suspicionless drug testing—subject, of course, to the few schools for which such a requirement might be a matter for collective bargaining. The procedures used when drug testing employees in nonpublic schools should be similar to those for students, especially when protecting the confidentiality of test results, because revealing confidential information about employees may lead to claims for invasion of privacy.[148]

If officials in nonpublic schools intend to introduce drug testing for students, it is difficult to argue why they should not also test employees. Even if students are not going to be tested, employees could still be tested on being hired. However, officials in nonpublic schools need to consider carefully whether suspicionless testing of employees thereafter, without also testing students, might send the wrong message to parents that the employees are a suspect group in need of constant monitoring.

Conclusion

School safety continues to be a driving force in school administrative decisions as it remains in the forefront of national discussions. The Omnibus Spending Bill passed by Congress and signed into law by President Trump in the spring of 2018 included $2.3 billion in new spending specifically for school safety.[149] These funds, administered through the departments of Justice,

---

[144] Jones v. Jenkins, 878 F.2d 1476 [54 Educ. L. Rep. 1138] (D.C. Cir. 1989) (permitting testing without probable cause).

[145] English v. Talladega Cnty. Bd. of Educ., 938 F. Supp. 775 [113 Educ. L. Rep. 291] (N.D. Ala. 1996).

[146] Cornette v. Commonwealth, 899 S.W.2d 502 [101 Educ. L. Rep. 474] (Ky. Ct. App. 1995).

[147] Aubrey v. School Bd. of Lafayette Parish, 148 F.3d 559 [127 Educ. L. Rep. 710] (5th Cir. 1998).

[148] See Hanssen v. Our Redeemer Lutheran Church, 938 S.W.2d 85 (Tex. Ct. App. 1996) (rejecting claims for both defamation, after church officials sent letters to all parents that the former secretary misappropriated school funds, and a false light invasion of privacy charge, because it was incorporated into defamation in Texas); see also Gosche v. Calvert Sch., 997 F. Supp. 867 [126 Educ. L. Rep. 219] (N.D. Ohio 1998) (rejecting an invasion of privacy claim against the head of a religious school who asked a teacher about an affair with the father of children in the school, where the investigation was pursuant to the school's religious values and the principal's conduct was not outrageous).

[149] Committee on Appropriations (2018a). House approves omnibus bill to fund federal government. Retrieved from https://appropriations.house.gov/news/documentsingle.aspx?DocumentID=395176

Education, and Health and Human Services, "include flexible funding for mental health programs designed by local governments and schools that will enable them to find creative solutions to improve school safety."[150] Devising solutions to school safety issues takes more than just money. Cooperation between and among school officials, government at all levels, and families is essential. In addition to funding for mental health services, schools need resources for policy development, planning, construction, and technological equipment. All of these innovations have one thing in common—they must remain within the bounds of the law.

Discussion Questions

1. What are the different elements of a crisis management plan for a private school? Why is important for a private school to have a crisis management plan?

2. What does the Every Student Succeed Act require in terms of school safety? Specifically address ESSA language about persistently dangerous schools.

3. Private schools operate under contract law. How does contract law affect private school officials' decision-making process concerning student searches?

4. Does the sniff of a drug dog constitute a search? Would the answer to this question be different in a private school instead of a public school?

5. Discuss the effects of cellphones on the legal landscape of private schools. Be sure to address both cyberspeech and searches of cellphones. What revisions to a private school's policy manual would you recommend in regard to students' cellphones?

6. What guidelines have the federal courts provided for conducting employee searches?

7. May private school officials conduct urinalysis drug testing of employees? Why or why not?

---

[150] Committee on Appropriations (2018b). FY 2018 Omnibus Fact Sheet- Labor, HHS, Education. Retrieved from https://appropriations.house.gov/uploadedfiles/ 03.21.18_fy18_omnibus_-_labor_hhs_education_-_one_pager.pdf n.p.

Key Words

Crime reporting
Crisis management plans
Drug testing
Safety codes
Searches

7

School Finance

Barbara M. De Luca and Steven A. Hinshaw

Contents

Introduction / 206
Constitutional and Legal Historical Background / 207
      Federal Funding / 207
      State Funding / 207
Revenues / 208
      Sources of Private Money / 208
            Tuition / 208
            Donations, Stewardship, Philanthropy / 210
      Public Money / 211
            Federal Level / 211
            State Level / 213
      Other Revenue Sources / 214
Budgets / 215
      Budget Objectives / 215
      Budget Allocations / 215
      Budget Approaches / 216
            Line Item Budgeting / 216
            Incremental Budgeting / 216
            Performance-Based Budgeting / 217
            Planning, Programming, and Budgeting Systems / 217
            Management by Objectives / 218
            Zero-based Budgeting / 218
            Cutback (Decremental) Budgeting / 219
            Weighted Student Funding as a Budgeting Approach / 219
      Budget Roles and Responsibilities / 220
      Capital Budgeting / 221
Conclusion / 221
Discussion Questions / 222
Key Words / 222

Introduction

School finance, whether private or public, depends on the number of schools involved and how many teachers and students are in those schools. The number of private schools of all types in the United States increased from 33,000 in fall of 1999 to 33,370 in 2009 and 34,580 in the fall 2015, while the number of students decreased from 6,018,280 in 1999 to 5,488,490 in 2009, but rebounded somewhat in 2015 to 5,750,520. At the same time, the number of full-time equivalent teachers increased from 408,400 in 1999 to 481,560 in 2015.[1]

During the 2015-2016 school year, 78.2% of students attending private schools went to schools with some religious affiliation.[2] In light of these numbers, this chapter reviews key issues relevant to finance in private or nonpublic schools, addressing whether public funds can be used in nonpublic PK-12 schools.

Because state and local governments are responsible for elementary and secondary education under the Tenth Amendment,[3] public schools are funded primarily by the states and local communities, with some categorical grant money coming from the federal government. While public PK-12 schools are funded with public tax money, private schools, whether sectarian or nonsectarian, are funded primarily by private money, usually by the households of the children attending them, in the form of tuition. Limited exceptions to this pattern exist. For example, in Wichita, Kansas, parishioners, with and without children in the schools, tithe 8% of their income to their Roman Catholic parishes, which contribute 10% of their income to the diocese. This provides funds for the diocese to subsidize the poor schools, freeing individual families in poor parishes from the requirement of paying tuition.[4]

Over time, critics and supporters have posed many arguments for and against allowing public funding for private schools. One of the arguments promoting state funding is that public education would face even more serious

---

[1] U.S. Department of Education (2016), National Center for Education Statistics. *Digest of education statistics.* Table 205.40. Number and percentage distribution of private elementary and secondary students, teachers, and schools, by orientation of school and selected characteristics: Fall 1999, Fall 2009, and Fall 2015. Retrieved from ed.gov/programs/digest/d16/tables/dt16_205.40asp.

[2] Stephen P. Brougham, Adam Rettig, & Jennifer Peterson, *Characteristics of private schools in the United States: Results from the 2015-16 Private School Universe survey first look* (NCES 2017-073) (August 2017). U.S. Department of Education. Washington, DC: National Center for Education Statistics at 6. Retrieved from http://nces.ed.gov/pubsearch. This chapter uses the terms religiously affiliated nonpublic schools, private religious schools, and faith-based schools interchangeably.

[3] *See, e.g.,* San Antonio Indep. Sch. Dist. v. Rodriguez, 411 U.S. 1, 35 (1973): "[e]ducation, of course, is not among the rights afforded explicit protection under our Federal Constitution. Nor do we find any basis for saying it is implicitly so protected;" Plyler v. Doe, 457 U.S. 202, 221 [4 Educ. L. Rep. 953] (1982), *reh'g denied*, 458 U.S. 1131, 91982) ("[p]ublic education is not a 'right' granted to individuals by the Constitution." (internal citations omitted).

[4] Valerie Schmalz, *Paying for Catholic School.* The Priest, 65(9), 10-14, 86-87 (2009).

financial challenges then it now confronts. More specifically, if private schools did not exist, states and local communities would have even more difficulty due to the financial support they would need to pay for the additional students who would populate the public schools. As interesting as this issue is, a discussion of whether private schools should survive is beyond the purview of this chapter. Rather, along with providing a brief glimpse of key cases on aid to nonpublic schools, the remainder of this chapter focuses on sound budgeting principles so that educational leaders and their lawyers can use their funds wisely to keep schools in operation.

Constitutional and Legal Historical Background

The Supreme Court upheld the right of private PK-12 schools to educate students in *Pierce v. Society of Sisters*, a dispute over a challenge to Oregon's compulsory attendance law.[5] This law required most children in Oregon, other than those who today would be classified as needing special education, to attend only public schools. Invalidating the statute as unconstitutional, the Court opened the door to allowing private schools to continue to educate children across the country. However, once private schools were deemed legal, public funding was, and continues to be, called into question.

Federal Funding

Issues surrounding funding for private religious schools focus largely on judicial interpretations of the U.S. Constitution, as the Supreme Court has interpreted a wide array of cases involving aid under the Establishment Clause. As interpreted by the Court, the Establishment Clause mandates separation of church and state, originally "intended to prohibit the federal government from declaring and financially supporting a national religion."[6] However, starting with *Everson v. Board of Education* (*Everson*) in 1947,[7] a lengthy line of Supreme Court cases have examined the parameters of the Establishment Clause over the constitutionally permissible use of public money for private religious schools.

State Funding

The earliest case on aid—albeit under the Fourteenth, rather than the First, Amendment—was *Cochran vs. Louisiana State Board of Education*. The Court affirmed an order of the Supreme Court of Louisiana upholding the constitutionality of a state law mandating the loans of secular textbooks to all students, regardless of where they attended school.

---

[5] 268 U.S. 510 (1925).

[6] Doug Linder, *Exploring Constitutional Conflicts, Introduction to the Establishment Clause.* Retrieved from http://law2.umkc.edu/faculty/projects/ftrials/conlaw/estabinto.htm (2001).

[7] 330 U.S. 1 (1947), *reh'g denied*, 347 U.S. 855 (1947) (upholding the constitutionality of a law from New Jersey which permitted local boards to reimburse parents for the cost of transporting their children to nonpublic schools).

In *Everson*, the Supreme Court, relying on the construct known as the Child Benefit Test, ruled that parents of students in private, religious schools in New Jersey could be reimbursed for the costs of transporting their children to school.[8] *Everson* was the initial case in which the Court based its judgment on the Establishment Clause of the First Amendment, thereby ushering in the modern era of its Establishment Clause jurisprudence.

The Child Benefit Test has had something of a checkered history, as the Supreme Court has gone through periods when it has not always upheld aid to faith-based schools and their students under its provisions. The differences emerged because the Court tended to interpret the tripartite *Lemon v. Kurtzman* test,[9] by far the most important case in this area, differently depending on the views of the Justices sitting at a particular time. The Child Benefit Test was rejuvenated, though, in *Agostini v. Felton*,[10] wherein the Justices allowed public school personnel in New York City to enter faith-based schools to assist students who were entitled to aid under Title I.

In *Zelman v. Simmons-Harris*,[11] the Supreme Court subsequently upheld the use of vouchers that allowed students in Cleveland, Ohio, to attend faith-based schools. In its analysis, the Justices pointed out that students attended the religious schools based on the free choices of their parents, rather than by operation of law. Chapter 3 includes a full discussion of the litigation at the Supreme Court with regard to religiously affiliated nonpublic schools and their students.

As indicated above, the sources of private school revenues are both public and private. Moreover, the cases just discussed, along with many others, provide the foundation for whether, and how much, public money can be spent in nonpublic schools. The following section reviews the public and private revenues of private schools.

Revenues

Sources of Private Money

Tuition

As perhaps could have been expected, the largest revenue source for private schools is tuition. The amount of tuition revenues schools realize is

---

[8] *Id.*

[9] 403 U.S. 602 (1971). According to the *Lemon* test: Every analysis in this area must begin with consideration of the cumulative criteria developed by the Court over many years. Three such tests may be gleaned from our cases. First, the statute must have a secular legislative purpose; second, its principal or primary effect must be one that neither advances nor inhibits religion; finally, the statute must not foster "an excessive government entanglement with religion." When dealing with entanglement, the Court identified three additional factors: "we must examine the character and purposes of the institutions that are benefitted, the nature of the aid that the State provides, and the resulting relationship between the government and religious authority." *Id.* at 615.

[10] 521 U.S. 203 (1997).

[11] 536 U.S. 639 (2002).

based on two factors: student enrollment numbers and the dollar value of the tuition. The average tuition for private schools for the 2017-2018 school year was $10,302 per student per year. The average tuition for elementary school children was $9263, while the average for secondary students was $14,017. Nebraska had the lowest average tuition, at $3155, and Connecticut the highest, at $24,171.[12] However, these numbers do not consider the cost of living, whether schools are religiously affiliated, whether schools are boarding or for day students, or other factors that can impact the amount of tuition school officials must charge.

The U.S. Department of Education reported that the highest average tuition in 2011-2012 was for nonsectarian schools, $21, 910, while the lowest was for Roman Catholic schools, $7020.[13] Much has been written about the size of tuition increases in private schools. For example, between 1996 and 2015 tuition increased 196% when not accounting for inflation.[14] Patrick Bassett, former president of the National Association of Independent Schools, said that one of the "factors great schools have in common" is that they "create a financially sustainable future by means other than persistently large annual tuition increases."[15] Yet, such tuition increases clearly are not sustainable in the long term.

Besides the increase in tuition each year, annual tuition dollars depend on the number of students in the schools. The student population in nonsectarian private schools increased from 19.65% of the total of all schoolchildren in 1995 to 24.33% in 2015. This amount also increased in all religious schools other than those that are Roman Catholic, from 35.39% to 39.45%. The student population in Catholic schools decreased from 44.95% of the total in 1995 to 36.22% in 2015,[16] evidencing a steady decline in enrollments that started in the

---

[12] Average Private School Tuition Cost (2017-2018). (2017). *Private School Review*. Retrieved from https://www.privateschoolreview.com/tuition-stats/private-school-cost-by-state.

[13] U.S. Department of Education, National Center for Education Statistics. *Digest of Educational Statistics 2013*, Table 205.50. Private elementary and secondary enrollment, number of schools, and average tuition, by school level, orientation, and tuition, selected years, 1999-2000 through 2011-2012. Retrieved from https://nces.ed.gov/programs/ digest/d13/tables/ dt13_205.50.asp (2013).

[14] William Daughtrey, William Hester, & Kevin Weatherill (2016). *Tuition Trends in Independent Day Schools, 2014-2015 National Association of Independent Schools*. Retrieved from https:// www.nais.org/ Articles/Documents/MemberCapstoneProject-Revised. pdf. p. 1-69. See also John Chubb & Clark Constance, TRENDBOOK 2014-2015, National Association of Independent Schools at 12 (2015).

[15] Patrick F. Bassett, 2013. *Twenty-five Factors Great Schools have in Common*. INDEPENDENT SCHOOL MAGAZINE, 72(2) (2013). Retrieved from https://www.nais.org/magazine/independent-school/winter-2013/twenty-five-factors-great-schools-have-in- comm-(1) at 9-10.

[16] U.S. Department of Education, National Center for Education Statistics. *Digest of Educational Statistics 2016*, Table 205.20. Enrollment and percentage distribution of students enrolled in private elementary and secondary schools, by school orientation and grade level: Selected years, Fall 1995 through Fall 2015. Retrieved from (2016).

late 1960s.[17] These increases for most of the schools translate into additional tuition revenues; decreases result in fewer tuition dollars.

One would think that raising tuition leads to further decreases in enrollment. Even so, there is little, if any, concrete evidence of such a trend. Because the cost of educating students is greater than the amount of tuition their parents pay, if school enrollments are small, there are insufficient revenues to keep them operating because per-pupil costs decrease as enrollment increases, based on economies of scale.

In 2015, 35% of the nonsectarian private schools had fewer than 150 students; about 34.4% of religious schools had less than 300 students.[18] When enrollment dips below the break-even point between revenues and expenditures, other sources of revenue are necessary to keep schools in business. As noted previously, when identifying financial practices of successful private schools, their officials must "[c]reate a financially sustainable future by means other than persistently large annual tuition increases."[19]

Donations, Stewardship, Philanthropy

Donations are the second most common source of revenue for private schools, especially religious schools. Most donations come from individuals, typically through regular contributions in weekly collections such as in Roman Catholic parishes; corporations/businesses; alumni; and religious organizations. Donations from these sources often go to financial aid to help families who are unable to pay the full tuition for their children. According to a report from the National Association of Independent Schools, in 2013, 92% of families received financial aid from at least one of the schools to which they applied.[20] Because philanthropy is critical to private schools, recommendations follow for increasing the number of donors and the dollar values of individual donations.

Research strongly suggests that school boards in private schools are crucial to successful fundraising; thus, individuals with development expertise

---

[17] "U.S. Catholic school enrollment reached its peak during the early 1960s when there were more than 5.2 million students in almost thirteen thousand schools across the nation .... Total Catholic school student enrollment for the current academic year [of 2016-2017] is 1,878,824. 1,309,429 in elementary/middle schools; 569,395 in secondary schools." National Catholic Education Association, Catholic School Data, Retrieved from http://www.ncea.org/NCEA/Proclaim/Catholic_School_Data/Catholic_School_Data.aspx (2018).

[18] U.S. Department of Education, National Center for Education Statistics. *Digest of Educational Statistics 2016*, Table 205.30 Percentage distribution of students enrolled in private elementary and secondary schools, by school orientation and selected characteristics for selected years, fall 2005 through Fall 2015. Retrieved from https://nces.ed.gov/programs/digest/d16/tables/dt16_205.30.asp (2016).

[19] Patrick F. Bassett, *Twenty-five Factors Great Schools have in Common*. INDEPENDENT SCHOOL MAGAZINE, *72*(2) (Winter, 2013). Retrieved from https://www.nais.org/magazine/independent-school/winter-2013/twenty-five-factors-great-schools-have-in- comm-(1), p.10.

[20] Mark Mitchell, *More Families Receiving Larger Financial Aid Package to Afford Private School*. National Association of Independent Schools (2015). Retrieved from larger-financial-aid-packa/.

should be asked to serve on boards.[21] Moreover, because board members must understand that they are expected to donate, some candidates for membership should come with previous donor lists. Policies should set clear expectations for the financial contributions of board members. Insofar as board members often are parents who are already paying tuition in parish schools, they may not have extra money for donating unless everyone on the board is wealthy. Regardless, board members should understand that fundraising is a priority. Having pointed this out, it is interesting that only 11% of respondents in one survey identified philanthropy as the highest priority for board members.[22]

The author of a white paper reviewed the research literature, including her own, in an effort to identify ways to increase donor dollars.[23] When fundraising, leaders should keep in mind that potential donors like to know that the schools or institutions raising money have "skin in the game," meaning they have contributed seed money. Donors also like to know how their money is being used and the value (nonmonetary) of their donations, meaning what project(s) their contributions funded. Interestingly enough, more money is contributed when donors must do something to be able to give, such as when some fundraisers plan races requiring runners to secure dollar-value pledges for each mile or kilometer they run.

Another tactic that officials can employ in attempts to raise more money, as well as increase the number of donors, is to provide donors with options such as allowing them to choose which projects they want portions of their money to support. Another point to keep in mind is that leaders planning fundraising campaigns must know their audiences; if school populations are less wealthy and the expectation is for smaller donations, it is important to remind donors of what can be done if everyone gives something, even if the "something" is small. On the other hand, if audiences are wealthy, leaders should promote the difference each donor can make. Additionally, research indicates that school leaders should find out what other large fundraising campaigns are occurring in nearby schools at the same time, in order to avoid overlaps. [24]

Public Money

Federal Level

In *Aguilar v. Felton*,[25] the Supreme Court forbade the on-site delivery of Title I services to students in religiously affiliated nonpublic schools as violating

---

[21] Marts & Lundy, *Setting a Curse for Sustainable Philanthropy: The Role of Boards and Fundraising in Independent Schools*. December, 2016, 1-20 Retrieved from FINAL_12_16. pdf.

[22] *Id.*

[23] Ashley V. Whillans, *A Brief Introduction to the Science of Fundraising*. CASE WHITE PAPER (2016). Retrieved from http://www.case.org/Publications_and_Products/White_Papers/ WP_Fundraising.html, 1-16.

[24] *Id.*

[25] 473 U.S. 402 (1985).

the Establishment Clause. However, twelve years later, in *Agostini v. Felton*,[26] the Court dissolved the injunction holding its earlier order in place, thereby opening the door for religious and nonreligious private schools to receive greater assistance from the federal government. Moreover, the Supreme Court's most recent judgment in *Trinity Lutheran Church v. Comer*,[27] which prohibits public officials from conferring or denying benefits to faith-based institutions or individuals solely due to their religious beliefs, seems to have opened a new door on the parameters of acceptable aid to faith-based institutions.

Since the passage of the Elementary and Secondary Education Act (ESEA) in 1965, the federal government, through local and state education agencies, has sought to provide equitable services to students and teachers of nonprofit private schools, including those that are religious in nature. Adjustments have been made in the reauthorization of ESEA in No Child Left Behind (NCLB) 2001 and Every Student Succeeds Act (ESSA).[28]

Under the ESSA, in a manner consistent with the Child Benefit Test, assistance cannot go directly to the schools; it can only go to students and teachers and, in some cases, other school personnel and parents. In order to qualify for federal grant money, students must attend private schools in public school districts eligible for the grants, meaning that they must be in low-income areas or in districts that are either failing or at risk of failing academically.

Under the ESSA, federal dollars go to local education agencies (LEAs) insofar as eligible students are included in the count of all local public district students. Among the programs in the ESSA that fund students from private schools are Title I – Improving the Academic Achievement of the Disadvantaged; Title II – Preparing, Training, and Recruiting High-quality Teachers and Principals; Title III – Language Instruction for LEP and Immigrant Students; Title IV – 21st Century Schools (Safe and Drug-free Schools and 21st Century Learning Centers); and Title V – Promoting Informed Parental Choice and Innovative Programs.[29]

Federal money may also provide benefits to students whose parents unilaterally place them in private schools under the Individuals with Disability Education Act (IDEA).[30] The IDEA "requires each state to ensure that a free appropriate public education (FAPE) is available to all eligible children

---

[26] 521 U.S. 203 (1997). *See also* VERN BRIMLEY, JR., & RULON R. GARFIELD, FINANCING EDUCATION IN A CLIMATE OF CHANGE, 8th Ed. (2002) at 254-255.

[27] For a commentary on this case, see William E. Thro & Charles J. Russo, *Odious to the Constitution: The Educational Implications of Trinity Lutheran Church v. Comer*, 346 EDUC. L. REP. 1 (2017).

[28] 20 U.S.C.A. §§ 6301 *et seq.*

[29] U.S. Department of Education. *ONPE General Issues Frequently Asked Questions Related to Nonpublic Schools.* Retrieved from https://www2.ed.gov/print/about/offices/ list/oii/nonpublic/faqgeneral.html (2015).

[30] 20 U.S.C.A. §§ 1400 *et seq.* Chapter 7 addresses issues associated with the IDEA and nonpublic schools.

with disabilities residing in that state."[31] The IDEA obligates LEAs to spend proportionate amounts of their federal special education funds on children in private schools, even though these services are neither identical to nor equal in amount to what their peers in public schools receive.[32]

State Level

Vouchers and tuition tax credits and deductions are currently the largest source of state revenue for private schools, especially secular schools. Tuition tax credits allow parents of students enrolled in private elementary and secondary schools to subtract the value of school tuition, and perhaps other costs, from the tax liabilities of their households, dollar-for-dollar. Tax deductions allow households to use tuition, and sometimes other costs such as books and transportation, as tax deductions, thereby reducing their taxable incomes. At the time of this writing, five states allowed tax credits or deductions: Alabama, Illinois, Iowa, Minnesota and South Carolina. Four states currently have tax deduction programs: Indiana, Louisiana, Minnesota and Wisconsin.[33] Both credits and deductions have largely withstood judicial challenges.[34]

State voucher programs give parents of students in public schools publicly funded vouchers worth specific dollar amounts to take to private schools, religious or otherwise, to pay for all or parts of the costs of attendance. Fifteen states and Washington, DC currently have at least one voucher program in place.[35]

In *Zelman v. Simmons-Harris* (*Zelman*),[36] the Supreme Court upheld Cleveland Ohio's voucher program as not violating the Establishment Clause because children attended religious schools, most of which were Roman Catholic, based on the choices of their parents rather than by operation of the law. Because *Zelman* is likely limited to its facts—meaning it is unlikely to apply in another case unless an urban school system that operated under a desegregation order and was taken over by the state seeks to create such a program—its direct impact has been negligible. Although participation eligibility varies from state to state and program to program, many voucher program participation

---

[31] U.S. Department of Education. The Individuals with Disabilities Education Act: Provisions Related to Children with Disabilities Enrolled by their Parents in Private Schools. Retrieved from https://www2.ed.gov/admins/lead/speced/privateschools/idea.pdf (2011) at 1.

[32] 20 U.S.C. § 1412(a)(10)(A)(i)(I); 34 C.F.R. § 300.133.

[33] EdChoice, *Fast Facts on School Choice*. Retrieved from http://www.edchoice.org/our-resources/fast-facts (2017).

[34] *See, e.g.*, Mueller v. Allen, 463 U.S. 388 (1983) (upholding a statute from Minnesota that granted all parents state income tax deductions for the actual costs of tuition, textbooks, and transportation associated with sending their children to K-12 schools.

[35] EdChoice, *Fast Facts on School Choice*, Retrieved from http://www.edchoice.org/ourresources/fast-facts. *See also* U.S. Department of Education (2017). National Center for Education Statistics. *State Education Reforms. Table 4.7. States with voucher programs, by state: 2017.* Retrieved from https://nces.ed.gov/programs/statereform/tab4_7.asp (2017).

[36] 536 U.S. 639 (2002).

requirements include household income caps, failing public schools, and/or students with special needs.

Many vouchers do not cover the total costs of tuition. Still, because vouchers increase enrollments, they often lead to increased total revenues for many private schools. For example, Ohio's EdChoice Scholarship (voucher) Program was worth $4650 for K-8 students and $6000 for students in grades 9-12 for 2017-18,[37] with the result that one Catholic school realized about one-half million dollars in revenue from the vouchers; others may receive even more. The major problem for schools that depend on state-funded vouchers is the risk of economic fluctuations, particularly downturns, impacting state finances. Put another way, when state funds decrease, it is possible that voucher funding will be curtailed or limited to some extent.

Other Revenue Sources

Although not a widespread practice, "The Stewardship Model"[38] in Wichita, Kansas, has generated enough revenue to pay the full tuition of all students in the diocese's schools.[39] A different take on donating, this model promotes the value of a Catholic school education, and, by doing so, raises full tuition from parishioners.

Renting school buildings, gymnasiums, cafeterias, and auditoriums is another potential revenue source. However, upkeep, maintenance, insurance, and other expenditures can exceed the revenue raised through such rentals, and so may not be cost-effective.

Many grants are available to private as well as public schools as a source of paying for their operating expenses. Foundations offer some grants, while the federal and state governments fund different programs. For instance, the FCC's e-rate grant "makes telecommunications and information services more affordable for schools and libraries."[40]

Another potential revenue source for private schools is state-funded transportation for students. By way of illustration, Ohio requires public school boards to transport all students living outside a two-mile radius of their schools to the public or private schools they attend.[41]

---

[37] Ohio Department of Education, *Nonpublic Education Options* (2017). Retrieved from http://education.ohio.gov/getattachment/Topics/Other-Resources/Scholarships/EdChoice-Scholarship-Program/How-to-Apply-1/2017_2018_ECFactSheet.pdf.aspx at 1.

[38] Valerie Schmalz, *Paying for Catholic School*. THE PRIEST, 65(9), 10-14 & 86-87 (2009).

[39] Bill Schmitt, Alliance for Catholic Education, *Wichita Parishioners Fund Full Tuition for Schools* (April 13, 2015). Retrieved from full-tuition-for-schools.

[40] Federal Communication Commission Consumer Guide. E-rate: Universal Service Program for Schools and Libraries, 1-2 (July, 2017). Retrieved from https://transition.fcc.gov/cgb/consumerfacts/usp_Schools.pdf.

[41] John Rau, *Transportation of Students*. MEMBERS ONLY, 127(6), 1-11 (August 31, 2007). Retrieved from https://www.lsc.ohio.gov/documents/reference/ current/ membersonlybriefs/127transportationofstudents.pdf .

With an understanding of the revenue sources for private schools, the next important piece of school finance is coming to grips with budgets, budget allocations, budget approaches, and budget responsibilities.

Budgets

Budget Objectives

Many private schools and related organizations annually report their audited financial information to the Internal Revenue Service (IRS) on the Form 990. IRS Form 990 collects revenue and expense information about nonprofit organizations. This financial information typically comes from annual audits of the financial activities of schools which is found on their financial statements such as balance sheets, income statements, and statements of cash flow. The Financial Accounting Standards Board (FASB) is "the independent, private-sector, not-for-profit organization…that establishes financial accounting and reporting standards for public and private companies and not-for-profit organizations that follow Generally Accepted Accounting Principles (GAAP)."[42]

The FASB explains that "budgets are particularly significant in the nonbusiness environment. Both business and nonbusiness organizations use budgets to allocate and control uses of resources."[43] The key purpose of school budgets is to allocate financial resources. Without budgets, school officials would not know where operating funds are coming from and where they are going. Budgets provide the structure needed to help ensure the schools meet their missions and purposes. Budgets also help establish policies set by governing boards that are carried out by the administrators in conjunction with faculty members and staff.

Budget Allocations

According to the National Association of Independent Schools *Facts at a Glance 2015-2016* report, almost 70% of total expenses in these schools are allocated to salaries and benefits for faculty, staff, and administration. Ten percent is allocated to instructional costs, athletics, technology, and professional development. A second 10% is allocated to debt service and auxiliary services, such as extended day services; the remaining 10% is allocated to possible physical plant replacement, plus renewal and special maintenance costs.[44] These figures are similar to the public school averages.

---

[42] Financial Accounting Standards Board (2017). Retrieved from http://www.fasb.org/jsp/ FASB/Page/SectionPage&cid=1176154526495. ¶1.

[43] Financial Accounting Standards Board (2008). *Statement of financial accounting concepts No. 4: Objectives of financial reporting by nonbusiness organizations*. Financial Accounting Standards Board at 10.

[44] National Association of Independent Schools. *Facts at a Glance 2015-2016* (2016). Retrieved from https://www.nais.org/Media/Nais/Statistics/Documents/NAISFactsAtA Glance201516.pdf.

As to public schools, the National Center for Education Statistics reports that "on a national basis in 2013-14, approximately 80% of current expenditures were for salaries and benefits for staff."[45] With these large allocations to compensation, the approach to entire budgets must be considered carefully.

Budget Approaches

Once officials in private schools determine the sources of their revenues, the next step in the budgeting process is to decide how to allocate revenues most effectively. As such, this section reviews commonly used key budgeting techniques and models.

Line Item Budgeting

Since 1906, various types of institutions have used line item budgeting to control and track their revenue and expenses. Originally designed by the New York City government, line item budgeting has been used by most businesses, schools, and governments. The accounting foundation is the approach on which different budgets are built.

Line item budgets present financial information on individual lines with charts of account numbers to explain specific revenues or expenses by departments or cost centers. An illustration of a line item budget is kindergarten teachers' salaries. Once salaries are funded to hire kindergarten teachers, the budget for these specific items is established and spending is tracked throughout fiscal years. It is important to recognize that a line item budget is an accounting function. How officials choose to allocate specific amounts of money to kindergarten teachers' salaries is a management function.

Incremental Budgeting

Widely considered the most popular budgeting approach,[46] incremental budgeting adds a percentage change, typically an increase, across all budget line items. The Consumer Price Index is an example of a measure used to determine the appropriate size of incremental increases. Incremental budgeting begins with the belief that a current budget is working well and is addressing a school's needs. Adding a percentage increase to all budget line items implies that the current model does not need significant changes or evaluations.

Incremental budgeting maintains stable relationships among the personnel tasked with budget responsibilities. This group of professionals can include governing boards, pastors, chief administrators, chief financial officers and school principals, along with faculty and staff members. The stability is found in the comfort one takes by not challenging the current budgetary model.

---

[45] U.S. Department of Education. National Center for Education Statistics. *Condition of Education* (2017) Retrieved from https://nces.ed.gov/programs/coe/pdf/coe_cmb.pdf. p. 2.

[46] Margaret J. Barr & George S. McClellan, Budgets and Financial Management in Higher Education (2011) 70-72. *See also* Janet M. Kelly & William C. Rivenbark, Performance Budgeting for State and Local Government (2015) 25-53.

If administrators decide that their existing budget models do not meet the needs of all constituents in their schools, they should employ other budgeting approaches.

Opening dialogues about allocating finite resources can destabilize relationships because, without additional revenues, increasing allocations to one part of a school will require a decrease in another part of its operations. In challenging incremental budgeting, a public budgeting theorist asked, "[o]n what basis shall it be decided to allocate X dollars to activity A instead of activity B?"[47] This essential question in budgeting theory demonstrates the delicate balance among people when building budgets. Who decides allocation amounts? Who decides which activities are funded? To help answer these questions, the critic quoted immediately above advocated for a more sophisticated model of budgeting than the simplistic line item budgeting and incremental budgeting. However, this perfect budgeting model does not exist because political realities and operational realities always seem to compete for budgetary dollars.

Performance-Based Budgeting

Performance-based budgeting (PBB) emerged in 1949 as the general public became increasingly critical of the federal government's focus on inputs. Critics advocated a budgetary system of linking inputs to outputs. Supporters of PBB presented this private sector-type efficiency model as a goal for the public sector. PBB establishes budgeting as a management function, not a clerical function. This approach is rather simplistic: link programs that are working to the budget. Schools would keep the programs that are working and drop those that are not succeeding. It is a cost-efficient budgetary approach.

The PBB approach requires an analysis of the programs schools offer, along with their priorities. Defining the measures to evaluate the relative success of each program can be difficult. The analysis discussion and measurement defining activity can lead to greater transparency among all of a school's stakeholders: administrators, faculty and staff members, parents, and students. Even so, each of those stakeholders may view the relative success of different programs from their individual perspectives and not in concert with entire school communities. Further, the political pressures in private schools may override the stakeholders' opinions of what constitutes successful programs.

Planning, Programming, and Budgeting Systems

President Lyndon B. Johnson mandated the Planning, Programming, and Budgeting Systems (PPBS) budgetary approach in a 1965 memo to government agencies. The system, which was based on that of the United States Department of Defense, assumed cost-benefit analysis should be decisive when creating budgets. The "PPBS places major emphasis on identification of program objectives and the measurement of 'results' or 'output' in quantitative

---

[47] Vladimer O. Key (1940). *The lack of a budgetary theory*. 34 THE AM. POL. SCI. REV. NO. 6, 1137-1144.

terms"[48] by comprehensively linking strategic planning and school-student programming to budgets.

Similar to performance-based budgeting, the PPBS approach can generate disagreements on what school goals are or should be in the face of competing goals. For example, schools may have both religious and college preparatory goals. Identifying results-oriented objectives to meet religious or college preparatory goals can be difficult, as these competing goals vie for finite financial resources. Despite the challenges it presents, the PPBS approach is relatively popular with officials who attempt to link strategic planning and program evaluations when planning their budgets.

Management by Objectives

The management by objectives (MBO) budgetary approach is a straightforward mechanism that has been used in many American corporations since the 1950s. Its premise is that it is "a process whereby the superior and subordinate managers of an organization jointly identify its common goals, define each individual's major areas of responsibility in terms of the results expected of him, and use these measures as guides for operating the unit and assessing the contribution of each of its members."[49]

Under MBO, organizational leaders and managers must jointly establish clear criteria for success without requiring additional resources. This is not an approach commonly found in educational settings, especially private schools, because the number of administrators, especially in private schools, is miniscule in comparison to the total of administrators in American corporations. Still, the joint identification of common goals among constituent groups makes MBO an appealing process for building budgets.

Zero-based Budgeting

As a direct attack on incremental budgeting, zero-based budgeting (ZBB) is the approach wherein organizations "prepare budgets from [a]zero base each year. This would allow funds to be allocated by collectively evaluating all programs on the basis of cost/benefit or some similar kind of evaluative analysis."[50] ZBB was popularized in the 1970s and integrated into various governmental agencies and American corporations.

Rather than incrementally adjusting each budgetary line item, the ZBB approach requires all line items to be justified annually when budgets are proposed. In theory, the justification creates a link between instructional activities and institutional goals. As a result, ZBB requires multiple budgets and written justification of each budget. Not surprisingly, this is a very labor-intensive

---

[48] Jack F. Hoover, *Planning, Programming, Budgeting System*, 21 J. OF RANGE MGMT No. 3, 123-125 at 123 (1968).

[49] George Odiorne, MANAGEMENT BY OBJECTIVES: A SYSTEM OF MANAGEMENT LEADERSHIP 55-56 (1965).

[50] James C. Wetherbe & Gary W. Dickson, *Zero-Based Budgeting: An Alternative to Chargeout Systems, Information & Management,* 2(5) (1979), 203-213, at 204.

process to establishing budgets. Because many private schools spend most of their financial resources on personnel costs, rendering much of the spending nondiscretionary, a down side to ZBB is that devoting time to justifying existing needs can be distracting for administrators. Consequently, it is more common for administrators to use ZBB in hybrid formats by justifying non-personnel costs or new personnel costs within their budgets.

Cutback (Decremental) Budgeting

The opposite of the incremental budgeting approach, cutback budgeting, employs a simple methodology: examine base budgets for cuts and make them. Similar to incremental budgeting, cutback budgeting can take the form of decreasing each budgetary line item by similar percentages.

When school officials need to cut their budgets, the process is often difficult because doing so is painful and can create "unstable coalitions and thus requires active leadership."[51] With this approach, budget reductions place programs in competition with each other for base allocations. When school officials use cutback budgeting, department heads can become intensely competitive and can ruin the stable relations between stakeholders that incremental budgeting seeks to maintain.

Weighted Student Funding as a Budgeting Approach

Weighted student funding (WSF) refers to a system whereby officials design formulae to attach weights to each student. The weights are based on student characteristics. Under WSF, identical weights are assigned to each student in districts or states having identical characteristics. For example, all students from low-income households would carry identical weights, as would all students with hearing impairments and all students with limited English proficiency.

The base weight assigned to all students, regardless of individual characteristics, is "1." A fixed number of dollars is assigned to this base weight, which is then multiplied times each student's individual weight. The resultant dollars would follow each student. This approach emerged in the late 1990s "as an alternative to traditional staff-based allocation policies. Student-weighted allocation uses student need, rather than staff placement, as the building block of school budgeting."[52]

As an allocation model, challenges arise to WSF. Determining appropriate "weights" for each level of student characteristic can be difficult. Many large, urban public school boards such as in Houston, Seattle, and Cincinnati have studied weights; yet, private schools have not published any work in this area. The roles of school administrators change under this model, as student weights become the primary functions in establishing school budgets. In order for this

---

[51] Robert D. Behn, *Cutback Budgeting*, 4 J. OF POL. ANALYSIS AND MGMT No. 2, 155-177 at 156 (1985).

[52] Karen H. Miles & Marguerite Roza, *Understanding Student Weighted Allocation as a Means to Greater School Resource Equity*. 81 PEABODY J. OF EDUC. No. 3, 39-62 at 39 (2006).

model to succeed, administrators must receive professional development on how to use it effectively.

Budget Roles and Responsibilities

Many school administrators do not commonly view working with their budgets as critical parts of their jobs. Other seemingly more important issues, such as those arising with students, faculty, staff members, and parents, often dominate administrators' days. However, understanding budgets and how schools' budgetary processes work can inform administrators about their responsibilities, while leading to more participatory forms of governance.

The size and organizational structure of schools often dictates the level of involvement of administrators, faculty and staff members, along with parents, in the budget process. Larger schools tend to be more bureaucratic, with many layers of people involved in budgeting. These schools may engage in site-based decision-making processes, whereby the site administrators have some input on budgets. Smaller schools tend to be more relational, with few layers of personnel involved in the budgeting process; leadership in these schools may request more input from site administrators. Faith-based schools tend to have more layers of budget responsibilities that are often divided among owners, whether dioceses or parishes, board members, administrators, plus teaching staff.[53] Independent schools tend to have fewer layers of budget responsibilities, which are often divided among boards of trustees and administrators.

Budget development is a continuous process usually led by a school's business officer, chief financial officer, or someone in a similar position. This person's job is typically to outline the budget process from gathering information, to the budget approach, to obtaining board approval. Once officials estimate the revenues for their budgets, the first step in the budget process typically is to determine a school's needs; this needs assessment can involve administrators and faculty members. The second step in the budget process is to develop goals; the goals should align with the schools' strategic plans or other vision and mission documents.

The third step in the budget process is to set objectives. Depending on a school's organizational structure, the personnel required to set objectives may include the governing board, administrators, and/or faculty members. The fourth step in the budget process is to identify the academic and non-academic programs and activities to be funded; because this planning is more operational in nature, it is usually the responsibility of administrators. The fifth step in the budget process is to develop the budget, a responsibility typically resting with a school's business officer. The sixth step is to evaluate a budget's effectiveness and start over at determining the needs. This collaborative effort is shared between and among members of the governing board and school administrators.

---

[53] Richard J. Burke, *Financial Planning for Catholic Secondary Schools: Essential But Not Determinative*. 2 CATHOLIC EDUC.: A J. INQUIRY AND PRACTICE No. 4, 479-490 (2013).

Capital Budgeting

The budgeting approaches discussed in this chapter are used for day-to-day operations. At the same time, though, private schools often have separate capital expense budgets titled "provision for plant replacement, renewal, and special maintenance." It is generally considered a good financial practice for school officials to budget 3% of the total costs of replacing their entire physical plants in capital budgets. This line item accounts for major investments in a school's physical plant. Examples of expenses include repairs and replacement of a school's roof; heating, ventilating, and air conditioning, commonly known as HVAC systems; windows; parking lots; athletic facilities; arts areas; and the like. Funding for these major capital investments can come from sources such as major donors, debt issuance, or operating budgets.

School officials handle capital budgeting differently than operational budgets. Different types of schools require different types of capital planning. For instance, boarding schools need to pay attention to dormitory conditions as the wants and needs of changing student populations evolve. Officials in day schools need to pay attention to common spaces used by parents and other non-student groups. And, of course, both types of schools require planning processes that consider instructional programming to determine how they can most effectively and efficiently use their facilities.

Conclusion

Private school finance has its unique challenges regarding revenue and allocation. Much of the school finance literature and debate has centered on public school finance and tax dollars. As demonstrated in this chapter, private schools do not rely heavily on public money to fund their operations. Cases such as *Everson v. Board of Education, Lemon v. Kurtzman, Agostini v. Felton*, and *Trinity Lutheran Church v. Comey* have all played, and continue to play, roles in funding private schools, whether through state or federal funds. However, as noted, public funds make up small percentages of the overall revenue of private schools; tuition, donations, stewardship, and/or philanthropy are the dominant revenue sources.

Allocating sources of revenue can vary greatly among private schools. There is no one preferred method of allocating resources, because there is no one governance model when it comes to budgeting. The largest use of funds continues to be for salaries and fringe benefits to faculty, staff, and administrators. How administrators in sectarian and nonsectarian nonpublic schools allocate and use their revenues is an important piece to their overall success and longevity in the United States.

Discussion Questions

1. What process would you use to select board members, keeping in mind their many roles, particularly as fundraisers?

2. Identify potential sources of financial aid for private schools to help students unable to afford full tuition.

3. What legal or fiscal policies do different states have that restricts or promote student access to private schools?

4. Describe your "ideal" budget process.

5. What factors that influence the budget can a budget manager control? Or should control?

6. Create a hybrid budgeting approach ideally suited to your department and skills.

Keywords

Budgeting
Public versus private funds
Revenues
School finance
School funding

8

Special Education and Students in Nonpublic Schools

Lynn M. Daggett

Contents

Introduction / 224

Overview of the Individuals with Disabilities Education Act and Students in Public Schools / 224

    Individuals with Disabilities Education Act Eligibility Requirements / 225

    The IDEA Eligibility Process / 226

    Alternative Eligibility under Section 504 of the Rehabilitation Act / 227

    Individualized Education Programs / 228

    Free Appropriate Public Education / 229

        Special Education Instruction / 231

        Related Services / 232

    Least Restrictive Environment / 233

    Procedural Safeguards / 235

        Parental Participation on Special Education Teams / 235

        Notice and Consent: Independent Educational Evaluations / 236

        Access to Special Education Records / 236

    Disciplining Special Education Students / 237

    Special Education Disputes / 238

The IDEA and Students in Private Schools / 240

    Child Find / 240

    Special Education and Students in Private Schools Generally / 241

    Children Placed in Private Schools by Public Agencies / 241

    Children Placed in Private Schools by Their Parents in FAPE Disputes with Public School Boards / 243

    Children Placed in Private Schools Due to Parental Preferences / 245

    Who Are the "Students in Private Schools" in This Category? / 245

        Proportionate Allocations of Federal IDEA Funds / 246

        Consultation Processes / 248

    Services Plan Requirement / 249

    Location of Services / 249

    Complaints by Parents Whose Children Attend Private Schools / 250

    By-Pass for Children in Private Schools / 251

    State Laws May Provide Additional Rights / 251

Private School Obligations under Section 504 / 252
Policy Issues / 257
Conclusion / 259
Discussion Questions / 260
Key Words / 260

Introduction

Congress enacted the first federal special education statute in 1975, the Education for all Handicapped Children's Act, now known as the Individuals with Disabilities Education Act (IDEA). The IDEA offers modest partial federal funding of special education costs to states, and thus their public school boards that agree to comply with its many requirements.

Because the IDEA regulates public, not private, schools, this chapter begins with an overview of the IDEA and the rights it grants to eligible students in public school. The chapter then turns to the more limited special education obligations public school boards owe to students in private schools. The IDEA's "child find" provision requires local school board officials to locate, evaluate, and identify all eligible students, including those in private schools. The obligations of public school boards to fund or provide special education services to students in private school are more limited, and vary depending on the reason(s) why parents enroll their children in private schools.

Many parents choose private schools for their children with disabilities because of religious beliefs, perceived quality of instruction, and/or concern for the safety of their children in their current placements. This chapter focuses primarily on students who attend private schools due to the preferences of their parents.

The IDEA entitles each IDEA-eligible student enrolled in public school to a free, appropriate public education (FAPE). However, the IDEA does not provide students with FAPEs or other individual entitlements if their parents enroll them in private schools. A public school board's obligation is limited to spending a proportionate amount of its modest federal IDEA funds on this group of IDEA-eligible students in private schools. Moreover, although officials in public schools are obligated to consult with staff members in private schools, and the parents of children enrolled in them, ultimately it is up to school board officials to determine what services to offer, where, and to which students.

Overview of the IDEA and Students in Public Schools

It is important for private school educators and students' parents to understand how special education works in public schools. Knowing how the IDEA works facilitates informed decision making about public school versus private school enrollment. Moreover, understanding the IDEA helps staff in private schools to better understand the experiences and expectations of their students who received special education services prior to enrollment in private schools, while also helping them to advocate for these students with public schools.

The IDEA[1] has been called "the last federal entitlement" because it provides both procedural and substantive individual rights to eligible students. The IDEA funds a small portion of special education costs,[2] leaving the great bulk of financial responsibility to state and local governments. In exchange for this federal funding, states and their local school boards agree to comply with IDEA's many requirements. The core requirements of the IDEA are:

1. Eligible students are entitled to a FAPE. Insofar as all special education students are unique, a team including school staff and parents writes an individualized education program (IEP) for the student to implement FAPE obligations.

2. Eligible students are entitled to be educated in the least restrictive environment (LRE), which means in general education with classmates who are not disabled, as appropriate.

3. Eligible students and their parents have extensive procedural safeguards to protect their IDEA rights, including participation in the special education teams; control over whether their children receive special education; limits on discipline; and the right to challenge any aspect of special education of their children in front of special education hearing officers, and ultimately in courts.

IDEA eligibility requirements

The IDEA sets out three requirements for eligibility:[3]

1. Age. Eligible students in most states are between ages 3 and 21 and have not yet graduated from high school.[4] In some states eligibility begins at age 5, and/or ends at age 18.[5] A different part of the IDEA provides services from birth.[6]

2. Disability. Students must be diagnosed as having one or more of the disabilities identified in the IDEA: intellectual disabilities, hearing impairments (including deafness), speech or language impairments, visual impairments (including blindness), serious emotional disturbance (referred to in this chapter as "emotional disturbance"), orthopedic impairments, autism, traumatic brain injury, other health impairments, or specific learning disabilities.[7] Younger children "experiencing developmental delays...

---

[1] 20 U.S.C. §§ 1400 *et seq*. regulations at 34 C.F.R. 300.1 *et seq*.

[2] Average costs for a special education student are roughly twice the cost of general education students. Federal funding has typically been about 8-10% of the total costs, or about 16-20% of the costs of special education above and beyond general education costs. *See generally* Clare McCann, *IDEA Funding, available at* http://www.edcentral.org/edcyclopedia/individuals-with-disabilities-education-act-funding-distribution/

[3] 20 U.S.C. § 1412(a)(1); 34 C.F.R. § 300.8.

[4] 20 U.S.C. § 1412(a)(1)(A).

[5] 20 U.S.C. § 1412(a)(1)(B); 34 C.F.R. § 300.102.

[6] IDEA Part C, 20 U.S.C. §§ 1431 *et seq*.

[7] 20 U.S.C. § 1401(3)(A); 34 C.F.R. § 300.8(a)(1).

in one or more of the following areas: physical development; cognitive development; communication development; social or emotional development; or adaptive development"[8] may be eligible without being diagnosed as having one of the conditions on the list.

3.   Need special education.[9] No disabilities are so severe as to render students ineligible under the IDEA.[10] On the other hand, some students with disabilities excel in school and so do not need special education. These students are ineligible under the IDEA.[11]

The IDEA Eligibility Process

The IDEA's "child find" requirements obligate public school officials to ensure that "all children with disabilities residing in the State, including children who are homeless or are wards of the State and children with disabilities attending private schools, regardless of the severity of their disability, and who are in need of special education and related services, are identified, located, and evaluated."[12] Among the child find activities public school boards employ are preschool screenings, newspaper announcements, and outreach to local day care centers, private schools, and preschools to identify potential IDEA students. School board staff members and/or parents[13] can also make referrals of children who may be eligible under the IDEA; unofficially, other persons such as pediatricians and day care, preschool, and private school staff may make referrals.

Once students have been identified as potentially IDEA-eligible, school officials consider existing information about them and decide whether to order evaluations, and if so, what kinds of evaluations to perform. For example, if educational officials suspect that a student has a specific learning disability, they might order a psychoeducational evaluation by a school psychologist. The child's parents must receive written notice of and consent in writing in advance of any evaluation.[14] Reevaluations must occur before any determinations can be made about change in eligibility, on parental or teacher requests or, in any case, at least every three years.[15] After evaluations are completed, teams convene to discuss the results and decide whether students are eligible under the IDEA. If so, the teams then proceed to write IEPs for the students.[16]

---

[8]   20 U.S.C. § 1401(3)(B); 34 C.F.R. § 300.8(b).

[9]   20 U.S.C. §§ 1401(3)(A)(ii); (B)(ii).

[10] *See* Timothy W. v. Rochester, N.H., Sch. Dist., 875 F.2d 954 [54 Educ. L. Rep. 74] (1st Cir. 1989).

[11] *Cf.* L.G. v. Pittsburg Unified Sch. Dist., 850 F.3d 996 [341 Educ. L. Rep. 60] (9th Cir. 2017) (deciding that a student who performed well due to the receipt of special education services provided was IDEA-eligible, suggesting he would not have qualified for IDEA services had he performed well without special education services).

[12] 34 C.F.R. § 300.111.

[13] 34 C.F.R. § 300.301(b).

[14] 34 C.F.R. §§ 300.304 (notice); 300.300 (consent)

[15] 34 C.F.R. §§ 300.303, 305.

[16] 34 C.F.R. § 300.306.

Alternative Eligibility Under Section 504 of the Rehabilitation Act

Some students who are not found to be eligible for special education under the IDEA can receive services under Section 504 of the Rehabilitation Act of 1973 (Section 504).[17] Section 504 prohibits disability discrimination in schools (including private schools, as well as higher education institutions) receiving federal education funds. Though not providing any specific funding for the costs of compliance, Section 504 covers a broader group of students than the IDEA. Under Section 504, individuals with disabilities are those with physical or mental impairments, not limited to the disabilities in the IDEA, that "substantially limit…major life activit[ies]" such as learning, reading, or walking, or who "have a record of such impairment[s]," or who are "regarded as having such impairment[s]."[18]

The Section 504 rights of students in private schools—which are limited to nondiscrimination and "minor adjustments" to their school programs—are discussed in detail later in this chapter. Section 504 students in K-12 public schools have IDEA-like entitlements to FAPE, LRE, and procedural safeguards.[19] For example, a public elementary school student with muscular dystrophy may need physical and occupational therapy, which are related services under the IDEA, but not special education instruction. Without a need for special education instruction, this student would be ineligible under the IDEA. The child would be eligible for the needed therapy under Section 504. Similarly, a student with a learning disability in reading who does not need special education instruction, but does require extra time on examinations, would be eligible for this accommodation under Section 504.

Section 504 protects students with histories of disabilities even if they are not currently disabled.[20] For instance, a student who was hospitalized for acute mental illness but is currently in good mental health is protected from discrimination based on that history. As such, officials in a private school could not reject this student because of her mental health history. Section 504 also protects students regarded as having disabilities even if there are no actual disabilities. Put another way, officials in a private school could not exclude a student because she lives in a household with a person who has AIDS and is perceived as being HIV-positive. Students with past and/or perceived disabilities would not normally need or be entitled to affirmative adjustments, but cannot be discriminated against.[21]

Section 504's discrimination ban extends to discrimination in all aspects of a school's operations. Among the areas covered are admissions, academics, testing, extracurricular activities, and nonacademic issues such as lunch and

---

[17] 29 U.S.C. § 794.

[18] 29 U.S.C. § 705(20)(B), incorporating 42 U.S.C. § 12102.

[19] *See* 34 C.F.R. §§ 104.31 *et seq.*

[20] *See* 29 U.S.C. §§ 705(9)(B); (20)(B) (incorporating the definition of the ADA Amendments).

[21] Dear Colleague Letter, 58 IDELR 79 (OCR 2012).

recess, counseling services, athletics, transportation, health services, clubs, and student employment.[22]

Individualized Education Programs

IEPs, the basic road maps for IDEA students, ordinarily cover a school year.[23] Because all IEPs are designed for individual students, no two are likely to be identical. IEPs identify students' starting points or current levels of performance, their desired ending points or annual goals, and specify how their progress toward these goals is to be measured. IEPs also specify the vehicles—namely special education instruction, related services, and testing or other accommodations—to enable students to make progress toward their annual goals. IEP teams consider various placements to ensure that students are educated in the LRE. Moreover, most IEPs include mileposts or short-term objectives, and measurement of progress toward them, to plan for and assess students' progress throughout school years.

The potential of IEPs to enable students to achieve educational success depends on three basic design and implementation concepts. The first is students' involvement and progress in general curricula, with appropriate special education and related services consistent with high academic standards and expectations for all students. The second is the involvement of parents and consideration of their views, as well as the information they provide in developing educational placements and plans for their children. The third is the preparation of students for transition from high school to adult life.[24] Once developed, IEPs are subject to review "periodically, but not less than annually, to determine whether the annual goals for the child are being achieved."[25]

The IDEA's procedural safeguards include requirements for members of IEP teams[26] and a timetable for their preparation. For initial IEPs, the meetings must follow within thirty days of determinations of eligibility, with implemen-

---

[22] 34 C.F.R. §§ 104.34(b); 104.37.

[23] For a comprehensive example of the content of IEPs, see MARK WEBER, RALPH MAWDSLEY, AND SARAH REDFIELD, SPECIAL EDUCATION LAW: CASES AND MATERIALS, (3d Ed.) 204-211 (LEXIS Nexis 2010).

[24] See 34 C.F.R. §§ 300.320 et seq. for details about the composition of IEP teams and the preparation of IEPs.

[25] 20 U.S.C. § 1414(d)(4)(A)(1).

[26] 20 U.S.C. § 1414 (d)(1)(B); 34 C.F.R. § 300.321. Those required at an IEP meeting are "the parents of a child with a disability; . . .regular education teacher of such child (if the child is, or may be, participating in the regular education environment); . . . special education teacher, or where appropriate, special education provider of such child; a representative of the local educational agency who is qualified to provide, or supervise the provision of, specially designed instruction to meet the unique needs of children with disability, is knowledgeable about the general curriculum, and is knowledgeable about the availability of resources of the local educational agency; and an individual who can interpret the instructional implications of evaluation results." In the discretion of parents or school officials, "other individuals who have knowledge or special expertise regarding the child, including related services personnel" may be included "as appropriate." The child with a disability is also to be included "whenever appropriate."

tation to begin as soon as possible after the IEP meetings end.[27] After that, IEPs are in place at the beginning of each school year for each student.[28] IEPs must be accessible by each special and regular education teacher and service provider responsible for its implementation.[29]

Free Appropriate Public Education

The IEP is the IDEA's mechanism used to determine what is a FAPE for each unique student. The IDEA defines FAPE as:

[S]pecial education and related services that

1. have been provided at public expense, under public supervision and direction, and without charge;
2. meet the requirements of the State educational agency;
3. include an appropriate preschool, elementary, or secondary school education in the State involved; and
4. are provided in conformity with the individualized education program required under section 1414(d).[30]

Section 504 FAPE requirements for public K-12 school students parallel those for the IDEA.[31]

Looking at each part of FAPE is helpful. The "free" part of FAPE requires boards to provide special education services under its provisions "at public expense"[32] and "at no cost to parents."[33] Thus, parents cannot be required to pay for any part of the special education of their children.[34] Still, "nothing relieves an insurer or similar third party from an otherwise valid obligation to provide or to pay for services provided to a child with a disability."[35]

The IDEA's regulations do permit school boards to ask parents to file claims with their medical insurers, or Medicaid for low-income families, to help defray costs, but parents must provide "informed consent" before public agencies can access private insurance funds.[36] School boards can use parental consent to access insurance only if there is no realistic threat that parents will experience financial losses.[37] Failure to notify parents adequately that billing programs are voluntary or that the billing can result in potential financial loss present actionable claims under Section 504.[38]

---

[27] 34 C.F.R. § 300.321(c)(1).

[28] 34 C.F.R. § 300.323(a).

[29] 34 C.F.R. § 300.321(d).

[30] 20 U.S.C. § 1401(9); *see* 34 C.F.R. § 300.17.

[31] 34 C.F.R. § 104.33.

[32] 20 U.S.C. § 1401(9)(A).

[33] 20 U.S.C. § 1401(29).

[34] *See* Miener v. Mo., 800 F.2d 749 [34 Educ. L. Rep. 1014] (8th Cir. 1986).

[35] 20 U.S.C. §§ 1412(a)(12); 1412(e); 34 C.F.R. § 300.154(d).

[36] 34 C.F.R. § 300.154(d).

[37] 34 C.F.R. § 300.154(d).

[38] Chicago (Ill.) Pub. Sch., 17 IDELR 124 (OCR 1990).

The "public" part of FAPE similarly means special education is at public expense and at no cost to families.[39] This does not mean that special education must in all cases be provided by public school boards. As discussed below, some school boards place, and fund, IDEA students in private schools that provide special education services unavailable in public schools.

The "education" part of FAPE includes academic, social, health, emotional, physical, and vocational needs.[40] This broad definition includes not only traditional academic skills, but also whatever skills will assist students in achieving independence as adults. For example, the IEPs of students with severe cognitive disabilities might focus on functional academics such as reading menus and making change; vocational skills developed through community placements with job coaches or other support; or daily living skills such as riding a bus or preparing meals. Similarly, the IEPs of students with emotional disabilities might focus on behavioral goals such as interactions with peers.

The statutory definition of a FAPE is not particularly helpful as to the level of education required for the "appropriate" part of FAPE. The Supreme Court, in both its first and most recent IDEA cases, examined what is "appropriate."

Initially, in *Board of Education of the Hendrick-Hudson School District v. Rowley (Rowley)*,[41] the Supreme Court resolved a case involving an elementary school student who was deaf. The student's board offered some tutoring and a hearing aid, but her parents requested a full-time sign language interpreter. Despite understanding only about 59% of what was said in her classroom, the student performed well and easily passed from grade to grade. The Court held that the board provided the student with an appropriate education, noting that it complied with the IDEA's procedural requirements, and had written an IEP that was "reasonably designed to confer educational benefit" on her, as evidenced by her being promoted from grade to grade.

After *Rowley*, lower courts and special education hearing officers struggled with how much educational benefit the IDEA requires. For instance, is a student who earns C and D grades receiving sufficient educational benefit? How is educational benefit to be measured in the case of a student who is not in general education and not receiving a report card? Is some progress on one IEP annual goal sufficient?

The Supreme Court's newest IDEA case offers some additional guidance. *Endrew F. v. Douglas County School District RE-1 (Endrew F.)*[42] involved a student with autism whose parents did not think their school board offered him an appropriate education. The parents then enrolled their son in a private school and sought tuition reimbursement from their board. While the standard for tuition reimbursement is discussed later in this chapter, it is worth noting

---

[39] 34 C.F.R. § 300.17(a).

[40] *See generally* County of San Diego v. Cal. Special Educ. Hearing Office, 93 F.3d 1458 (9th Cir. 1996).

[41] 458 U.S. 176 [5 Educ. L. Rep. 34] (1982).

[42] 137 S. Ct. 988, 996 (2017) (ruling that an IEP must be "reasonably calculated to enable a child to make progress appropriate in light of the child's circumstances") (internal citations omitted).

that, in part, it requires parents to show that their public school boards did not offer appropriate educations.

In *Endrew F.* the Supreme Court rejected the "merely more than de minimis"[43] educational benefit standard the Tenth Circuit relied on and which the parents challenged; some lower courts also considered this level to be sufficient for FAPEs under the IDEA. The Court found that in order to be appropriate, IEPs should be "ambitious" and reasonably designed to allow students to make "appropriate progress"[44] in light of their circumstances. This standard, while nebulous, appears to heighten the standard for "appropriate." Even so, the Court indicated that deference was owed to the judgment of school officials. It is also important to acknowledge that the IDEA defines a FAPE as including both special education, described as "specially designed instruction . . . to meet the unique needs of a child with a disability"[45] and related services.[46]

Special Education Instruction

IDEA students may receive special education in a variety of settings, both designed and implemented by an array of persons. Some IDEA students are educated in special schools, hospitals, or at home. School boards may operate "self-contained" special education classes; these are typically small, with perhaps ten or so students, all of whom are IDEA students. Self-contained classes are taught by certificated special education teachers, often with the assistance of one or more paraprofessionals. IEPs may place IDEA students in self-contained classes either part time or full time. Boards also operate "resource rooms" operated by special education teachers. IEPs may call for students to be removed from general education to spend time in resource rooms, so that children with learning disabilities in reading may be assigned to resource rooms for one hour per day to get special education instruction and extra assistance in reading.

In general education, some IDEA students work under different lesson plans than their peers in their classes. By way of illustration, IDEA students with intellectual disabilities in general education fourth-grade classes in which other children are reading chapter books and writing book reports might listen to books being read aloud and dictate reports on their contents. These adapted lesson plans and instruction may be designed by special education teachers or general education teachers with training. A paraprofessional, a general education teacher, or an itinerant special education teacher might deliver instruction under these lesson plans. Sorting out these issues in students' IEPs is a difficult and complicated balance of predicted progress under various options, with LRE obligation, as will be explained later.

---

[43] *Id.* at 1001.

[44] *Id.* at 999.

[45] 20 U.S.C. § 1401(29).

[46] 20 U.S.C. § 1401(9).

Related Services

Some students need support services to benefit from special education, labeled "related services" by the IDEA. Students in wheelchairs may need special transportation, while children with cerebral palsy may require physical therapy. The IDEA defines "related services" as "transportation, and such developmental, corrective, and other supportive services . . . as may be required to assist a child with a disability to benefit from special education." Those services include:

> speech-language pathology and audiology services, interpreting services, psychological services, physical and occupational therapy, recreation, including therapeutic recreation, social work services, school nurse services designed to enable a child with a disability to receive a free appropriate public education as described in the individualized education program of the child, counseling services, including rehabilitation counseling, orientation and mobility services, and medical services, except that such medical services shall be for diagnostic and evaluation purposes only . . . and includes the early identification and assessment of disabling conditions in children.[47]

As a component of FAPE, school boards must provide these services without cost to parents or children.[48] Many legal cases deal with claims for reimbursement or compensatory services because of denial of specific related services.[49]

The IDEA includes medical evaluations, if IEP teams determine they are necessary. For example, special education teams might order neurological evaluations of students suspected as having traumatic brain injuries. Further, the IDEA includes school health services such as providing insulin medication to students who are diabetics. However, the IDEA explicitly excludes "medical services" from the definition of related services. Accordingly, if students with traumatic brain injuries need surgery, boards are not responsible for paying for the operations. Drawing a line between IDEA-required school health services and IDEA-excluded medical services has proved difficult, resulting in two Supreme Court cases.

The Supreme Court ruled that services which can be provided by nurses and other non-physician health care providers are IDEA-required school health services, even if students' needs for them are extensive. Thus, the Court pointed out that IDEA-required related services include clean intermittent catheterization (CIC), as in *Irving Independent School District v. Tatro*,[50] and suctioning of

---

47 20 U.S.C. § 1401(26).

48 *See* 20 U.S.C. § 1401(8).

49 For an overview of the case law, see Mark C. Weber, Special Education Law and Litigation Treatise, Chapter 8 (4th ed. 2017).

50 468 U.S. 883 [18 Educ. L. Rep. 138] (1984).

a tracheotomy tube and ambu-bag ventilation, as in *Cedar Rapids Community School District v. Garrett F.*[51]

Related services generally do not include equipment. The IDEA expressly excludes the provision of surgically implanted devices such as cochlear implants, the optimization of their functioning (such as via mapping), their maintenance, or their replacement, from the definition of a related service.

In a case on point, a federal trial court in the District of Columbia rationalized the exclusion of cochlear implant mapping from the scope of related services. The court explained that "the decision to exclude mapping was the result of a reasoned analysis by the Department, taking into account such factors as the fact that 'mapping does not have to be done in school or during the school day in order to be effective,' the financial burden associated with mapping, and the high skill level required to provide mapping services."[52] Yet, nothing prevents school board personnel from conducting routine checks of external components of surgically implanted devices to make sure they are functioning properly.[53]

Least Restrictive Environment

The IDEA requires that, as appropriate, IDEA students be educated with children not having disabilities; this requirement is referred to as the least restrictive environment (LRE).[54] The statutory standard is:

> To the maximum extent appropriate, children with disabilities, including children in public or private institutions or other care facilities, are educated with children who are not disabled, and special classes, separate schooling, or other removal of children with disabilities from the regular educational environment occurs only when the nature or severity of the disability of a child is such that education in regular classes with the use of supplementary aids and services cannot be achieved satisfactorily.[55]

As with FAPE, the standard centers on "appropriate," which remains undefined. Still, the IDEA clearly contemplates individualized LRE decisions. School board officials cannot, for example, automatically place students with Down syndrome in self-contained classes, but must consider various options from non-restrictive general education, perhaps with paraprofessionals or other support, to increasingly more restrictive resource rooms, self-contained classes, and special schools for each student.

At the same time, the statute also contemplates that some IDEA students will be in separate classes or schools. Consequently, the IDEA does not

---

[51] 526 U.S. 66 [132 Educ. L. Rep. 40] (1999).

[52] Petit v. U.S. Dep't of Educ., 578 F. Supp. 2d 145 [238 Educ. L. Rep. 616] (D.D.C. 2008).

[53] 34 C.F.R. § 300.34.

[54] For a more comprehensive discussion, see Mark Weber, Ralph Mawdsley, and Sarah Redfield, Special Education Law: Cases and Materials 261-291 (LEXIS 2010).

[55] 20 U.S.C. § 1412(a)(5)(A).

embrace the "full inclusion" or "regular education initiative" philosophies of some educators and parents that all students with IEPs must be placed full time in general education. Nonetheless, within the range of possible settings from more restrictive and less integrated, to less restrictive and more integrated, the less restrictive are to be preferred.

The IDEA's regulations require IEPs to contain "[a]n explanation of the extent, if any, to which the child will not participate with nondisabled children in the regular class and in the activities described in . . . this section."[56] Additionally, the IDEA mandates requires consideration of a "continuum of alternative placements" and "provision for supplementary services (such as resource room or itinerant instruction) to be provided in conjunction with regular class placement."[57] Other LRE-related IDEA provisions include:

- "The child's placement [must be] . . . as close as possible to the child's home."[58]
- "Unless the IEP of a child with a disability requires some other arrangement, the child [must be] educated in the school that he or she would attend if nondisabled."[59]
- "In selecting the LRE, consideration [must be] given to any potential harmful effect on the child or on the quality of services that he or she needs."[60]
- "A child with a disability [must] not [be] removed from education in age-appropriate regular classrooms solely because of needed modifications in the general curriculum."[61]

In providing or arranging for the provision of nonacademic and extracurricular services and activities, including meals, recess periods, and activities. . . set forth in § 300.107 [(b): "counseling services, athletics, transportation, health services, recreational activities, special interest groups or clubs sponsored by the public agency, referrals to agencies that provide assistance to individuals with disabilities, and employment of students, including both employment by the public agency and assistance in making outside employment available"], each public agency must ensure that each child with a disability participates with nondisabled children in those services and activities to the maximum extent appropriate to the needs of that child.[62]

The Section 504 regulations for public K-12 school students set out LRE requirements similar to those in the IDEA.[63]

Insofar as the Supreme Court has not addressed an LRE case, there is no national LRE standard. Federal appeals courts, though, have announced varying LRE standards commonly involving balancing the benefits and burdens of

---

[56] 34 C.F.R. § 300.320(a)(5).
[57] 34 C.F.R. § 300.115.
[58] 34 C.F.R. § 300.116(b)(3).
[59] 34 C.F.R. § 300.116(c).
[60] 34 C.F.R. § 300.116(d).
[61] 34 C.F.R. § 300.116(e).
[62] 34 C.F.R. § 300.117.
[63] 34 C.F.R. § 104.34.

placement options with varied restrictiveness. For example, in a case about a young student with an intellectual disability, the Ninth Circuit balanced the academic benefits she received in general and special education, the social and other nonacademic benefits she obtained in general and special education, and whether placing her in general education would have monopolized the teacher's time or disrupted learning for other children.[64]

Procedural Safeguards

The IDEA affords parents extensive procedural rights, including limiting special education decision-making authority to teams including them while adopting hearing procedures to challenge team decisions with which they disagree. Parental rights normally transfer to the student at age of eighteen.[65] These procedural rights allow parents to advocate for their children and ensure compliance with the IDEA; in part, they are premised on the importance of parental involvement to the academic success of their children. Indeed, violations of some IDEA procedural rights that limit parent participation can amount to denials of FAPEs.

Parental Participation on Special Education Teams

All decisions about the special education programs of students must be made by teams of persons who are knowledgeable about the children under consideration. Parents have a right to participate in all IEP team meetings about their children[66] with the groups of persons who make eligibility and placement decisions.[67] Parents must receive advance written notice of team meetings, which must be scheduled at mutually convenient times.[68] School officials must use their best efforts to get parents to attend team meetings and must document their efforts to ensure parental attendance.

If parents cannot be convinced to attend meetings, school officials must attempt to allow them to participate by phone or otherwise, and/or provide information after the meetings. Teams must meet at least annually to review to revise IEPs. Parents may request IEP team meetings about their children at any time, and officials "should grant any reasonable request for such a meeting."[69] If parents will not attend team meetings, officials are not excused from going

---

[64] Sacramento City Unif. Sch. Dist. Bd. of Educ. v. Rachel H., 14 F.3d 1398 [89 Educ. L. Rep. 57] (9th Cir. 1994). For a commentary on this case, see Ralph Julnes, *The New Holland and Other Tests For Resolving LRE Disputes*, 91 Educ. L. Rep. 789 (1994).

[65] 34 C.F.R. § 300.520.

[66] 34 C.F.R. §§ 300.321, 300.322.

[67] *See, e.g.* 34 C.F.R. § 300.306 (eligibility determinations); 300.327 (placement decisions).

[68] 34 C.F.R. § 300.322.

[69] 34 C.F.R. Part 300 Appendix C Response to Question 11.

forward with meetings and preparing IEPs.[70] Failure to involve parents may amount to denials of FAPEs.[71]

Notice and Consent: Independent Educational Evaluations

Parents must consent in writing to initial evaluations to determine IDEA eligibility.[72] Consent is also required for reevaluations, with some limits.[73] Any such consent must be "fully informed."[74] Specifically, parents must "understand" the activities to which they are consenting. If parents do not consent, school officials may, but are not required, to initiate due process hearings to ask special education hearing officers to order initial evaluations.[75]

Parents who disagree with the evaluation of their children performed by school officials may request an "Independent Educational Evaluation" (IEE).[76] On request by parents, boards must pay for the IEEs or initiate special education hearings to defend the appropriateness of their evaluations.[77] In any case, IEP teams must consider the IEE results.[78] School officials may establish reasonable guidelines on IEEs' cost and evaluator qualifications.[79]

Parents must also consent in writing to initial placements in special education.[80] School officials override parental failure to consent to initial placements in special education. If parents refuse to agree or revoke consent to special education, boards may not initiate due process to override their refusals.[81] If parents revoke consent, their actions are not retroactive.[82] Once parents revoke consent, school boards do not owe students FAPEs or IEPs, and need not convene IEP team meetings.[83]

Access to Special Education Records

The IDEA requires school boards to grant access to parents, their representatives, or eligible students "without unnecessary delay" and before IEP meet-

---

[70] 34 C.F.R. § 300.322(d).
[71] *See, e.g.,* J.T. v. Dep't of Educ., 2012 WESTLAW 1995274 (D. Haw. 2012) (treating failure to consider IEEs and meeting without parents as violations for which compensatory education can be awarded), *rev'd on other grounds,* 695 F. App'x 227 (9th Cir. 2017).
[72] 34 C.F.R. § 300.300.
[73] 34 C.F.R. § 300.300(c)(2).
[74] 34 C.F.R. § 300.9.
[75] 34 C.F.R. § 300.300(a)(3).
[76] 34 C.F.R. § 300.502.
[77] 34 C.F.R. § 300.502(b).
[78] 34 C.F.R. § 300.502(c).
[79] 34 C.F.R. § 300.502(e).
[80] 34 C.F.R. § 300.300(b).
[81] *Id.*
[82] 34 C.F.R. § 300.9(c)(2).
[83] 34 C.F.R. § 300.300(b)(4).

ings or due process hearings.[84] IDEA confidentiality violations, including those of incorporated FERPA requirements, may be actionable through the IDEA.[85]

Disciplining of Special Education Students

Improperly disciplining students for conduct caused by their disabilities is a form of illegal disability discrimination. If IDEA-eligible students engage in misconduct and school officials are considering suspensions of more than ten days, or expulsions, IEP teams must decide whether to subject them to discipline or to treat such incidents as educational programming issues. Such students may be excluded for up to ten days as "cooling off" periods while the IEP team meets.

IEP teams must use a two-part test when deciding whether to discipline IDEA students. IEPs teams must first ask whether students' (mis)conduct was caused by, or had a direct and substantial relationship to, their disabilities. Second, teams must consider whether the (mis)conduct was the direct result of school officials' failure to implement the students' IEPs.[86] If the IEP team answers either question "yes," the (mis)behavior is a manifestation of a disability. IEP teams must then conduct functional behavioral assessments (FBAs) if they have not already done so, and implement behavioral intervention plans (BIPs), while considering changes such as adding or modifying behavioral goals or strategies to deal with the behavior.[87]

If the (mis)behaviors are not manifestations of disabilities, students theoretically can be punished, up to and including expulsion, but must still be provided FAPEs even if expelled.[88] If parents file for due process under the IDEA to challenge expulsions, typically claiming that the misconduct was, in fact, a manifestation of a disability, stay put is not triggered such that students remain expelled in the interim.

In the event students facing discipline may claim they are disabled, whether they are entitled to the IDEA's protections depends on educators' knowledge of their conditions.

If public school officials had knowledge that students may be disabled before their alleged misconduct occurred, such as when parents inform them in writing of their concerns that their children are disabled and/or request evaluations to determine eligibility, or staff members suggest that children may be disabled, they gain IDEA discipline protections.[89] If school officials lack such "knowledge," they may proceed simultaneously with the discipline

---

[84] 34 C.F.R. § 300.613.

[85] *See, e.g.*, C.M. v. Bd. of Educ., 128 F. App'x 876, 880 [198 EDUC. L. REP. 58] (3d Cir. 2005) (determining that if the plaintiff had not been provided access to specified information in her school records, injunctive relief under IDEA may have be appropriate even though she had graduated).

[86] 20 U.S.C. § 1415(k)(1)(E).

[87] 20 U.S.C. § 1415(k)(1)(F).

[88] 20 U.S.C. § 1415(k)(1)(C).

[89] 20 U.S.C. § 1415(k)(5).

and expedited evaluations/eligibility determinations. On the other hand, if parents refused consent for special education evaluations or placements, or if IEP teams determined that children were ineligible, officials are not deemed to have "knowledge" that students are or may be disabled.[90]

Special Education Disputes

Parents who disagree with IEP teams on any matter concerning their special education of their children may seek impartial due process hearings, appealable to courts.[91] Filing for due process triggers the IDEA's "stay put" provision.[92] This means that while due process and any judicial appeals are pending, unless the parties agree otherwise, students "stay put" in their last uncontested placements.

The IDEA establishes alternative interim placements for some unsafe behaviors, including an expanded, forty-five-school-day alternate "stay put" placement for students who bring firearms or other weapons to school or school functions; knowingly use, possess, sell, or distribute illegal drugs at schools or school functions; or "inflict serious bodily injury upon another person while at school, on school premises, or at a school function."[93] In such cases, IEP teams determine the alternate placements.

Before due process hearings begin, state-assigned mediators are available to help the parties resolve their disputes.[94] If disputes proceed to hearings, state hearing officers with training in both law and special education conduct formal evidentiary proceedings[95] that are appealable to state or federal courts. Absent unusual circumstances, parents must proceed through the administrative hearing before going to court, a process known as exhaustion of (administrative) remedies.[96]

Monetary damages are not available for IDEA violations, but injunctive-type relief, such as ordering placements in specific programs or IEPs with specific terms, is common. Compensatory education—that is, extra time in special education—is an IDEA remedy.[97] As discussed below, reimbursement for unilateral private school placements by parents may be ordered. The IDEA is also a fee-shifting statute, meaning that parents who prevail in litigation are entitled to reasonable reimbursement of their attorney fees and costs, not including expert witness fees.[98] Parents represented by free attorneys can still recover fees at market rates.

---

[90] 20 U.S.C. § 1415(k)(5)(C).

[91] 20 U.S.C. §1415; 34 C.F.R. §§ 300.507 *et seq.*

[92] 20 U.S.C. § 1415(j); 34 C.F.R. § 300.518.

[93] 20 U.S.C. § 1415(k)(G).

[94] 34 C.F.R. § 300.506.

[95] 34 C.F.R. § 300.511(c).

[96] 20 U.S.C. § 1415(l); *see generally* Fry v. Napoleon Cmty. Sch., 137 S. Ct. 743 [340 Educ. L. Rep. 19] (2017).

[97] *See, e.g.,* Reid v. District of Columbia, 401 F.3d 516 [196 Educ. L. Rep. 402] (D.C. Cir. 2005).

[98] 20 U.S.C. § 1415(i)(3)(B).

The IDEA also makes state complaint processes available.[99] Anyone may file a complaint with the state education agency, which is responsible for investigating complaints and taking appropriate actions.

Section 504 has a somewhat different approach to disputes with internal complaints, Office of Civil Rights (OCR) complaints, and litigation options. School officials are required to establish informal internal grievance processes for Section 504 complaints.[100] Students who believe that officials in their schools violated their Section 504 rights, such as when educators at their private schools engage in discrimination by not providing requested minor adjustments, by not meeting physical accessibility requirements, or by retaliating against them for asking for such adjustments, may, but are not required to, use these internal grievance processes.

Parties may file complaints with the OCR in the federal Department of Education if they believe that Section 504 rights have been violated.[101] On receipt of complaints, OCR officials notify school officials, ask for responses, and otherwise investigate. Investigations may involve on-site visits to school with reviews of students' files and interviews of school employees. There is no hearing.

If the OCR finds a violation, its officials work with educators to obtain voluntary compliance and can issue summary letters which are publicly available.[102] The OCR can refer cases to the Department of Justice, which can file suit. If school officials do not comply voluntarily, OCR can also initiate hearings to cease providing federal education funds to schools, or can institute compliance reviews against schools, regardless of whether they received complaints.

Plaintiffs can initiate litigation under Section 504 alleging disability discrimination. Remedies include compensatory damages if they can prove that educators acted with bad faith or gross misjudgment as to their Section 504 rights.[103] Punitive damages are not available.[104] As with the IDEA, prevailing students are eligible for reimbursement of reasonable attorney fees from their schools.[105]

---

[99] 34 C.F.R. §§ 300.151 *et seq.*

[100] 34 C.F.R. § 104.7(b).

[101] For an overview of this process and complaints, see http://www.ed.gov/about/offices/list/ocr/docs/howto.html?src=rt; 34 C.F.R. § 104.61, incorporating *id.* at 100.7–100.9.

[102] Normally the names of complaining students are redacted but the names of schools are not. *See* 34 C.F.R. § 104.61, incorporating *id.* at 100.7(e).

[103] *See, e.g.,* M.P. v. Independent Sch. Dist., 439 F.3d 865 [206 Educ. L. Rep. 846] (8th Cir. 2006). For an overview of claims and remedies under Section 504, see Mark Weber, *Procedures and Remedies Under Section 504 and the ADA for Public School Children with Disabilities*, 32 J. Nat'l Ass'n Admin. L. Judiciary 611 (2012).

[104] Barnes v. Gorman, 536 U.S. 181 (2002).

[105] 29 U.S.C. § 794a.

The IDEA and Students in Private Schools

As discussed above, the IDEA provides modest funds to states and public school boards, while according rights to eligible students enrolled in public schools. Generally, the IDEA applies to public, but not private, schools. While the IDEA requires officials in public schools to identify and evaluate eligible students, including those enrolled in private schools, it does not afford students in private schools individual rights to special education services.

The IDEA formerly required an "equitable opportunity to participate" by students in private schools, interpreted by some as providing them with individual rights.[106] The IDEA currently imposes full child find obligations on public school board personnel to identify and evaluate IDEA-eligible students who attend private schools, are homeschooled, or are not enrolled in schools. Officials in private schools and other parents may use the IDEA's due process hearings and other dispute resolution mechanisms to assert child find violations.

As to special education services, the IDEA only requires public school boards to spend a proportionate amount of their modest federal IDEA funds on students in private schools. These students lack individual entitlements to services or to use IDEA hearings to challenge the special education services (not) provided to them. However, state law may offer these students enhanced rights, such as to enroll part time in public schools to receive special education and related services.

Child Find

States and their public school boards must identify, locate, and evaluate children with disabilities, specifically including "children with disabilities in the State who are enrolled in private, including parochial, elementary and secondary schools."[107] This includes students in for-profit private schools.[108] Insofar as the "child find" responsibility is ongoing, the failure to identify and evaluate children at any age who display behaviors indicating disabilities can be a child find violation.[109] In fact, child find applies to all children, even those in instructional settings not identified as "private schools" by states, such as homeschools or those not enrolled in schools,[110] and to all who attend school in

---

[106] Under this language, the Supreme Court treated the IDEA as a statute of general applicability, thereby making services equally available without regard to where the student attended school, even though it did not actually rule on this issue. Zobrest v. Catalina Foothills Sch. Dist., 509 U.S. 1 [83 Educ. L. Rep. 930] (1993).

[107] 20 U.S.C. §§ 1412 (a)(3), (a)(10)(A)(ii); 34 C.F.R. §§ 300.133(d); 300.111.

[108] *Questions and Answers on Serving Children with Disabilities Placed by Their Parents in Private Schools*, 111 LRP 32532 at O-1 (OSERS 2011).

[109] Dep't of Educ. State of Haw. v. Cari Rae S., 158 F. Supp. 2d 1190 [156 Educ. L. Rep. 924] (D. Haw. 2001) (treating the failure to exercise child find as retroactive violation of the IDEA even after a child graduated to cover parental expenses that might not have been necessary if school board officials had evaluated the child).

[110] 34 C.F.R. § 300.111.

a district, including nonresident students in local private schools.[111] The IDEA reevaluation and IEE obligations also apply to students in private schools and other children as part of child find.[112]

Students in private schools and elsewhere can bring child find claims using the IDEA's due process hearing system.[113] Child find violations that caused students to not receive special education as required by the IDEA may result in awards of compensatory education to make up for lost services.[114]

Special Education and Students in Private Schools Generally

Students with disabilities attending private schools fall into three categories. First, public school boards may place, and pay for, IDEA students in private schools. These students have full IDEA rights.

Second, parents may enroll their children in private schools because they believe public school officials have not offered their children IEPs providing them with FAPEs. These parents may use the IDEA's due process hearing process to seek reimbursement of private school tuition from their public school boards. The IDEA provides for tuition reimbursement if public boards failed to offer FAPEs and the private schools provide appropriate programs.

Third, and most commonly, some parents enroll their children in private schools as matters of preference, whether for religious or other reasons. Some of these students may receive limited special education services from their public school boards, but have no individual entitlements under the IDEA.

Children Placed in Private Schools by Public Agencies

Some private schools are designed to serve special education students with needs the public schools cannot meet. For example, some residential private schools serve children with acute mental illnesses. Publicly placed students in private schools are funded by their public school boards and have the same statutory rights to IEPs and related services as children in public schools.

Placements of IDEA students are often limited to state-approved private schools, as the IDEA provides that "the State educational agency shall determine whether such schools and facilities meet standards that apply to State and local educational agencies and that children so served have all the rights they would have if served by such agencies."[115] However, the now-superseded highly qualified teacher requirements in the No Child Left Behind Act did not apply

---

[111] *See* 34 C.F.R. § 300.131(f).

[112] *Questions and Answers on Serving Children with Disabilities Placed by Their Parents in Private Schools*, 111 LRP 32532 at B-12 (IEE); B-8 (reevaluation) (OSERS 2011).

[113] 34 C.F.R. § 300.140(b).

[114] *See, e.g.,* Lakin v. Birmingham Pub. Sch., 70 F. App'x 295 [179 EDUC. L. REP. 640] (6th Cir. 2003).

[115] 20 U.S.C. § 1412(a)(10)(B)(2).

to these placements.[116] Moreover, states must provide opportunities for input by officials in private schools into state standards impacting their schools.[117]

As discussed earlier, the "public" part of the FAPE requirement mandates that special education services be provided "under public supervision and direction."[118] Under the IDEA, if officials of public agencies place children in private schools, they are considered to be receiving public educations and have "all of the rights of a child with a disability who is served by a public agency."[119] In particular, representatives of private schools must be invited to be part of IEP teams.[120]

Even if public school boards contract with officials in private schools to provide educational services, the boards are still responsible if these children do not receive appropriate special education services.[121] Thus, in some states where public boards do not have high schools and must contract for services with private schools, the contracts with the nonpublic schools and payment of tuition by the public boards does not exculpate them of their responsibilities under the IDEA.

Placing children with disabilities in private schools does not make them responsible for carrying out the IDEA's requirements. As illustrated by a case from Ohio, parents unsuccessfully argued that because a private school received federal assistance, it was liable under the IDEA for not providing their son with special education services necessary to address his hearing impairment and learning disability. The Sixth Circuit affirmed that because only a public school board, and not private schools, could receive funds under the IDEA, only the former could be liable under the IDEA for the child's failure to receive services.[122] While the private school in this case might have been liable under Section 504, it could not have been responsible under the IDEA.[123]

---

[116] 34 C.F.R. § 300.146(b).

[117] 34 C.F.R. § 300.147(c).

[118] 20 U.S.C. § 1401(9)(A); 34 C.F.R. § 300.142(b)(2).

[119] 20 U.S.C. § 1412(a)(10)(B)(ii); 34 C.F.R. § 300.146(c).

[120] See, e.g., 34 C.F.R. § 300.321 (IEP teams must include a person who provides special education or related services to students); S.H. v. Plano Sch. Dist., 487 F. App'x 850 [287 Educ. L. Rep. 721] (5th Cir. 2012) (observing that the failure to invite a representative from a private school to an IEP team meeting, instead relying on a teacher who had not worked with the student, resulted in the development of an inappropriate IEP, thereby denying him a FAPE; also ordering $15,000 in extended year services).

[121] See St. Johnsbury Acad. v. D.H., 240 F.3d 163 [151 Educ. L. Rep. 74] (2d Cir. 2001) (upholding a private school's performance requirements that did not permit a child with disabilities to be placed in its mainstream academic classes as not violating the IDEA because it was not subject to the IDEA).

[122] Ullmo v. Gilmour Acad., 273 F.3d 671 [159 Educ. L. Rep. 521] (6th Cir. 2001).

[123] Id., but see St. Johnsbury Academy v. D.H., 240 F.3d 163 [151 Educ. L. Rep. 74] (2d Cir. 2001) (did not raise Section 504 issues, holding that a student with disabilities was not "otherwise qualified" under Section 504 because he failed to meet the private school's essential minimum requirement for admission into the mainstream curriculum, insofar as he was unable to read at the fifth-grade level).

As in the Sixth Circuit case in the preceding paragraph, private schools in such disputes typically contract with public school boards. In these situations, contract provisions usually require compliance with the IEP and IDEA provisions and may permit private schools to indemnify the public school boards.[124] In addition, these private schools may face breach of contract claims filed by public school boards.

Children Placed in Private Schools by Their Parents in FAPE Disputes with Public School Boards

Public school boards are not required to pay for, or reimburse, unilateral parental placements "if that agency made a free appropriate education available to the child and the parents elected to place the child in such private school or facility."[125] However, the failure of public school boards to make FAPEs available prior to unilateral parental placements in private schools which afford appropriate educations can make the public boards responsible for the costs of the private education.[126]

Parents who place their children in private schools have frequently made these claims, resulting in a Supreme Court case and amendments to the IDEA. In *Schaffer v. Weast*,[127] the Supreme Court held that insofar as parents who unilaterally placed their son in a private school challenged the services he received in the public school under his IEP, they bore the burden of proof challenging its appropriateness.

In order for parents to be eligible for reimbursements, they must prove that the IEPs offered by their public school boards did not provide FAPEs and that their children received appropriate educations in the private schools. Courts review "appropriate" private school placements chosen by parents based on the understanding that they are not education experts. Thus, for example, in *Florence County School District v. Carter*,[128] the Supreme Court found that a private school placement was appropriate where the student was making

---

[124] *See, e.g.*, Koehler v. Juniata Cty. Sch. Dist., 2008 WL 1787632 (M.D. Pa. 2008) (involving such a contract).

[125] 20 U.S.C. § 1412 (a)(10)(C)(i).

[126] *See* School Comm'n of Burlington v. Dep't of Educ. of Mass., 471 U.S. 359 [23 Educ. L. Rep. 1189] (1985) (interpreting the IDEA as implicitly authorizing reimbursement for a private placement where a school board failed to provide a FAPE and that reimbursement did not constitute damages because they are impermissible under the IDEA); Florence Cty. Sch. Dist. v. Carter, 510 U.S. 7 [86 Educ. L. Rep. 41] (1993) (finding that a public school board was liable for tuition expenses for parents' private school placement because it failed to provide a FAPE; also, refusing to read the IDEA's definition of FAPE as applying to parental placements and not barring reimbursement because the program the parents chose in the private school did not meet the IDEA's definition of a FAPE).

[127] 546 U.S. 49 [203 Educ. L. Rep. 29] (2005).

[128] 510 U.S. 7 [86 Educ. L. Rep. 41] (1993) (explaining that a parental placement in a private school can be appropriate and qualify for tuition reimbursement under the IDEA even if the private school does not employ state-certified teachers). *See also* 34 C.F.R. § 300.148(c) ("A parental placement may be found to be appropriate by a hearing officer or a court even if it does not meet the State standards that apply to education provided by the SEA and LEAs.").

good progress, although some teachers were not state-certified. In this and other cases, the testimony of private school teachers and other staff members about students' progress was crucial in determining the appropriateness of the private school placements the parents chose.

In *Forest Grove School District v. T.A.* (*Forest Grove*),[129] the Supreme Court decided that IDEA language purportedly restricting reimbursements to parents "who previously received special education and related services under the authority of a public agency"[130] did not prevent parents from seeking reimbursements even if their children had not received services. Again, the Court made it clear that parents have some leeway from technical requirements; what is important is that children receive FAPEs. If public school personnel fail to identify students in need of evaluations, or do not evaluate them comprehensively, boards may be responsible under *Forest Grove* for some or all expenses at private schools.[131] After *Forest Grove*, lower courts focused on whether the parents' private placements are providing the services they considered to be deficient in the public schools or missing in the IEPs.[132]

The IDEA recognizes reasons for reducing or denying reimbursement to parents, including failure to give advance notice, failure to make the child available for evaluation, and unreasonable actions by parents. In general, as to advance notice, parents have two options. First, they must notify board officials at the most recent IEP meetings they attended prior to removing their children from the public schools and the reasons why, while announcing their intent to enroll their children in private schools at public expense.[133] Second, ten business days prior to removing their children from public schools, parents must give the public school boards notice of their intent.[134]

Parental failure to provide notice might not bar their being reimbursed if they are illiterate or do not speak English, or where enforcement would result in emotional harm to children. Further, reimbursement is not barred if school personnel prevented notice from reaching parents, where parents were not informed about the notice requirements, or where enforcement would result in physical harm to the children.[135]

In some cases, parents must make their children available for evaluation by their public school boards in order to be eligible for reimbursement. Put another way, before parents removed their children from public schools, if

---

[129] 557 U.S. 230 [245 Educ. L. Rep. 551] (2009).

[130] 20 U.S.C.A. § 1412(a)(10)(C)(ii).

[131] For an analysis of *Forest Grove*, see Ralph D. Mawdsley, *The Supreme Court's Reassessment of Parental Placement Under the IDEA: Forest Grove School District v. T.A.*, 251 Educ. L. Rep. 1 (2010).

[132] *See, e.g.,* Davis v. Wappingers Cent. Sch. Dist., 772 F. Supp. 2d 500 [269 Educ. L. Rep. 110] (S.D.N.Y. 2010).

[133] 20 U.S.C. § 1412(a)(10) (C)(iii)(I)(aa).

[134] 20 U.S.C. § 1412(a)(10)(C)(iii)(I)(bb). *See* C.H. v. Cape Henlopen Sch. Dist., 606 F.3d 59 [257 Educ. L. Rep. 39] (3d Cir. 2010) (parents were not entitled to reimbursement where they failed to provide notice).

[135] 20 U.S.C. § 1412(a)(10)(C)(iv).

board officials had informed them of their intent to evaluate their children, they must make them available for such evaluations.[136] Parents' eligibility for full reimbursements may also be lost if there have been judicial findings of unreasonableness with respect to their actions.[137]

Children Placed in Private Schools Due to Parental Preferences

As noted, some students with disabilities are enrolled in private schools because their parents want them to receive religious education, perceive that the private schools provide higher quality educations, view the private schools as better fits for their children, or similar reasons. Some of these students may receive limited special education services from their public school boards, but the IDEA does not provide them with individual entitlements to special education.

Public school boards must spend a proportionate share of their federal IDEA funds on students in private schools. Moreover, public boards must consult with staff and parents in local private schools, but the decisions about which students get services, and whether they are provided at public schools or private schools, are left to the public school boards. Students in private schools cannot challenge the services they (do not) receive under the IDEA's due process procedures. State law may provide additional rights to these students, such as to enroll on a part- time basis in the public schools to be educated.

Who Are the "Students in Private Schools" in This Category?

The IDEA leaves defining private schools to state law,[138] thereby offering states latitude on whether to include homeschooling in their definitions for IDEA purposes.[139] It is also up to states to determine what preschool and day care programs may be included as private schools. However, as to services for students in private schools, the IDEA excludes for-profit private schools. Thus, students attending for-profit private schools are included in child find, but are not eligible for services.[140]

Ordinarily, state law defines private schools in compulsory attendance statutes and may include homeschools, as well as regular sectarian and non-sectarian schools.[141] Moreover, states may distinguish between and among kinds of nonpublic schools. For example, Florida defines home education as

---

[136] 20 U.S.C. § 1412(a)(10)(C) (iii)(II).

[137] 20 U.S.C. § 1412(a)(10)(C)(iii)(III).

[138] *See* Hooks v. Clark Cty. Sch. Dist., 228 F.3d 1036 [147 Educ. L. Rep. 870] (9th Cir. 2000), *cert. denied*, 532 U.S. 971 (2001).

[139] *See* Letter to Williams, 18 IDELR 742 (OSEP 1992).

[140] *Questions and Answers on Serving Children with Disabilities Placed by Their Parents in Private Schools*, 111 LRP 32532 at O-1 (OSERS 2011).

[141] *See, e.g.,* Tex. Educ. Code Ann. § 25.086 (exempting children from compulsory attendance laws who attend "a private or parochial school that includes in its course a study of good citizenship"). Private schools under this definition were interpreted in Texas Education Agency v. Leeper, 893 S.W.2d 432 [98 Educ. L. Rep. 491] (Tex. 1994) as including instruction in a home school.

meeting the state's compulsory attendance requirement, but does not classify homeschools as private schools.[142] Under this approach, public school boards would not include students who are homeschooled students in the number of children with disabilities in private schools for the purpose of calculating the proportionate amount of funds to allocate for services to those children. While public boards would have child find obligations to students who are homeschooled, there is no IDEA obligation to provide them with special education services.[143]

State law may provide additional rights to children who are not "students in private schools." For instance, an appellate court in New Jersey affirmed that even though a homeschooled student lacked an entitlement to IDEA speech therapy services because he was not in a private school as defined under state law, he had a right to these services under the state constitution.[144] The court found a state constitutional equal protection violation when officials in public schools provided services to students in private schools, but not to those who were homeschooled. Nevada has addressed the issue of special education services for homeschooled students through legislation, mandating that "[t] he board of trustees of each school district shall provide programs of special education and related services for children who are exempt from compulsory attendance pursuant to the home-education exemption and receive instruction at home."[145]

Proportionate Allocations of Federal IDEA Funds

Public school boards are obligated to expend funds for students with disabilities in private schools equal to proportionate amounts of federal funds available under the IDEA.[146] This amount includes neither money spent on child find nor administrative costs.[147] The IDEA requires consultation with staff of private schools and parents before determining the number of children with disabilities and the proportionate amount of federal IDEA funds to be allocated to them.[148] State and local funds may be used for this consultative process.

---

[142] *Cf.* FLA. STAT. ANN. § 1002.41 (stating that home-educated students must meet the requirements of a "home education program" for purposes of satisfying compulsory attendance) *with* FLA. STAT. ANN. § 1002.01 (declaring that a "home education program" is explicitly excluded from the definition a "private school," which can include "a parochial, religious, denominational, for-profit, or nonprofit school"). *See also* VA. CODE ANN. § 22.1-254 ("Instruction in the home of a child or children by the parent, guardian or other person having control or charge of such child or children shall not be classified or defined as a private, denominational or parochial school"); COLO. REV. STAT. ANN. § 22-33-104.5 (2) (a) ("Nonpublic home-based educational program . . . does not qualify as a private and nonprofit school").

[143] Forstrum v. Byrne, 775 A.2d 65 [155 EDUC. L. REP. 608] (N.J. Super. Ct. App. Div. 2001).

[144] Nev. Rev Stat. § 392.072(1).

[145] Hooks v. Clark County Sch. Dist., 228 F.3d 1036 [148 EDUC. L. REP. 870] (9th Cir. 2000), *cert. denied,* 532 U.S. 971 (2001).

[146] 20 U.S.C. § 1412(a)(10)(A)(i)(I); 34 C.F.R. § 300.133.

[147] 34 C.F.R. § 300.131(d).

[148] 20 U.S.C. § 1412(a)(10)(A)(i)-(iii).

Public school boards may choose to spend additional state or local funds on students in private schools, but are not required to do so. The IDEA expressly provides that "[s]tate and local funds may supplement and in no case shall supplant the proportionate amount of Federal funds required to be expended under this subparagraph."[149]

Let us say a hypothetical public school board receives $150,000 in federal IDEA money and identifies 100 IDEA students, including ten IDEA-eligible students in private schools. This board must spend 10/100 (10%) of its $150,000, or $15,000, on this group of students in private schools. No one student in this group is entitled to FAPE, LRE, any specific services, or to services costing the equivalent of an individual share, here $1500, of the proportionate federal IDEA funds allocation. Obviously, at this level of funding, the services provided fall far short of providing any students in private schools with FAPEs.[150]

Services provided to children with disabilities who are parentally placed must "be secular, neutral and nonideological."[151] Services cannot benefit the private schools, nor be provided to meet the general instructional needs of the private schools or their student bodies.[152] If services are provided at public schools or other common sites, there cannot be separate classes for students from the public and private schools.[153] Accordingly, public school boards may not establish separate resource rooms at public schools to serve students from private schools. All funds and services provided to children with disabilities whose parents placed them in private schools must be administered by the public school board, which must retain title to all "materials, equipment, and property purchased with [IDEA] funds."[154]

The IDEA's specific language on the limited obligations to students in private schools includes:

1. No private school child with a disability "has an individual right to receive some or all of the special education and related services the child would receive if enrolled in a public school."[155]

2. "Private school children with disabilities may receive a different amount of services than children with disabilities in public schools."[156]

3. After consulting with representatives of private schools on these matters, each public school board will determine which children

---

[149] 20 U.S.C. § 1412 (a)(10)(A)(i)(IV).

[150] *See, e.g.,* Board of Educ. of the Appoquinimink Sch. Dist. v. Johnson, 543 F. Supp.2d 351 [231 Educ. L. Rep. 794] (D. Del. 2008) (noting that the board's proportionate share of federal IDEA funds for students in private schools was $3693; yet, the full-time interpreter the student in the private school sought would have cost $37,000, or more than ten times the total amount available for all students in private schools).

[151] 20 U.S.C. § 1412 (a)(10)(A)(vi)(II).

[152] 34 C.F.R. § 300.141.

[153] 34 C.F.R. § 300.143.

[154] 20 U.S.C. § 1412 (a)(10)(A)(vii).

[155] 34 C.F.R. § 300.137(a).

[156] 34 C.F.R. § 300.138(a)(2).

from private schools are to receive services, what services are to be provided, how and where the services are to be provided, and how the services provided are to be evaluated.[157]

4. Once public school boards decide to provide services to students in private schools, personnel providing those services must meet "the same standards as personnel providing services in public schools," other than highly qualified teacher requirements[158]

As noted, students in private schools lack individual rights to services[159] or to FAPEs. In one such case, the Seventh Circuit explained that the 1997 IDEA amendments "unambiguously show that participating states and localities have no obligation to spend their money to ensure that disabled children who have chosen to enroll in private schools will receive publicly funded education generally 'comparable' to those provided to public-school children." [160]

Consultation Processes

Officials in public schools must consult with their counterparts in local private schools and the parents of their students on various issues, including the following six items.[161]

1. Parents who have placed their children in nonpublic schools, as well as teachers and school officials in private schools, must be informed of the child find process.[162]

2. Public school officials must consult with officials from private schools and parents who placed their children with disabilities in private schools over the proportionate amount of federal funds available to these children.[163]

3. This consultative process must continue throughout the school year "to ensure that parentally placed private school children with disabilities identified through the child find process can meaningfully participate in special education and related services."[164]

4. Consultation on what types of services are to be provided for parentally placed children with disabilities, including "how such services will be apportioned if funds are insufficient to serve all children and how and when these decisions will be made."[165]

5. If parents who placed their children with disabilities in private schools disagree with public school boards about the allocation of services,

---

[157] 34 C.F.R. §§ 300.134(d); .138(b)(2).

[158] 34 C.F.R. § 300.138(a).

[159] 34 C.F.R. § 300.137(a). *See* Foley v. Special Sch. Dist. of St. Louis Cnty., 153 F.3d 863 [128 EDUC. L. REP. 1049] (8th Cir. 1998).

[160] K.R. v. Anderson Cmty. Sch. Corp., 125 F.3d 1017, 1019 [121 EDUC. L. REP. 490] (7th Cir. 1997).

[161] 20 U.S.C. § 1412 (a)(10)(A)(iii).

[162] 20 U.S.C. § 1412 (a)(10)(A)(iii)(I).

[163] 20 U.S.C. § 1412 (a)(10)(A)(iii)(II).

[164] 20 U.S.C. § 1412 (a)(10)(A)(iii)(III).

[165] 20 U.S.C. § 1412 (a)(10)(A)(iii)(IV).

the boards must "provide to the private school officials a written explanation of the reasons why the local educational agency [board] chose not to provide services directly or through a contract."[166]

6. Each school board must provide its state department of education "a written affirmation signed by the representatives of participating private schools" that meaningful consultation has occurred, and if representatives are not willing to sign such an affirmation, "the local educational agency shall forward the documentation of the consultation process to the State educational agency."[167]

7. Parents and private schools may file complaints with their state educational agencies if they are not satisfied with the consultative process or the services that are (not) provided and if dissatisfied with state decisions, can appeal to the U.S. Secretary of Education.[168]

Services Plan Requirement

Students whose parents have enrolled them in private schools and are selected by public school boards to receive some special education services are not entitled to IEPs. Rather, these students are entitled to services plans. A services plan "describes the specific special education and related services that the LEA [public board] will provide to the child in light of the services that the LEA has determined . . . it will make available to parentally placed private school children with disabilities."[169] Service plans lack the detail and road-map nature of IEPs, but do need to identify the services provided, the locations where they are to be provided, and must be developed, reviewed, and revised consistent with the requirements for IEPs.[170] Representatives of the private schools and parents of the students being served must be involved in developing service plans.[171]

Location of Services

It is up to officials of public school boards to decide whether to bring services to private schools, have students come to the public schools, or have them come to neutral locations. Services can be provided on-site at private, including religious, schools "to the extent consistent with law."[172] The Supreme Court has interpreted the Constitution as not prohibiting public school officials

---

[166] 20 U.S.C. § 1412 (a)(10)(A)(iii)(V).
[167] 20 U.S.C. § 1412 (a)(10)(A)(iv).
[168] 20 U.S.C. § 1412 (a)(10)(A)(v).
[169] 34 C.F.R. §§ 300.138(b)(1), 37.
[170] 34 C.F.R. § 300.138(c).
[171] 34 C.F.R. §300.137(c)(2).
[172] 34 C.F.R. § 300.139(a).

from delivering services on site to students in private religious schools.[173] However, some state constitutions may prohibit such arrangements.[174] School boards may pay employees of the private schools to perform the services as long as an "employee performs the services outside of his or her regular hours of duty, and the employee performs the services under public supervision and control."[175] Public school officials may place property, equipment, and supplies at private school sites for delivery of services to their students, but the items must be removed if they are no longer needed or if doing so is necessary to prevent their unauthorized use.[176]

It is not clear whether states can choose to provide on-site services at nonsectarian but not sectarian schools. The Eighth Circuit indicated that while states do not have to provide special education services on-site in private schools, their officials cannot discriminate against religious schools by providing services only to nonreligious schools.[177] The court emphasized that while states could decide to prohibit all services on-site to private schools, they cannot exhibit a "religious animus" toward them. The status of this holding is unclear in the wake of *Locke v. Davey*[178] and *Trinity Lutheran Church of Columbia v. Comer*,[179] wherein the Supreme Court ruled that faith-based institutions cannot be denied generally available aid simply because they are religious.

A related issue pertains to transportation. Students in private schools who receive services off-site are entitled to transportation, as necessary, to the service sites and back to their private schools or homes, but not between their homes and private schools.[180]

Complaints by Parents Whose Children Attend Private Schools

Parents of students in private schools are not entitled to use the IDEA's impartial due process hearing procedures except to challenge the alleged failures of local school boards to employ the child find provisions to identify,

---

[173] *See, e.g.,* Agostini v. Felton, 521 U.S.203 [119 Educ. L. Rep. 29] (1997) (permitting the on-site delivery of Title I remedial services at private religious schools); Zobrest v. Catalina Foothills Sch. Dist., 509 U.S.1 [83 Educ. L. Rep. 930] (1993) (permitting a government-funded sign language interpreter for an IDEA-eligible student whose parents enrolled him in a faith-based school); *cf.* Mitchell v. Helms, 530 U.S. 793 [145 Educ. L. Rep. 44] (2000) (permitting government-funded computers and library books to be used in faith-based schools).

[174] *See, e.g.,* Wash. Const. Art. 9 Section 4 ("All schools maintained or supported wholly or in part by the public funds shall be forever free from sectarian control or influence.").

[175] 34 C.F.R. § 300.142(b).

[176] 34 C.F.R. § 300.144.

[177] Peter v. Wedl, 155 F.3d 992 [129 Educ. L. Rep. 594] (8th Cir. 1998).

[178] 540 U.S. 712 [185 Educ. L. Rep. 30] (2004) (state scholarship program including academic religious study, but excluding theological study, is constitutional).

[179] 137 S. Ct. 2012 (2017) (invalidating a state playground grants program that excluded religious-affiliated applicants as unconstitutional). For a discussion of this case, see William E. Thro & Charles J. Russo, *Odious to the Constitution: The Educational Implications of Trinity Lutheran Church v. Comer*, 346 Educ. Law Rep. 1 (2017).

[180] 34 C.F.R. § 300.139(b).

locate, and/or evaluate students.[181] For all other complaints, such as denials of services or failure to implement services plans, state complaint processes are available.[182] Within sixty days of when parents file state complaints, officials must conduct investigations and issue written decisions including any necessary corrective measures.[183]

By-pass for Children in Private Schools

In jurisdictions where state law prohibits children who attend private schools from participating in special education services, the federal Department of Education arranges for direct provision of services. This delivery of services is subject to the condition that the amounts of money available cannot exceed the sum derived from dividing the state's total amount of dollars received for the fiscal year by the total number of students receiving services.[184] Such decisions by the Secretary of Education are reviewable by federal circuit courts.[185]

State Laws May Provide Additional Rights

In some jurisdictions, state law provides IDEA-eligible students with additional rights. For example, some states give private and homeschooled students the right to enroll part time in local public schools for classes, activities, special education, and other services unavailable in their private schools or homeschool programs.[186] In this event, officials in public school would have special education obligations to the students who are enrolled on a part-time basis that are not limited to proportionate spending of federal IDEA funds, and the IDEA due process hearing system is available.

State law may provide for FAPEs for students in private schools under some circumstances. In such a case, the Eighth Circuit interpreted Minnesota's "shared time" statute for a student from a faith-based school with a learning disability who attended public school for part of the day.[187] State law made the public school board responsible for a FAPE to the extent the student attended the public school, also allowing him, through his parents, to challenge denial of this FAPE right in an IDEA due process hearing.

Some states make vouchers available to students in special education placements. For instance, Florida has enacted the McKay Scholarships for

---

[181] *See* 34 C.F.R. § 300.140.

[182] *Id.*

[183] 34 C.F.R. §§ 300.151 *et seq.*

[184] 20 U.S.C. § 1412(f). See 34 C.F.R. §§ 300.190 *et seq.*

[185] 20 U.S.C. § 1412(f)(3)(B).

[186] For example, in Washington, private school and homeschool students have a state law right to enroll part time in public schools for any program, course, service, or activity not offered in their private or homeschool. So, for example, students could enroll part time in public schools to receive needed special education instruction or related services. States receive prorated state education funding for services for these students. *See* R.C.W. § 28A.150.350; WA. Admin. Code § 392-134-002 *et seq.*

[187] Special Sch. Dist. No. 1 v. R.M.M., 861 F.3d 769 [344 Educ. L. Rep. 766] (8th Cir. 2017).

Students with Disabilities Program, a special education voucher system.[188] The program allows families to use vouchers to send their children either to public schools or participating secular or religious private schools. Still, the participating private schools are not necessarily covered by disability and other discrimination laws.

The amount of the vouchers in the Florida program is the lesser of private school tuition or the sum of money public school boards would have spent on the students. Parents are responsible for transportation to private schools and decide whether their children will participate in state standardized testing. Perhaps most significantly, participating families waive their IDEA rights. Critics have questioned this program for allegedly lacking accountability, the ability of private schools to engage in disability and other discrimination, and its less than full funding of special education costs.

Private School Obligations under Section 504

Private schools receiving federal education funds are covered by Section 504,[189] which bans disability-based discrimination. Regardless of funding, because private schools are also defined as places of public accommodation they are governed by the Americans with Disabilities Act (ADA),[190] which bans disability discrimination; even so, the Act includes a broad exclusion for religious schools.[191] This leaves private religious schools not receiving federal education funds as not directly subject to either Section 504 or the ADA.

In federally funded private schools, or secular private schools, though, it is unlawful disability discrimination to engage in stereotype-driven decision making such as denying admission to students with disabilities or IEPs. Further, Section 504 and the ADA mandate physical accessibility for students in wheelchairs or with other mobility impairments.[192]

Section 504's ban on discrimination includes some education-related requirements. As discussed earlier in this chapter, Section 504 prohibits discrimination in all aspects of school operations: admissions, academics, testing, extracurricular activities and non-academics such as lunch and recess, counseling services, athletics, transportation, health services, clubs, and student employment. For example, in counseling, schools must not steer students with disabilities toward more restrictive career objectives.[193] In physical education and athletics, school officials must afford students equal opportunities to participate in intramural, club, and interschool sports, including reasonable

---

[188] http://www.fldoe.org/schools/school-choice/k-12-scholarship-programs/mckay/; FL. STAT. ANN. § 1002-39.

[189] 29 U.S.C. § 794.

[190] 42 U.S.C. § 12101 *et seq.*

[191] 42 U.S.C. § 12181(7)(j); 28 C.F.R. §§ 36.102, 104.

[192] 34 C.F.R. §§ 104. 21-23.

[193] 34 C.F.R. § 104.37(b) states in part: "The recipient shall ensure that qualified handicapped students are not counseled toward more restrictive career objectives than are nonhandicapped students with similar interests and abilities."

modifications. The regulation governing athletics applies to both public and private schools.[194]

An OCR guidance letter on point, aimed at public schools,[195] reminds officials of their obligation to make reasonable modifications for athletes with disabilities. Modifications might include visual cues for athletes who are deaf, assistance getting to the mat for a wrestler who is blind, allowing a swimmer with one hand to substitute a one-hand touch and the other arm outstretched as a modification of two-hand touch requirement to finish races (if doing so does not provide an advantage), allowing an athlete with asthma to use an inhaler, and providing for glucose testing and insulin administration for an athlete with diabetes. Modifications which provide advantage to athletes with disabilities, or which alter essential aspect of sports, are not reasonable. Schools can adopt safety and skill/performance standards for all athletes, but cannot make decisions about athletic participation based on stereotypes.

The ban on disability discrimination includes freedom from harassment and bullying. Research indicates that students with disabilities are disproportionately the victims of bullying and harassment.[196]

The ban on discrimination also includes LRE requirements.[197] Because private schools not providing special education do not have self-contained special education classes or other more restrictive placements, the LRE requirements have limited applicability. However, it seems that officials would be liable for LRE violations if they required a student with food allergies to eat lunch by herself in a separate room.

Turning to discipline, the nondiscrimination obligations of schools include not punishing students for conduct caused by their disabilities. For example, applying a conduct rule forbidding cursing to a private school student with Tourette syndrome who has a verbal tic involving involuntary cursing would be unlawful discrimination. In one case, a state court granted a preliminary injunction against a private school that expelled a high school senior with a bleeding disorder who cursed when she cut herself with a knife in class.[198]

The disability discrimination laws do not require private schools not offering special education to begin doing so. The Section 504 requirement for non-special education private schools is one of "minor adjustments."[199]

---

[194] *See* 34 C.F.R. §§ 104.37(c); 104.39(c).

[195] Dear Colleague Letter, 62 IDELR 185 (OCR 2013).

[196] Dear Colleague Letter, 55 IDELR 174 (OCR 2010). *See generally* Charles J. Russo & Allan G. Osborne, *Bullying and Students with Disabilities: How Can We Keep Them Safe?* 36 EDUC. L. REP. 1 (2015); Mark Weber, *Disability Harassment in the Public Schools*, 43 WM. & MARY L. REV. 1079 (2002).

[197] 34 C.F.R. § 104.34.

[198] Thomas v. Davidson Acad., 846 F. Supp. 611 [90 EDUC. L. REP. 132] (M.D. Tenn. 1994) (involving a senior honors student with an otherwise good record).

[199] 34 C.F.R. § 104.39. For a comprehensive review of these obligations, see Lynn M. Daggett, *"Minor adjustments" and other not-so-minor obligations: Section 504, private religious K-12 schools, and students with disabilities*, 52 U. LOUISV. L. REV. 301 (2014).

The ADA requirement of reasonable modifications[200] presumably is similar. A Section 504 regulation also explicitly provides that private schools may charge families for special services involving substantial costs, [201] explaining that they cannot charge Section 504 students more except when they have "substantial increase in cost."

One court attempted a general definition of "minor adjustments," holding that "it is clear that minor adjustments is less than a reasonable accommodation. Minor indicates a minimal burden and adjustment implies a small correction."[202] In applying this standard, the court balanced the burden of the requested adjustment, namely, a mandatory scent-free environment, on the school with the benefit to the student. The court found that the mandatory scent-free environment would have been burdensome and unworkable given the large school facility, the presence of visitors and other outsiders, the small administrative staff, and the difficulty of monitoring compliance, such that officials were not required to make this "minor adjustment."

"Minor adjustments" should be understood in the context of Section 504's nondiscrimination mandate. First, to the extent private school officials make adjustments for individual students for non-disability reasons, they are likely obligated to make those same modifications as necessary for students with disabilities. By way of illustration, if officials at a private school gave a student a leave of absence and make-up examination to travel with her family, they may be obligated to do the same for students with disabilities who are hospitalized or are otherwise too ill to attend school.

If officials at private schools waived attendance requirements for students who attended school-related events such as Boys or Girls Nation, family vacations during school days, or athletes attending away games, they may be obligated to do so to a similar extent for students with disabilities. Private schools that allow students who are not yet fluent in English extra time on examinations, or vary their formats (such as when giving reading tests to these children and recording their oral responses), may be obligated to make similar adjustments as necessary for students with disabilities.

The kinds of adjustments educators in private schools make for students who do not have disabilities also suggests what is feasible for their schools, and thus what may be "minor" for them under Section 504. The arrangements school officials have with other students provides important evidence about what is "minor" for their purposes. To this end, officials might offer varied test formats to students to allow them to demonstrate their knowledge in formats demonstrating their strengths, such as allowing students who are not good at multiple choice questions to answer in essay formats, or vice versa. Such actions appear to reflect the feasibility of adjusting examination formats and so may make similar adjustments required "minor" ones under Section 504.

---

[200] 42 U.S.C. § 12182(b)(2)(A)(ii).

[201] 34 C.F.R. § 104.39(b).

[202] Hunt v. St. Peter Sch., 963 F. Supp. 843 [118 EDUC. L. REP. 663] (W.D. Mo. 1997).

In contrast, some school officials never vary examination formats, perhaps because they want to compare all students' performance on the same tasks, or maybe because they view such modifications as imposing too great a burden on their teachers. In these cases, officials appear to have decided that format adjustments are not feasible and so likely would not be minor ones for those schools. Similarly, extensive personal tutoring for Section 504 student seems on its face to be more than a minor adjustment. However, if officials provide extensive tutoring to non-Section 504 students, such as some student-athletes, it may be discriminatory not to make the same tutoring services available to Section 504 students, in that this tutoring is a "minor adjustment" for that school.

Examples of minor adjustments may include "tutorial services [voluntarily made available by private school officials], extra time to take examinations, special seating arrangements, and other [noncontent] modifications,"[203] modifications to school disciplinary policies,[204] breaks for snacks for students with diabetes,[205] and leaves of absence. Other examples are time extensions to complete diplomas or other requirements, daily notes to parents describing homework assignments for students with Attention Deficit Disorder (ADD), extra time on examinations, and low-distraction environments for students with ADD.

Modifications to essential academic requirements of private schools would render students unqualified under Section 504[206] and so are not required under the minor adjustments standard. Examples of non-required academic accommodations are modifications of minimum GPAs or core academic requirements,[207] creation of new curricula,[208] or waivers of minimum achievement levels for admission.[209]

Generally, special education instruction or related services are beyond required minor adjustments.[210] Yet, scheduling modifications allowing Section 504 students to receive special education services on-site at their private

---

[203] Benedictine (GA) Military Sch., 22 IDELR 643 (OCR 1995).

[204] Thomas v. Davidson Acad., 846 F. Supp. 611 [90 EDUC. L. REP. 132 (M.D. Tenn. 1994).

[205] *See, e.g.,* Springboro (OH) Cmty. City Sch. Dist., 39 IDELR 41 (OCR 2003).

[206] 34 C.F.R. § 104.3(l); *see also* Ireland v. Kan. Dist. of the Wesleyan Church, 1994 WL 413807 (D. Kans. 1994) (finding that a student with disabilities who has not achieved daycare's required combination of age and developmental milestones may not have been otherwise qualified).

[207] *Cf.* Axelrod v. Phillips Acad., 46 F. Supp.2d 72 [135 EDUC. L. REP. 461] (D. Mass. 1999) (noting that under the ADA's reasonable modifications standard, school officials agreed to waive the foreign language requirement, but not for mathematics, for a student with ADHD who was eventually dismissed for academic reasons; the court deferred to educators' academic judgment that the student was not making sufficient effort).

[208] *See, e.g.,* Kendall (DC) Demonstration Elementary Sch., 107 LRP 36725 (OCR 2006) (deciding that officials in a nonpublic school for students who were deaf was not required to create functional curriculum for students with lower levels of intellectual functioning).

[209] St. Johnsbury Acad. v. D.H., 240 F.3d 163 [151 EDUC. L. REP. 74] (2d Cir. 2001) (ruling that a school policy requiring all student to achieve at the fifth-grade level did not violate Section 504).

[210] *See* Benedictine (GA) Military Sch., 22 IDELR 643 (OCR 1995); Life Christian (WA) School, 352 IDELR 523 (OCR 1987).

schools or at local public schools appear to be required minor adjustments. For example, if a student with a speech disability enrolled in a private school, its officials should be open to scheduling arrangements allowing the child to receive speech therapy from a private provider, or publicly provided at either the private school or the local public school.

School officials are not obligated to make adjustments imposing significant burdens such as those necessitating additional staffing.[211] Further, in most cases, modifications posing health and/or safety risks are beyond minor adjustments.[212] As a corollary, modifications which are significantly disruptive of school operations are likely beyond required minor adjustments.[213]

Private schools may pass on substantial charges for individual modifications to families. It appears that individual modifications involving substantial charges which families are not willing to bear go beyond required minor adjustments. However, allowing families to make and pay for on-site services involving substantial charges, such as having a private sign language interpreter on site to interpret for a hearing-impaired child, likely would be required minor adjustments. School officials likely cannot use this provision to charge for services in discriminatory ways. That is, officials likely cannot charge Section 504 students for tutoring services which are provided for free to athletes or other students. It is also notable that this section refers to passing on costs which are "substantial" without reference to the financial means of schools or the burdens which would be imposed on them if they absorbed these expenses. It appears that private schools may pass on "substantial" costs to families for adjustments for students with disabilities, even if the tuition charged is substantial and/or the private schools could afford to pay the substantial costs themselves.

The burden is on students, and their families, to document their disabilities and to request adjustments. Documentation should not be required for obvious, permanent disabilities such as blindness and quadriplegia.[214] Under the IDEA's child find procedures, public school officials may have evaluated a student and documented the disability. Documentation of the disability may also include

---

[211] *See, e.g.,* Lynnfield (MA) Pub. Sch., 108 LRP 21716 (OCR 2007) (pointing out that officials in a private school were not required to add a full-time nurse for student with diabetes, but that a care plan, dissemination of information, and training constituted required minor adjustments).

[212] *See* St. Peter's (PA) Child Development Center, 352 IDELR 479 (OCR 1987) (treating admission of an asymptomatic hepatitis carrier, where the school's population included Down syndrome students particularly susceptible to hepatitis, went beyond required minor adjustments).

[213] *See, e.g.,* Life Christian School (WA), 352 IDELR 523 (OCR 1987) (refusing to treat the determination of officials in a private school that the needs of two students with cerebral palsy and limited communication skills in wheelchairs—who also demonstrated disruptive behavior to special education instruction and related services, were more than its staff could handle, and that the parent's presence as an aide was disruptive—as pretexts for discrimination).

[214] In a 2012 letter, OCR indicated that "the nature of many impairments is such that in virtually every case, a determination of disability will be made" and suggested that schools should not require significant documentation to determine that students with diabetes, epilepsy, bipolar disorder, or autism had disabilities under Section 504. Dear Colleague Letter, 58 IDELR 79 (OCR 2012).

recommended adjustments.[215] The obligation of private schools is to use the documentation supplied by students and their parents, along with the expertise of their staff, to decide on and implement required minor adjustments.

Creation of individual plans by teams—the process required by the IDEA and Section 504 for public school students— is not expressly required for private schools, but may be good practice. Individual plans centralize information about students and utilize collective academic and other expertise within schools, likely enhancing the quality of decision making. The use of teams also facilitates consistency of decisions. Moreover, the expertise represented by teams may cause courts to defer to the teams' judgments about what adjustments to (not) make, particularly if core academic requirements are involved and team members have significant academic expertise.

Notably, the OCR partially resolved a complaint involving a private school by agreeing to convene a committee to consider possible adjustments for a student with diabetes.[216] At the same time, school official should understand that failure to implement agreed-on minor adjustments are almost per se violations of Section 504. As such, officials should be careful to ensure that all plans are implemented fully.[217] Options for resolving minor adjustments and other disputes under Section 504 are discussed earlier in this chapter.

Policy Issues

Public school boards are obligated to evaluate students with disabilities in private schools and identify them as eligible for special education. These boards must also spend a proportionate share of their modest federal special education funds on students in private schools. While public board officials must consult with their counterparts in private schools and parents before deciding how to spend this proportionate share of federal special education funds, the decisions are left to their discretion.

Students in private schools lack individual rights to receive special education services. In fact, when public school board officials decide to offer students in private schools some special education services, with only modest federal funds available, the services provided likely will fall far short of providing any students in private schools with FAPEs. Moreover, decisions about where to offer services, such as at local public schools, at the private schools, or elsewhere, is one for public school officials to make.

---

[215] Private school staff and parents should understand that many evaluators are used to recommending services which would be part of FAPEs for public school students, or which would be reasonable accommodations for employees or students in higher education, and so may recommend modifications and services well beyond the minor adjustments private schools are capable of providing.

[216] Akron (OH) Public Schools, 111 LRP 28345 (OCR 2010).

[217] Cf. Doe v. Withers, 20 IDELR 422 (W.Va. Cir. Ct. 1993) (finding a teacher personally liable for compensatory and punitive damages for failing to implement an IEP's provisions for testing accommodations and belittling a student in front of her classmates).

This current approach has both pros and cons. On the one hand, the current approach is consistent with that of general education. Parents are free to enroll their children in private schools, but, generally, the government does not fund their choices. Instead, parents are responsible for paying private school tuition. Nor do students in private schools generally have the right to access public school courses or services selectively. Similarly, parents may enroll their children with disabilities in private schools, but the consequences of doing so are financial responsibility for the chosen private school educations, as well as the loss of rights to access public school special education services selectively.

The current approach avoids federal and state constitutional concerns. If students in private schools had individual entitlements to FAPE, public school officials would have to work closely with their counterparts in private schools, a situation which might lead to unconstitutional levels of entanglement with benefits to, and possible loss of autonomy of, religious private schools. Further, some state constitutions explicitly forbid any government support of religious schools.

The current approach avoids perceived or actual federal overreach. Through the IDEA, Congress funds only a small portion of special education costs, in exchange for compliance with hefty FAPE, LRE, and procedural safeguards requirements. Any IDEA mandate for students in private schools would be paid for with largely state and local government funds. The current approach leaves states free to do more than the IDEA requires. And, some states do considerably more, such as providing more services than are required on ad hoc bases, creating voucher programs, or enacting state laws permitting students in private schools to enroll part time in public school to receive special education.

The current approach allows private schools to continue to operate without significant special education obligations. Public school boards must serve special education students and are limited in their ability to exclude them for disciplinary reasons. Religious private schools cannot engage in disability discrimination only if they receive federal education funds. Even so, religious private schools have limited special education obligations. In this way, private schools are generally free to deny admission to special education pupils they are not equipped to serve and are generally free to expel these, and other, students for misconduct.

On the other hand, the current approach leaves many students in private schools with disabilities not receiving FAPEs, harming not only children with disabilities, but also society. FAPE and acquisition of academic and life skills obviously is essential to the long-term independence, success, and happiness of special education students. Moreover, receiving FAPEs is important for society; more adult services and a larger social safety net benefits will be required for students with disabilities who do not acquire academic and life skills sufficient for adult independence and success.

The current approach limits the numbers of students with disabilities that nonpublic schools are able to attract and retain. This, in turn, restricts family choice to educate their children with disabilities in private schools in ways that choice is not limited for children without disabilities. For example, unless they are wealthy and able to pay for private special education services, parents who seek faith-based educations for their children are unlikely to be able to do so for children with significant disabilities. If parents choose public schools for their children with disabilities, the education they receive may, in some respects, be inconsistent with their own faiths. Yet, there is no entitlement to a religious education to prepare students for adult life in faith communities.[218]

The current approach does not seem to be the only one permitted by current federal constitutional analysis. The Supreme Court has upheld the constitutionality of vouchers used in private secular and religious schools,[219] as well as significant secular aid to private secular and religious schools.[220] In addition, the Court has found that religious schools and government officials working closely together is not unconstitutional, as long as neither controls or influences the other.[221]

The current approach also does not incorporate innovations by states. Congress could adopt approaches that states have pioneered, such as allowing IDEA-eligible students to enroll part time in public schools to receive special education, or a special education voucher system. Finally, the current approach is inconsistent with the approach of some other countries which directly fund private schools.[222]

Conclusion

Certainly, reasonable persons can disagree about whether congressional failure to establish individual entitlements to special education for students in private schools furthers public policy. Aware of congressional inaction, Secretary of Education Betsy DeVos is a strong supporter of school choice and has praised Florida's special education voucher program. Whether programs such as the one in Florida will grow to others states is part of a discussion that will surely continue.

---

[218] M.L. v. Smith, 867 F.3d 487 [346 Educ. L. Rep. 667] (4th Cir. 2017) (interpreting the IDEA as not requiring instruction in the tenets of Orthodox Judaism for a student with Down syndrome, but requiring officials to make reasonable accommodations for his faith).

[219] Zelman v. Simmons-Harris, 536 U.S. 639 [166 Educ. L. Rep. 30] (2002).

[220] Mitchell v. Helms, 530 U.S. 793 [145 Educ. L. Rep. 44] (2000).

[221] Agostini v. Felton, 521 U.S. 203 [119 Educ. L. Rep. 29] (1997).

[222] See Ralph Mawdsley and Lisa Ehrich, *Religious K-12 Schools and Disability Discrimination: An Australia-United States Comparison*, 147 Educ. L. Rep. 1 (2000) (comparing the U.S. approach with Australia's, where states provide funds for children directly to all nonpublic schools, including those with religious affiliations).

Discussion Questions

1. Both the IDEA and the Establishment Clause of the Constitution permit, but do not require, public school boards to provide on-site services in religious schools. Should the IDEA be changed to require the on-site delivery of special education services in religious schools?

2. Should the IDEA be amended to require FAPEs for students in private schools? What are the pros and cons of such an amendment?

3. Should the IDEA be modified to eliminate the obligations of public school officials both to engage in child find activities for students in private schools and to spend proportionate shares of the federal IDEA funds of their boards on these children?

4. Reimbursement for parent placements are considered by some to be a rich person's remedy because many parents are unable to afford the cost of private education, especially if it is for residential or private special education schools. Other parents must rely on compensatory education, which obligates public school boards to provide extra time in special education to make up for deficiencies. Should the IDEA be amended to remove the reimbursement option, leaving compensatory education as the only remedy available to all parents?

5. Many parents who unilaterally place their children in private schools send their children to schools specializing in providing special education services that often result in significant academic progress. Should the IDEA's "least restrictive environment" requirements be considered in claims for tuition reimbursement when parents unilaterally place their children in these schools?

Key Words

Americans with Disabilities Act (ADA)
Child find
Consultation process
Discrimination
Due process hearings
Eligibility
Equipment
Evaluation
Facilities
Free appropriate public education (FAPE)
Homeschooling
Individualized education program (IEP)
Least restrictive environment (LRE)
Minor adjustments

Parent special education rights
Part-time enrollment
Placement
Private school
Procedural safeguards
Rehabilitation Act of 1973, Section 504
Related services
Special education
State complaint process
Students
Unilateral parent placement
Vouchers

9

Government Regulation of Nonpublic Schools

Bryan H. Beauman

Contents

Introduction / 264
Basis for State Regulation and Restrictions on Governmental Authority / 264
    Free Exercise Expanded: *Wisconsin v. Yoder* / 265
    Free Exercise Limited: *Employment Division Department of Human Resources of Oregon v. Smith* / 266
    Free Exercise Targeted: *Church of the Lukumi Babalu Aye v. City of Hialeah* / 268
    Free Exercise Excluded: *Trinity Lutheran Church of Columbia v. Comer* / 270
    Protected Liberty Interests / 271
    Expanding Public School Requirements / 272
Government Regulation of Admission and Hiring in Nonpublic Schools / 274
    The Church Autonomy Doctrine / 275
    Religiosity to Qualify for the Ministerial Exemption / 276
    Hosanna-Tabor Evangelical Lutheran Church and *School v. Equal Employment Opportunities Commission* Affirms the Constitutional Rule / 277
    Qualifying for the Ministerial Exemption / 279
Participation by Nonpublic School Students in Public School Courses and Activities / 282
    Nonpublic Schools Participating in State Activities / 282
    Public School Opportunities for Students in Private Schools / 285
Governmental Regulation of Home Instruction / 287
    Home Instruction Generally / 287
    Opportunities in Public Schools for Students who are Homeschooled / 289
    Legislative and Organizational Involvement Public School Activities / 290
Conclusion / 291
Discussion Questions / 291
Key Words / 292

Introduction

Nonpublic schools hold no privilege from governmental oversight. Yet, nonpublic schools do enjoy a variety of constitutional checks on governmental regulation. Two primary constitutional protections apply to limit the way the federal government can regulate nonpublic schools. First, for religious nonpublic schools, the Free Exercise Clause prevents governmental regulation from interfering with their operations. Second, parents have the ability to direct the education of their children under the protection of the Fourteenth Amendment.

The protections afforded nonpublic schools are best illustrated in the context of their employment and admissions practices, as well as the ability of their students to participate in associational or extracurricular activities sponsored by public schools; it is also evident in the arena of home schooling/education. Against this background, this chapter addresses the authority and limitations of governmental regulations in these contexts.

Basis for State Regulation and Restrictions on Governmental Authority

In *Pierce v. Society of Sisters* (*Pierce*) the Supreme Court reinforced the authority of states to regulate education as implied in the Tenth Amendment of the Federal Constitution:

No question is raised concerning the power of the state reasonably to regulate all schools, to inspect, supervise and examine them, their teachers and pupils to require that all children of proper age attend some school, that teachers shall be of good moral character and patriotic disposition, that certain studies plainly essential to good citizenship must be taught, and that nothing be taught which is manifestly inimical to the public welfare.[1]

The grant of governmental authority is, of course, limited by other restrictions elsewhere in the Constitution. In *Pierce*, the Supreme Court ruled that Oregon's legislative act requiring all students to attend public schools violated the Fourteenth Amendment liberty interests of parents to direct the education of their children.[2]

States have considerable regulatory authority over nonpublic schools. Thus, while the *Pierce* Court invalidated the State of Oregon's attempt to legislate nonpublic schools out of existence, it left for a future date the question as to the limits of the extensive regulatory power of states over nonpublic schools.

---

[1] 268 U.S. 510, 534 (1925).

[2] "…nor shall any state deprive any person of life, liberty, or property, without due process of law…"

Free Exercise Expanded: *Wisconsin v. Yoder*

Forty-seven years after *Pierce*, in *Wisconsin v. Yoder* (*Yoder*),[3] the Supreme Court revisited the subject of state control over nonpublic education, addressing the regulatory authority of the State to impose its compulsory attendance statute[4] on children whose parents refused to permit them to attend high school once they completed eight years of education in Amish schools. At issue were the two to three years between the completion of eighth grade, when students were 13 or 14, and the compulsory attendance age of 16. Three Amish parents who were convicted of truancy for refusing to permit their children to attend a public high school and were fined $5 challenged the state law, giving rise to this situation.

In presenting their case, the Amish parents had the advantage of relying on the Free Exercise Clause which, even though omnipresent in the First Amendment, had not yet been applicable to the states at the time of *Pierce*.[5] Analyzing the Amish parents' free exercise claim, the Supreme Court first inquired whether the compulsory education law substantially burdened their religious practices. The Court emphasized that "to have the protection of the Religion Clauses," the parents' "claims must be rooted in religious belief."[6] The Court easily found that the Amish way of life, that they claimed the compulsory education laws undermined, was a product of their religious convictions:

> [T]he record in this case abundantly supports the claim that the traditional way of life of the Amish is not merely a matter of personal preference, but one of deep religious conviction, shared by an organized group, and intimately related to daily living.[7]

The Justices also decided that the compulsory education law imposed a severe burden on the religious practices of the Amish. The Court specified that exposure to secondary education would "substantially interfer[e] with the religious development of the Amish child and his integration into the way of life of the Amish faith community."[8] Moreover, the Court thought that the statute placed an impermissible burden on the Amish parents because the

---

[3] 406 U.S. 205 (1972).

[4] Wis. Stat. Ann. § 118.15 provided in part: (1)(a) Unless the child has a legal excuse or has graduated from high school, any person having under his control a child who is between the ages of 7 and 16 years shall cause such child to attend school regularly during the full period and hours, religious holidays excepted, that the public or private school in which such child should be enrolled is in session until the end of the school term, quarter or semester of the school year in which he becomes 16 years of age. . . . .(5) Whoever violates this section . . . may be fined not less than $5 nor more than $50 or imprisoned not more than 3 months or both.

[5] The Free Exercise Clause was incorporated to the states under the due process clause of the Fourteenth Amendment in *Cantwell v. Connecticut*, 310 U.S. 296 (1940).

[6] *Id. at* 215. The Court noted that claims that are "philosophical and personal," rather than religious, are not protected by the Free Exercise Clause. *Id.* at 216.

[7] *Id.*

[8] *Id.* at 218.

compulsory education law compelled them "to perform acts undeniably at odds with fundamental tenets of their religious beliefs."[9]

Having reasoned that Wisconsin's compulsory education law placed a substantial burden on practitioners of the Amish religion, the Supreme Court called on its lawyers to show that the statute served "a state interest of sufficient magnitude to override the interest claiming protection under the Free Exercise Clause."[10] Wisconsin's lawyers failed to make such a showing in their primary argument that the compelling interest at stake, to ensure the proper education of all children in the state, was so strong that the practices of the Amish had to give way.

Wisconsin's lawyers unsuccessfully contended that insofar as compulsory education was imperative to the mental and physical well-being of all children and their ability to function as productive members of society, they would have been at a disadvantage if deprived of these benefits. Rejecting this argument, the Supreme Court observed that allowing Amish children to forgo one or two years of compulsory education "will not impair the physical or mental health of the child, or result in an inability to be self-supporting or to discharge the duties and responsibilities of citizenship, or in any other way materially detract from the welfare of society."[11] In the end, the Court refused to treat Wisconsin's interest in compulsory education as sufficiently compelling "to justify the severe interference with [the] religious freedom" of the practitioners of the Amish religion.[12]

Free Exercise Limited: *Employment Division Department of Human Resources of Oregon v. Smith*

In *Employment Division Department of Human Resources of Oregon v. Smith* (*Smith*),[13] the Supreme Court was of the opinion that the Free Exercise Clause was no longer a defense to "a neutral, generally applicable regulatory law."[14] The Justices were unwilling to interpret the Free Exercise Clause as prohibiting the application of a drug law from Oregon in a dispute over the ceremonial ingestion of peyote. In so doing, the Court refused to order the reinstatement of two Native American drug counselors who were dismissed from their jobs for ingesting peyote. The Court allowed Oregon officials, consistent with the Free Exercise Clause, to deny the claimants unemployment compensation for work-related misconduct in the form of ingesting peyote.

---

[9] *Id.*

[10] *Id.* at 214. The Court described the requisite state concern as an "interest of the highest order" that is "not otherwise served." *Id.* at 215.

[11] *Id.* at 234.

[12] *Id.* at 227.

[13] 494 U.S. 872 (1990). For commentaries on this case, see Ralph D. Mawdsley, *Employment Division v. Smith Revisited: The Constriction of Free Exercise Rights Under The United States Constitution*, 76 Educ. L. Rep. 1 (1992); Ralph D. Mawdsley, *Has Wisconsin v. Yoder been Reversed? Analysis of Employment Division v. Smith*, 63 Educ. L. Rep. 11 (1990).

[14] *Id.* at 880.

Smith effected a wholesale change in how courts analyze "free exercise" claims. In the past, plaintiffs raising free exercise claims had been able to rely on strict scrutiny review of governmental restrictions impairing their religious practices merely by demonstrating that the challenged limitations imposed substantial burdens on practices motivated by sincere religious beliefs. Under *Smith*, free exercise plaintiffs faced a much higher hurdle to obtain strict scrutiny review of governmental actions purportedly burdening their religious practices. Litigation continues to highlight the way to bring successful free exercise claims in the post-*Smith* era.[15] Most important among these cases are *Church of the Lukumi Babalu Aye v. City of Hialeah*[16] and *Trinity Lutheran Church of Columbia v. Comer.*[17]

Smith established a new rule for free exercise claims. As the Justices succinctly put it,

> [T]he right of free exercise does not relieve an individual of the obligation to comply with a "valid and neutral law of general applicability on the ground that the law proscribes (or prescribes) conduct that his religion prescribes (or proscribes)."[18]

In other words, if challenged laws are neutral and equally applicable to all, courts do not subject them to strict scrutiny review even if they substantially limit individuals' religious practices.

As noted, in *Smith*, the plaintiffs were members of the Native American Church who were fired from their jobs as drug counselors because they ingested peyote during a religious ceremony. When the plaintiffs applied for unemployment benefits, officials denied their claims because they were fired for misconduct. At the time, Oregon law proscribed the "knowing or intentional possession of a 'controlled substance' unless the substance ha[d] been

---

[15] This discussion focuses on making a federal constitutional challenge under the Free Exercise Clause. In response to *Smith*, in 1993 Congress enacted the Religious Freedom Restoration Act (RFRA), to restore the compelling interest test to restrictions placed on religious freedom. The Supreme Court later held that the federal RFRA could not apply to the states, only the federal government in City of Boerne v. Flores, 521 U.S. 507 (1997). In response to *City of Boerne*, states enacted their own legislation to strengthen religious liberty protection and restore the "compelling interest" test. "Since 1993, 21 states have enacted state RFRAs. These laws are intended to echo the federal RFRA, but are not necessarily identical to the federal law." National Conference of State Legislatures, available at http://www.ncsl.org/research/civil-and-criminal-justice/state-rfra-statutes.aspx. In addition, "Nine states ha[d] Religious Freedom Restoration Act (RFRA) legislation pending in 2017" http://www.ncsl.org/research/civil-and-criminal-justice/2017-religious-freedom-restoration-act-legislation.aspx. These laws, enacted or pending, offer greater religious liberty protection than the federal counterpart. *Smith* then had no current effect on those states' laws. A discussion about the application of a federal or state RFRA or other state law protection must be conducted on a state-by-state basis, a subject not addressed here. For discussion of this case, see Ralph D. Mawdsley, *Flores v. City of Boerne: Testing the Constitutionality of the Religious Freedom Restoration Act*, 115 EDUC. L. REP. 593 (1997).

[16] 508 U.S. 520 (1993).

[17] 137 S. Ct. 2012 (2017).

[18] *Smith*, 494 U.S. at 879 (internal citation omitted).

prescribed by a medical practitioner."[19] Peyote qualified as such a "controlled substance."

The Supreme Court described Oregon's controlled substance law as an "across-the-board criminal prohibition on a particular form of conduct."[20] Because the law was neutral and generally applicable, the Justices rejected the plaintiffs' free exercise claims. As the Court indicated, where the burdening of religious practices is "merely the incidental effect of a generally applicable and otherwise valid provision, the First Amendment has not been offended."[21]

Smith does not end a free exercise inquiry. Plaintiffs raising free exercise claims can still seek to prove that the laws allegedly burden their religious practices by proving they are neither neutral nor generally applicable, or showing that the laws regulate religious beliefs.

Free Exercise Targeted: *Church of the Lukumi Babalu Aye v. City of Hialeah*

Church of the Lukumi Babalu Aye v. City of Hialeah (*Lukumi*)[22] reveals that *Smith* acts as a gatekeeper for free exercise claims insofar as "law[s] burdening religious practice[s]" that are neither neutral nor not generally applicable need to pass through *Smith*'s gate and must undergo "the most rigorous of scrutiny."[23] In *Lukumi*, the Court explicitly declared that once Free Exercise claims get through the gate erected in *Smith*, they are entitled to a true compelling interest standard that is not "'water[ed] down' but 'really means what it says.'"[24] *Lukumi* demonstrates how laws can lack neutrality, general applicability, or both.

As the Supreme Court explained in *Lukumi*, "[t]here are...many ways of demonstrating that the object or purpose of a law is the suppression of religion or religious conduct."[25] The Court identified the minimum requirement of neutrality as being that "a law not discriminate [against religion] on its face."[26] However, the Court pointed out that a finding of "facial neutrality is not determinative."[27] Additionally, the Court remarked that the Free Exercise Clause "forbids subtle departures from neutrality, and covert suppression of particular religious beliefs."[28] "Official action that targets religious conduct for distinctive treatment cannot be shielded by mere compliance with the

---

[19] *Id.* at 874.

[20] *Id.* at 884.

[21] *Id.* at 878. The Court also put it this way: "We have never held that an individual's religious beliefs excuse him from compliance with an otherwise valid law prohibiting conduct that the State is free to regulate." *Id.* at 878–79.

[22] 508 U.S. 520 (1993).

[23] *Id.* at 546 (1993).

[24] *Id.* (internal citations omitted).

[25] *Id.* at 533.

[26] *Id.*

[27] *Id.* at 534.

[28] *Id.* (internal citations and quotation marks omitted).

requirement of facial neutrality. The Free Exercise Clause protects against governmental hostility which is masked, as well as overt."[29]

In *Lukumi*, there was a bevy of evidence of "covert" discrimination against the religious practices of the plaintiffs. The plaintiffs were adherents of Santeria, which practices animal sacrifices as an expression of religious devotion to the spirits they worship. When officials in the City of Hialeah, Florida, learned of the plaintiffs' plan to establish a Santeria Church within city limits, they enacted ordinances aimed at restricting the practice of animal sacrifice. While the Court was convinced that these ordinances were facially neutral, it nonetheless concluded that they lacked neutrality because in operation and effect they achieved a "religious gerrymander" aimed solely at the Santeria religion.[30]

In its analysis, the Supreme Court commented that one of the ordinances prohibited the sacrifice of animals, but defined "sacrifice" as "'to unnecessarily kill . . . an animal in a public or private ritual or ceremony not for the primary purpose of food consumption.'"[31] The Justices posited that this Ordinance was carefully drawn to effectuate a "religious gerrymander" because the "net result . . . is that few if any killings of animals are prohibited other than Santeria sacrifice, which is proscribed because it occurs during a ritual or ceremony and its primary purpose is to make an offering to the [spirits], not food consumption."[32] The Court concluded that the other ordinances operated in a similar fashion, and that they all worked together "to suppress Santeria religious worship."[33]

Lukumi also demonstrated how laws are not generally applicable: laws that are either underinclusive in relation to the purposes they were adopted to serve, or permit governmental officials to make individualized assessments in granting exemptions to otherwise generally applicable and neutral statutes. The Justices wrote that a law is underinclusive when the government "fail[s] to prohibit nonreligious conduct that endangers [its] interests in a similar or greater degree than" the prohibited religious practice.[34] In *Lukumi*, the city officials claimed that the ordinances at issue passed served the interests of preventing cruelty to animals and protecting public health.

At the same time, the ordinances were woefully underinclusive in relation to these purposes. The Supreme Court acknowledged that "[d]espite the city's proffered interest in preventing cruelty to animals, the ordinances are drafted with care to forbid few killings but those occasioned by religious sacrifice. Many types of animal deaths or kills for nonreligious reasons are either not prohibited or approved by express provision."[35]

As to the city's proffered interest in protecting public health, the Supreme Court noted that the "health risks posed by the improper disposal of animal

---

[29] *Id.*

[30] *Id.* at 535.

[31] *Id.* at 535-36 (quoting Ordinance 87-81).

[32] *Id.* at 536.

[33] *Id.* at 540.

[34] *Id.* at 543.

[35] *Id.*

carcasses are the same whether Santeria sacrifice or some nonreligious kill-ing preceded it."[36] Nonetheless, the record revealed that city officials did not regulate how hunters or restaurants disposed of animal carcasses, even while they did so for Santeria. The Court was satisfied that the ordinances were underinclusive since they left unregulated nonreligious conduct impairing the city's proffered interests to the same or greater degree as analogous religious conduct. Because the ordinances in *Lukumi* burdened religious practice and were not generally applicable, the Court applied strict scrutiny.

In sum, laws are underinclusive when they fail to restrict "nonreligious conduct that endangers"[37] the purposed interests challenged laws were adopted to serve "in a similar or greater degree"[38] than the prohibited religious conduct. Such laws are subject to strict scrutiny.

A more straightforward challenge to governmental regulations under the Free Exercise Clause is to demonstrate that challenged laws target religious beliefs for disparate treatment. In *Smith*, the Supreme Court held that the Free Exercise Clause prohibits "regulation of religious *beliefs* as such," including in this prohibited category laws that "compel affirmation of religious belief, punish the expression of religious doctrines [the government] believes to be false, impose special disabilities on the basis of religious views or religious status, or lend [the government's] power to one or the other side in controversies over religious authority or dogma."[39]

Free Exercise Excluded: *Trinity Lutheran Church of Columbia v. Comer*

Trinity Lutheran Church of Columbia v. Comer[40] demonstrates how governmental programs can violate the Free Exercise Clause for religious schools. At issue was a program under which Missouri's Department of Natural Resources provided grants to public and nonpublic schools to purchase play-ground surfaces made from recycled tires.[41] Because Trinity Lutheran Church of Columbia, Missouri, operated a Child Learning Center serving about ninety preschool-aged children, including a basic playground, it sought to replace the gravel surface by participating in the recycled tire program.[42]

Due to limited resources, Missouri was unable to award grants to all applicants. Officials thus devised a ranking system. Even though Trinity Lutheran ranked fifth among the forty-four applicants, state officials deemed it ineligible to participate in the program because of the Center's affiliation

---

[36] *Id.* at 544.

[37] *Id.* at 543

[38] *Id.*

[39] Oregon v. Smith, 494 U.S. 872, 877 (1990).

[40] 137 S. Ct. 2012 (2017). For a representative commentary on this case, see William E. Thro & Charles J. Russo, *Odious to the Constitution: The Educational Implications of Trinity Lutheran Church v. Comer*, 346 Educ. L. Rep. 1 (2017).

[41] *Id.* at 2017.

[42] *Id.*

with the church and the officials' concern to avoid providing monetary governmental aid to a church.[43]

The Supreme Court rejected Missouri's approach because officials "expressly den[ied] a qualified religious entity a public benefit solely because of its religious character. Under our precedents, that goes too far."[44] The Court ruled that the program placed the Center in the position of choosing between its religious character or participation in a governmental program available to the general public.[45]

The Supreme Court highlighted the harmony of its judgment with *Smith* and *Lukumi*:

> In recent years, when this Court has rejected free exercise challenges, the laws in question have been neutral and generally applicable without regard to religion. We have been careful to distinguish such laws from those that single out the religious for disfavored treatment.[46]

In this way, *Trinity Lutheran* reaffirms that the Free Exercise Clause protects against governmental regulation treating religious nonpublic schools and institutions differently or targeting them for special disabilities based on their religious status.[47] The simple rule is that state officials cannot deny generally available governmental programs or benefits to nonpublic schools based solely on their religious identities.[48]

Protected Liberty Interests

In other contexts, the Fourteenth Amendment's protection of the liberty rights of parents to direct the education of their children continues to maintain some viability against arbitrary state actions. In a case from Texas, the Fifth Circuit addressed a dispute wherein officials denied a public school teacher a promotion to a job as an assistant principal because she enrolled her children in a private school. The court decided that the teacher had a claim that officials violated her right to educate her children in a private school.[49] A subsequent jury verdict, upheld on appeal, awarded the teacher $35,000 in damages plus $650,000 in costs and fees.[50]

A like case arose in Ohio when an elementary teacher alleged that a superintendent repeatedly denied him a job because his child attended a

---

[43] *Id.* at 2018.

[44] *Id.* at 2024.

[45] *Id.* ("The State in this case expressly requires Trinity Lutheran to renounce its religious character in order to participate in an otherwise generally available public benefit program, for which it is fully qualified").

[46] *Id.* at 2020.

[47] *Id.* at 1919; *see also Lukumi*, 508 U.S. 533, 542.

[48] That is, unless the government can justify the highest state interest in doing so. *Id.*

[49] Barrow v. Greenville Indep. Sch. Dist., 332 F.3d 844 [177 EDUC. L. REP. 922] (5th Cir. 2003), *cert. denied* sub nom. Smith v. Barrow, 540 U.S. 1005 (2003).

[50] Barrow v. Greenville Indep. Sch. Dist., 480 F.3d 377 [217 EDUC. L. REP. 116] (5th Cir. 2007).

religious school. The Sixth Circuit affirmed that the teacher was entitled to a trial as to whether the superintendent violated his rights to child-rearing.[51] Both the Fifth and Sixth Circuits agreed that the law was so well established as to parental choices of the venue for the educations of their children that the superintendents were not entitled to qualified immunity for their actions in denying the applicants the positions.[52]

At issue in a dispute from Idaho was a superintendent's reassignment of an elementary school principal to a teaching position because he homeschooled his children. The Ninth Circuit affirmed that the superintendent violated the principal's right to the free exercise of religion. While conceding that the superintendent might have "a compelling interest if well-informed persons understood Peterson's action as a vote of no confidence in the school system rather than as the practice of his religion," the court rejected the assumption that "a religiously-motivated school principal following his conscience as to his own children would somehow be the object of scorn or distrust of his faculty or parent patrons...trammel[ed] his exercise of religion without compelling reason."[53] The court also agreed that there was sufficient general evidence of the former principal's desperate struggle to survive following his reassignment to teaching that supported a jury's award of $300,000 in his favor.

Expanding Public School Requirements

Smith merits one final topic for discussion: applying public school teacher certification requirements to nonpublic schools.[54] The Supreme Court of Michigan, ascertaining that applying the state's teacher certification requirement to homeschooling parents violated their rights to the free exercise of religion,

---

[51] Barrett v. Steubenville City Schs., 388 F.3d 967 [193 Educ. L. Rep. 124] (6th Cir. 2004), *cert. denied*, 546 U.S. 813 [202 Educ. L. Rep. 27] (2005).

[52] *See also* the Sixth Circuit's discussion of *Pierce*, *Yoder* and other cases, *id.* at 972-974 ("it is clearly established that parents have a fundamental right to direct the education of their children. ... There is also a clearly established law that forbids employers from denying one employment based only on 'person's involvement in activity shielded by the constitutionally protected rights of privacy and liberty." In *Barrow*, 332 F.3d at 848, the Fifth Circuit similarly decreed that "[t]he state cannot take an adverse employment action against a public-school employee for exercising this right unless it can prove that the employee's selection of private school materially and substantially affects the state's educational mission."

[53] Peterson v. Minidoka Cnty. Local Sch. Dist., 118 F.3d 1351, 1357 [120 Educ. L. Rep. 71] (9th Cir. 1997), *as amended*, 132 F.3d 1258 (9th Cir. 1997).

[54] *See also* New Life Baptist Church Acad. v. E. Longmeadow, 885 F. 2d 940 [56 Educ. L. Rep. 82] (1st Cir. 1989) (reversing an earlier order that standardized testing was a satisfactory replacement for on-site visits, observing that "we cannot say that standardized testing is *no* less burdensome than the School Committee's proposal, but neither can we see how it substantially alleviates the burden on the free exercise of religion, nor how it can represent a *major* improvement") (emphasis in original). *See also* Johnson v. Charles Cmty. Schs., 368 N.W.2d 79 [25 Educ. L. Rep. 524] (Iowa 1985) (refusing to apply the "Amish" exception to homeschooling); State v. Baptist Church, 301 N.W.2d 571 (Neb. 1981) (refusing to consider student testing as a satisfactory alternative to teacher certification).

distinguished the state's interest in education and its enforcement of teacher certification as a necessary means to achieve this end. According to the court:

> The state has focused on the incorrect governmental interest. The state's interest is not ensuring that the goals of compulsory education are met, because the state does not contest that the DeJonges are succeeding at fulfilling such aims. Rather, the state's interest is simply the certification requirement of the private school act, not the general objectives of compulsory attendance. The interest the state pursues is the manner of education, not its goals.[55]

In general, state and lower federal courts fail to agree about compliance of nonpublic schools with state approval, curriculum, and teacher certification requirements. For example, the Supreme Court of Ohio determined that officials unreasonably applied the state's compulsory attendance requirement, obligating children to attend schools with certificated teachers, to a non-Amish child in an Amish school.[56]

On the other hand, the Eighth Circuit was of the view that a statute from Iowa exempting Amish schools from teacher certification requirements was inapplicable to a Baptist school.[57] Further, in a case from Maine, the federal trial court thought that the state's Department of Education lacked express statutory authority under the compulsory attendance law to impose direct sanctions against unapproved private schools.[58] The Supreme Court of Nebraska, though, affirmed that enforcement of the state's compulsory attendance laws included the authority to enjoin operation of a school and to incarcerate a pastor for operating a church school in violation of state statutes.[59]

Case law regarding compliance with state curricular requirements presents similarly mixed results. The Supreme Court of Ohio invalidated state curricular requirements regulating not only the courses to be offered, but also the amount of instructional time to be allocated to the subjects taught, as unreasonable.[60] Conversely, the Supreme Court of North Dakota affirmed that regulations from the state department of education specifying the courses to be offered in a faith-based school were reasonable.[61]

On a related issue, the Supreme Court of Kentucky interpreted a provision in the commonwealth's constitution providing that no man shall "be compelled to send his child to any school to which he may be conscientiously opposed" as prohibiting public officials from both requiring certification for teachers in nonpublic schools and identifying which basic texts had to be used in private or parochial schools.[62] However, Massachusetts' highest court observed that

---

[55] People v. DeJonge 501 N.W.2d 127,137 [83 EDUC. L. REP. 773] (Mich. 1993).

[56] State v. Olin, 415 N.E.2d 279 (Ohio 1980).

[57] Fellowship Baptist Church v. Benton, 815 F.2d 485 [38 EDUC. L. REP. 893] (8th Cir. 1987).

[58] Bangor Baptist Church v. State of Me., 576 F. Supp. 1299 [15 EDUC. L. REP. 759] (D. Me. 1983).

[59] Sileven v. Tesch, 326 N.W.2d 850 [7 EDUC. L. REP. 1013] (Neb. 1982).

[60] State of Ohio v. Whisner, 351 N.E.2d 750 (Ohio 1976).

[61] State v. Shaver, 294 N.W.2d 883 (N.D. 1980).

[62] Ky. State Bd. v. Rudasill, 589 S.W.2d 877, 879 (Ky. 1979), *cert. denied*, 446 U.S. 938 (1980).

a statutory provision, whereby school committees "shall not withhold such approval [to operate nonpublic schools] on account of religious teaching," did not exempt parents engaged in home instruction from the duty to furnish outlined curricula, materials to be used in teaching, and information about the qualifications of instructors.[63]

In many jurisdictions, legislatures intervened by enacting laws freeing nonpublic schools from many of the more onerous state requirements.[64] This confrontation has largely moved on to new issues such as requirements for postsecondary institutions[65] and considerations of whether the Free Exercise Clause or the liberty protection of the Fourteenth Amendment entitle students in nonpublic schools to participate in specific courses and extracurricular activities in public schools, a topic discussed later in this chapter.

Government Regulation of Admission and Hiring in Nonpublic Schools

Chapter 10 reviews the myriad federal nondiscrimination laws applicable to nonpublic schools. Related issues more broadly applicable to issues in this chapter address the extent to which governmental regulations impact student enrollment and employment practices in nonpublic schools.

In *Bob Jones University v. United States* (*Bob Jones*)[66] the Supreme Court introduced the concept of fundamental public policy to education law. In *Bob Jones*, the Court upheld the Internal Revenue Service's revocation of the university's tax-exempt status because, at that time, it had rules based on its interpretation of the Bible prohibiting interracial dating and marriage among faculty, staff, and students. The university has since changed its policies and regained its tax-exempt status.

Bob Jones added yet another layer of government control over nonpublic schools in what the Supreme Court referred to as "fundamental public

---

[63] Care and Protection of Charles, 504 N.E.2d 592, 597 [37 Educ. L. Rep. 934] (Mass. 1987).

[64] *See also* People v. Bennett, 501 N.W.2d 106 [83 Educ. L. Rep. 752] (Mich. 1993) (upholding the state's authority to charge parents with truancy because teacher certification requirements did not violate their Liberty Clause rights; even so, prior to the trial, the parents were entitled to a hearing as to whether their educating their children as homes satisfied the state's Private and Parochial Schools Act); Michigan Dep't of Soc. Servs. v. Emmanuel Baptist Preschool, 455 N.W.2d 1 Mich. 1990) (upholding a state licensure requirement for employees of a church daycare while also prohibiting corporal punishment, but forbidding the state from imposing accreditation or program content).

[65] *See* Illinois Bible Colls. Ass'n v. Anderson, 870 F.3d 631 [347 Educ. L. Rep. 121] (7th Cir. 2017) (upholding the application of state statutes governing postsecondary schools to private bible colleges); Newport Int'l Univ. v. State Dept. of Educ., 186 P.3d 382 [233 Educ. L. Rep. 944] (Wyo. 2008) (rejecting equal protection and due process claims challenging a state statute requiring all private post-secondary institutions to be accredited); Galen Instit. v. Lewis, 392 F. Supp.2d 357 [203 Educ. L. Rep. 687] (D. Conn. 2005) (dismissing charges against state employees alleging that licensure inspections resulted in having to make unnecessary changes in the institution's programs).

[66] 461 U.S. 574 [10 Educ. L. Rep. 918] (1983).

policy."[67] The governmental interest advanced in *Bob Jones*, "eradicating racial discrimination in education,"[68] was different qualitatively from the teacher certification used to measure the quality of nonpublic school instruction in other litigation. Yet, the lingering question after *Bob Jones* is whether the Court's order might have become the vehicle to elevate other, or all, compelling interests, such as gender and sexuality, into fundamental public policies. This debate continues despite the Court's ruling that Colorado's Civil Rights Commission failed to comply with the Free Exercise Clause's requirement of religious neutrality in finding against a baker for refusing to design a custom-baked wedding cake for a same-sex couple in *Masterpiece Cakeshop, Ltd. v. Colorado Civil Rights Commission.*[69]

As discussed in Chapter 10, federal law prohibits employment discrimination based on race, color, religion, sex, national origin, or age. Even so, officials of religious organizations may consider the religious beliefs of applicants or employees in hiring and firing.[70] Moreover, under the ministerial exception, officials in religious schools and other qualifying institutions are exempt from employment nondiscrimination laws for hiring and firing ministerial employees, those tasked with performing organizational religious rituals as well as teaching and/or explaining their beliefs.[71] It is critical, then, that officials in religious schools develop criteria for their employees, students, and volunteers, particularly for those institutions whose beliefs may not be harmonious with governmental policies concerning gender and sexuality.

The Church Autonomy Doctrine

To begin, governmental regulation should not be able to address the propriety of the religious beliefs of schools in terms of the rightfulness or wrongfulness of their policies. The church autonomy doctrine is a legal construct the courts use when resolving disputes between religious institutions and the government grounded in the Free Exercise and Establishment clauses;[72] it precludes courts from becoming intervening in internal issues integral to religious institutions, including their ecclesiastical polity.[73] In other words,

---

[67] *See id.* at 596, n.1.

[68] *Id.* at 604.

[69] ___ S. Ct. ___, 2018 WL 2465172 (2018).

[70] *See* 42 U.S.C. § 2000e-1(a); 42 U.S.C. § 2000e-2(e)-(2); *see also* Hosanna-Tabor Evangelical Lutheran Church & Sch. v. Equal Employment Opportunities Comm'n, 132 S. Ct. 694, 710 (2012); McClure v. Salvation Army, 460 F.2d 553, 558 (5th Cir. 1972), *cert. denied*, 409 U.S. 896 (1972) (affirming that Title VII prevented the courts from becoming involved in a dispute over gender-based discrimination between a "church and its minister" in which a female officer completed professional training).

[71] *Id.* Hosanna-Tabor, at 694; McClure at 558-61; Scharon v. St. Luke's Episcopal Presbyterian Hosp., 929 F.2d 360 (8th Cir. 1991).

[72] *See* Watson v. Jones, 80 U.S. (13 Wall/.) 679 (1872).

[73] *See* Kedroff v. St. Nicholas Cathedral, 344 U.S. 94, 116 (1952) (interpreting the First Amendment as including "a spirit of freedom for religious organizations, an independence from secular control or manipulation – in short, power to decide for themselves, free from state interference matters of church government as well as those of faith and doctrine.").

the fact that religious institutions profess particular views on God's intended design of marriage, or of human sexuality, for example, are beyond the State's ability to regulate.

Religiosity to Qualify for the Ministerial Exemption

Closely related to the church autonomy doctrine is the ministerial exemption from governmental regulations; it is also rooted in the First Amendment. Before claiming such an exemption, though, institutions must actually be religious in nature. The seminal case as to whether an organization is sufficiently religious so as to be able to invoke the ministerial exemption arose in Washington. In resolving the case, the Ninth Circuit identified the following factors in concluding that an organization was religious for the purposes of the exemption. The court asked whether the organization

- was for-profit or not-for-profit;
- produced a secular product;
- a government agency had determined its status;
- its articles of incorporation or other documents stated a religious purpose;
- represented itself as a secular or sectarian body;
- had a church intimately involved in its management, day-to-day operations, and financial affairs;
- obtained support from a church or is affiliated with the entity;
- adheres to or deviates from an original religious purpose;
- requires its employees to subscribe to a statement of faith; and/or
- conducts religious activities, services, or instruction. [74]

---

[74] Spencer v. World Vision, 633 F.3d 723 (9th Cir. 2011).

Courts have split on the application of these factors.[75] Still, the ministerial exception is a judicially recognized exception flowing from the First Amendment, applicable broadly to all antidiscrimination laws.

Hosanna-Tabor Evangelical Lutheran Church and *School v. Equal Employment Opportunities Commission* Affirms the Constitutional Rule

In *Hosanna-Tabor Evangelical Lutheran Church and School v. Equal Employment Opportunities Commission* (*Hosanna-Tabor*),[76] a unanimous Supreme Court reasoned that the ministerial exception was constitutionally valid, albeit under the Americans with Disabilities Act (ADA)[77] rather than Title VII.

Hosanna-Tabor was initiated by a teacher at Lutheran school that was operated by a church in Michigan who started out as "lay," but later, after undergoing training through her synod, became "called."[78] In addition to instruction in secular subjects, the plaintiff taught a religion class, led her students in daily prayer and devotional exercises, and took them to a weekly school-wide chapel service. The teacher led the chapel service herself about twice a year.

Because she developed narcolepsy, the teacher took a disability leave of absence. When the teacher sought to return to work, officials expressed concerns that she was not ready to do so, informing her they already contracted with a substitute for the rest of the year. Even so, the teacher attempted to come back to work and refused to leave when asked to do so. When officials

---

[75] *See* Killinger v. Samford Univ., 113 F.3d 196 [118 Educ. L. Rep. 48] (11th Cir. 1997) (treating the university as religious because it was founded by and received funding from the Baptist state convention, its trustees had to be Baptists, it reported financially to the Baptist convention, all faculty were required to subscribe the Baptist Faith & Message, and the charter stated its chief purpose was promotion of Christianity); LeBoon v. Lancaster Jewish Cmty. Ctr. Ass'n, 503 F.3d 217, 226 (3d Cir. 2007) (treating the center as a religious organization based on factors similar to *Killinger* and because it displayed religious symbols in its buildings, offered religious instructional programs, observed Jewish holidays, began meetings with Bible readings, and used rabbis from local congregations as advisors); Hall v. Baptist Mem'l Health Care Corp., 215 F.3d 618, 624–25 (6th Cir.2000) (affirming that the religious exemption applied after considering various factors in determining the organization's purpose and atmosphere). *But see* EEOC v. Townley Engineering & Mfg. Co., 859 F.2d 610 (9th Cir. 1988) (refusing to treat a business as religious because of its profit motive and production of a secular product); EEOC v. Kamehameha Schs./Bishop Estate, 990 F.2d 458 (9th Cir. 1993) (rejecting the claim that a school was religious based on the general picture and because it was not controlled by a religious organization, not affiliated with church denomination or religious association of schools, and its religious nature was minimal); Fike v. United Methodist Children's Home, 547 F. Supp. 286 (E.D. Va. 1982) (refusing to treat the home as religious because it did not incorporate religious symbols or services into its program, theological instruction involved multiple viewpoints including atheism, and attendance at religious services was voluntary).

[76] 565 U.S. 171 (2012). For a commentary on this case, see Ralph D. Mawdsley & & Allan G. Osborne, Jr., *Shout Hosanna: The Supreme Court Affirms the Free Exercise Clause's Ministerial Exception*, 278 Educ. L. Rep. 693 (2012).

[77] 42 U.S.C.A. §§ 12101 *et seq.*

[78] *Id.* at 177. For another case reaching the same outcome involving a "called teacher," see Herzog v. St. Peter Lutheran Church, 884 F. Supp. 2d 668 [288 Educ. L. Rep. 668] (N.D. Ill. 2012).

told the teacher she would likely be fired for her conduct, she threatened to sue if dismissed. On being dismissed, the teacher filed suit claiming retaliation under the ADA.

On further review of orders from the Equal Employment Opportunities Commission, a federal trial court, and Sixth Circuit, the Supreme Court reversed in favor of the church.[79] The Court explained that to require

> a church to accept or retain an unwanted minister, or punishing a church for failing to do so, intrudes on more than a mere employment decision. Such action interferes with the internal governance of the church, depriving the church of control over the selection of those who will personify its beliefs. By imposing an unwanted minister, the state infringes the Free Exercise Clause, which protects a religious group's right to shape its own faith and mission through its appointments.[80]

The Justices noted that the basis of the ministerial exception was rooted in both religion clauses of the First Amendment. The Court acknowledged that "[b]oth Religion Clauses bar the government from interfering with the decision of a religious group to fire one of its ministers."[81] Put another way, the Court asserted that the purpose of the exception is not to safeguard the actions of churches in firing ministers only when they do so for religious reasons. Rather, the Court added that the exception ensures that the authority to select and control who ministers to the faithful—a matter 'strictly ecclesiastical'—belongs to churches alone."[82]

In addition to this constitutional restriction, most jurisdictions provide exemptions for religious organizations in their complementary state statutory civil rights acts. Many states provide this statutory exemption in three contexts. First, all employers, regardless of whether they are religious, may take employment actions on the basis of religion when religion is a bona fide occupational qualification for a job. Second, religious employers may hire individuals on the basis of religion to perform work connected with the carrying out of their religious activities. Third, officials in religious schools may employ persons of a particular religion if they are owned, supported, controlled or managed by religious organizations, or if the schools are directed toward the propagation of a particular religion, and its choice of employees is calculated to promote the religious principles for which it was established or maintained.[83]

---

[79] EEOC v. Hosanna-Tabor Evangelical Lutheran Church and Sch., 597 F.3d 769 (6th Cir. 2010), *reh'g and reh'g en banc denied, cert. granted,* 563 U.S. 903 (2011).

[80] 565 U.S. *Id.* at 188.

[81] *Id.* at 181.

[82] *Id.* at 195 (internal citations omitted).

[83] For a discussion of this issue, see Charles J. Russo, *Religious Freedom in a Brave New World: How Leaders in Faith-Based Schools Can Follow their Beliefs in Hiring.* 45 UNIV. TOLEDO L. REV. 457 (2014).

Qualifying for the Ministerial Exemption

In *Hosanna Tabor*, the Supreme Court was unwilling to adopt a rigid formula for determining who qualifies as a minister for purposes of the ministerial exception. Rather, the Court examined four factors in the teacher's employment that led to it to treat her as a minister for purposes of the ministerial exception. First, church leaders held the teacher out as a minister, with a role distinct from that of most of its ministers. Second, the teacher's title reflected a significant degree of religious training, followed by a formal process of commissioning. Third, the teacher identified herself out as a minister by accepting the formal call to religious service, according to its terms and by her actions in other ways. Fourth, the teacher's job duties evidenced a role in conveying the church's message and carrying out its mission.

The Supreme Court refused to place much emphasis on the teacher's performance of secular duties, writing

> [t]he issue before us, however, is not one that can be resolved by a stopwatch. The amount of time an employee spends on particular activities is relevant in assessing that employee's status, but that factor cannot be considered in isolation, without regard to the nature of the religious functions performed and the other considerations discussed above."[84]

In *Hosanna Tabor*, the Supreme Court did not address whether the ministerial exception applies to other suits, such as employees alleging breach of contract or tortious conduct by their religious employers.[85] After *Hosanna-*

---

[84] *Id.* at 193-94.

[85] For post *Hosanna-Tabor* litigation allowing defendants to rely on the ministerial exception in rejecting claims by former employees, see, e.g., Fratello v. Roman Catholic Archdiocese of N.Y., 863 F.3d 190 (2d Cir. 2017) (denying a former principal's gender discrimination and retaliation claims because she was a minister for the purposes of Title VII; DeBruin v. St. Patrick Congregation, 816 N.W.2d 878 (Wis. 2012) (rejecting the breach of contract claim of a Director of Faith Formation in a Catholic Church); Mills v. Standing General Comm'n on Christian Unity, 958 N.Y.S. 2d 880 (N.Y. Sup. Ct. 2013) (rejecting the wrongful dismissal claims a former Associate General Secretary).

Tabor, courts have reached different results as to whether an employee's position qualified for the ministerial exception.[86]

When courts apply the ministerial exception, it is absolute such that religious entities do not have to justify their employment decisions to a secular court.[87] The ministerial exception covers all aspects of employment relationships, not just hiring and firing, and has been treated as an exception to Title VII,[88] the Age Discrimination in Employment Act,[89] the ADA,[90] the Family

---

[86] *See* Demkovich v. St. Andrew the Apostle Parish, Calumet City, 2017 WL 4339817 (N.D. Ill. 2017) (applying the ministerial exception to deny claims of a music director of a Catholic parish who was terminated after entering a same-sex marriage); Conlon v. InterVarsity Christian Fellowship, 777 F.3d 829 (6th Cir. 2015) (applying the ministerial exception to claims of an employee with the title "spiritual director" whose duties included "leading others toward Christian maturity" and cultivating "intimacy with God and growth in Christ-like character through personal and corporate spiritual disciplines"); Cannata v. Catholic Diocese of Austin, 700 F.3d 169, 179 (5th Cir. 2012) (interpreting the ministerial exception as barring claims of a church "music director" despite the absence of any formal training in Catholic doctrine because of "the important part his ostensibly secular duties" in coordinating all the musical aspects of services "played in furthering the mission and message of the church at Mass"); Ciurleo v. St. Regis Parish, 214 F. Supp.3d 647, 652 [342 EDUC. L. REP. 185] (E.D. Mich. 2016) (relying on the ministerial exception to bar claims even though only the last of the four Hosanna–Tabor factors applied because providing daily religious instruction and leading morning prayers "are the hallmark of religious exercises through which religious communities transmit their received wisdom and heritage to the next generation of believers."). *But see* Richardson v. Northwest Christian Univ., 242 F. Supp. 3d 1132 (D. Or. 2017) (rejecting the ministerial exception for an exercise science instructor); Herx v. Diocese of Ft. Wayne–South Bend., 48 F.Supp.3d 1168, 1177 [315 EDUC. L. REP. 169] (N.D. Ind. 2014) (declining to apply the ministerial exception to a "lay teacher" at a Catholic school who had no special religious training and never held herself out as a minister, even though her job duties included attending and participating in prayer and religious services with students); Dias v. Archdiocese of Cincinnati, 2013 WL 360355 *4 (S.D. Ohio 2013) (ascertaining that a non-Catholic teacher at a Catholic school was not a minister because she "was not permitted to teach Catholic doctrine."). *See also* Jessica L. Waters, *Testing Hosanna–Tabor: The Implications for Pregnancy Discrimination Claims and Employees' Reproductive Rights*, 9 STAN. J. C.R. & C.L. 47, 67 (2013) (noting the judicial split over how much to defer to employers' characterizations of employees' position as ministerial, predicting that "*Hosanna–Tabor's* limited guidance may be of little use to lower courts attempting to define the contours of the exception in specific cases").

[87] *See* Bollard v. Cal. Province of Soc'y. of Jesus, 196 F.3d 940, 946 (9th Cir. 1999) ("[I]t would offend the Free Exercise Clause simply to require the church to articulate a religious justification for its personnel decisions."); Werft v. Desert Southwest Annual Conference, 377 F. 3d 1099, 1103 (9th Cir. 2004) ("If [the plaintiff] is allowed to proceed, the Church would necessarily be required to provide a religious justification for its [employment decision] and this is an area into which the First Amendment forbids us to tread.").

[88] McClure v. Salvation Army, 460 F.2d 553, 560 (5th Cir. 1972), *cert. denied*, 409 U.S. 896 (1972).

[89] Scharon v. St. Luke's Episcopal Presbyterian Hosps., 929 F.2d 360 (8th Cir. 1991); Minker v. Baltimore Annual Conference of United Methodist Church, 894 F.2d 1354 (D.C. Cir. 1990); Sanchez v. Catholic Foreign Soc'y of Am., 82 F. Supp. 2d 1338 (M.D. Fla. 1999); Powell v. Stafford, 859 F. Supp. 1343 (D. Colo. 1994).

[90] Hosanna-Tabor Evangelical Lutheran Church and School v. Equal Employment Opportunities Comm'n, 565 U.S. 171 (2012). Starkman v. Evans, 198 F.3d 173 (5th Cir. 1999); Rosati v. Toledo, Ohio Catholic Diocese, 233 F. Supp. 2d 917 (N.D. Ohio 2002).

and Medical Leave Act,[91] Section 1981,[92] and the Fair Labor Standards Act,[93] along with state and local antidiscrimination laws and ordinances.[94]

The ministerial exception applies to more than just the formal term "minister." Earlier cases broadened the exception to include the press secretary for a Catholic Church,[95] the principal of a Catholic elementary school,[96] the administrator of a Salvation Army rehabilitation center,[97] the music director and part-time music teacher for a Catholic church,[98] the choir director for a Methodist church,[99] a teacher in a Catholic elementary school,[100] a nun who taught canon law at a Catholic University,[101] the Kosher supervisor of a Jewish nursing home,[102] and the chaplain of a church-affiliated hospital.[103]

Hosanna-Tabor and the ministerial exemption present a key element in understanding how officials in religious schools may apply their beliefs about marriage, gender, and sexuality in their school communities. In *United States v. Commonwealth of Virginia (V.M.I.)*,[104] for instance, the Supreme Court used an intermediate equal protection standard, "exceedingly persuasive

---

[91] Fassl v. Our Lady of Perpetual Help Roman Catholic Church, 2005 WL 2455253 (E.D. Pa. 2005)

[92] Bogan v. Miss. Conference of the United Methodist Church, 433 F. Supp. 2d 762 (S.D. Miss. 2006).

[93] Shaliehsabou v. Hebrew Home of Greater Wash., 363 F.3d 299 (4th Cir. 2004).

[94] Werft v. Desert Southwest Annual Conference of the United Methodist Church, 377 F.3d 1099, 1100 at note 1 (9th Cir. 2004) ("Just as there is a ministerial exception to Title VII, there must also be one to any federal or state cause of action that would otherwise impinge on the Church's prerogative to choose its ministers"); Stately v. Indian Cmty. Sch. of Milwaukee, 351 F. Supp. 2d 858 [195 EDUC. L. REP. 164] (E.D. Wis. 2004); Schmoll v. Chapman Univ., 83 Cal.Rptr. 2d 426 [133 EDUC. L. REP. 206] (Cal. Ct. App. 1999); Malichi v. Archdiocese of Miami, 2006 WL 3207982 (Fla. Dist. Ct. App. 2006); Pardue v. Ctr. City Consortium of the Archdiocese of Wash., 875 A.2d 669 [199 EDUC. L. REP. 287] (D.C. 2005).

[95] Alicea-Hernandez v. Catholic Bishop of Chicago, 320 F.3d 698, 704 (7th Cir. 2003) (discrimination based on national origin and sex).

[96] Pardue v. Ctr. City Consortium of the Archdiocese of Wash., 875 A.2d 669 [199 EDUC. L. REP. 287] (D.C. 2005) (involving discrimination based on race).

[97] Schleicher v. Salvation Army, 518 F.3d 472 (7th Cir. 2008).

[98] EEOC v. Roman Catholic Diocese of Raleigh, 213 F.3d 795, 803 (4th Cir. 2000) (discrimination based on sex and retaliation); *see also* Starkman v. Evans, 198 F.3d 173 (5th Cir. 1999).

[99] Starkman v. Evans, 198 F.3d 173, 174 (5th Cir. 1999) (involving disability discrimination); Miller v. Bay View United Methodist Church, 141 F. Supp. 2d 1174, 1175 (E.D. Wis. 2001) (concerning racial discrimination).

[100] Coulee Catholic Schs. v. Labor & Indus. Rev. Comm'n, 768 N.W. 2d 868 (Wis. 2009).

[101] EEOC v. Catholic Univ. of Am., 83 F3d 455 [109 EDUC. L. REP. 568] (D.C. Cir. 1996). For a commentary on this case, see Charles J. Russo, *The Camel's Nose In the Tent: Judicial Intervention in Tenure Disputes at Catholic Universities*, 117 EDUC. L. REP. 813 (1997).

[102] Shaliehsabou v. Hebrew Home of Greater Wash., 363 F.3d 299, 301 (4th Cir. 2004) (discussing a Fair Labor Standards Act claim for unpaid overtime).

[103] Scharon v. St. Luke's Episcopal Presbyterian Hosps., 929 F.2d 360, 361 (8th Cir. 1991); *see also* Petruska v. Gannon Univ., 462 F.3d 294 (3rd Cir. 2006).

[104] 518 U.S. 515 (1996). For a commentary on this case, see Charles J. Russo & Susan J. Scollay, *All Male State-Funded Military Academies: Anachronism or Necessary Anomaly?* 82 EDUC. L. REP. 1073 (1993).

justification,"[105] to strike down the Virginia Military Institute's exclusion of women. Still, the Court stopped short of equating gender-based discrimination with the race-based discrimination in *Bob Jones University*.[106]

Nonetheless, *V.M.I.* raised the visibility of gender issues that can arise in religious schools. For instance, school officials may adopt policies addressing intimate sexual activity confined to marriages between one man and one woman. When officials learn of breaches of policies, such as when a teacher in a faith-based school has an out-of-wedlock pregnancy,[107] or an employee enters into a same-sex marriage,[108] they may view these as conflicts with the religious missions of their schools. If school officials seek to act in these situations, it is important that they engage in an analysis of the Free Exercise Clause, as informed through *Hosanna-Tabor*.

Participation by Nonpublic School Students in Public School Courses and Activities

Questions increasingly arise over whether students and their nonpublic schools have rights to participate in state associational activities with public schools. While this question ordinarily arises in the context of athletics, a variety of other highly competitive extracurricular activities exist, such as trying out for school plays. In the same vein, students who are homeschooled seek to participate in activities of their local public schools.

Nonpublic Schools Participating in State Activities

In a case from Arkansas, officials at a Christian school unsuccessfully filed suit alleging that the state activities association's requirement conditioning membership on state accreditation standards violated the Free Exercise Clause and the school's constitutionally protected liberty interest. Among the accreditation requirements were that schools had to teach minimum numbers of units of specific courses, have a minimum number of books in their libraries, and have teachers teach a majority of the school day in their areas of certification. Pursuant to a tenet of their religion that "religious matters (including education) are subject to divine governance only,"[109] school officials claimed

---

[105] *Id.* at 531.

[106] It is worth keeping in mind that *V.M.I.* has no direct impact on nonpublic schools because it was resolved under the Equal Protection Clause of the Fourteenth Amendment.

[107] Boyd v. Harding Acad. of Memphis, 88 F.3d 410 [110 Educ. L. Rep. 981] (6th Cir. 1996) (upholding the dismissal of a teacher in a faith-based school who was pregnant out of wedlock where she failed to prove that officials applied the policy against premarital sex in a discriminatory manner).

[108] *See, e.g.,* Demkovich v. St. Andrew the Apostle Parish, Calumet City, 2017 WL 4339817 (N.D. Ill. 2017) (applying the ministerial exception to bar claims by music director of Catholic parish who was terminated after entering a same-sex marriage); Richardson v. Northwest Christian Univ., 242 F. Supp. 3d 1132 (D. Or. 2017) (rejecting the ministerial exception for an exercise science college instructor).

[109] Windsor Park Baptist Church v. Ark. Activities Ass'n, 658 F.2d 618, 620 (8th Cir. 1981).

that by requiring accreditation as a condition for participation in the activities association, "the State [was] thus imposing a cost on plaintiff's members' exercise of their religion"[110] in violation of the First Amendment.

Affirming a judgment in favor of the association, the Eighth Circuit determined that pursuant to *Pierce*, the requirements were reasonable, and under *Yoder* that the state sought neither to punish parents nor close down the school. Unlike *Yoder*, the court commented that the state was not seeking to prosecute parents and was willing to allow the school to satisfy the compulsory attendance requirements with its uncertified teachers. In the end, the significance of this case was that it dealt with extracurricular activities with school officials not claiming that any "interscholastic activity is an integral part of [the] plaintiff's religion, in the sense that education in the home was a part of the Amish belief."[111]

It is important to bear in mind that the activities association in Arkansas was not attempting to exclude the nonpublic school; in fact, the school had been a member of the association on a probationary basis for years. This case illustrates one of the tensions facing officials in religious schools, namely how to provide controlled religious environments for their students while being part of organized activities in public schools.[112]

Related issues arise when state athletic associations prevent nonpublic schools from becoming members, a necessity for students to participate in a range of competitive activities. In such a case from Virginia, the Fourth Circuit invalidated an injunction ordering the state-level athletic association to accept a religious school as a member.[113] The court found that the athletic association's classifications limiting membership to public schools, while excluding private schools, was rational under the Equal Protection Clause due to the lack of specifically designed private school drawing areas and the difficulties in enforcing transfer rules. In other words, the court remarked that not only could private schools attract students from broad geographic areas, but those transferring into them would have automatically been ineligible for one semester because their parents would have no way to establish residence.

The Fourth Circuit was also convinced of the merit of the athletic association's concern about its anti-proselytizing rule "that students not be subjected to pressures by coaches, fans and other interested parties to attend one school over another."[114] In effect, the court endorsed the notion that because private schools are perceived as the most likely source of violations of the transfer

---

[110] *Id.*

[111] *Id.* at 622.

[112] *See, e.g.,* Valley Christian Sch. v. Mont. Pub. High Sch. Ass'n, 86 P.3d 554 [186 Educ. L. Rep. 543] (Mont. 2004) (upholding an association bylaw removing a school from the state athletic association where officials hired teachers who were not certified, rejecting the claim that its certification requirement violated the right of free exercise because it was facially neutral and generally applicable).

[113] Denis J. O'Connell High Sch. v. Va. High Sch. League, 581 F.2d 81 (4th Cir. 1978), *cert. denied,* 440 U.S. 936 (1979).

[114] *Id.* at 86.

rule, they need to be eliminated entirely from even the possibility of causing problems by not permitting them to become members of the association.[115]

Other courts have adopted this rationale. For instance, in a case from Delaware, the Third Circuit summarily affirmed that an athletic conference's refusal to permit a religious school to join did not violate the Equal Protection Clause or impermissibly burden its free exercise rights.[116] The trial court had posited that the association's exclusion of private schools was supported by legitimate interests in preventing athletic recruiting and maintaining a competitive balance among member schools.

In Maryland, an appellate court applied heightened scrutiny and a compelling-interest test in rejecting the claims of students from a religious high school who were not allowed to take part in an all-county music program offered only to full-time students enrolled in the public schools. Relying on *Yoder* and *Pierce*, the court explained that "this right to attend parochial school does not in our view necessarily establish a concomitant right for these children to remain eligible for participation in public school programs."[117] The court pointed out that if the officials had to admit the plaintiffs, "there would be no device to preclude, for example, a private school having difficulty securing a qualified chemistry teacher from unilaterally deciding to transport the entire student body to a nearby public school for their chemistry education."[118]

Once nonpublic schools are permitted to join state athletic or activities associations, they are entitled to the same constitutional fairness in interpreting organizational rules as are public school members. In *Brentwood Academy v. Tennessee School Athletic Association,*[119] the Supreme Court decided that a state athletic association was a state actor and could be sued by a religious school it penalized for allegedly violating its "undue influence" rule. The Court later interpreted the recruitment rule and its enforcement as not violating the school's First Amendment or due process rights.[120]

Membership in athletic associations means that private schools are governed by the same rules applicable to public schools. In such a case from Pennsylvania, the coach of the girls' basketball team at a Catholic high school unsuccessfully challenged her one-year suspension, alleging that an anti-

---

[115] *See id.* at 87 ("At present a student who desires to engage in League-sponsored tournaments is not exposed to a potentially tempting choice of schools; of the public schools, he is usually eligible to attend only the one serving the district in which he lives, and private schools are ineligible for League tournament competition.")

[116] Valencia v. Blue Hen Conference, 476 F. Supp. 809 (D. Del. 1979), *aff'd without opinion*, 615 F.2d 1355 (3d Cir. 1980). *See also* Christian Bros. Inst. of N.J. v. N.J. Interscholastic League, 432 A.2d 26 (N.J. 1981) (refusing to treat an athletic association's denial of a religious school's application as a violation of equal protection, citing to Valencia v. Blue Hen Conference).

[117] Thomas v. Allegany Cnty. Bd. of Educ., 443 A.2d 622, 625 [3 EDUC. L. REP. 670] (Md. Ct. Spec. App. 1982).

[118] *Id.* at 626.

[119] 531 U.S. 288 [151 EDUC. L. REP. 18] (2001) *on remand*, 304 F. Supp. 2d 981 [186 EDUC. L. REP. 180] (M.D. Tenn. 2003).

[120] Tennessee Secondary Sch. Athletic Ass'n v. Brentwood Acad., 551 U.S. 291 [220 EDUC. L. REP. 39] (2007).

recruiting rule violated her right to free speech. Association officials considered the coach's repeatedly paying attention to an eighth-grade player as being intended to influence her to attend the school. The court rejected the coach's free speech claim, emphasizing that contacts with a player are not matters of public concern, and even if they were, the association had an overriding interest in "promoting academics over athletics, protecting students from exploitation, and maintaining competitive equity."[121]

In a case from Illinois, the Seventh Circuit held that an associational rule against head coverings that prohibited athletes from wearing yarmulkes during games did not violate the free exercise right of Orthodox Jewish basketball players. While the court observed that Jewish players "[had] no constitutional right to wear yarmulkes insecurely fastened by bobby pins," it ordered the federal trial court to retain jurisdiction so "the plaintiffs can have an opportunity to propose to the [a]ssociation a form of secure head covering that complies with Jewish law yet meets the [a]ssociation's safety concerns."[122] The court pointedly warned that "if the [a]ssociation proves to be so obdurate—if it refuses to accommodate the indisputably sincere beliefs of a religious group though it can do so at no cost to the only objective, safety, that the rule in question is claimed to have—it will be standing on constitutional quicksand."[123]

Conversely, the Fifth Circuit, in a case from Texas, affirmed that a school board's interests in teaching hygiene, preventing disruptions, instilling discipline, and avoiding safety hazards were not compelling interests that required males to wear their long hair in buns or tucked inside their shirts.[124] The court agreed that when students have sincerely held religious beliefs in wearing their hair visibly long, officials cannot rely on general platitudes but must show exactly how their religious practices jeopardize their stated goals.[125]

Opportunities in Public Schools for Students from Private Schools

In cases involving participation by students from nonpublic schools in public school courses and activities, courts have focused on whether state laws permit dual enrollments and, if not, whether doing so is required under the First or Fourteenth Amendments. Dual enrollment statutes permit students who attend nonpublic schools to enroll in public schools to take selected courses and/or participate in extracurricular activities. Generally, these courses or activities occur in the public schools, but not always.

---

[121] Rottman v. Pa. Interscholastic Athletic Ass'n, 349 F. Supp. 2d 922, 931 [194 EDUC. L. REP. 892] (W.D. Pa. 2004).

[122] Menora v. Ill. Athletic Ass'n, 683 F.2d 1030, 1035 (7th Cir. 1982), *cert. denied*, 459 U.S. 1156 (1983).

[123] *Id.* at 1034.

[124] A.A. ex rel. Betenbaugh v. Needville Indep. Sch. Dist., 611 F.3d 248, 269 [269 EDUC. L. REP. 955] (5th Cir. 2010).

[125] *Id.* at 268.

In the first of a pair of cases from Indiana, a state statute permitted partial subsidies for public school boards when students from nonpublic schools participated in dual enrollment programs. The courses were provided on-site in private, including religious, schools for the dual-enrolled students in fitness and health, art, foreign language, study skills, verbal skills, music, and computer technology, including internet services. According to the Supreme Court of Indiana, the statute did not violate either the federal Constitution's Establishment Clause or the state constitutional provision[126] that "[n]o money shall be drawn from the treasury, for the benefit of any religious or theological institution."[127] The court indicated that insofar as the program provided educational benefits to students, any savings realized by private schools were merely incidental.

As reflected by the second case, the Indiana Supreme court has gone further in clarifying direct versus incidental beneficiaries. The court approved the use of school vouchers at private and parochial schools, ruling that that the direct beneficiaries were the children who used them rather than their schools which received funding from the vouchers.[128]

A dispute arose when a student in a private, nondenominational Christian academy sought to enroll in a public school elective band class. The student hoped to take the course when it was offered in the public school, with her parents transporting her to and from the class. Upholding the student's right to enroll in the class, the Supreme Court of Michigan wrote that the statutory right to public education in the state "[was] not conditioned on full-time attendance."[129] The court added that nonessential elective classes that the state does not require officials to offer in nonpublic schools, such as band, art, domestic science, shop, advanced mathematics, and science classes, are the kinds of courses that, if offered in public schools, "must also be offered to resident nonpublic school students."[130]

It its analysis, the court acknowledged that the public school board failed to present evidence that participation by the student from the nonpublic school would have resulted in a decrease in full-time public school student attendance. This is noteworthy because the court indicated that the student's participation on a part-time basis did not result in the public school being denied state school aid for the child. Insofar as the court identified support for allowing the student from the nonpublic school to enroll in the class, it did not address the constitutional issues she raised, other than declaring that having a pupil from a religious school attend a public school on a part-time basis did not violate the Establishment Clause.[131]

---

[126] Embry v. O'Bannon, 798 N.E.2d 157 [182 Educ. L. Rep. 325] (Ind. 2003).

[127] Ind. Const., art. I, § 6.

[128] Meredith v. Pence, 984 N.E.2d 1213 [290 Educ. L. Rep. 998] (Ind. 2013).

[129] Snyder v. Charlotte Sch. Dist., 365 N.W.2d 151, 159 [24 Educ. L. Rep. 466] (Mich. 1984).

[130] Id. at 162.

[131] See id. at 162-168 (declaring that all of the instruction the student received would have been secular and would occur in the public school).

The Supreme Court of Montana, although relying on a different rationale than the dispute from Maryland discussed earlier,[132] reached the same result.[133] A student who was denied permission to participate in public school athletic activities claimed that this violated the state constitutional provision that: "[i]t is the goal of the people to establish a system of education which will develop the full educational potential of each person. Equality of educational opportunity is guaranteed to each person of the state."[134]

Applying a mid-tier analysis of the student's rights under this provision, the court asserted that "the right to participate must be balanced against the School District's interests in restricting participation to students enrolled in the public school system."[135] Affirming the denial of the student's claim, the court agreed with the board that "providing a unified program in which required academic courses, elective courses and extracurricular activities are 'integrated' so as to complement each other."[136]

Governmental Regulation of Home Instruction

Home Instruction Generally

Between 1999 and 2012, the percentage of homeschooled students doubled, from 1.7 % to 3.4%.[137] Data collected in 2016 indicate that about 3.3% of children are homeschooled.[138] For a sense of perspective, in 2003, "more children are educated at home than are educated in the public schools of Wyoming, Vermont, Delaware, North Dakota, Alaska, South Dakota, Rhode Island, Montana and Hawaii—combined. In fact, the total number of children educated in homeschools outnumbers the aggregate of children educated in the public schools of 41 individual states."[139]

States have recognized interests in regulating homeschooling. Challenges to state statutes setting requirements for homeschooling are typically unsuccessful.[140] All fifty states accept homeschools as a means of satisfying their

---

[132] *See* Thomas v. Allegany Cnty. Bd. of Educ., *supra* note 117.

[133] Kaptein v. Conrad Sch. Dist., 931 P.2d 1311 [116 Educ. L. Rep. 435] (Mont. 1997).

[134] Mont. Const. art. X, sec. 1.

[135] Kaptein, 931 P.2d at 1316.

[136] *Id.* at 1317.

[137] National Center for Education Statistics, Parent and Family Involvement in Education: Results from the National Household Education Surveys Program of 2016 (2017). *See* Table 8, available at https://nces.ed.gov/pubsearch/pubsinfo.asp?pubid=2017102.

[138] *Id.*

[139] Brad Colwell and Brian Schwartz, *Implications for Public Schools: Legal Aspects of Homeschools*, 173 Educ. L. Rep. 381 (2003).

[140] *See, e.g.,* Combs v. Homer-Center Sch. Dist., 540 F.3d 231, 243 (3d Cir. 2008) (conceding that the state had "a legitimate interest in ensuring children taught under home education programs are achieving minimum educational standards and are demonstrating sustained progress in their educational program.").

compulsory attendance requirements, the majority by statute.[141] States differ widely in the amount of regulation, though. Parents desirous of homeschooling their children need to review the statutory requirements in their states before undertaking this venture. The penalty for noncompliance with a state's compulsory attendance is generally a truancy charge.[142] Courts have also upheld a wide range of regulatory methods affecting homeschools.[143]

States vary about whether homeschools can be treated as private schools, with courts split over this issue.[144] A number of states have enacted statutes specifically addressed to homeschooling that have tended to reduce confusion

---

[141] *See, e.g.*, ARK. CODE ANN. § 6–15–501; COL. REV. STAT. ANN. § 22–33–104.5; DEL. CODE ANN. tit. 14 § 2703; LA. REV. STAT. ANN. tit. 17 § 236.1; ME. REV. STAT. ANN. 20–A, § 5001–A(3)(A)(3); MICH. COMP. LAWS ANN. § 380.1561(3)(f); N.J. STAT. ANN. § 18A: 38–25; OHIO REV. CODE ANN. § 3321.04(A)(2); PA. STAT. ANN. tit. 24 § 13–1327.1.

[142] For cases upholding truancy convictions, *see, e.g.*, State v. Patzer, 382 N.W.2d 631 [30 EDUC. L. REP. 1265] (N.D. 1986); State v. Edgington, 663 P.2d 374 [1 EDUC. L. REP. 301] (N.M. Ct. App. 1983); Burrow v. State, 669 S.W.2d 441 [17 EDUC. L. REP. 997] (Ark. 1984); State v. Lowrey, 383 P.2d 962 (Kan. 1963); In Interest of Sawyer, 672 P.2d 1093 [14 EDUC. L. REP. 1126] (Kan. 1983).

[143] *See, e.g.*, Goulart v. Meadows, 345 F.3d 239 [181 EDUC. L. REP. 75] (4th Cir. 2003) (upholding the refusal of park service officials to permit students who were homeschooled to use facilities for homeschooling instruction); Battles v. Arundel Cnty. Bd. of Educ., 904 F. Supp. 471 [105 EDUC. L. REP. 93] (D. Md.1995), *aff'd*, 95 F.3d 41 (4th Cir. 1995) (upholding a state monitoring system including parental maintenance of portfolios in established curricular areas plus a requirement that a representative of the state department of education observe teaching on-site); Brunelle v. Lynn Pub. Schs., 702 N.E.2d 1182 [130 EDUC. L. REP. 1322] (Mass. 1998) (upholding the right of local public schools to oversee homeschooling curricula and parental teaching qualifications, but rejecting the claim that a superintendent could conduct on-site visits); State v. DeLaBruere, 577 A.2d 254 [61 EDUC. L. REP. 984] (Vt. 1990) (upholding a reporting law as neither violating free exercise nor substantive due process, and as not being unconstitutionally vague).

[144] For cases recognizing homeschools as private schools, see Jonathan L. v. Superior Ct., 81 Cal. Rptr.3d 571 [235 EDUC. L. REP. 492] (Cal. Ct. App. 2008); Texas Educ. Agency v. Leeper, 893 S.W.2d 432 [98 EDUC. L. REP. 491] (Tex. 1995); Conclara v. State Bd. of Educ., 501 N.W.2d 88 [83 EDUC. L. REP. 734] (Mich. 1993); People v. Levisen, 90 N.E.2d 213 (Ill. 1950). For cases refusing to treat homeschools as private schools, see State v. Superior Ct., 346 P.2d 999 (Wash. 1960); State v. Lowrey, 383 P.2d 962 (Kan. 1963); State v. M.N., 407 So. 2d 987 [2 EDUC. L. REP. 314] (Fla. Dist. Ct. App. 1982); State v. Morrow, 343 N.W.2d 903 [16 EDUC. L. REP. 260] (Neb. 1984); State v. Bigelow, 334 N.W.2d 444 [11 EDUC. L. REP. 650] (Neb. 1983).

about comparisons to private schools.[145] Homeschool statutes usually require some form of notification and/or child assessment.[146]

Opportunities in Public Schools for Students who are Homeschooled

Parental interests in affording their children who are homeschooled opportunities to participate in public school activities have grown significantly in recent years. Four cases illustrate the concern of the public schools and their associations.

In a case from Oklahoma, the Tenth Circuit affirmed that a board policy in Oklahoma prohibiting part-time attendance did not violate a homeschooled student's right to the free exercise of religion.[147] The student had sought to take foreign language, vocal music, and science courses in a public school. As to free exercise, the court viewed the policy of not permitting part-time students to enroll as a neutral, generally applicable rule, motivated largely by the fact it would not have received funding for such children.

Conceding that decisions "as to how to allocate scarce resources, as well as what curriculum to offer or require, are uniquely committed to the discretion of local school authorities,"[148] the Tenth Circuit refused to translate the parental right to direct the education of their daughter into one allowing them "to send their children to public school on a part-time basis, and to pick and choose which courses their children will take from the public school."[149]

The federal trial court in Maine rejected the claim that the parental right to direct the education of their children extended to obligating local educational officials to permit a student who was homeschooled to compete in an interschool athletic event on behalf of a Christian school. The parents rejected the option of having their son compete on the team of his local public high

---

[145] *See, e.g.*, CAL. EDUC. CODE § 48222; ILL. COMP. STAT. ANN. 105 5/26–1; MASS GEN. LAWS ANN. Ch. 76 § 1; TEX. EDUC. CODE ANN. § 25.086.

[146] *See, e.g.*, Colo. Rev. Stat. Ann. § 22-33-104.5 (requiring parents to notify school board officials that they are establishing home-based educational programs including curricula covering specified subject matter areas, including evaluations by nationally standardized achievement test at end of specified grades, the maintenance of grades and vaccination records, and at least 172 days of instruction; even so, parents are not subject to state teacher licensing laws); LA. REV. STAT. ANN. § 17:236 (mandating that home study programs be approved by the State Board of Elementary and Secondary Education to evaluate whether they offer sustained curricula of a quality at least equal to that offered by public schools at the same grade level); Minn. Stat. Ann. § 120A.22 & 24) (obligating homeschool curricula to include specific subject matter areas; student must be assessed annually by "a nationally norm-referenced standardized achievement examination," but parents are not required to meet teaching qualifications called for in private school); N.C. GEN. STAT. § 115C-564 (requiring home instructors to have high school diplomas and students to take annual standardized achievement tests).

[147] Swanson by and through Swanson v. Guthrie Indep. Sch. Dist. No. I-L, 135 F.3d 694 [123 EDUC. L. REP. 1087] (10th Cir. 1998).

[148] *Id.* at 700.

[149] *Id.*

school because they did not want him doing so for religious reasons.[150] Denying the family's request for injunctive relief, the court concluded that for the purposes of the free exercise of religion, the rules for competition were neutral and generally applicable, even though they incidentally burdened the religious beliefs of the parents and their son.

In a case from Pennsylvania, the Third Circuit affirmed that a student who attended a cyber-school lacked a right to participate in interscholastic basketball.[151] The student was educated at home for third through eighth grades and began ninth grade as homeschooled before enrolling in the charter school. The court agreed that forbidding the student from competing because she failed to meet the board's eligibility criteria was rationally related to its legitimate interest in ensuring that all students were educated. The court was persuaded that officials did not violate the student's right to equal protection because participation in extracurricular activities is not fundamental right.

An appellate court in Michigan affirmed that students who were homeschooled lacked a right to participate in the extracurricular sports programs sponsored by their local board because they failed to meet its enrollment criteria.[152] As in the other cases, the court agreed that the enrollment rule was neutral and generally applicable. The court declared not only had the parents made a choice between extracurricular activities and homeschooling, but also that their

> desire to have their children participate in extracurricular interscholastic athletic activities runs counter to their stated religious purpose to ensure that the education provided to their children integrates their religious beliefs on a curriculum-wide basis and to minimize the influence of other world-views (e.g. secular humanism/scientific naturalism) and other persons (e.g. peers and other authority figures) which threaten to undermine those sincerely held religious beliefs.[153]

Legislative and Organizational Involvement Public School Activities

A growing number of states have enacted legislation,[154] while athletic associations have adopted rules allowing students who are homeschooled to

---

[150] Pelletier v. Maine Principals' Ass'n, 261 F. Supp. 2d 10 [177 Educ. L. Rep. 992] (D. Me. 2003).

[151] Angstadt v. Midd-West Sch. Dist., 377 F.3d 338 [190 Educ. L. Rep. 48] (3d Cir. 2004).

[152] Reid v. Kenowa Hills Pub. Schs., 680 N.W.2d 62 [188 Educ. L. Rep. 438] (Mich. Ct. App. 2004). For an earlier case reaching the same result, see Bradstreet v. Sobol, 650 N.Y.S.2d 402 [114 Educ. L. Rep. 927] (N.Y. App. Div. 1996).

[153] Id. at 69-70.

[154] See, e.g., Colo. Rev. Stat. § 22–33–104.5; Fla. Stat. Ann. §§ 1002.20, 41; Me. Rev. Stat. Ann. 20–A, § 5021.4–5; Minn. Stat. Ann. § 123B.49(4)(a); N.H. Rev. Stat. Ann. § 193:1–c; OHIO REV. CODE ANN. § 3313.5312; Or. Rev. Stat. Ann. § 339.460.

participate in public school extracurricular activities to varying degrees.[155] Under Colorado law, for instance,

> a child who is participating in a nonpublic home-based educational program shall have the same rights as a student enrolled in a public school of the school district in which the child resides or is enrolled and may participate on an equal basis in any extracurricular or interscholastic activity offered by a public school or offered by a private school, at the private school's discretion.[156]

In a more limited vein, in 2016 the Alabama High School Athletic Association amended its bylaws to permit students who are homeschooled to participate in interscholastic athletics.[157] Officials in many states take case-by-case approaches, allowing individual boards to consider the levels of involvement afforded students who are homeschooled if they wish to participate in extracurricular activities.[158]

Conclusion

Governmental regulation of nonpublic schools is well established. Governmental regulations must be neutral to religious schools and cannot single them out for special rules, nor may governmental regulations be made or enforcement officials act with animus toward nonpublic schools. Instead, the governmental must take an approach of neutrality. If so, then officials in nonpublic schools are required to abide by those neutral and generally applicable regulations overseeing school administration, operations, curricula, and the like. However, in some limited areas, even neutral and generally applicable regulations cannot violate specified functions of particular schools and families in the education of their children, especially pertaining to those of ministerial functions. In these areas, then, nonpublic schools and home education families may be exempt from governmental regulations.

Discussion Questions

1. Is my school, a religious school?
   - Do we have a statement of faith?
   - Do we maintain religious employment criteria?
   - Do we have a religious purpose?
   - Do we practice religion at school?
   - Does the school present itself as religious?
2. What are my controlling state laws for homeschool education?

---

[155] For a commentary on this issue, see Charles J. Russo & Allan G. Osborne, *Sports Participation and Home Schooling: A Game Changer?* 301 EDUC. L. REP. 8 (2014).

[156] Colo. Rev. Stat. Ann. § 22-33-104.5(6)(b)(1).

[157] Available at http://www.ahsaa.com/Portals/0/PDF's/AHSAA/Home%20School/Memo-%20for%20link%20to%20Non-traditional%20school%20laws%20changes.pdf?ver=2016-04-12-170214-927

[158] For a current review of each state status see: https://hslda.org/content/docs/nche/Issues/E/Equal_Access.pdf

Key Words

Church autonomy doctrine
Compelling interest
Establishment Clause
Extracurricular activities
Fourteenth Amendment
Free Exercise Clause
Governmental regulation
Homeschooling
Liberty interests
Ministerial exception
Neutral, generally applicable law
Substantial burden

10 Federal Antidiscrimination Legislation

William E. Thro

Contents

Introduction / 293
Title VII / 296
    Overview / 296
    The Ministerial Exception May Exempt Some Employees from Title VII / 296
    Faith-Based Schools May Require Employees to Adhere to the Faith / 296
    Faith-Based Schools May Have to Accommodate Employees' Religious Beliefs / 297
    Liability Theories for Title VII / 297
        Intentional Discrimination / 297
        Disparate Impact / 299
        Harassment / 299
Americans with Disabilities Act / 300
    Employment / 300
        Reasonable Accommodation / 301
        Drug Use / 301
        Exemption for Selected Religious Tasks / 302
    Participation in Educational Programs and Activities / 302
Age Discrimination in Employment Act / 303
The Equal Pay Act / 303
The Family Medical Leave Act / 304
    Special Rules for Classroom Teachers / 305
Retaliation Claims / 306
Conclusion / 306
Discussion Questions / 307
Key Words / 307

Introduction

With respect to federal antidiscrimination laws, faith-based schools and other nonpublic schools have to be aware of three basic propositions.

First, when employees of faith-based schools are "ministers," federal antidiscrimination laws do not apply.[1] Although the Establishment Clause and the Free Exercise Clause "often exert conflicting pressures,"[2] and there is frequently an "internal tension ... between the Establishment Clause and the Free Exercise Clause,"[3] the Supreme Court unanimously held that "[b]oth Religion Clauses bar the government from interfering with the decision of a religious group to fire one of its ministers."[4]

Emphasizing both the right of "hierarchical religious organizations to establish their own rules and regulations for internal discipline and government, and to create tribunals for adjudicating disputes over these matters,"[5]

---

[1] Hosanna-Tabor Evangelical Lutheran Church and School v. Equal Employment Opportunities Comm'n (*Hosanna-Tabor*), 563 U.S. 903 (2011).

[2] Cutter v. Wilkinson, 544 U.S. 709, 719 (2005).

[3] Tilton v. Richardson, 403 U.S. 672, 677 (1971) (Burger, C.J., joined by Harlan, Stewart, & Blackmun, J.J., announcing the judgment of the Court).

[4] *Hosanna-Tabor,* 565 U.S. at 171. Interpreting the Religion Clauses as requiring the ministerial exceptions, the Supreme Court rejected two arguments made by both the teacher and the Obama Administration. First, with respect to the contentions that the case should have turned exclusively on the freedom of association and the Religion Clauses as not providing a basis for a ministerial exception, the Court found it "hard to square with the text of the First Amendment itself, which gives special solicitude to the rights of religious organizations. We cannot accept the remarkable view that the Religion Clauses have nothing to say about a religious organization's freedom to select its own ministers." *Hosanna-Tabor,* 565 U. S. at 189. The necessary inference is that while religious organizations enjoy the same associational freedoms as secular organizations, religious organizations, through the Religion Clauses, have greater associational freedoms.

Second, concerning the assertion that exempting religious organizations from antidiscrimination laws contradicted Employment Div., Dep't of Human Resources of Oregon v. Smith, 494 U.S. 872 (1990), the Court limited *Smith* to "government regulation of only outward physical acts." In *Smith,* the Court held the "right of free exercise does not relieve an individual of the obligation to comply with a valid and neutral law of general applicability on the ground that the law proscribes (or prescribes) conduct that his religion prescribes (or proscribes)." *Id.* at 879. Because the antidiscrimination and retaliation provisions are valid and neutral laws of general applicability, *Smith* seems to require religious organizations to comply. *Hosanna-Tabor*, 565 U.S. Ct. at 190. Yet, because *Hosanna-Tabor* "concerns government interference with an internal church decision that affects the faith and mission of the church itself," the Court rejected the "contention that *Smith* forecloses recognition of a ministerial exception rooted in the Religion Clauses." *Id.*

[5] Serbian Eastern Orthodox Diocese for the U.S. and Canada v. Milivojevich, 426 U.S. 696, 724 (1976).

the Supreme Court explained that there is such a ministerial exception.[6] "The members of a religious group put their faith in the hands of their ministers. Requiring a church to accept or retain an unwanted minister, or punishing a church for failing to do so, intrudes upon more than a mere employment decision."[7]

Second, for employees who are not considered "ministers," a variety of federal statutes—including Title VII, the Americans with Disabilities Act, the Age Discrimination in Employment Act, the Equal Pay Act, and the Family & Medical Leave Act—apply to faith-based and other nonpublic schools.[8] Moreover, the Americans with Disabilities Act will have some applications to students. All of these laws have retaliation provisions protecting individuals who complain about violations of these statutes.

Third, if faith-based or nonpublic schools receive federal funds, then a variety of antidiscrimination statutes, including Title VI (race), Title IX (sex), and Section 504 (disability), apply. Although virtually all private higher education institutions receive federal funds, very few private elementary and secondary schools do so. Consequently, this chapter does not address the statutes impos-

---

[6] *Hosanna-Tabor*, 565 U.S. at 188. While the decision was unanimous, two concurrences concerned the breadth of the ministerial exception. First, Justice Thomas wrote, "separately to note that, in my view, the Religion Clauses require civil courts to apply the ministerial exception and to defer to a religious organization's good-faith understanding of who qualifies as its minister." *Id.* at 196 (Thomas, J., concurring). "Judicial attempts to fashion a civil definition of 'minister' through a bright-line test or multi-factor analysis risk disadvantaging those religious groups whose beliefs, practices, and membership are outside of the 'mainstream' or unpalatable to some." *Id.* at 197 (Thomas, J. concurring). Second, Justice Alito, joined by Justice Kagan, emphasized "it would be a mistake if the term "minister" or the concept of ordination were viewed as central to the important issue of religious autonomy that is presented in cases like this one. Instead, courts should focus on the function performed by persons who work for religious bodies." *Id.* at 198 (Alito, J., joined by Kagan, J., concurring). Therefore, "religious groups must be free to choose the personnel who are essential to the performance of these functions." *Id.* at 199 (Alito, J., joined by Kagan J., concurring). "If a religious group believes that the ability of such an employee to perform these key functions has been compromised, then the constitutional guarantee of religious freedom protects the group's right to remove the employee from his or her position." *Id.* (Alito, J., joined by Kagan, J., concurring)

[7] *Id.* In reaching this outcome, the Court relied on *both* the Free Exercise and the Establishment Clauses. "By imposing an unwanted minister, the state infringes the Free Exercise Clause, which protects a religious group's right to shape its own faith and mission through its appointments." *Hosanna-Tabor,* 565 U.S. at 188. "According the state the power to determine which individuals will minister to the faithful also violates the Establishment Clause, which prohibits government involvement in such ecclesiastical decisions." *Id.* at 199-89. While the Court declined "to adopt a rigid formula for deciding when an employee qualifies as a minister," it did observe "that the exception covers [the employee who brought the suit], given all the circumstances of her employment." *Id.* at 190. In particular, the Court emphasized that both the employee and the Church represented that she was a minister. *Id.* at 191-92. Moreover, the Court stressed that the employees' performances of some secular duties or that lay people often performed similar duties at the school was not significant. *Id.* at 192-94.

[8] As discussed in more detail below, Title VII is inapplicable to some employees who are not necessarily ministers, but who perform religious functions.

ing conditions on the receipt of federal funds. If institutions receive federal funds, their leaders should consult legal counsel.

The remainder of this chapter offers a detailed overview of these key federal statutes: Title VII, the Americans with Disabilities Act, the Age Discrimination in Employment Act, the Equal Pay Act, the Family & Medical Leave Act, and the associated retaliation provisions, applicable to all schools. The chapter rounds out with a conclusion.

Title VII

Overview

If faith-based schools have more than fifteen employees,[9] then Title VII of the Civil Rights Act of 1964[10] prohibits discrimination *in employment* based on race, color, religion, sex, and national origin. It is applicable to all races, not just racial minorities, and to both sexes, not just women.

The Ministerial Exception May Exempt Some Employees from Title VII

As noted in the introduction, the Religion Clauses of the First Amendment mandate a "ministerial exception" to other applicable federal laws, including discrimination laws. Thus, if an employee is a "minister," then Title VII's prohibitions do not apply.

In Some Instances, Faith-Based Schools May Require Employees to Adhere to the Faith

Title VII generally prohibits religious discrimination. Even so, Title VII grants exceptions that may allow faith-based schools to discriminate against those who do not share their religious tenets.

First, if an institution is "in whole or in substantial part, owned, supported, controlled or managed by a particular religious corporation, association, or society, or if the curriculum of such school, college, religious school, or other educational institution or institution of learning is directed toward the propaga-

---

[9] Title VII does not apply to employers with fewer than fifteen employees. 42 U.S.C. § 2000e (b). In many cases, when faith-based schools function as units of church, courts must use a four-part test under a judicially constructed "single employer doctrine" to determine whether employees of different parts of ministries should be counted together for purposes of Title VII jurisdiction: interrelations of operations; common management; centralized control of labor relations; and common ownership or financial control.

[10] 42 U.S.C. § 2000e.

tion of a particular religion," it is exempt.[11] The amount of control or support necessary to invoke this exemption is not that considerable.[12]

Second, Title VII exempts hiring, discharge, or classification based on religion, sex, or national origin where "religion is a bona fide occupational qualification (BFOQ) reasonably necessary to the operations of that particular business or enterprise."[13] The burden is on employers to prove BFOQ exemptions.

Third, Title VII exempts "a religious corporation, association, educational institution, or society with respect to the employment of individuals of a particular religion to perform work connected with the carrying on by such corporation, association, educational institution, or society of its activities."[14]

In Some Instances, Faith-based Schools May Have to Accommodate an Employee's Religious Beliefs

Title VII requires employers to "reasonably accommodate" employees' religious needs, as long as they can do so "without undue hardship." Most of the conflicts in the area of accommodating employees' religious needs occur either in the scheduling of work, particular work assignments, or employees' requests to wear religious attire at work.[15]

Liability Theories for Title VII

Intentional Discrimination

In intentional discrimination cases, plaintiffs claim that schools treated them differently and the bases for doing so were their race, gender, religion, or disability. Plaintiffs must first establish a prima facie case in order to recover

---

[11] 42 U.S.C. § 2000e-2(e)(2).

[12] *See* Killinger v. Samford Univ., 113 F.3d 196 [118 EDUC. L. REP. 48] (11th Cir. 1997) (despite the Alabama Baptist Convention's having discontinued control of the university in terms of appointing members of the board, its $4,000,000 annual contribution constituted substantial support, even though it was only 7% of the university's annual budget); Hall v. Baptist Mem'l Health Care Corp., 27 F. Supp. 2d 1029, 1037 [131 EDUC. L. REP. 385] (W.D. Tenn. 1998), *aff'd*, 215 F.3d 618 [145 EDUC. L. REP. 216] (6th Cir. 2000) (treating a single three-hour course in religion required by the college controlled by the corporation as sufficient under the Title VII exemption; "the College does not have to hire only Baptists or follow a strict policy of religious discrimination to be eligible for the Title VII exemption").

[13] 42 U.S.C. § 2000e-2 (e)(1).

[14] 42 U.S.C. 2000e-1 (a).

[15] In Trans World Airlines v. Hardison, 432 U.S. 63 (1977), over the employee's refusal to work on Friday nights, the Supreme Court narrowly construed this provision, deciding that it would have been an undue hardship to require an employer to bear more than a minimal cost in order to accommodate an employee's religious beliefs or worship requirements. In Ansonia Bd. of Educ. v. Philbrook, 479 U.S. 60 (1986), the Court ruled that employers need not provide the accommodations requested by employees if the accommodations they actually offered met the test of reasonableness. In other words, the Court indicated that employers do not have to prove that the accommodations sought by their employees are undue hardship, but merely that the accommodations they offered are reasonable.

for intentional discrimination. In its landmark opinion in *McDonnell Douglas Corp. v. Green*,[16] the Supreme Court held that a prima facie case consists of the following elements:

1. A plaintiff belongs to a protected class under the applicable civil rights statute.
2. A plaintiff applied for and met stated qualifications for the position for which the employer was seeking applicants.
3. Despite having the qualifications, the plaintiff was rejected.
4. After the plaintiff was rejected, the position remained open, and the employer continued to seek applications from persons with the plaintiff's qualifications.

In many cases alleging intentional discrimination in violation of Title VII, defendant employers present evidence of both discriminatory and nondiscriminatory motives ("mixed motives" or "dual motives") for adverse employment actions. In *Desert Place, Inc. v. Costa*,[17] the Supreme Court ruled that Title VII, as amended by the Civil Rights Act of 1991, did not require direct evidence of discrimination; it was sufficient in a mixed-motive case if plaintiffs could show sufficient evidence that "race, color, religion, sex, or national origin was a motivating factor for any employment practice."[18]

If plaintiffs can establish prima facie cases, then the burden of *production* shifts to the officials of faith-based schools, who have the responsibility to articulate legitimate, nondiscriminatory reasons for acting.[19] However, it must be noted this burden is one of production, not persuasion; it "can involve no credibility assessment."[20] Indeed, "[t]he ultimate burden of persuading the trier of fact that the defendant intentionally discriminated against the plaintiff remains at all times with the plaintiff."[21]

If officials of the faith-based schools articulate legitimate, nondiscriminatory reasons for acting, then the plaintiffs "must be afforded the "opportunity to prove by a preponderance of the evidence that the legitimate reasons offered by the defendant were not its true reasons, but were a pretext for discrimination."[22] However, even if plaintiffs demonstrate that actions of their faith-based employer's nondiscriminatory reasons are pretextual, they do not necessarily

---

[16] 411 U.S. 792 (1973).

[17] 539 U.S. 90 (2003).

[18] 42 U.S.C. §2000 e-2(m).

[19] *See* Texas Dep't. of Cmty. Affairs v. Burdine, 450 U.S. 248 (1981).

[20] St. Mary's Honor Ctr. v. Hicks, 509 U.S. 502, 509 (1993).

[21] *Burdine*, 450 U.S. at 253.

[22] Reeves v. Sanderson Plumbing, 530 U.S. 133, 144 (2000) (citations omitted).

prevail.[23] In other words, plaintiffs bear the ultimate responsibility to prove intentional discrimination. Refuting the legitimate, nondiscriminatory reasons offered by their faith-based schools may help plaintiffs prove intentional discrimination, but it is not conclusive proof of such discrimination.

Disparate Impact

In disparate impact discrimination cases, plaintiffs typically challenge the impact of otherwise neutral requirements. For example, plaintiffs may challenge the validity of tests or requirements that they possess specific educational credentials.

Under the *Uniform Guidelines on Employee Selection Procedures*,[24] plaintiffs can prove prima facie cases of disparate impact discrimination if they can show that the pass rate for their group is less than four-fifths the pass rate for the highest group. For example, if one hundred percent of another group passed the examination, then plaintiffs will be required to show that in their groups less than eighty percent, or four-fifths of one hundred percent, passed. However, in applying the four-fifths rule, a court must first ascertain that the sample size is sufficiently large to be valid.[25] If officials of faith-based schools use multiple factors in determining eligibility, then plaintiffs must identify which factors have a disparate impact and must show that these factors, in fact, have a disparate impact.[26]

Once plaintiffs have established that particular factors have a disparate impact, the burden of articulation shifts to officials in the faith-based schools to demonstrate that the challenged factors sufficiently relate to successful job performance so that reasonable people would rely on the challenged factors when making employment decisions.

Harassment

The most common forms of harassment are those based on sex and race. Even so, Title VII's prohibition against harassment has been extended to

---

[23] As the Supreme Court observed: The fact finder's rejection of the employer's legitimate, nondiscriminatory reason for its action does not *compel* judgment for the plaintiff. The ultimate question is whether the employer intentionally discriminated, and proof that "the employer's proffered reason is unpersuasive, or even obviously contrived, does not necessarily establish that the plaintiff's proffered reason ... is correct." In other words, "[i]t is not enough ... to *dis*believe the employer; the fact finder must *believe* the plaintiff's explanation of intentional discrimination." In reaching this conclusion, however, we reasoned that it is *permissible* for the trier of fact to infer the ultimate fact of discrimination from the falsity of the employer's explanation. . . . . Proof that the defendant's explanation is unworthy of credence is simply one form of circumstantial evidence that is probative of intentional discrimination, and it may be quite persuasive. *Reeves*, 530 U.S. at 146-47 (citations and block quotation omitted).

[24] 29 C.F.R. § 1607.

[25] *See* Clady v. County of Los Angeles, 770 F.2d 1421 (9th Cir. 1985).

[26] *See* 42 U.S.C. § 2000d-2(k)(1)(B).

religious, age, and disability harassment.[27] The standards set forth below apply to *all* forms of harassment under Title VII.

First, if the harassment results in a tangible employment action, then faith-based schools are strictly liable for the harassment.[28] Examples of tangible employment actions include decisions causing significant changes in benefits and work assignments.[29]

Second, if the harassment does not result in a tangible employment action, then the faith-based school may avoid liability by demonstrating that their officials exercised reasonable care to prevent and promptly correct any harassing behaviors and that the employee(s) unreasonably failed to take advantage of any preventive or corrective opportunities provided by their employers or to avoid harm otherwise.[30] Thus, the prudent course for faith-based employers to avoid liability for harassment under Title VII is to promulgate anti-harassment policies/complaint procedures and to make all employees aware of their existence.

Americans with Disability Act

For faith-based schools, the Americans with Disability Act (ADA) prohibits discrimination against "a qualified individual with a disability because of the disability."[31] The nature of the disability under the ADA applies to both employees and students:

1. A physical or mental impairment that substantially limits one or more of the major life activities of such individual;
2. a record of such impairment; or
3. being regarded as having such an impairment.[32]

The ADA addresses both employment, in its Title I, along with access to programs and activities as places of "public accommodation," in its Title III.[33]

Employment

With respect to employment, Title I prohibits employers with fifteen or more employees from discriminating against individuals with disabilities in "job application procedures, hiring, firing, advancement, compensation, job training, and other terms, conditions, and privileges of employment."[34] The requirement of fifteen or more employees is jurisdictional, and whether

---

[27] *See* Hafford v. Seidner, 167 F.3d 1074, 1080 (6th Cir. 1999) (religion); Breeding v. Arthur J. Gallagher and Co., 164 F.3d 1151, 1158 (8th Cir. 1999) (age); Wallin v. Minnesota Dep't of Corrections, 153 F.3d 681, 687 (8th Cir. 1999) (disability).

[28] *See* Farragher v. City of Boca Raton, 524 U.S. 775 (1998); Burlington Industries v. Ellerth, 524 U.S. 742 (1998).

[29] *See Farragher, id.*, at 778-89; *Ellerth, id.* at 760-61.

[30] *See Farragher*, 524 U.S. at 807-08; *Ellerth*, 118 S. Ct. at 2270.

[31] 42 U.S.C. § 12112.

[32] 42 U.S.C. § 12102.

[33] 42 U.S.C. §§ 12101 *et seq.*

[34] 42 U.S.C. § 12112(a).

church and school employees can be counted together depends on the amount of church control over a given school. Individual employees cannot be sued under the ADA.

Reasonable Accommodation

Officials in faith-based schools are required to make reasonable accommodations to the disabilities of employees, unless doing so would constitute "undue hardship."[35] Reasonable accommodations are broadly defined as making existing facilities used by employees readily accessible to and usable by individuals with disabilities; job restructuring; part-time or modified work schedules; reassignments to vacant positions; acquisitions or modification of equipment or devices; appropriate adjustments or modification of examinations, training materials or policies; the provision of qualified readers or interpreters; or other similar accommodations for individuals with disabilities.[36]

Even with reasonable accommodations, though, employees must still be able to perform essential job functions. Employees with disabilities are responsible to identify reasonable accommodations, at which point employers can request medical documentation of disabilities and then either provide the accommodations suggested by the employees or provide alternative accommodations. Whether employer accommodations are reasonable is a question of law. Where multiple accommodations are possible to permit employees to perform essential job functions, employers are entitled to select the one that is the least expensive.

Drug Use

The ADA does not protect "any employee or applicant who is currently engaging in the illegal use of drugs,"[37] but cover individuals who have completed, or are completing, supervised drug rehabilitation programs and are not engaging in the use of illegal drugs.[38] The ADA expressly protects individuals with communicable diseases, except that employers "may refuse to assign or

---

[35] 42 U.S.C. § 12111 (10). In evaluating whether actions would result in undue burdens, the factors to be considered include: (1) The nature and cost of the action needed under this part;(2) The overall financial resources of the site or sites involved in the action; the number of persons employed at the site; the effect on expenses and resources; legitimate safety requirements that are necessary for safe operation, including crime prevention measures; or the impact otherwise of the action upon the operation of the site; (3) The geographic separateness, and the administrative or fiscal relationship of the site or sites in question to any parent corporation or entity;(4) If applicable, the overall financial resources of any parent corporation or entity; the overall size of the parent corporation or entity with respect to the number of its employees; the number, type, and location of its facilities; and (5) If applicable, the type of operation or operations of any parent corporation or entity, including the composition, structure, and functions of the workforce of the parent corporation or entity. 28 C.F.R. § 36.104.

[36] 42 U.S.C. § 12111 (9).

[37] 42 U.S.C. § 12114 (a).

[38] 42 U.S.C. § 12114 (b).

continue to assign [individuals with communicable diseases] to a job involving food handling."[39]

Exemption for Selected Religious Tasks

Faith-based schools are exempted from the ADA only as to "giving preference in employment to individuals of a particular religion to perform work connected with the carrying on by such [religious employer]."[40] Consequently, persons with disabilities who otherwise meet employers' religious requirements must be given the same consideration as other job applicants or current employees.

Participation in Educational Programs and Activities

Title III of the ADA protects students in public accommodations from disability discrimination. Included in the definition of a public accommodation is "a nursery, elementary, secondary, undergraduate, or postgraduate private school, or other place of education."[41] Individuals with disabilities are "qualified" when "with or without reasonable modification[s] to rules, policies, or practices, the removal of architectural, communication, or transportation barriers, or the provision of auxiliary aids and services, [they] meet the essential eligibility requirements for the receipt of services or his participation in programs or activities provided by a public entity."[42]

Title III focuses on ten areas of institutional activity and applies its nondiscrimination requirements to private institutions: eligibility criteria for the services provided by colleges and universities; modifications of policies, practices, or procedures, such as parking regulations; auxiliary aids and services, such as interpreters; removal of architectural barriers; alternatives to barrier removal; personal devices and services which the law does not require institutions to provide; conditions under which public accommodations must provide accessible or special goods on request; accessible seating in assembly areas; accessibility to and alternatives for examinations and courses that reflect the individuals' abilities rather than their impairments; and accessible transportation. These requirements affect a wide array of institutional policies and practices, such as admissions policies, accessibility of residence halls and classrooms, the actions of individual faculty members with respect to formats of tests or ways of communicating information, and the offering of public performances and events.

At the same time, the ADA exempts "any religious entity,"[43] defined as "a religious organization, including a place of worship,"[44] from the definition of public accommodation. Religious elementary and secondary schools are free

---

[39] 42 U.S.C. § 12113 (d)(2).
[40] 42 U.S.C. § 12113 (c).
[41] 42 U.S.C. § 12181 (7).
[42] 42 U.S.C. § 12131.
[43] 28 C.F.R. § 36.102 (e).
[44] 28 C.F.R. § 36.104.

under the ADA to refuse admission to students with disabilities and to dismiss such students, even if the conduct is a manifestation of their disabilities. To reiterate, Title III exempts faith-based schools from discrimination liability for students, not employees.

The Age Discrimination in Employment Act

The Age Discrimination in Employment Act (ADEA) prohibits hiring, discharging, classifying, or engaging in wage-rate discrimination of employees over 40 years old.[45] The ADEA has four exemptions or affirmative defenses: treatment "based on reasonable factors other than age;"[46] discharge or discipline "for good cause;"[47] treatment based on "a bona fide occupational qualification reasonably necessary to the normal operation of the particular business;"[48] and observance of the terms of a bona fide seniority or employee benefit plan.[49]

The Equal Pay Act

The Equal Pay Act (EPA) prohibits employers from engaging in sex discrimination by paying men and women differently.[50] The EPA exempts differential wage payments made pursuant to "(1) a seniority system; (2) a merit system; (3) a system which measures earnings by quantity or quality or production; or (4) a differential based on any other factor than sex."[51] Even though the ministerial exception would apply to employees who are ministers, the EPA contains no exemption for religious organizations that allege their religious beliefs regarding the relative positions of men and women require men to receive higher pay or greater benefits than women.

---

[45] 29 U.S.C. § 623. In order to establish prima facie cases, employees must allege: (1) they experienced unfavorable employment actions; (2) they were least 40; (3) a person or persons younger than themselves received favorable treatment; or (4) allegations revealing evidence from which the inference can be drawn that the reason for employers' actions were the claimants' ages. As with Title VII, once employees establish prima facie cases, the burden shifts to school officials to establish nondiscriminatory reasons for acting. If this occurs, then the burden shifts back to employees, to establish by clear and convincing evidence that employers' reason(s) for acting demonstrated discriminatory pretext.

[46] 29 U.S.C. § 623 (f)(1).

[47] 29 U.S.C. § 623 (f)(3).

[48] 29 U.S.C. § 623 (f)(1).

[49] 29 U.S.C. § 623 (f)(2).

[50] Specifically, the Act prohibits employers from: paying wages to employees . . . at a rate less than the rate at which he pays wages to employees of the opposite sex . . . for equal work on jobs the performance of which required equal skill, effort and responsibility, and which are performed under similar working conditions. 29 U.S.C. § 206 (d)(1).

[51] *Id.*

The Family Medical Leave Act

Congress enacted the Family Medical Leave Act (FMLA) to provide leave for employees who need to care for family members or themselves. The FMLA, applies to "any private elementary or secondary school and an eligible employee of that school."[52] Although the FMLA would not apply to employees who are "ministers," it contains no exemptions for faith-based schools.[53]

The FMLA defines employer as persons engaging in commerce with fifty or more employees;[54] yet, there is no indication that the fifty employees could not also include those in other controlling organizations, such as churches. The FMLA regulations add the term "telecommuting" to the regulations,[55] clarifying that "virtual" employees who work out of their home do not have their personal residences as their work site; rather, they are considered to work in the "office to which they report and from which assignments are made."[56] The FMLA regulations now provide for exigency leave where employees' spouses, children, or parents are on covered active duty.[57]

Employee are eligible for medical and family leave benefits if they have performed at least 1250 hours of service during the previous twelve months for their employers.[58] Leave is twelve work weeks during any twelve-month period and can be used for the following:

1. The birth of a son or daughter of the employee . . . and to care for the child;
2. placement of a child with the employee for adoption or foster care;
3. care for the spouse, son, daughter, or parent of the employee if such spouse, son, daughter, or parent has a serious medical condition; or
4. an employee's serious health condition that makes the employee unable to perform the functions of the position.[59]

If employers provide paid leave for fewer than twelve work weeks, employees may take the balance as unpaid leave.[60] However, if employees elect to take paid leave, they must follow the paid leave policies of their employers with respect to use of leave.[61] Employers must continue to provide group health plan coverage during FMLA leave under the same terms as offered to

---

[52] 29 U.S.C. § 2618 (1)(1)(B).

[53] See the discussion of the ministerial exception in the introduction to this chapter.

[54] 29 U.S.C. § 2611 (4)(A).

[55] 29 C.F.R. § 825.111(a)(2).

[56] Id.

[57] 29 C.F.R. § 825.126(a).

[58] 29 U.S.C. § 2611 (2)(A)(i). See Rollins v. Wilson Cnty. Gov't, 967 F. Supp. 990 (M.D. Tenn. 1997) (declaring that the time an employee worked for the school system could not be aggregated with time she worked for the county government to establish eligibility where two employing entities were created by different state acts, they performed differing governmental functions, they were administered separately, and her terms of employment changed when she began working for the county).

[59] 29 U.S.C. § 2612 (a)(1).

[60] 29 U.S.C. § 2612 (d)(1).

[61] 29 U.S.C. § 2612(d)(2); 29 C.F.R. § 825.207(a).

employees not on leave[62] and employee entitlements to benefits other than group health plan coverage during FMLA leave is determined by employers' established policies for providing such benefits during other forms of leave.[63]

When leave for medical treatment, birth, or adoption is "foreseeable" according to standards in the FMLA, "the employee shall provide the employer with not less than thirty days' notice."[64] However, where medical treatment, birth, or adoption must occur in fewer than thirty days, employees are required to provide only such "notice as is practicable."[65] Under specified conditions, employers may require "certification issued by the health care provider of the eligible employee or of the son, spouse, or parent of the employee, as appropriate."[66]

On returning from the FMLA leave, except for specific highly compensated employees, individuals are to be restored "to the position of employment held by the employee when the leave commenced . . . or . . . to an equivalent position with equivalent employment benefits, pay, and other terms and conditions of employment."[67] Employees maintain this right to reinstatement even if they have been replaced or their positions have been restructured to accommodate their absences.[68] The FMLA regulations have requirements pertaining to pay increases and bonuses.[69]

Special Rules for Classroom Teachers

The FMLA contains special exceptions for individuals who work primarily as classroom teachers or in other roles that are predominately instructional. If teachers request intermittent or reduced schedule leaves for foreseeable medical care and are likely to be absent for more than 20% of the total working days during leave periods, school officials have two options. First, school officials may either require teachers to take leaves for periods not in excess of the length of their planned treatments. Alternatively, officials may temporarily transfer teachers to other jobs with equivalent pay and benefits.[70]

Similarly, three exceptions apply to teachers who wish to take leaves near the end of school terms. These exceptions are designed to prevent the disruption of teachers leaving for multiple weeks and then returning. First, if teachers wish to take leaves of more than three weeks, but intend to return during the last three weeks of school terms, educational officials may require teachers to wait until the end of the terms. Second, if teachers request leaves of more than two weeks during the last five weeks of terms and intend to return during

---

[62] 29 U.S.C. § 2614(c)(1).

[63] 29 C.F.R. § 825.209(h).

[64] 29 U.S.C. § 2612 (e)(1).

[65] 29 U.S.C. §§ 2612 (e)(1), (2)(B).

[66] 29 U.S.C. § 2613 (a).

[67] 29 U.S.C. § 2614 (a).

[68] 29 C.F.R. § 825.214(a).

[69] See 29 C.F.R. § 825.216(a), (b).

[70] 29 U.S.C.A. § 2618(c).

the last two weeks of the term, school officials may require them to postpone their leaves until after terms end. Finally, if teachers request leaves of at least five working days during the last three weeks of school terms, school officials may require them to not take a leave until the end of the terms.[71]

Retaliation Claims

The federal antidiscrimination laws contain independent prohibitions against retaliation. Under Title VII, for example, the antiretaliation provision makes it unlawful for an employer:

> to discriminate against any of his employees or applicants for employment ... because [such employee or applicant] has opposed any practice made an unlawful employment practice by this subchapter, or because he has made a charge, testified, assisted, or participated in any manner in an investigation, proceeding, or hearing under this subchapter.[72]

Similar provisions appear in the Americans with Disabilities Act[73] and the Age Discrimination in Employment Act.[74] As with the substantive discrimination statutes, the antiretaliation provisions are inapplicable to individual employees who are "ministers."[75]

Conclusion

Even if they do not receive federal funds, faith-based and other nonpublic schools are subject to many federal antidiscrimination laws including the Americans with Disabilities Act, the Age Discrimination in Employment Act, the Equal Pay Act, and the Family and Medical Leave Act. While the constitutionally mandated "ministerial exception" means that these statutes are inapplicable to some employees in faith-based schools, the statutes are applicable to all other employees and, in the case of the Americans with Disabilities Act, to students. Additionally, when employees assert rights under these statutes, school officials may not retaliate. Accordingly, officials in all faith-based and other nonpublic schools should carefully monitor their obligations under these statutes, making every effort to comply with their provisions.

---

[71] 29 U.S.C.A. § 2618(d).

[72] 42 U.S.C. §2000e-3(a). In 2013, the Supreme Court ruled that "Title VII retaliation claims must be proved according to traditional principles of but-for causation, not the lessened causation test stated in [the statutory text]. This requires proof that the unlawful retaliation would not have occurred in the absence of the alleged wrongful action or actions of the employer." Univ. of Tex. SW. Med. Ctr. v. Nassar, 570 U.S. 338, 360 (2013).

[73] 42 U.S.C. § 12203(a), (b).

[74] 29 U.S.C. § 623(d).

[75] For a discussion of the ministerial exception, see the introduction to this chapter.

Discussion Questions

1. What steps should officials in faith-based schools take to ensure that an employee is covered by the ministerial exception?

2. What steps should officials in faith-based schools take to require that some of its employees are required to adhere to the faith tenets of the school?

3. What steps should officials in faith-based schools take to comply with the Americans with Disabilities Act as applied to employees?

4. What steps should officials in faith-based schools take to comply with the Americans with Disabilities Act as applied to students?

5. What steps should officials in faith-based schools take to avoid retaliation claims?

Key Words

Americans with Disabilities Act
Antidiscrimination
Equal Pay Act
Family & Medical Leave Act
Ministerial exception
Title VII

11

Special Topics

Charles J. Russo

Contents

Introduction / 309
Copyright / 309
       Copyright Protection / 309
       Fair Use / 311
       Works for Hire / 313
       Educational-Use Exemption / 314
       Multiple Photocopying / 315
       Civil Penalties / 316
       Digital Millennium Copyright Act of 1998 / 316
       The Technology, Education, and Copyright Harmonization Act / 317
Immigration and Reform Control Act / 318
Family Educational Rights and Privacy Act / 319
Conclusion / 325
Discussion Questions / 325
Key Words / 325
Appendices A, B, C, D / 326–333

Introduction

This chapter reviews three special topics that arise with some frequency in nonpublic schools, but are not dealt with elsewhere in this book: copyright, immigration law in institutional hiring and student loans, and student records. While these issues are infrequently litigated in nonpublic schools, boards, educational leaders, and their lawyers can stay ahead of the proverbial curve in helping their schools to function effectively within the boundaries of the law by developing sound policies and procedures associated with these topics.

Copyright

Copyright Protection

Under the Copyright Act of 1976, copyrights are automatic. In order to have copyright protection, individuals are neither obligated to register their works with the United States Copyright Office nor to place copyright notices on their works. Copyright protection in the United States applies to published and unpublished original[1] works fixed in tangible media of expression that can be "perceived, reproduced, or otherwise communicated."[2]

"Works of authorship include the following categories: (1) literary works; (2) musical works, including any accompanying words; (3) dramatic works, including any accompanying music; (4) pantomimes and choreographic works; (5) pictorial, graphic, and sculptural works; (6) motion pictures and other audiovisual works; (7) sound recordings; . . .."[3] Copyright protection does not extend to "any idea[s]" or facts.[4]

Congress amended the Copyright Act in 2008, providing that "no civil action for infringement of the copyright in any United States work shall be instituted until preregistration or registration of the copyright claim has been made in accordance with this title."[5] A copyright notice

> consists of the following three elements: (1) the symbol © (the letter C in a circle), or the word "Copyright", or the abbreviation "Copr."; (2) the year of first publication of the work [with special rules for compilations or derivative works]; and, (3) the name of the owner of copyright in the work.[6]

Copyrights entitle their owners to "a bundle of exclusive rights," among which are reproduction of their works; preparation of derivatives or adaptations based on the original works; distribution of copies of the works to the public by sales, gifts, rentals, leases, or lending; performance of the works publicly; and displays of the works publicly.[7] The Copyright Act created special rights for authors of visual art, including not to have their names identified as the creators of visual arts that have been distorted, mutilated, or modified.[8]

The duration of copyright protection has expanded over time, most recently with the Sonny Bono Copyright Term Extension Act of 1989. Works created after January 1, 1978 are protected for the lives of their author or creators plus seventy years; for corporate authors, copyright is the shorter of 95 years from a work's first publication, or 120 years from when it was created. For works

---

[1] Feist Publications v. Rural Telephone Serv. Co., 499 U.S. 340, 354 (1991), ruling that protected works must be original to authors and must possess "at least some minimal degree of creativity," explaining that the amount of effort involved is irrelevant because what matters is the originality and transformative value of new works. The Court defended the rights of users, adding that "copyright assures authors the right to their original . . . expression, but encourages others to build freely upon the ideas and information conveyed by a work." *Feist*, at 349-350.

[2] 17 U.S.C.A. § 102(a).

[3] *Id.*

[4] 17 U.S.C.A. §102(b). *See also* Feist Publications v. Rural Telephone Serv. Co., 499 U.S. 340, 344 (1991) ("facts are not copyrightable").

[5] 17 U.S.C.A. § 411(a).

[6] 17 U.S.C.A. § 401(b)(1-3).

[7] 17 U.S.C.A. § 106.

[8] 17 U.S.C.A. § 106A(a).

created prior to 1978, the term is whichever is shorter: the life of the author plus 70 years, or December 31, 2047.[9]

Fair Use

Perhaps no change in the law impacted education more than the 1976 Copyright Act, the cornerstone of copyright law, which established the fair use doctrine. While copyright owners have the right to reproduce their works, users may be able to make copies by claiming "fair use" under specified situations.

The Copyright Act provides that reproduction of copyrighted material for "criticism, comment, news reporting, teaching (including multiple copies for classroom use), scholarship or research, is not an infringement of copyright."[10] The Copyright Act assesses fair use according to four factors:

(1) the purpose and character of the use, including whether such use is of a commercial nature or is for nonprofit educational purposes;

(2) the nature of the copyrighted work;

(3) the amount and substantiality of the portion used in relation to the copyrighted work as a whole; and

(4) the effect of the use upon the potential market for or value of the copyrighted work.[11]

Unfortunately, the Act does not definitively define fair use, though. Moreover, because it was written prior to the advent of personal computers and the Internet, this section has engendered a great deal of confusion about what constitutes fair use in today's media-rich educational institutions.

On a related issue, the Copyright Act does not limit the remedies federal courts can award in enforcing its provisions in affording the judiciary broad authority to grant injunctive relief.[12] Whether injunctive relief is awarded to copyright holders for alleged copyright fair use violations depends on weighing all four factors, not all of which have equal value such that a prevailing party need not win on all four.[13]

---

[9]   17 U.S.C.A. § 302

[10] 17 U.S.C.A. § 107.

[11] *Id.*

[12] 17 U.S.C.A. § 502(a). *See* Perfect 10 v. Amazon.com, 508 F.3d 1146, 1154, n.1 (9th Cir. 2007) (…"the Copyright Act gives courts broad authority to issue injunctive relief. *See* 17 U.S.C. § 502(a)"…).

[13] *See* Harper & Row, Publishers v. Nation Enters., 471 U.S. 539 (1985) (upholding an award of damages where the magazine's unauthorized publication of verbatim quotes from essentially the "heart" of unpublished presidential memoirs, even though only 300 copyrightable words, amounted to 13% of the infringing article and was intended to supplant copyright the holders' commercially valuable right of first publication). For cases involving education, see NXIVM Corp. v. Ross Inst., 364 F.3d 471 (2d Cir. 2004) (denying injunctive relief for the producer of seminar materials against a website owner that posted seminar materials on its website where only the second factor weighed in favor of the copyright owner; the second, third, and fourth in favor of the owner of the letters); Educ. Testing Serv. v. Katzman, 793 F.2d 533 (3d Cir. 1986) (upholding an injunction against the use of test questions similar to those of the plaintiff in preparing students scoring higher on the Scholastic Aptitude Test, uncovering likely violations of all four factors in rejecting the defense that the materials were used for teaching purposes).

In a case on point from Illinois, the Seventh Circuit balanced the copyright interest of a school board in creating and copyrighting a series of standardized tests, the "Chicago Academic Standards Exams" (CASE), with a teacher's interest in publishing the materials "because he thought them bad tests and he could best demonstrate this by publishing them in full."[14] The court began its analysis by observing that "[t]here is no analytical difference between destroying the market for a copyrighted work by producing and selling cheap copies and destroying the subsequent years' market for a standardized test by blowing its cover."[15]

The court conceded that the school board was correct that the teacher "[had done] it harm going beyond the force of his criticisms [by printing the full tests]."[16] The court further noted that "[c]opyright should not be a means by which criticism is stifled with the backing of the courts."[17] Acknowledging that the Copyright Act's four fair use factors "are not exhaustive and do not constitute an algorithm that enables decisions to be ground out mechanically,"[18] the best the court could offer as a judicial standard is that fair use copiers must copy no more than is reasonably necessary to enable them to pursue aims the law recognizes as proper, in this situation criticizing the copyrighted work effectively.

Rounding out its rationale, the court explained that the school board's tests qualified as "secure tests"[19] under the Copyright Act. As such, the court ordered that, on remand, an injunction should "enjoin the defendants, and those in privity with them or with notice of the injunction, just from copying or publishing or otherwise distributing copies of secure Chicago public school tests, in whole or substantial part, in which the school board has valid and subsisting copyright, without the board's authorization."[20]

Litigation involving fair use in the classroom is rare. In a case from California, when a teacher who had written and copyrighted a thirty-five-page booklet on cake decorating sold it to her students for $2.00, a colleague sued her, alleging that the teacher violated her rights under copyright law by having taken most of the materials from her book. Treating this as a copyright violation, the Ninth Circuit determined that the defendant violated the first and third fair use factors. As to the first factor, the court pointed to a "strong indication of no fair use," where the book was copied for the same intrinsic

---

[14] Chicago Bd. of Educ. v. Substance, 354 F.3d 624, 627 [184 Educ. L. Rep. 112] (7th Cir. 2003), *cert. denied*, 543 U.S. 816 [192 Educ. L. Rep. 302] (2004).

[15] *Id.*

[16] *Id.* at 629.

[17] *Id.* at 628.

[18] *Id.* at 629.

[19] According to 37 C.F.R. § 202.20(b)(3), "The term[] secure test ... ha[s] the meaning[] set forth in" 37 C.F.R. 202.13(b)(1): (1) A secure test is a nonmarketed test administered under supervision at specified centers on scheduled dates, all copies of which are accounted for and either destroyed or returned to restricted locked storage following each administration.

[20] *Chicago Bd.*, 354 F.3d at 632.

purpose "for which the copyright owner intended it to be used" [21] and where the defendant failed to secure permission or provide attribution to the plaintiff. As to the third factor, the court reasoned the "defendant had engaged in virtually verbatim copying," [22] insofar as the 50% of her booklet taken from the plaintiff's constituted the substance of the latter's work.

Works for Hire

The Copyright Act identifies two categories of works made for hire.[23] The first involves works prepared by employees within the scope of employment that is ordinarily considered the property of their employers, unless the parties signed written agreements to the contrary. In a case from New York, the Second Circuit affirmed that because a teacher's prepared tests, quizzes, and homework problems developed for classroom use were works for hire, once he was suspended from work and did not take the materials with him when he left the building, he could not rely on a subpoena to recover the items.[24] The court concluded that because the teacher prepared the materials for use in his classes, they were the property of the school as works for hire.

On the other hand, a year later, a federal trial court in New York was convinced that a triable question of fact existed as to whether the manual a high school teacher developed to teach a new course involving science research was a work for hire.[25] The legal theory at issue is interesting, because the board raised the work-for-hire claim in arguing essentially that since the teacher developed the manual for use in his class, it was a work for hire, thereby precluding his copyright infringement claim. The plaintiff eventually prevailed in part and was awarded some damages for a copyright infringement.[26] This case is a reminder that materials developed and used by teachers for classes can be subject to "work for hire" challenges to copyright protection.[27]

The second kind of work for hire is one "specially ordered or commissioned for use as a contribution to a collective work, as a part of a motion picture or other audiovisual work, as a translation, as a supplementary work, as a compilation, as an instructional text, as a test, as answer material for a test, or as an atlas, if the parties expressly agree in a written instrument signed by them that the work shall be considered a work made for hire.[28] These items

---

[21] Marcus v. Rowley , 695 F.2d 1171, 1175 [8 Educ. L. Rep. 258] (9th Cir. 1983).
[22] *Id.* at 1177.
[23] 17 U.S.C.A.§ 101.
[24] Shaul v. Cherry Valley-Springfield Cent. Sch. Dist., 363 F.3d 177 [186 Educ. L. Rep. 604] (2d Cir. 2004).
[25] Pavlica v. Behr, 397 F. Supp. 2d 519 [204 Educ. L. Rep. 560] (S.D.N.Y. 2005).
[26] Pavlica v. Behr, 2006 WL 1596763 (S.D.N.Y. 2006).
[27] *See* Shaul v. Cherry Valley-Springfield Cent. Sch. Dist., 363 F.3d 177 [186 Educ. L. Rep. 604] (2d Cir. 2004). *But see* Weinstein v. Univ. of Ill., 811 F.2d 1091 [37 Educ. L. Rep. 1089] (7th Cir. 1987) (affirming that work for hire is inapplicable to publications in higher education even though faculty members are required to publish).
[28] 17 U.S.C.A. § 101.

are not considered to be works for hire unless the parties have signed written agreements designating the materials as such.

Educational-Use Exemption

The Copyright Act permits the performance or display of a work by instructors or pupils in the course of face-to-face teaching activities of a nonprofit educational institution, in a classroom or similar place devoted to instruction, unless, in the case of a motion picture or other audiovisual work, the performance, or the display of individual images, is given by means of a copy that was not lawfully made under this title, and that the person responsible for the performance knew or had reason to believe was not lawfully made.[29]

This permitted use includes the "performance of a nondramatic literary or musical work or of a dramatico-musical work of a religious nature, or display of a work, in the course of services at a place of worship or other religious assembly."[30] As noted, this definition excludes audiovisual works not "lawfully made under this title, and that the person responsible for the performance knew or had reason to believe was not lawfully made."[31]

The use of face-to-face instruction has been extended to include online classes transmitted by means of interactive digital networks, including "[b]y faculty of massive open online courses (MOOCs) offered by accredited nonprofit educational institutions."[32] For post-secondary institutions, accreditation is defined as regional or national accreditation organizations approved by the Council of Higher Education Accreditation or the United States Department of Education.[33] For elementary and secondary schools, accreditation means recognition "by the applicable state certification or licensing procedures."[34]

The e-course exemption allows teachers to both perform and display, via digital technology, entire nondramatic literary and musical works, as well as reasonable and limited portions of any type of audiovisual work. This expanded range of educational use of materials is inapplicable to materials designed for distance-learning markets or works not lawfully made or acquired; materials not directly related to teaching content and limited to reception for students in classes for which the transmission is being made; materials not analogous to typical classrooms; transmissions lacking safeguards to prevent student retention and redistribution of transmitted materials; or the making of digital copies used for other than authorized transmissions.[35]

---

[29] 17 U.S.C.A. § 110(1).

[30] 17 U.S.C.A. § 10(3).

[31] 17 U.S.C.A. § 110(1). Relatively little attention is given in the Copyright Act to the definition of what has been "lawfully made." The Supreme Court, in Sony Corp. v. Universal City Studio, 464 U.S. 417 (1984), ruled that off-the-air copying of commercial television for time-shifting would be "lawfully made" and, presumably, could be used in teaching students in classrooms. *See* 17 U.S.C.A.§ 109 (c).

[32] 37 C.R.R. § 201.40(b)(1)(v).

[33] 17 U.S.C.A. § 110(11A).

[34] 17 U.S.C.A. § 110(11B).

[35] 17 U.S.C.A. § 110 (2) (A)-(D).

At the same time, the Copyright Act permits the making of copies of digital works and digitizing them to portions of analog works. However, the conversion of analog or print works into digital formats is impermissible unless no digital version of the analog version is available or "the digital version of the work that is available to the institution is subject to technological protection measures that prevent its use for [lawful transmission under] section 110(2)."[36]

Multiple Photocopying

Section 107 of the Copyright Act indicates that multiple photocopying for classroom distribution is fair use.[37] This type of photocopying is controlled by an agreement negotiated among groups representing authors, publishers, and educators. In addition, a music educators and music publishers negotiated a separate agreement regarding music copying. These agreements are in Appendix B.

The music limitations are much more narrowly drawn and much clearer than the classroom guidelines. Section 108 of the Copyright Act limits library photocopies to one copy of items to be used for "private study, scholarship, or research."[38] In addition, libraries are required to have, at the location where copies are made, "a warning of copyright in accordance with requirements that the Register of Copyrights shall prescribe by regulation."[39] The Agreement On Guidelines For Classroom Copying in Not-For-Profit Educational Institutions is in Appendix B at the end of this chapter.

Civil Penalties

Copyright infringement litigation can involve actions for injunctive relief and/or damages. Copyright owners can elect to prove actual damages or can use the measure of statutory damages provided in the act. Once copyright owners elect a measure of damages, either actual or statutory, this becomes the exclusive remedy.[40] Actual damages can be recovered for lost profits and lost royalties.[41]

The range of statutory damages depends on the willfulness of violations. Damages for non-willful infringements range from a minimum of $750 to a

---

[36] 17 U.S.C.A. § 112 (f)(2).

[37] 17 U.S.C.A. § 107 (…the fair use of a copyrighted work, including such use by reproduction in copies or phonorecords or by any other means specified by that section, for purposes such as criticism, comment, news reporting, teaching (including multiple copies for classroom use), scholarship, or research, is not an infringement of copyright.").

[38] 17 U.S.C.A. § 108 (d)(1).

[39] 17 U.S.C.A. § 108 (e)(2). The warning authorized under the Copyright Act is promulgated as 37 C.F.R. § 201.14(b); it appears as Appendix A at the end of this chapter.

[40] See Basic Books v. Kinko's Graphics Corp., 758 F. Supp. 1522, 1543 [66 Educ. L. Rep. 983] (S.D.N.Y. 1991).

[41] See, e.g., Applied Innovations v. Regents of Univ. of Minn., 876 F.2d 626, 637 [54 Educ. L. Rep. 146] (8th Cir. 1989) (affirming a damages award of $226,598 to the licensee for lost profits and $162,161 to the copyright owner for lost royalties from a computer software developer for infringements of copyrighted psychological test materials).

maximum of $30,000 for each violation.[42] Awards for willful violations can be as high as $150,000 per charge.[43] In the case of copyright infringements where the "infringer was not aware and had no reason to believe that his or her acts constituted an infringement of copyright," courts, in their discretion, may reduce awards of statutory damages to sums not less than $200 for each violation.[44] For agents or employees of educational institutions acting in the scope of their employment who "believed or had reasonable grounds for believing that his or her use of copyrighted work was fair use," courts "shall remit statutory damages."[45]

Digital Millennium Copyright Act of 1998

Congress enacted the Digital Millennium Copyright Act of 1998 in order to set criteria regarding the copyright liability of online service providers (OSP), logical access providers, and users.[46] The act responded to earlier case law suggesting that OSPs might be vicariously liable for copyright infringements by users.[47] Along with providing safe havens for transitory communications,[48] systems caching,[49] information residing on systems or networks at the direction of users,[50] and information location tools,[51] the act limits liability for nonprofit educational institutions.

The infringing activities of faculty members and students cannot be imputed to their institutions if online access has not been provided as part of required course materials during the preceding three years, institutions have not received more than two notifications of infringements during the prior three years, and institutions provide all system users with notice of copyright law compliance.

One provision in the act should be of particular interest to instructional personnel. A regulation promulgated pursuant to the act allows teachers to incorporate "short portions of motion pictures into new works for the purpose of criticism or comment."[52]

---

[42] 17 U.S.C.A. § 504(c)(1).

[43] 17 U.S.C.A. § 504(c)(2).

[44] *Id.*

[45] 17 U.S.C.A. § 504 (c)(1).

[46] 17 U.S.C. §§ 512, 1201-1205, 1301-1332, 4001.

[47] *See* Fonovisa v. Cherry Auction, 76 F.3d 259 (9th Cir. 1996) (imposing liability on the owner-operator of a swap meet where pirated tapes were sold; the concept of rendering the owner of space where copyright violations occurred liable arguably applies to OSPs providing online technology space).

[48] 17 U.S.C.A. § 512(a) (limits liability of OSPs that transmit information at the request of subscribers).

[49] 17 U.S.C.A. § 512 (b) (limits liability of OSPs that retain a copy of online material placed there other than by the OSP and then transmitted to a subscriber).

[50] 17 U.S.C.A. § 512 (c) (exempts OSPs from liability if, on notification by the copyright owner of infringement, they remove or block access to infringing material).

[51] 17 U.S.C.A. § 512 (d) (exempts logical access providers, including web search engines, on the same bases as OSPs).

[52] 37 C.F.R. § 201.40.

The Technology, Education, and Copyright Harmonization Act

Aware of the growing reliance on online distance education via the Internet and cyber schools, Congress enacted the Technology, Education, and Copyright Harmonization (TEACH) Act of 2002, expanding copyright exceptions for educational and library users.[53] "This important legislation updates sections 110(2) and 112 of the Copyright Act to allow the same activities to take place using digital delivery mechanisms that were permitted under the policy balance that was struck by Congress when the law was enacted in 1976, while introducing safeguards to minimize the additional risks to copyright owners that are inherent in exploiting works in a digital format."[54]

The TEACH Act expands fair use by affording distance learning educators easier access to copyrighted materials as long as school officials satisfy its requirements. The key provisions associated with the TEACH Act are that that schools must remain accredited and not-for-profit; develop and enforce copyright policies; ensure that students and staff are aware of their policies; install safeguards to protect copyrighted materials from external dissemination; and limit the use of copyrighted materials to reasonable, mediated instructional use for classes.

Immigration and Reform Control Act

The Immigration and Reform Control Act (IRCA), enacted in 1974, made all employers part of the Immigration and Naturalization Service (INS) enforcement process.[55] Effective March 2018, a regulation promulgated pursuant to the IRCA requires employers or those acting on their behalf to do two things within three business days of newly hiring individuals.[56] First, someone must "[p]hysically examine the documentation presented by the individual establishing identity and employment authorization ... [to] ensure that the documents presented appear to be genuine and to relate to the individual."[57] Second, someone must "[c]omplete section 2—"Employer Review and Verification"—on the Form I–9 within three business days of the hire and sign the attestation with a handwritten signature or electronic signature...."[58]

Different rules apply to individuals seeking to establish identities and work authorizations, identities only, and work authorizations only. This information appears as Appendix C at the end of this chapter.

---

[53] Technology, Education, and Copyright Harmonization Act, Pub. L. No. 107–273, § 13301, 116 Stat. 1758, 1910 (2002), codified at 17 U.S.C.A. 101 §§ 110, 112, 802.

[54] Statement of Marybeth Peters, The Register of Copyrights before the Senate Committee on the Judiciary United States Senate, 107th Congress, 1st Session, March 13, 2001, Technology, Education and Copyright Harmonization ("TEACH") Act (S. 487), available at https://www.copyright.gov/docs/regstat031301.html

[55] 8 U.S.C.A. §§ 1324, 1324a, 1324b.

[56] 8 C.F.R. § 274a.2(b)(1)(i)(B)(ii). The list of verification requirements for employers hiring individuals who were previously employed appears at C.F.R. § 274a.2(c).

[57] 8 C.F.R. § 274a.2(b)(1)(i)(B)(ii)(A).

[58] 8 C.F.R. § 274a.2(b)(1)(i)(B)(ii)(B).

A regulation incident to the IRCA adds that employers must preserve the I-9, along with verification documents for "three years after the date of the hire or one year after the date the individual's employment is terminated, whichever is later."[59] I-9 forms are subject to inspection by authorized agencies of the federal government "with at least three business days notice prior to an inspection."[60]

Civil penalties for failure to comply with the IRCA include progressive fines from the maximum $2,000 for first-time offenses for each unauthorized alien up to the maximum $10,000 fine for repeat employer offenders.[61] Criminal penalties include fines up to $3,000 and a six-month imprisonment for each violation.[62]

The IRCA also addresses issues involving students receiving federal financial assistance under Title IV of the Higher Education Act of 1965.[63] In order to be eligible for Title IV funds, all students must declare, under penalty of perjury, whether they are citizens of the United States and, if not, whether they have immigrant status not rendering them ineligible for grants, loans, or work assistance under Title IV. The Act mandates specific procedures for verifying the immigration status of students. The federal regulation detailing these procedures is in Appendix D at the end of this chapter

If alien students have improperly received Title IV funds, educational institutions are protected from the imposition of penalties by the Secretary of Education if their officials relied on the INS verification of eligibility procedures or were awaiting INS verification of student.[64] In cases involving guaranteed student loans, guarantees are not voided or payments nullified if they were made prior to prompt notification from educational officials about individuals' ineligibility to the entities making the loans.[65]

The IRCA prohibits discrimination based on national origin or citizenship status. Employers of more than three employees are prohibited from discriminating in hiring or discharging of persons because of individuals' national origin or because they are United States citizens or intending to become citizens.[66] However, the IRCA adds that "it is not an unfair immigration-related employment practice for a person or other entity to prefer to hire, recruit, or refer an individual who is a citizen or national of the United States over another individual who is an alien if the two individuals are equally qualified."[67]

---

[59] 8 C.F.R. § 274a.2(b)(2)(i)

[60] 8 C.F.R. § 274a.2(b)(2)(ii).

[61] 8 U.S.C.A. § 1324a(e)(4).

[62] 8 U.S.C.A. § 1324a(f)(1).

[63] Codified at 20 U.S.C.A. §§ 1070-1091.

[64] 20 U.S.C.A. § 1091(h).

[65] 20 U.S.C.A. § 1091(i).

[66] 8 U.S.C.A. § 1324b(a).

[67] 8 U.S.C.A. § 1324b (a)(4).

Family Educational Rights and Privacy Act

All educational institutions receiving federal assistance administered by the Secretary of Education are subject to the requirements of Family Educational Rights and Privacy Act (FERPA),[68] also known as the Buckley Amendment after its primary sponsor, then-New York Senator James Buckley, and its regulations.[69] However, FERPA "does not apply to an educational agency or institution solely because students attending that agency or institution receive non-monetary benefits under a program [administered by the Secretary of Education], if no funds under that program are made available to the agency or institution."[70] While this definition excludes all religious elementary and secondary schools, because the benefits they receive are non-monetary, post-secondary institutions whose students receive Title IV student grants or loans are subject to FERPA.[71]

FERPA provides parents and eligible students access to their educational records while restricting access to those lacking permission. Under FERPA, on reaching the age of 18 or attending post-secondary institutions, students gain sole control over their educational records.[72] According to one of FERPA's regulations, educational records are those directly related to students and maintained by educational agencies or institutions, or by parties acting for the agencies or institutions.[73] This regulation specifies that records are "any information recorded in any way, including, but not limited to, handwriting, print, film, microfilm, and microfiche."[74]

Items such as student grades or written parental comments become educational records only when school officials exercise control over those items. In *Owasso Independent School Dist. No. I-011 v. Falvo (Falvo)*,[75] a unanimous Supreme Court clarified that the privacy protection attaches to documents under FERPA only when they "are maintained by an educational agency or institution or by a person acting for such agency or institution."[76] At issue in *Falvo* was a teacher's use of peer-grading whereby students grade the papers of their classmates and call out the marks to their teachers. Rejecting a mother's challenge that this practice violated FERPA, the Court held that because the

---

[68] 20 U.S.C.A. § 1232g(d).

[69] 34 C.F.R. §§ 99.1 *et seq.*

[70] 34 C.F.R. § 99.1(b).

[71] 34 C.F.R. § 99.1(c).

[72] 20 U.S.C.A. § 1232g(d).

[73] 34 C.F.R. § 99.3.

[74] 34 C.F.R. § 99.3.

[75] 534 U.S. 426 [161 Educ. L. Rep. 33] (2002). For commentaries on this case, see Ralph D. Mawdsley & Charles J. Russo, *FERPA, Student Privacy and The Classroom: What Can Be Learned from Owasso School District v. Falvo?* 171 Educ. L. Rep. 397 (2003); Ralph D. Mawdsley & Charles J. Russo, *Limiting The Reach of FERPA into The Classroom: Owasso School District v. Falvo,* 165 Educ. L. Rep. 1 (2002).

[76] 20 U.S.C.A. § 1232g (a)(4)(A).

students were not agents for their schools, the grades were not "maintained" by school officials during peer grading.

The *Falvo* Court permitted the mother's case to proceed as a private right of action, an issue it clarified in *Gonzaga University v. Doe (Gonzaga)*.[77] In *Gonzaga*, an undergraduate male filed suit alleging that university officials violated his FERPA rights when, in the face of apparently unsubstantiated accusations of sexual misconduct involving a female, they released his records to state officials without his knowledge or consent. State officials then denied the man's application for certification as a public school teacher.

Absent Congressional intent permitting the student, or anyone, to do so, in *Gonzaga* the Supreme Court ruled that the plaintiff could not file a private right of action against university officials. The upshot is that individuals who are dissatisfied with the contents of their educational records can seek redress only by filing complaints with the Federal Department of Education. Insofar as FERPA does not permit private causes of action, damages claims under Section 1983 for such violations likewise are impermissible.[78]

A case from a federal trial court in Louisiana explored the meaning of "record," applying FERPA's protections to a letter a mother sent to her son's teacher. The letter stated the mother's views on an unspecified politically sensitive issue, while requesting that her son be excluded from school activities that exposed him to teachings contrary to her own opinions.[79] When the mother later ran for political office, the teacher released the letter to the media. The court decided that the mother had claims under common-law invasion of privacy; additionally, school officials had a duty not to violate her rights to procedural due process and under FERPA by providing her notice prior to releasing the letter to her son's teacher to the media. Although the mother no longer had a private claim under FERPA after *Gonzaga*,[80] she still would have had an invasion of privacy tort charge.

According to one of FERPA's regulations, education records are those "kept in the sole possession of the maker, [and] are used only as a personal memory aid, and are not accessible or revealed to any other person except a temporary substitute for the maker of the record;"[81] student employment records;[82] medical records on a student at least eighteen years of age and

---

[77] 536 U.S. 273 [165 EDUC. L. REP. 457] (2002) (eliminating $450,000 of the judgment, but still leaving $655,000 in tort claim recovery). For a commentary on this case, see Ralph D. Mawdsley, *A Section 1983 Cause of Action under IDEA? Measuring the Effect of* Gonzaga University v. Doe, 170 EDUC. L. REP. 425 (2002).

[78] For a discussion of this issue, see Ralph D. Mawdsley, *A Section 1983 Cause of Action under IDEA? Measuring the Effect of* Gonzaga University v. Doe, 170 EDUC. L. REP. 425 (2002).

[79] Warner v. St. Bernard Parish Sch. Bd., 99 F. Supp.2d 748 [145 EDUC. L. REP. 257] (E.D. La. 2000).

[80] 536 U.S. 273 [165 EDUC. L. REP. 457] (2002) (the plaintiff in *Gonzaga* recovered $100,000 for invasion of privacy, a charge not affected by denial of the FERPA claim).

[81] 34 C.F.R. § 99.3 (b)(1).

[82] 34 C.F.R. § 99.3 (b)(3).

attending a higher education institution;[83] and law enforcement records.[84] FER-PA permits educational officials to include "disciplinary action taken against student[s] for conduct that posed a significant risk to the safety or well-being of that student, other students, or other members of the school community" in files and to reveal this information to teachers and school officials, both in the students' schools and elsewhere if they "have legitimate educational interests in the behavior of the student[s]."[85]

FERPA's regulations describe the process by which students and/or their parents have "opportunit[ies] for ... hearing[s] ... to challenge the content[s] of . . . [their] education records."[86] Dissatisfied parties can seek hearings that officers must conduct and resolve within reasonable time periods.[87] If hearing officers agree that challenged materials are inaccurate, misleading, or violate the rights of students to privacy, they can order officials to amend them, informing students and/or their parents in writing that this has been done.[88] If hearing officers think the materials are not inaccurate, misleading, or in violation of students' privacy rights, the records need not be amended.[89] Parents and/or students who still disagree with the materials at issue can add to the records statements explaining their objections. These statements must be kept with the contested information for as long as the records are kept on file.[90]

Disclosure of information in students' educational records, either to themselves or others, means "to permit access to or the release, transfer, or other communication of education records, or the personally identifiable information contained in those records, to any party, by any means, including oral, written, or electronic means."[91] "Personally identifiable information" protects the students' identities and includes, but is not limited to—

(a) The student's name;

(b) The name of the student's parent or other family members;

(c) The address of the student or student's family;

(d) A personal identifier, such as the student's social security number, student number, or biometric record;

(e) Other indirect identifiers, such as the student's date of birth, place of birth, and mother's maiden name;

(f) Other information that, alone or in combination, is linked or linkable to a specific student that would allow a reasonable person in the school community, who does not have personal knowledge of the relevant circumstances, to identify the student with reasonable certainty; or

---

[83] 34 C.F.R. § 99.3 (b)(4).

[84] 34 C.F.R. § 99.3 (b)(2).

[85] 20 U.S.C.A.§ 1232g(h).

[86] 20 U.S.C.A. § 1232g(a)(2).

[87] 34 C.F.R. § 99.22.

[88] 34 C.F.R. §§ 99.21(b)(1), 300.620(a).

[89] 34 C.F.R. §§ 99.21(b)(2), 300.620(b).

[90] 34 C.F.R. §§ 99.21(c), 300.620(c).

[91] 34 C.F.R. § 99.3.

(g) Information requested by a person who the educational agency or institution reasonably believes knows the identity of the student to whom the education record relates. [92]

In order to facilitate the normal operation of an educational institution subject to FERPA, the kinds of information that are generally not considered to be harmful or invasions of privacy, if disclosed, are referred to as "directory information." Directory information can be revealed without securing permission each time the materials are released:

(a) Directory information includes, but is not limited to, the student's name; address; telephone listing; electronic mail address; photograph; date and place of birth; major field of study; grade level; enrollment status (e.g., undergraduate or graduate, full-time or part-time); dates of attendance; participation in officially recognized activities and sports; weight and height of members of athletic teams; degrees, honors, and awards received; and the most recent educational agency or institution attended.

(b) Directory information does not include a student's—

(1) Social security number; or

(2) Student identification (ID) number, except as provided in paragraph (c) of this definition.

(c) In accordance with paragraphs (a) and (b) of this definition, directory information includes—

(1) A student ID number, user ID, or other unique personal identifier used by a student for purposes of accessing or communicating in electronic systems, but only if the identifier cannot be used to gain access to education records except when used in conjunction with one or more factors that authenticate the user's identity, such as a personal identification number (PIN), password or other factor known or possessed only by the authorized user; and

(2) A student ID number or other unique personal identifier that is displayed on a student ID badge, but only if the identifier cannot be used to gain access to education records except when used in conjunction with one or more factors that authenticate the user's identity, such as a PIN, password, or other factor known or possessed only by the authorized user. [93]

Educational officials have the duty to notify parents or eligible students annually of the kinds of information considered to be "directory information," [94] usually via statements in student handbooks; unless parent or qualified student objects, they can reveal this information. Apart from directory information,

---

[92] 34 C.F.R. § 99.3.

[93] 34 C.F.R. § 99.3. This section further defines other terms within this definition. "Attendance" can be "in person or by correspondence [or] working under a work-study program." "Dates of attendance" means a period of time such as "an academic year, a spring semester, or a first quarter," but does not mean "specific daily records of a student's attendance at an educational agency or institution."

[94] 20 U.S.C.A.§ 1232g (a)(5)(B); 34 C.F.R. § 99.6 (a)(6).

FERPA contains exceptions permitting student information to be revealed without student disclosure or consent. Key items not subject to consent include granting access to records to officials in schools to which students applied;[95] federal, state, and local officials for law enforcement purposes;[96] those evaluating student eligibility for financial aid;[97] organizations conducting studies on behalf of educational agencies or institutions;[98] accrediting agencies;[99] parents of dependent children;[100] persons who protect the health and safety of students or others in emergency situations;[101] subpoenaed records;[102] Secretary of Agriculture and other officials of the Food and Nutrition Service;[103] and caseworkers or representatives of child welfare agencies[104]

FERPA permits officials in institutions of higher education to reveal to parents the alcohol and drug violations of their children if they are under the age of 21 and if their actions also constitute disciplinary violations.[105] As part of the War on Terrorism, FERPA permits a person at a position no lower than the Assistant Attorney General to secure an ex parte order to "collect . . . retain, disseminate, and use" education records for the purpose of investigating or prosecuting offenses involving "an act of domestic or international terrorism."[106]

Officials in educational institutions must comply with requests for records within forty-five days and cannot destroy records once requests are made.[107] Institutional officials can charge fees for duplication of requested records, unless doing so "prevents [an] eligible student from exercising the right to inspect [his or her] education records. . . ."[108] When personally identifiable information has been disclosed, the parties to whom the information has been disclosed cannot then share it with third parties without the consent of parents or eligible students.[109]

FERPA permits the disclosure of disciplinary information to other students under specified circumstances. Post-secondary institutions are permitted to notify the victims of crimes of violence[110] or nonforcible sex offenses about "the final results of any disciplinary proceeding conducted by such institution

---

[95] 20 U.S.C.A. § 1232g(b)(1)(B) (with appropriate notice).

[96] 20 U.S.C.A. §§ 1232g(b)(1)(C), (E).

[97] 20 U.S.C.A. § 1232g(b)(1)(D).

[98] 20 U.S.C.A. § 1232g(b)(1)(F).

[99] 20 U.S.C.A. § 1232g(b)(1)(G).

[100] 20 U.S.C.A. § 1232g(b)(1)(H).

[101] 20 U.S.C.A. § 1232g(b)(1)(I).

[102] 20 U.S.C.A. § 1232g(b)(1)(J) (with appropriate notice).

[103] 20 U.S.C.A. § 1232g(b)(1)(K) (also calling for the destruction of personally identifiable data no longer needed for program purposes).

[104] 20 U.S.C.A. § 1232g(b)(1)(L).

[105] 20 U.S.C.A. § 1232g(i).

[106] 20 U.S.C.A. § 1232g(j). *See* 18 U.S.C.A. § 2232b(g)(5)(B) for a list of the areas of concern in collecting information.

[107] 20 U.S.C.A.§ 1232g(a)(1)(A); 34 C.F.R. § 99.10.

[108] 34 C.F.R. § 99.11.

[109] 34 C.F.R. § 99.33.

[110] *See* 18 U.S.C.A. § 16 for definition of crimes of violence.

against the alleged perpetrator of such crime or offense with respect to such crime or offense."[111]

In addition, officials of post-secondary institutions presumably can disclose, to students who are generally on campuses, the final results of disciplinary proceedings involving crimes of violence or nonforcible sex offenses. Officials can release this information "if the institution determines as a result of that disciplinary proceeding that the student committed a violation of the institution['s] rules or policies with respect to such crime or offense."[112]

FERPA further clarifies that "final results" means "the name of the student, the violation committed, and any sanction imposed by the institution on that student," but includes the name of another student such as a victim or witness "only with [their] written consent."[113] Moreover, officials in post-secondary institutions can disclose the names of registered sex offenders revealed to them under the Jacob Wetterling Crimes Against Children and Sexually Violent Offender Registration Program Act.[114]

Most elementary and secondary nonpublic schools are not subject to FERPA. Still, officials in these schools need to consider whether adherence, if not to the letter then at least to the spirit of the law as spelled out in FERPA, serves the best interests of their school communities. Providing students or their parents access to their records is an effective method of assuring that they are correct and current. Anecdotal comments about students' behaviors in elementary grades, when they demonstrated good conduct in high school, hardly seem worth keeping. At the very least, students or their parents should be able to submit responses to challenged information in their files, at which point school officials may want to reconsider whether retaining the information is really necessary.

Conclusion

As noted at the introduction to this chapter, litigation involving copyright, immigration law in institutional hiring and student loans, and student records is uncommon in educational institutions. Still, the better informed that boards, educational leaders, and their attorneys are by devising sound policies and procedures, then the better able they will be to meet the needs of their faculties, staffs, and students on these potentially important questions.

---

[111] 20 U.S.C.A. § 1232g (b)(6)(A).

[112] 20 U.S.C.A. § 1232g (b)(6)(B).

[113] 20 U.S.C.A. § 1232g(b)(6)(C).

[114] 20 U.S.C.A. § 1232g(b)(7)(A); 42 U.S.C.A. §§ 14072 (e), (j).

Discussion Questions

1. What would you do to help building-level educators better understand the parameters of copyright law, especially with regard to copying materials for use in class?

2. Has a situation or controversy ever arisen in your educational institution, regardless of its level, about the application of works for hire in terms of the fruits of the labors of educators in your school, college, and/or university?

3. Do you know who is responsible in your school, or school system, for ensuring compliance with the Immigration and Reform Control Act?

4. Do you think it wise that FERPA transfers sole control over their records to students when the turn 18 years of age or attend post-secondary institutions?

5. Do you think that FERPA should be made fully applicable to faith-based and other nonpublic schools?

Key Words

Copyright
Fair use,
Immigration
Photocopying
Student records
Works for hire

Appendix A

The warning authorized under the Copyright Act, 37 C.F.R. § 201.14(b):

(b) Contents. A Display Warning of Copyright and an Order Warning of Copyright shall consist of a verbatim reproduction of the following notice, printed in such size and form and displayed in such manner as to comply with paragraph (c) of this section:

NOTICE WARNING CONCERNING COPYRIGHT RESTRICTIONS

The copyright law of the United States (title 17, United States Code) governs the making of photocopies or other reproductions of copyrighted material.

Under certain conditions specified in the law, libraries and archives are authorized to furnish a photocopy or other reproduction. One of these specific conditions is that the photocopy or reproduction is not to be "used for any purpose other than private study, scholarship, or research." If a user makes a request for, or later uses, a photocopy or reproduction for purposes in excess of "fair use," that user may be liable for copyright infringement.

This institution reserves the right to refuse to accept a copying order if, in its judgment, fulfillment of the order would involve violation of copyright law.

(c) Form and manner of use.

(1) A Display Warning of Copyright shall be printed on heavy paper or other durable material in type at least 18 points in size, and shall be displayed prominently, in such manner and location as to be clearly visible, legible, and comprehensible to a casual observer within the immediate vicinity of the place where orders are accepted.

(2) An Order Warning of Copyright shall be printed within a box located prominently on the order form itself, either on the front side of the form or immediately adjacent to the space calling for the name or signature of the person using the form. The notice shall be printed in type size no smaller than that used predominantly throughout the form, and in no case shall the type size be smaller than eight points. The notice shall be printed in such manner as to be clearly legible, comprehensible, and readily apparent to a casual reader of the form.

Appendix B

AGREEMENT ON GUIDELINES FOR CLASSROOM COPYING IN NOT-FOR-PROFIT EDUCATIONAL INSTITUTIONS[115]

WITH RESPECT TO BOOKS AND PERIODICALS

The purpose of the following guidelines is to state the minimum and not the maximum standards of educational fair use under section 107 of H.R. 2223 [this section]. The parties agree that the conditions determining the extent of permissible copying for educational purposes may change in the future; that certain types of copying permitted under these guidelines may not be permissible in the future; and conversely that in the future other types of copying not permitted under these guidelines may be permissible under revised guidelines.

Moreover, the following statement of guidelines is not intended to limit the types of copying permitted under the standards of fair use under judicial decision and which are stated in section 107 of the Copyright Revision Bill [this section]. There may be instances in which copying, which does not fall

---

[115] H.R. Rep. No. 94-1476, 94th Cong., 2nd Sess. 68-70, reprinted in (1976) U.S. Code Cong. & Ad. News 5659, 5682-83.

within the guidelines stated below, may nonetheless be permitted under the criteria of fair use.

GUIDELINES

I. Single Copying for Teachers

A single copy may be made of any of the following by or for a teacher at his or her individual request for his or her scholarly research or use in teaching or preparation to teach a class:

A. A chapter from a book.

B. An article from a periodical or newspaper.

C. A short story, short essay or short poem, whether or not from a collective work.

D. A chart, graph, diagram, drawing, cartoon or picture from a book, periodical, or newspaper.

II. Multiple Copies for Classroom Use

Multiple copies (not to exceed in any event more than one copy per pupil in a course) may be made by or for the teacher giving the course for classroom use or discussion, provided that:

A. The copying meets the tests of brevity and spontaneity as defined below; *and,*

Brevity

i. Poetry: (a) A complete poem if less than 250 words and if printed on not more than two pages or, (b) from a longer poem, an excerpt of not more than 250 words.

ii. Prose: (a) Either a complete article, story or essay of less than 2,500 words, or (b) an excerpt from any prose work of not more than 1,000 words or 10 percent of the work, whichever is less, but in any event a minimum of 500 words.

[Each of the numerical limits stated in "i" and "ii" above may be expanded to permit the completion of an unfinished line of a poem or of an unfinished prose paragraph.]

iii. Illustration: One chart, graph, diagram, drawing, cartoon or picture per book or per periodical issue.

iv. "Special" works: Certain works in poetry, prose or in "poetic prose" which often combine language with illustrations and which are intended sometimes for children and at other times for a more general audience fall short of 2,500 words in their entirety. Paragraph "ii" above notwithstanding such "special works" may not be reproduced in their entirety; however, an excerpt comprising not more than two of the published pages of such special work and containing not more than 10% of the words found in the text thereof, may be reproduced.

Spontaneity

i. The copying is at the instance and inspiration of the individual teacher, and

ii. The inspiration and decision to use the work and the moment of its use for maximum teaching effectiveness are so close in time that it would be unreasonable to expect a timely reply to a request for permission.

B. Meets the cumulative effect test as defined below; and,

Cumulative Effect

i. The copying of the material is for only one course in the school in which the copies are made.

ii. Not more than one short poem, article, story, essay or two excerpts may be copied from the same author, nor more than three from the same collective work or periodical volume during one class term.

iii. There shall not be more than nine instances of such multiple copying for one course during one class term.

[The limitations stated in "ii" and "iii" above shall not apply to current news periodicals and newspapers and current news sections of other periodicals.]

C. Each copy includes a notice of copyright.

III. Prohibitions as to I and II Above

Notwithstanding any of the above, the following shall be prohibited:

A. Copying shall not be used to create or to replace or substitute for anthologies, compilations or collective works. Such replacement or substitution may occur whether copies of various works or excerpts therefrom are accumulated or reproduced and used separately.

B. There shall be no copying of or from works intended to be "consumable" in the course of study or of teaching. These include workbooks, exercises, standardized tests and test booklets and answer sheets and like consumable material.

C. Copying shall not:

i. substitute for the purchase of books, publishers' reprints or periodicals;

ii. be directed by higher authority;

iii. be repeated with respect to the same item by the same teacher from term to term.

D. No charge shall be made to the student beyond the actual cost of the photocopying.

Agreed March 19, 1976.

GUIDELINES FOR EDUCATIONAL USES OF MUSIC

The purpose of the following guidelines is to state the minimum and not the maximum standards of educational fair use under Section 107 of H.R. 2223 [this section]. The parties agree that the conditions determining the extent of permissible copying for educational purposes may change in the future, that certain types of copying permitted under these guidelines may not be permissible in the future, and conversely that in the future other types of copying not permitted under these guidelines may be permissible under revised guidelines.

Moreover, the following statement of guidelines is not intended to limit the types of copying permitted under the standards of fair use under judicial decision and which are stated in Section 107 of the Copyright Revision Bill [this section]. There may be instances in which copying which does not fall within the guidelines stated below may nonetheless be permitted under the criteria of fair use.

A. Permissible Uses

1. Emergency copying to replace purchased copies which for any reason are not available for an imminent performance provided purchased replacement copies shall be substituted in due course.

2. (a) For academic purposes other than performance, multiple copies of excerpts of works may be made, provided that the excerpts do not comprise a part of the whole which would constitute a performable unit such as a section, movement, or aria, but in no case more than 10 percent of the whole work. The number of copies shall not exceed one copy per pupil.

(b) For academic purposes other than performance, a single copy of an entire performable unit (section, movement, aria, etc.) that is, (1) confirmed by the copyright proprietor to be out of print or (2) unavailable except in a larger work, may be made by or for a teacher solely for the purpose of his or her scholarly research or in preparation to teach a class.

3. Printed copies which have been purchased may be edited or simplified provided that the fundamental character of the work is not distorted or the lyrics, if any, altered or lyrics added if none exist.

4. A single copy of recordings of performances by students may be made for evaluation or rehearsal purposes and may be retained by the educational institution or individual teacher.

5. A single copy of a sound recording (such as a tape, disc, or cassette) of copyrighted music may be made from sound recordings owned by an educational institution or an individual teacher for the purpose of constructing aural exercises or examinations and may be retained by the educational institution or individual teacher. (This pertains only to the copyright of the music itself and not to any copyright which may exist in the sound recording.)

B. Prohibitions

1. Copying to create or replace or substitute for anthologies, compilations or collective works.

2. Copying of or from works intended to be "consumable" in the course of study or of teaching such as workbooks, exercises, standardized tests, answer sheets, and like material.

3. Copying for the purpose of performance, except as in A(1) above.

4. Copying for the purpose of substituting for the purchase of music, except as in A(1) and A(2) above.

5. Copying without inclusion of the copyright notice which appears on the printed copy.

Appendix C

8 C.F.R. § 274a.2(b)(v)(A)

Documents that establish both identity and work authorization are,

(1) A United States passport;

(2) An Alien Registration Receipt Card or Permanent Resident Card (Form I–551);

(3) A foreign passport that contains a temporary I–551 stamp, or temporary I–551 printed notation on a machine-readable immigrant visa;

(4) An Employment Authorization Document which contains a photograph (Form I–766);

(5) In the case of an individual who is employment-authorized incident to status or parole with a specific employer, a foreign passport with an Arrival/Departure Record, Form I–94 (as defined in 8 CFR 1.4) or Form I–94A, bearing the same name as the passport and containing an endorsement by DHS indicating such employment-authorized status or parole, as long as the period of endorsement has not yet expired and the employment is not in conflict with the individual's employment-authorized status or parole;

(6) A passport from the Federated States of Micronesia (FSM) or the Republic of the Marshall Islands (RMI) with Form I–94 or Form I–94A indicating nonimmigrant admission under the Compact of Free Association Between the United States and the FSM or RMI;

(7) In the case of an individual lawfully enlisted for military service in the Armed Forces under 10 U.S.C. 504, a military identification card issued to such individual may be accepted only by the Armed Forces.

8 C.F.R. § 274a.2(b)(v)(B)

The following documents establish identity only:

(B) The following documents are acceptable to establish identity only:

(1) For individuals 16 years of age or older:

(i) A driver's license or identification card containing a photograph, issued by a state (as defined in section 101(a)(36) of the Act) or an outlying possession of the United States (as defined by section 101(a)(29) of the Act). If the driver's license or identification card does not contain a photograph, identifying information shall be included such as: name, date of birth, sex, height, color of eyes, and address;

(ii) School identification card with a photograph;

(iii) Voter's registration card;

(iv) U.S. military card or draft record;

(v) Identification card issued by federal, state, or local government agencies or entities. If the identification card does not contain a photograph, identifying information shall be included such as: name, date of birth, sex, height, color of eyes, and address;

(vi) Military dependent's identification card;

(vii) Native American tribal documents;

(viii) United States Coast Guard Merchant Mariner Card;

(ix) Driver's license issued by a Canadian government authority;

(2) For individuals under age 18 who are unable to produce a document listed in paragraph (b)(1)(v)(B)(1) of this section, the following documents are acceptable to establish identity only:

(i) School record or report card;

(ii) Clinic doctor or hospital record;

(iii) Daycare or nursery school record.

(3) Minors under the age of 18 who are unable to produce one of the identity documents listed in paragraph (b)(1)(v)(B)(1) or (2) of this section are exempt from producing one of the enumerated identity documents if:

(i) The minor's parent or legal guardian completes on the Form I–9 Section 1—"Employee Information and Verification" and in the space for the minor's signature, the parent or legal guardian writes the words, "minor under age 18."

(ii) The minor's parent or legal guardian completes on the Form I–9 the "Preparer/Translator certification."

(iii) The employer or the recruiter or referrer for a fee writes in Section 2—"Employer Review and Verification" under List B in the space after the words "Document Identification #" the words, "minor under age 18."

(4) Individuals with handicaps, who are unable to produce one of the identity documents listed in paragraph (b)(1)(v)(B)(1) or (2) of this section, who are being placed into employment by a nonprofit organization, association or as part of a rehabilitation program, may follow the procedures for establishing identity provided in this section for minors under the age of 18, substituting where appropriate, the term "special placement" for "minor under age 18", and permitting, in addition to a parent or legal guardian, a representative from the nonprofit organization, association or rehabilitation program placing the individual into a position of employment, to fill out and sign in the appropriate section, the Form I–9. For purposes of this section the term individual with handicaps means any person who

(i) Has a physical or mental impairment which substantially limits one or more of such person's major life activities,

(ii) Has a record of such impairment, or

(iii) Is regarded as having such impairment.

(C) The following are acceptable documents to establish employment authorization only:

(1) A Social Security account number card other than one that specifies on the face that the issuance of the card does not authorize employment in the United States;

(2) Certification or report of birth issued by the Department of State, including Forms FS–545, DS–1350, FS–240;

(3) An original or certified copy of a birth certificate issued by a State, county, municipal authority or outlying possession of the United States bearing an official seal;

(4) Native American tribal document;

(5) United States Citizen Identification Card, Form I–197:

(6) Identification card for use of resident citizen in the United States, Form I.

8 C.F.R. § 274.2 (b)(1)(v)(C)

The following documents evidence employment authorization only:

(1) A Social Security account number card other than one that specifies on the face that the issuance of the card does not authorize employment in the United States;

(2) Certification or report of birth issued by the Department of State, including Forms FS–545, DS–1350, FS–240;

(3) An original or certified copy of a birth certificate issued by a State, county, municipal authority or outlying possession of the United States bearing an official seal;

(4) Native American tribal document;

(5) United States Citizen Identification Card, Form I–197:

(6) Identification card for use of resident citizen in the United States, Form I–179:

(7) An employment authorization document issued by the Department of Homeland Security.

(8) An employment authorization document issued by the Department of Homeland Security.

Appendix D

Verification of the immigration status of students
20 U.S.C.A. § 1091(g).

(g) Verification of immigration status

(1) In general

The Secretary shall implement a system under which the statements and supporting documentation, if required, of an individual declaring that such individual is in compliance with the requirements of subsection (a) (5) shall be verified prior to the individual's receipt of a grant, loan, or work assistance under this subchapter.

(2) Special rule

The documents collected and maintained by an eligible institution in the admission of a student to the institution may be used by the student in lieu of the documents used to establish both employment authorization and identity under section 1324a(b)(1)(B) of Title 8 to verify eligibility to participate in work-study programs under part C of this subchapter.

(3) Verification mechanisms

The Secretary is authorized to verify such statements and supporting documentation through a data match, using an automated or other system, with other Federal agencies that may be in possession of information relevant to such statements and supporting documentation.

(4) Review

In the case of such an individual who is not a citizen or national of the United States, if the statement described in paragraph (1) is submitted but the documentation required under paragraph (2) is not presented or if the documentation required under paragraph (2)(A) is presented but such documentation is not verified under paragraph (3)--

(A) the institution--

(i) shall provide a reasonable opportunity to submit to the institution evidence indicating a satisfactory immigration status, and

(ii) may not delay, deny, reduce, or terminate the individual's eligibility for the grant, loan, or work assistance on the basis of the individual's immigration status until such a reasonable opportunity has been provided; and

(B) if there are submitted documents which the institution determines constitute reasonable evidence indicating such status--

(i) the institution shall transmit to the Immigration and Naturalization Service either photostatic or other similar copies of such documents, or information from such documents, as specified by the Immigration and Naturalization Service, for official verification,

(ii) pending such verification, the institution may not delay, deny, reduce, or terminate the individual's eligibility for the grant, loan, or work assistance on the basis of the individual's immigration status, and

(iii) the institution shall not be liable for the consequences of any action, delay, or failure of the Service to conduct such verification.

Case Index

A.A. ex rel. Betenbaugh v. Needville Indep. Sch. Dist. / 285

A.N. ex rel. Niziolek v. Upper Perkiomen Sch. Dist. / 192

Aaris v. Las Virgenes Unified Sch. / 139

Adams v. Cado Parish Sch. Bd. / 122

Agostini v. Felton / 86, 94, 99, 102, 104, 208, 221, 250, 259

Aguilar v. Felton / 104, 211, 212

Albert v. Carovano / 44, 46

Albritton v. Neighborhood Ctrs. Ass'n for Child Dev. / 134

Alicea-Hernandez v. Catholic Bishop of Chicago / 281

Allan v. Caspar / 61

Altimore v. Mount Mercy Coll. / 37

Alvarez v. Fountainhead / 151

Am. and Foreign Ins. Co. v. Church Schs. of Diocese of Va. / 135

Am. Univ. Sys. v. Am. Univ. / 31

American Fed'n of Teachers-West Va. AFL-CIO v. Kanawha Cnty. Bd. of Educ. / 201

Amos v. Corporation of the Presiding Bishop / 166

Anable v. Ford / 191

Anders v. Ft. Wayne Cmty. Schs. / 186

Anderson v. Strong Mem'l Hosp. / 119

Andre v. Pace Univ. / 57

Angstadt v. Midd-West Sch. Dist. / 290

Anonymous v. Lyman Ward Military Acad. / 142

Ansonia Bd. of Educ. v. Philbrook / 297

Ansorian v. Zimmerman / 117

Applied Innovations v. Regents of Univ. of Minn. / 316

Archbishop Coleman F. Carroll High Sch. v. Maynoldi / 122

Archbishop Stepinac High Sch. / 148

Aronson v. Horace Mann-Barnard Sch. / 131

Aronson v. North Park Coll. / 51

Association of Zone A and B Homeowners' Subsidiary v. Zoning Bd. / 167

Aubrey v. School Bd. of Lafayette Parish / 201

Axelrod v. Phillips Acad. / 255

B.C. v. Plumas Unified Sch. Dist. / 188

Bache Halsey Stuart v. Univ. of Houston / 74

Ballaban v. Bloomington Jewish Cmty. / 53

Ballou v. Ravena-Coeymans-Selkirk Sch. / 131

Bane v. Hebrew Acad. of Five Towns and Rockaway / 34

Bangor Baptist Church v. State of Me. / 273

Banks v. Fritsch / 118

Barnes v. Gorman / 239

Barr v. United Methodist Church / 85, 91

Barrett v. Steubenville City Schs. / 272

Barrie Sch. v. Patch / 36, 38, 59

Barrow v. Greenville Indep. Sch. Dist. / 271

Basic Books v. Kinko's Graphics Corp. / 316

Battig v. Hartford Accident and Indem. Co. / 140

Battles v. Arundel Cnty. Bd. of Educ. / 288

Beauchene v. Mississippi Coll. / 49

Becker v. City Univ. of Seattle / 47

Beeching v. Levee / 118

Bell v. Board of Educ. of the City of N.Y. / 148

Bell v. Itawamba Cnty Bd. of Educ. / 193

Bella v. Davis / 116

Bellefonte Ins. Co. v. Queen / 140

Bender v. Alderson Broaddus Coll. / 34

Bendig v. Bethpage Union Free Sch. Dist. / 131

Benitez v. New York City Bd. of Educ. / 127, 130, 131

Benjamin v. Sparks / 56

Ben-Yonatan v. Concordia Coll. Corp. / 47

Bernard v. EDS Noland Episcopal Day Sch. / 49

Berrios v. Inter-Am. Univ. / 45

Bethel School District v. Fraser / 39

Bischoff v. Brothers of the Sacred Heart / 64

Bishop v. Westminster Schs. / 60

Bisignano v. Harrison Cent. Sch. Dist. / 114

Black v. St. Bernadette Congregation of Appleton / 53

Blackburn v. Fisk Univ. / 44

Blank v. Board of Higher Educ. of City of N.Y. / 64

Bleich v. Maimonides Sch. / 75

Blum v. Yaretsky / 42

Board of Curators of Univ. of Mo. v. Horowitz / 62

Board of Educ. of Kiryas Joel Village Sch. Dist. v. Grumet 103

Board of Educ. of the Appoquinimink Sch. Dist. v. Johnson / 247

Board of Educ. of the Hendrick-Hudson School District v. Rowley / 230

Board of Educ. of Central Sch. Dist. No. 1 v. Allen / 24, 97, 98, 100

Board of Educ. of Indep. Sch. Dist. No. 92 of Pottawatomie Cnty. v. Earls / 194

Bob Jones Univ. v. Johnson / 75

Bob Jones Univ. v. United States / 75, 274, 275, 282

Bogan v. Miss. Conference of the United Methodist Church / 281

Bollard v. Cal. Province of Soc'y. of Jesus / 280

Boyd v. Harding Acad. of Memphis / 282

Bradford v. Norwich City Sch. Dist. / 193

Bradley T. v. Cent. Catholic High Sch. / 116

Bradstreet v. Sobol / 290

Branch v. Stehr / 133

Brannen v. Kings Local Sch. Dist. Bd. of Educ. / 200

Braun v. Glade Valley Sch. / 56

Breeding v. Arthur J. Gallagher and Co. / 300
Brennan v. Bd. of Trs. for Univ. of La. Sys. / 197
Brenner v. Little Red Sch. House / 60
Brentwood Acad. v. Tenn. Sch. Athletic Ass'n, / 42, 43, 284
Bright v. Isenbarger / 44
Britt v. Chestnut Hill Coll. / 56
Brousseau v. Town of Westerly / 180
Brown ex rel. Brown v. Ramsey / 113
Browns v. Mitchell / 44
Brugger v. Joseph Acad. / 116, 123, 137
Brunelle v. Lynn Pub. Schs. / 288
Bruner v. Univ. of S. Miss. / 88
Brzica v. Trustees of Dartmouth Coll. / 81
Burge ex rel. Burge v. Colton Sch. Dist. 53 / 192, 193
Burlington Industries v. Ellerth / 300
Burrow v. State / 288
Butler v. La. Bd. of Educ. / 153
C.H. v. Cape Henlopen Sch. Dist. / 244
C.M. v. Bd. of Educ. / 237
Calvary Christian Sch. v. Huffstuttler / 32
Campbell v. Gahanna-Jefferson Bd. of Educ. / 114
Cannata v. Catholic Diocese of Austin / 280
Cantwell v. Connecticut / 94
Care and Protection of Charles / 274
Catholic High Sch. Ass'n of Archdiocese of N.Y. v. Culvert / 76
Cavaliere v. Duff's Bus. Inst. / 58
Caviness v. Horizon Cmty. Learning Ctr. / 41, 45
Cedar Rapids Community School Dist. v. Garret F. / 152, 233
Central Catholic Educ. Ass'n v. Archdiocese of Portland / 76
Centre Coll. v. Trzop / 40, 49
Cerny v. Cedar Bluffs Junior/Senior Pub. Sch. / 127
Chicago Bd. of Educ. v. Substance / 312, 313
Childress v. Madison v. Madison Cnty. / 139
Christian Bros. Inst. of N.J. v. N.J. Interscholastic League / 284
Christian v. Eagles Landing Christian Acad. / 131
Church of the Lukumi Babalu Aye v. City of Hialeah / 267, 268, 269, 270, 271
City of Boerne v. Flores / 267
Ciurleo v. St. Regis Parish / 84, 280
Clady v. County of Los Angeles / 299
Clayborn v. Bankers Standard Life Ins. Co. / 134
Clayton v. Trs. of Princeton Univ. / 30, 54
Cleveland Board of Education v. Loudermill / 39
Cochran v. Louisiana State Board of Education / 96, 98, 207
Collins v. Bossier Parish Sch. Bd. / 124
Colorado State Bd. of Educ. v. Taxpayers for Pub. Educ. / 106
Combs v. Homer-Center Sch. Dist. / 287

Committee for Public Education and Religious Liberty v. Nyquist / 100
Commonwealth v. J.B. / 181
Commonwealth v. Snyder / 181
Conclara v. State Bd. of Educ. / 288
Conlon v. InterVarsity Christian Fellowship / 280
Connecticut Department of Public Safety v. Doe / 169
Connick v. Myers / 39
Conway v. Pacific Univ. / 56
Cormier v. City of Lynn / 115
Cornette v. Commonwealth / 201
Cornfield by Lewis v. Consol. High Sch. Dist. No. 230 / 182, 189
Corporation of Mercer Univ. v. Smith / 82
Corporation of Presiding Bishop of Church of Jesus Christ of Latter Day Saints
    v. City of West Linn / 167
Coulee Catholic Schs. v. Labor & Indus. Rev. Comm'n / 84, 281
Covington County v. G.W. / 186
Cox v. Barnes / 149
Cox v. DeJarnette / 133
Craft v. Vanderbilt Univ. / 43
Creative Cnty. Day Sch. of Sandy Spring v. Montgomery Cnty. Bd. of Appeals
    / 167
Crenshaw v. Columbus City Sch. Dist. Bd. of Educ. / 155
Crevlin v. Board of Educ. of City Sch. Dist. of City of Niagara Falls / 117
Culver v. Port Allegany Reporter Argus / 120
Cunningham v. Helping Hands / 131
Cutter v. Wilkinson / 294
D.J.M. ex rel. D.M. v. Hannibal Pub. Sch. Dist. No. 60 / 192
D.M.A. v. Hungerford / 135
Dabbs v. Aron Security / 146
Dahlman v. Oakland Univ. / 33
Daniels v. Fluette / 121
Davenport v. Cotton Hope Plantation Horizontal Regime / 138
David v. City of N.Y. / 149
Davis v. Lutheran S. High Sch. Ass'n of St. Louis / 121
Davis v. Monroe Cnty. Bd. of Educ. / 112, 116
Davis v. Wappingers Cent. Sch. Dist. / 244
Dawkins v. Biondi Educ. Ctr. / 47
Dayton Christian Schs. v. Ohio Civil Rights Comm'n / 33
DeBruin v. St. Patrick Congregation / 279
Dec v. Auburn Enlarged Sch. Dist. / 118
DeMarco v. Holy Cross High Sch. / 53, 83
Demkovich v. St. Andrew the Apostle Parish, Calumet City / 280, 282
Denis J. O'Connell High Sch. v. Va. High Sch. League / 283
Dep't of Educ. State of Haw. v. Cari Rae S. / 240
Desert Place, Inc. v. Costa / 298
DeShaney v. Winnebago County Dep't of Soc. Servs. / 124

Desilets v. Clearview Bd. of Educ. / 185

Diana G. v. Our Lady Queen of Martyrs Sch. / 127

Dias v. Archdiocese of Cincinnati / 280

District of Columbia v. Doe / 125

Doe v. Archbishop Stepinac High Sch. / 111, 123, 140

Doe v. Brouillette / 113

Doe v. Corp. of the President of the Church of Latter Day Saints / 156

Doe v. Gonzaga Univ. / 120

Doe v. High-Tech Inst. / 197

Doe v. Renfrow / 188

Doe v. Western New England Univ. / 51

Doe v. Withers / 257

Dr. Perkins Sch. v. Freeman / 60

Duffy v. Long Beach City Sch. Dist. / 132

Dunfey v. Roger Williams Univ. / 33

Earley v. DiCenso / 99

Edson v. Barre Supervisory Union #61 / 129

Educ. Testing Serv. v. Katzman / 312

Edwards v. Saul / 136

EEOC v. Catholic Univ. of Am. / 53, 281

EEOC v. Hosanna-Tabor Evangelical Lutheran Church and Sch. / 278

EEOC v. Kamehameha Schs./Bishop Estate / 77, 78, 277

EEOC v. Roman Catholic Diocese of Raleigh / 281

EEOC v. Townley Engineering & Mfg. Co. / 277

Ehlers-Renzi v. Connelly Sch. of the Holy Child / 165

Eiseman v. State / 169

Ellerbee v. Mills / 118

Embry v. O'Bannon / 286

Employment Div., Dep't of Human Resources of Oregon v. Smith / 266, 267. 270, 272, 294

Endrew F. v. Douglas County School District RE-1 / 230, 231

English v. Talladega Cnty. Bd. of Educ. / 201

Enright by Enright v. Busy Bee Playschool / 127

Ette v. Linn-Mar Cmty. Sch. Dist. / 150, 179

Eulitt ex rel. Eulitt v. Maine, Dep't of Educ. / 105

Evans v. Tacoma Sch. Dist. No. 10 / 157

Everson v. Board of Education / 93, 97, 98, 207, 208, 221

F.S.E. v. State / 186

Faieta v. World Harvest Church / 114

Farragher v. City of Boca Raton / 300

Farrington v. Tokushige / 96

Fassl v. Our Lady of Perpetual Help Roman Catholic Church / 281

Faur v. Jewish Theological Seminary of Am. / 33

Fazzolari v. Portland Sch. Dist. No. IJ / 125

Feist Publications v. Rural Telephone Serv. Co. / 310

Fellheimer v. Middlebury Coll. / 51, 54

Fellowship Baptist Church v. Benton / 273
Fernandez v. Florida Nat'l Coll. / 122
Fewless v. Bd. of Educ. of Wayland Union Schs. / 179, 189
Fike v. United Methodist Children's Home / 277
Fischer v. Driscoll / 44
Fitzer v. Greater Greenville S.C. YMCA / 134
Flint v. St. Augustine High Sch. / 40, 48
Florence Cty. Sch. Dist. v. Carter / 243
Flynn v. Estevez / 50
Foley v. Special Sch. Dist. of St. Louis Cnty. / 248
Fonovisa v. Cherry Auction / 316
Forest Grove School District v. T.A. / 244
Forest Hills Early Learning Ctr. v. Grace Baptist Church / 167
Forstrum v. Byrne / 246
Foster v. Houston General Ins. Co. / 148
Fraad-Wolf v. Vassar Coll. / 54
Franchi v. New Hampton Sch. / 81
Frank v. Orleans Parish Sch. Bd. / 114
Franklin v. Leland Stanford, Jr. Univ. / 40
Fratello v. Roman Catholic Archdiocese of N.Y. / 79, 279
Frugis v. Bracigliano / 146
Fry v. Napoleon Cmty. Sch. / 238
Fuller v. Lakeview Acad. / 37
G.C. v. Owensboro Pub. Sch. / 192
Galen Instit. v. Lewis / 274
Galiani v. Hofstra Univ. / 54
Gallimore v. Henrico Cnty. Sch. Bd. / 192
Gallo v. Salesian Soc'y / 30
Gamble v. Vanderbilt Univ.) / 88
Garcetti v. Ceballos / 39
Gardiner v. Mercyhurst Coll. / 45
Gardiner v. Tulia Indep. Sch. Dist. / 194
Gatto v. St. Richard Sch. / 63, 117
Gebser v. Lago Vista Indep. Sch. Dist. / 112
Geraci v. St. Xavier High Sch. / 44, 49, 51
Gilbert v. McLeod Infirmary / 80
Godoy v. Cent. Islip Union Free Sch. Dist. / 132
Golian v. New York City Admin. for Children Servs. / 156
Gonzaga University v. Doe / 320
Gonzales v. Passino / 147
Gorman v. St. Raphael's Acad. / 42
Gosche v. Calvert Sch. / 52, 201
Goss v. Lopez / 39
Gossett v. Jackson / 120
Goulart v. Meadows / 288
Grace Methodist Church v. City of Cheyenne / 167

Grafton v. Brooklyn Law Sch. / 43
Green v. Kennedy / 20
Green v. Orleans Parish Sch. Bd. / 127
Greening v. Sch. Dist. of Millard / 129
Griffin v. Arkansas / 154
Griffin v. Sch. Bd. of Prince Edward Cnty. / 18
Griffith v. City of N.Y. / 129
Guinan v. Roman Catholic Archdiocese of Indianapolis / 53, 83
Gylten v. Swalboski / 150
Hafford v. Seidner) / 300
Hall v. Baptist Mem'l Health Care Corp. / 277, 297
Hammond v. Bd. of Educ. of Carroll Cnty. / 128, 138
Hanssen v. Our Redeemer Lutheran Church / 201
Hardwicke v. American Boychoir Sch. / 113
Harper & Row, Publishers v. Nation Enters. / 312
Harrison v. Day, 106 S.E.2d 636 (1959) / 18
Hart v. Electronic Arts / 120
Hart v. State of N. C. / 105
Hartz v. Administrators of Tulane Educ. Fund / 33
Harvey v. Palmer Coll. of Chiropractic / 40, 54
Harwood v. Johns Hopkins Univ. / 38
Hazelwood School District v. Kuhlmeier / 39
Hearn v. Bd. of Pub. Educ. / 200
Heartland Acad. Cmty. Church v. Waddle / 31
Hebert v. LaRocca / 153
Heisler v. New York Med. Coll. / 62
Helm v. Prof'l Children's Sch. / 58
Helms v. Picard / 102
Henry v. Red Hill Evangelical Lutheran Church of Tustin / 52
Hentosh v. Herman M. Finch Univ. of Health Sci. / 35
Hershman v. Muhlenberg Coll. / 31
Herx v. Diocese of Ft. Wayne–South Bend / 280
Herzog v. St. Peter Lutheran Church / 277
Higgins v. Am. Soc'y of Clinical Pathologists / 30
Hill v. Cal. / 177
Hill-Murray Fed'n of Teachers, St. Paul, Minn. v. Hill-Murray High Sch.,
    Maplewood, Minn. / 76
Hoeffner v. The Citadel / 131
Honig v. Doe / 39
Hooks v. Clark Cty. Sch. Dist. / 245, 246
Hope v. Pelzer / 189
Horton v. Goose Creek Indep. Sch. Dist. / 188
Hosanna-Tabor Evangelical Lutheran Church and School v. Equal Employment
    Opportunities Commission / 79, 275, 277, 279, 280, 281, 282, 294, 295
Houston v. Mile High Adventist Acad., 872 F. Supp. 829 / 58
Howard v. Pine Forge Acad. / 42

Hu v. Am. Bar Ass'n / 45
Huff v. Notre Dame High Sch. / 42, 44
Hungerford v. Portland Sanitarium and Benevolent Ass'n / 134
Hunt v. St. Peter Sch. / 254
Hustler Magazine v. Falwell / 118
Hutcheson v. Grace Lutheran Sch. / 54
I.H. by and through Hunter v. Oakland School for Arts / 45
Idrees v. Am. Univ. of the Caribbean / 57
Illinois Bible Colls. Ass'n v. Anderson / 274
Imperiale v. Hahneman Univ. / 45
In Interest of Dumas / 181
In Interest of Sawyer / 288
In re Adam / 178
In re Beychok / 81
In re Billingsley / 64
In re F.B. / 187
In re Parkman / 64
In re S.D. / 156
In re St. Thomas High Sch. / 50
Ingraham v. Wright / 113
Ireland v. Kan. Dist. of the Wesleyan Church / 255
Irving Indep. Sch. Dist. v. Tatro /153, 232
J.D.B. v. North Carolina / 194
J.K. v. UMS-Wright Corp. / 84
J.S. ex rel. Snyder v. Blue Mountain Sch. Dist. / 192
J.S. v. Bethlehem Area Sch. Dist. / 193
J.T. v. Dep't of Educ. / 236
Jackson v. Strayer Coll. / 41
James v. Unified Sch. Dist. No. 512 / 186
Jane Doe-3 v. McLean Cnty. Unit Dist. No. 5 Bd. of Dirs. / 143
Jenkins by Hall v. Talladega City Bd. of Educ. / 189
Jenkins v. Talladega City Bd. of Educ. / 182
Jobe v. City of Orange / 167
Johnson v. Charles Cmty. Schs. / 272
Johnson v. Newburgh Enlarged Sch. Dist. / 146
Jonathan L. v. Superior Ct. / 288
Jones v. Graham Cnty. Bd. of Educ. / 201
Jones v. Howe Military Sch. / 54
Jones v. Jenkins / 201
Jordan v. World Pub. Co. / 118
Joy v. Penn-Harris-Madison Sch. Corp. / 195
Juran v. Independence Cent. Sch. Dist. 13J / 191
K.R. v. Anderson Cmty. Sch. Corp. / 248
Kahn v. East Side Union High Sch. Dist. / 131
Kakaes v. George Washington Univ. / 35
Kaptein v. Conrad Sch. Dist. / 287

Kedroff v. St. Nicholas Cathedral / 275

Kelley v. Bonney / 118

Kelly v. McCarrick / 131

Kent State Univ. v. Ford / 36

Key v. Coryell / 58

Killinger v. Samford Univ. / 277, 297

Kleinknecht v. Gettysburg Coll. / 123

Kloth v. Southern Christian Univ. / 31

Klump v. Nazareth Area Sch. Dist. / 192

Knipmeyer v. Diocese of Alexandria / 55

Knisley v. Pike Cnty. Joint Vocational Sch. Dist. / 190

Knox Cnty. Educ. Ass'n v. Knox Cty. Bd. of Educ. / 201

Koch v. Adams / 192

Koehler v. Juniata Cty. Sch. Dist. / 243

Konop v. Northwestern Sch. Dist. / 181, 191

Kowalski v. Berkeley Cnty. Schs. / 192

Kuehn v. Renton Sch. Dist. / 185

Ky. Sch. Bds. Ins. Trust v. Bd. of Educ. of Woodford Cnty. / 135

Ky. State Bd. v. Rudasill / 273

L.G. v. Pittsburg Unified Sch. Dist. / 226

L.R. ex rel. N.R. v. Sch. Dist. of Philadelphia / 116, 129

LaCross v. Cornerstone Christian Acad. / 52, 65

Lake Ridge Acad. v. Carney / 60

Lakin v. Birmingham Pub. Sch. / 241

Landry v. Ascension Parish Sch. Bd. / 146

Laney v. Farley / 191

Larson v. Cuba Rushford Cent. Sch. Dist. / 132

Lawrence v. Grant Parish Sch. Bd. / 126

Layshock v. Heritage Sch. Dist. / 192

Leahy v. Sch. Bd. of Hernando County / 115

Leake v. Murphy / 172

LeBoon v. Lancaster Jewish Cmty. Ctr. Ass'n / 277

Lee v. Weisman / 95

Lemon v. Kurtzman / 94, 97, 99, 100, 166, 221

Leo v. Mount St. Michael Acad. / 121, 123

Leventhal v. Knalek / 200

Levitt v. Committee for Public Education and Religious Liberty / 101

Lewis v. Loyola Univ. of Chicago / 35

Liedtke v. Carrington / 156

Lifton v. Board of Educ. of City of Chicago / 116

Linke v. Northwestern Sch. Corp. / 194, 195, 197

Little v. Yale Univ. / 62

Litz v. Clinton Cent. Sch. Dist. / 131

Locke v. Davey / 250

Lockett v. Bd. of Educ. for Sch. Dist. No. 189 / 133

Logan v. Bennington Coll. / 45

Logiodice v. Trs. of Me. Cent. Inst. / 42, 45, 46
Love v. Duke Univ. / 33
Lovell v. Poway Unified Sch. Dist. / 193
Loving Savior Church v. U.S. / 86
Luina v. Katharine Gibbs Sch. N.Y. / 124
Lynch v. Donnelly / 95
M.L. v. Smith / 259
M.P. v. Independent Sch. Dist. / 239
Magana v. Charlotte-Mecklenburg Bd. of Educ. / 90
Malichi v. Archdiocese of Miami / 281
Mancha v. Field Museum of Natural History / 148
Manno v. St. Felicitas Elem. Sch. / 52
Marcus v. Rowley / 313
Marner v. Eufala City Sch. Bd. / 200
Martin v. Pratt Inst. / 38
Martin v. Univ. of New Haven / 43, 45
Masterpiece Cakeshop, Ltd. v. Colorado Civil Rights Commission / 2, 3, 275
McClure v. Salvation Army / 275, 280
McClyde v. Archdiocese of Indianapolis / 111, 123
McCollin v. Roman Catholic Archdiocese of N.Y. / 123, 124
McConnell v. Le Moyne Coll. / 34
McDonald v. Mass. Gen'l Hosp. / 133
McDonald v. Terebonne Parish Sch. Bd. / 145
McDonnell Douglas Corp. v. Green / 298
McEnroy v. St. Meinard Sch. of Theology / 53
McGrath v. Dominican Coll. of Blauvelt / 41
McGuire-Welch v. House of the Good Shepherd / 53
McKelvey v. Pierce / 134
Meek v. Pittenger / 99, 102, 103
Meier v. Salem-Keizer Sch. Dist. / 154
Menora v. Ill. Athletic Ass'n / 285
Meredith v. Pence / 105, 286
Meyer v. Naperville Manner / 139
Michigan Dep't of Soc. Servs. v. Emmanuel Baptist Preschool / 274
Mid-Vermont Christian Sch. v. Dep't of Employment and Training / 75
Miener v. Mo. / 229
Milkovich v. Lorain Journal Company / 117
Miller v. Bay View United Methodist Church / 281
Miller v. Wilkes / 197
Milligan v. Harborfields Cent. Sch. Dist. / 127
Mills v. Standing General Comm'n on Christian Unity / 279
Milonas v. Williams / 42
Minker v. Baltimore Annual Conference of United Methodist Church / 280
Minnesota Baptist Convention v. Pillsbury Acad. / 72
Mirand v. City of N.Y. / 110, 124
Missert v. Trs. of Boston Coll. / 42, 45

Mitchell v. Helms / 102, 250, 259
Mitchell v. Pruden / 118
Moffice v. Oglethorpe Univ. / 33
Moghimzadeh v. College of St. Rose / 45
Moore v. Vanderloo / 58
Morehouse Coll. v. McGaha / 34
Morris v. State Farm Ins. / 76
Morse v. Frederick / 39
Moses v. Skandera / 106
Moyse v. Runnels Sch. / 59, 60
Mt. Healthy City Bd. of Educ. v. Doyle / 39, 40
Mueller v. Allen / 101, 213
Muick v. Glenayre Electronics / 200
Muniz v. Warwick Sch. Dist. / 132
Munn v. Hotchkiss Sch. / 141
Murphy v. Bajjani / 172, 174
Murphy v. Villanova Univ. / 43
Myers v. Drozda / 134
Nampa Charter Sch. v. DeLaPaz / 117
Napolitano v. Trs. of Princeton Univ. / 30, 40, 63
Nat'l Indem. Co. of the South v. Consolidated Ins. Servs. / 136
National Treasury Employees Union v. Von Raab / 201
NCAA v. Tarkanian / 42
Neal v. Fulton Cnty. Bd. of Educ. / 113, 114
New Jersey v. T.L.O. / 39, 176, 177, 180, 181, 182, 183, 185, 189, 198
New Life Baptist Church Acad. v. E. Longmeadow / 272
New Mexico Ass'n of Non-public Schs. v. Moses / 106
New York Times Co. v. Sullivan / 118
Newport Int'l Univ. v. State Dept. of Educ. / 274
Nims v. Harrison / 119
NLRB v. Catholic Bishop of Chicago / 76
NLRB v. Hanna Boys Ctr. / 76
Nobles v. Ala. Christian Acad. / 45
Nolan v. Memphis City Schs. / 114
Norwood v. Harrison / 19
Nugent v. Diocese of Rockville Centre / 57
Nunn v. State / 58
Nussbaumer v. State / 156
NXIVM Corp. v. Ross Inst. / 312
O'Brian v. Langley Sch. / 61
O'Connor v. Burningham / 118
O'Connor v. Hewlett-Woodmere Union Free Sch. Dist. / 131
O'Connor v. Ortega / 39, 198, 199, 200, 201
O'Heron v. Blaney / 156
Obergefell v. Hodges / 2
Odem v. Pace Acad. / 51

Oliver v. Hofmeister / 105
Oliver v. McClung / 190
Opulent Life Church v. City of Holly Springs, MS / 168
Orr v. Brigham Young Univ. / 153
Owasso Independent School Dist. No. I-011 v. Falvo / 320
Owens v. Colorado Cong. of Parents, Teachers and Students / 105
Paladino v. Adephi Univ. / 58
Palmer v. Bennington Sch. Dist. / 118
Paragas v. Comsewogue Union Free Sch. Dist. / 127
Pardue v. Ctr. City Consortium of the Archdiocese of Wash. / 281
Parham v. Raleigh Cnty. Bd. of Educ. / 146
Parizek v. Roncalli Catholic High Sch. of Omaha / 36, 60
Partin v. Vernon Parish Sch. Bd. / 125
Patti Ann H. v. New York Med. Coll. / 62
Pavlica v. Behr / 313
Peavy v. Harman / 117
Pelletier v. Maine Principals' Ass'n / 290
Pelotte v. Simmons / 88
Penn-Harris-Madison Sch. Corp. v. Joy / 196, 197
People v. Bennett / 274
People v. DeJonge / 273
People v. Levisen / 288
Perez v. Aerospace Acad. / 61
Perez v. New York City Dep't of Educ. / 131
Perfect 10 v. Amazon.com / 311
Peter v. Wedl / 250
Peter W. v. S.F. Unified Sch. Dist. / 58
Peterson v. Minidoka Cnty. Local Sch. Dist. / 272
Petit v. U.S. Dep't of Educ. / 233
Petruska v. Gannon Univ. / 281
Philippou v. Baldwin Union Free Sch. Dist. / 131
Phillips v. Lincoln Cnty. Sch. Dist. / 128
Pickering v. Board of Educ. of Twp. High Sch. Dist. 205 / 39, 40
Pierce v. Society of Sisters of the Holy Names of Jesus and Mary / 12, 42, 96,
    207, 264, 265, 283
Pierce v. Yakima Valley Mem'l Hosp. Ass'n, / 134
Pierre v. Univ. of Dayton / 50
Plyler v. Doe / 206
Potter v. N.C. Sch. of the Arts / 123
Powell v. District of Columbia / 124
Powell v. Stafford / 280
Princeton Montessori Soc'y v. Leff / 59, 60
Public Education and Religious Liberty v. Regan / 101
R.L. v. Central York Sch. Dist. / 193
R.S. v. State / 156
Raethz v. Aurora Univ. / 62

Raleigh v. Indep. Sch. Dist. No. 625 / 149

Ramirez v. Genovese / 146

Randi W. v. Muroc Joint Unified Sch. Dist. / 143

Reardon v. Lemoyne / 83

Berthiaume v. McCormack / 83

Reeves v. Sanderson Plumbing / 298

Reid v. District of Columbia / 238

Reid v. Kenowa Hills Pub. Schs. / 290

Rendell-Baker v. Kohn / 43, 45, 46, 47

Reynolds v. Sterling Coll. / 34

Rhodes v. Guarricino / 183

Richardson v. Northwest Christian Univ. / 280, 282

Richland Sch. Dist. v. Mabton Sch. Dist. / 144

Riehm v. Engelking / 193

Riester v. Riverside Cmty. Sch. / 41

Rinker v. Sipler / 181

Robert S. v. Stetson Sch. / 47

Roberts v. Board of Educ. / 117

Roberts v. Wake Forest Univ. / 35

Rollins v. Wilson Cnty. Gov't / 304

Roman Catholic Church v. Kennan / 134

Rooney v. Tyson / 35

Rosati v. Toledo, Ohio Catholic Diocese / 280

Ross v. Creighton Univ. / 58, 59

Rottman v. Pa. Interscholastic Athletic Ass'n / 285

Ruegsegger v. Jefferson Cnty. Sch. Dist. R-1 / 146

Rupp v. Bryant / 115

Russell v. Salve Regina Coll. / 55, 119

S.B. v. St. James Sch. / 84, 119

S.H. v. Plano Sch. Dist. / 242

Sacramento City Unif. Sch. Dist. Bd. of Educ., v. Rachel H. / 235

Safford Unified Sch. Dist. No. 1 v. Redding / 154, 182, 189, 190

Safon v. Bellmore-Merrick Cent. High Sch. Dist. / 131

Sain v. Cedar Rapids Cmty Sch. Dist. / 58

Salter v. Natchitoches Chiropractic Clinic / 58

San Antonio Indep. Sch. Dist. v. Rodriguez / 206

Sanchez v. Catholic Foreign Soc'y of Am. / 280

Schaffer v. Weast / 243

Schaill v. Tippicanoe County Sch. Corp. / 197

Scharon v. St. Luke's Episcopal Presbyterian Hosps. / 275, 280, 281

Schleicher v. Salvation Army / 281

Schmoll v. Chapman Univ. / 281

School Comm'n of Burlington v. Dep't of Educ. of Mass. / 243

School District of Abington Township v. Schempp and Murray v. Curlett / 94, 99

Schultz v. Boy Scouts of Am. / 134

Scott v. Indep. Sch. Dist. No. 709 / 121

Scott v. Mid-Del Sch. Bd. of Educ. / 111

Scott v. Pacific Gas & Electric Co. / 61

Seal v. Morgan / 179

Serbian Eastern Orthodox Diocese for the U.S. and Canada v. Milivojevich / 294

Shaliehsabou v. Hebrew Home of Greater Wash. / 281

Shannon v. Bepko / 33

Sharick v. Southeastern Univ. of the Health Sci. / 30

Sharpe v. Quality Educ. / 133

Shaul v. Cherry Valley-Springfield Cent. Sch. Dist. / 199, 312, 314

Sheridan v. Trs. of Columbia Univ. / 38

Shields v. The Sch. of Law, Hofstra Univ. / 63

Sibley v. St. Albans Sch. / 38, 119

Sileven v. Tesch / 273

Simmons ex rel. Simmons v. Columbus Cnty. Bd. of Educ. / 133

Simmons v. Parkette Nat'l Gymnastic Training Ctr. / 139

Simmons–Harris v. Goff / 105

Sirohi v. Lee / 58

Sisters of the Holy Child Jesus at Old Westbury v. Corwin / 36, 38, 58, 86

Sivaslian v. Rawlins / 140

Skinner v. R.R. Labor Executives Ass'n / 201

Sloan v. Lemon / 100

Smith v. Alameda County Soc. Agency / 58

Smith v. Archbishop of St. Louis / 123, 125

Smith v. Doe / 169

Smith v. Dorsey / 81

Smith v. Duquesne Univ. / 43

Smith v. Roman Catholic Church of Archdiocese of New Orleans / 123

Snyder v. Charlotte Sch. Dist. / 286

South Gibson Sch. Bd. v. Sollman / 179

Spacek v. Charles / 111

Spark v. Catholic Univ. of Am. / 43

Spears on Behalf of Spears v. Jefferson Parish Sch. Bd. / 129

Special Sch. Dist. No. 1 v. R.M.M. / 251

Spell v. Bible Baptist Church / 54

Speller v. Toledo Pub. Sch. Dist. Bd. of Educ. / 110

Spencer v. World Vision / 276

Squires v. Sierra Educ. Found. / 57

St. Johnsbury Acad. v. D.H. / 242, 255

St. Mary's Honor Ctr. v. Hicks / 298

Starkman v. Evans / 280, 281

State ex rel Gaydos v. Blaeuer / 117

State ex rel. Galford v. Mark Anthony B. / 189

State ex rel. Marianist Province of the U.S. v. Ross / 113

State of Ohio v. Whisner / 273

State v. Baptist Church / 272

State v. Bigelow / 288
State v. Brown / 155
State v. DeLaBruere / 288
State v. Edgington / 288
State v. Glenn / 156
State v. Lowrey / 288
State v. M.N. / 288
State v. Morrow / 288
State v. Motherwell / 155
State v. Olin / 273
State v. Patzer / 288
State v. Polashek / 156
State v. Shaver / 273
State v. Superior Ct. / 288
Stately v. Indian Cmty. Sch. of Milwaukee / 281
Stead v. Unified Sch. Dist. No. 259, Sedgwick Cnty., Kan. / 120
Stern v. Webb Hays Nat'l Training Sch. for Deaconesses and Missionaries / 82
Stone v. Dartmouth Coll. / 43
Struble v. Blytheville Sch. Dist. / 155
Struble v. Valley Forge Military Acad. / 130
Sullivan v. Boston Architectural Ctr. / 34
Susan M. v. New York Law Sch. / 63
Swanson by and through Swanson v. Guthrie Indep. Sch. Dist. No. I-L / 289
Swanson v. Wabash Coll. / 122
Swartley v. Hoffner / 55
Swidryk v. St. Michael's Med. Ctr. / 58
T.K. v. Simpson Cnty. Sch. Dist. / 146
Tacka v. Georgetown Univ. / 34
Tannahill v. Lockney Indep. Sch. Dist. / 194
Tavolini v. Mt. Sinai Med. Ctr. / 45
Taxpayers for Pub. Educ. v. Douglas Cnty. Sch. Dist. / 106
Taylor v. Bd. of Educ. of City of Chicago / 155
Taylor v. Calvary Baptist Church / 116
Tedeschi v. Wagner Coll. / 54
Tennessee Secondary Sch. Athletic Ass'n v. Brentwood Acad. / 284
Texas Dep't. of Cmty. Affairs v. Burdine / 298
Texas Education Agency v. Leeper / 245, 288
Theodore v. Delaware Valley Sch. Dist. / 197
Thomas ex rel. Thomas v. Roberts / 189
Thomas Jefferson Sch. v. Dapros / 60
Thomas v. Allegany Cnty. Bd. of Educ. / 284, 287
Thomas v. Clayton Sch. Dist. / 189
Thomas v. Davidson Acad. / 253, 255
Tilton v. Richardson / 294
Timothy W. v. Rochester, N.H., Sch. Dist. / 226
Tinker v. Des Moines Indep. Sch. District / 39

Tinkham v. Kole / 114
Todd v. Rush County Schs. / 194
Tollefson v. Roman Catholic Bishop of San Diego / 61
Tollenaar v. Chino Valley Sch. Dist. / 123
Tomic v. Catholic Diocese of Peoria / 53, 83
Traficienti v. Moore Catholic High Sch. / 123
Trans World Airlines v. Hardison / 297
Transport Careers v. Nat'l Home Study Council / 42
Tree of Life Christian Schs. v. City of Upper Arlington / 167
Trinidad Sch. Dist. v. Lopez / 195
Trinity Lutheran Church of Columbia v. Comer / 2, 3, 75, 95, 106, 212, 221,
    250, 267, 270, 271
Troknya v. Cleveland Chiropractic Clinic / 34, 57
Trustees of Trinity Coll. v. Ferris / 132
Tunkl v. Regents of Univ. of Cal. / 139
Tuomala v. Regent Univ. / 35
Turner v. Atlanta Girls' Sch. / 36, 38
Ullmo v. Gilmour Acad. / 33, 242
United States v. Commonwealth of Virginia (V.M.I.) / 281, 282
United States v. Simons / 200
United States v. Slanina / 200
Unity Christian Sch. of Fulton, Ill. v. Rowell / 75
Univ. of Tex. SW. Med. Ctr. v. Nassar / 306
Univ. Preparatory Sch. v. Huitt / 128
Valencia v. Blue Hen Conference / 284
Valley Christian Sch. v. Mont. Pub. High Sch. Ass'n / 283
Van Loock v. Curran / 57
Vanderbilt Univ. v. DiNardo / 36
Velez v. Our Lady of Victory Church / 123, 125
Verkel v. Indep. Sch. Dist. No. 709 / 124
Verni v. Cleveland Chiropractic Coll. / 34
Vernonia School District 47J v. Acton / 194
Victory Outreach Ctr. v. Melso / 41
Vincent v. W. Technical Corp. / 42
Wagenblast v. Odessa School District / 138
Wahba v. New York Univ. / 43
Walker v City of N.Y. / 125
Wall v. Tulane Univ. / 33
Wallace v. Batavia Sch. Dist. / 147
Waller v. Moore / 81
Wallin v. Minnesota Dep't of Corrections / 300
Walters-Southland Inst. v. Walker / 87
Walz v. Tax Commission of New York City / 99
Warner v. St. Bernard Parish Sch. Bd. / 321
Warren v. Bd. of Regents of Univ. Sys. of Ga. / 82
Watson v. Jones / 275

Watts v. St. Mary's Hall / 52

Wayne Twp. of Sch. Comm's v. Indiana Ins. Co. / 135

Webb v. McCullough / 186

Weber v. William Floyd Sch. Dist. / 131

Weinstein v. Univ. of Ill. / 314

Weisfeld v. Peterseil Sch. Corp. / 37, 61

Wells v. Harrisburg Area Sch. Dist. / 124

Welter v. Seton Hall Univ. / 55

Werft v. Desert Southwest Annual Conference of the United Methodist Church / 280, 281

Wesly v. Nat'l Hemophilia Found. / 31

Westchester Day Sch. v. Village of Mamaroneck / 167

Western Reserve Acad. v. Franklin / 36

White v. City of Troy / 137

Whitney v. Bd. of Educ. of Grand Cnty / 35

Whittington v. Sowela Tech. Inst. / 150

Widdoes v. Detroit Pub. Schs. / 114

Wilcher v. State / 180

Williams ex rel. Williams v. Ellington / 189

Williams v. Cahill / 133

Williams v. Cambridge Bd. of Educ. / 179

Williams v. Discovery Day Sch. / 43

Williams v. Ellington / 182

Williams v. Howard Univ. / 43, 44

Williams v. Junior Coll. Dist. of Cent. Southwest Mo. / 133

Willis v. Anderson Cmty. Sch. Corp. / 194

Wilson v. Darr / 121, 156

Windsor Park Baptist Church v. Ark. Activities Ass'n / 282

Wisch v. Sanford Sch. / 44

Wisconsin v. Yoder / 265, 283

Wolman v. Walter / 98, 99, 101, 102, 103

Woods v. Wills / 112

Words of Faith Fellowship v. Rutherford Cnty. Dep't of Social Servs. / 155

Wu v. Shattuck-St. Mary's Sch. / 139

Yarbrough v. East Wake First Charter Sch. / 90

Yates v. Mansfield Bd. of Educ. / 144

Zelman v. Simmons–Harris / 86, 105, 208, 213, 259

Zelnick v. Morristown-Beard Sch. / 50

Ziegler v. Martin Cnty. Sch. Dist. / 191

Zimmerman v. Poly Prep Country Day Sch. / 84

Zivich v. Mentor Soccer Club / 139

Zobrest v. Catalina Foothills Sch. Dist. / 97, 98, 103, 240, 250